EDUCATION, POLITICS, AND PUBLIC LIFE

Series Editors:
Henry A. Giroux, McMaster University
Susan Searls Giroux, McMaster University

Within the last three decades, education as a political, moral, and ideological practice has become central to rethinking not only the role of public and higher education, but also the emergence of pedagogical sites outside of the schools—which include but are not limited to the Internet, television, film, magazines, and the media of print culture. Education as both a form of schooling and public pedagogy reaches into every aspect of political, economic, and social life. What is particularly important in this highly interdisciplinary and politically nuanced view of education are a number of issues that now connect learning to social change, the operations of democratic public life, and the formation of critically engaged individual and social agents. At the center of this series will be questions regarding what young people, adults, academics, artists, and cultural workers need to know to be able to live in an inclusive and just democracy and what it would mean to develop institutional capacities to reintroduce politics and public commitment into everyday life. Books in this series aim to play a vital role in rethinking the entire project of the related themes of politics, democratic struggles, and critical education within the global public sphere.

SERIES EDITORS:

HENRY A. GIROUX holds the Global TV Network Chair in English and Cultural Studies at McMaster University in Canada. He is on the editorial and advisory boards of numerous national and international scholarly journals. Professor Giroux was selected as a Kappa Delta Pi Laureate in 1998 and was the recipient of a Getty Research Institute Visiting Scholar Award in 1999. He was the recipient of the Hooker Distinguished Professor Award for 2001. He received an Honorary Doctorate of Letters from Memorial University of Newfoundland in 2005. His most recent books include *Take Back Higher Education* (coauthored with Susan Searls Giroux, 2006), *America on the Edge* (2006), *Beyond the Spectacle of Terrorism* (2006), *Stormy Weather: Katrina and the Politics of Disposability* (2006), *The University in Chains: Confronting the Military-Industrial-Academic Complex* (2007), and *Against the Terror of Neoliberalism: Politics Beyond the Age of Greed* (2008).

SUSAN SEARLS GIROUX is Associate Professor of English and Cultural Studies at McMaster University. Her most recent books include *The Theory Toolbox* (coauthored with Jeff Nealon, 2004) and *Take Back Higher Education* (coauthored with Henry A. Giroux, 2006), and *Between*

Race and Reason: Violence, Intellectual Responsibility, and the University to Come (2010). Professor Giroux is also the Managing Editor of *The Review of Education, Pedagogy, and Cultural Studies.*

Sport, Spectacle, and NASCAR Nation

Consumption and the Cultural Politics of Neoliberalism

Joshua I. Newman

and

Michael D. Giardina

SPORT, SPECTACLE, AND NASCAR NATION

First published in 2011 by
PALGRAVE MACMILLAN®
in the United States—a division of St. Martin's Press LLC,
175 Fifth Avenue, New York, NY 10010.

Where this book is distributed in the UK, Europe and the rest of the world,
this is by Palgrave Macmillan, a division of Macmillan Publishers Limited,
registered in England, company number 785998, of Houndmills,
Basingstoke, Hampshire RG21 6XS.

Palgrave Macmillan is the global academic imprint of the above companies
and has companies and representatives throughout the world.

Palgrave® and Macmillan® are registered trademarks in the United States,
the United Kingdom, Europe and other countries.

ISBN: 978–0–230–11519–4

Library of Congress Cataloging-in-Publication Data

Newman, Joshua I., 1976–
    Sport, spectacle, and NASCAR nation : consumption and the cultural
politics of neoliberalism / Joshua I. Newman, Michael D. Giardina.
        p. cm.—(Education, politics and public life)
        ISBN 978–0–230–11519–4 (hardback)
        1. Stock car racing—Social aspects—United States. 2. Stock car
racing—Politcal aspects—United States. 3. NASCAR (Association)
I. Giardina, Michael D., 1976– II. Title.

GV1029.9.S74N48 2011
796.720973—dc22   2011011016

A catalogue record of the book is available from the British Library.

Design by Newgen Imaging Systems (P) Ltd., Chennai, India.

First edition: October 2011

10 9 8 7 6 5 4 3 2 1

Printed in the United States of America.

Dedication
For Joe Kincheloe

CONTENTS

FIGURES

ACKNOWLEDGMENTS

First and foremost, we thank our series editors, Susan Searls Giroux and Henry Giroux, for their enthusiastic support of this project. Their progressive vision can be seen running through each of the excellent books in this series. At Palgrave Macmillan, we thank Burke Gerstenschlager for assisting us in the early stages of the book's development; Kaylan Connally for providing expert production assistance throughout the process; and our copy editors Rohini Krishnan and Sumathi Ellappan, for helping strengthen the text with considered attention to detail.

A number of friends and colleagues were also instrumental in the theoretical, methodological, and practical creation of this book. Adam Beissel was a superior research assistant and co-conspirator over the long course of our endeavors, accompanying us to numerous events and contributing critical observations; Juliet Preston and Katie Flanagan provided sage proofreading of the final manuscript; Doug Booth, Dean of the School of Physical Education at the University of Otago, provided essential funding support for the book at a key point in its development; Keith Hunter, pro-vice chancellor for the Division of Sciences at Otago, for similarly availing resources needed to complete the project; Towson University's Faculty Development Research Grant Committee, for a grant to fund part of our early travels. Norman K. Denzin, Shirley Steinberg, and the much-missed Joe Kincheloe were early supporters of this project, publishing versions of Chapters Four and Six in their edited venues. Thanks also to David Andrews; Mark Falcous; Ryan King-White; Andy Grainger; Steve Jackson; Janelle Joseph; Jennifer L. Metz; and Michael Silk.

Joshua also thanks his friends, colleagues, and mentors at the University of Memphis, the University of Maryland, Towson University, and the University of Otago, especially Carolyn Albright,

John Amis, Hannah Booker, Bryan Bracey, Jessica Braunstein, Lisette Burrows, Chris Button, Ik-Young Chang, Jessica Chin, Brian Cook, Michael Friedman, James Govan, Hamish Gould, Allen Hill, Ken Hodge, John Hyden, Koji Kobayashi, Geoff Kohe, Alex Kolb, Richard Irwin, Woo-Young Lee, Brian Loeffler, Russ McSwain, Robert Pitter, Elaine Rose, Mike Sam, Sally Shaw, Jon Shemmell, Jennifer Sterling, Lisa Swanson, Alapasita Teu, Luiz Uehara, Bruno Watkins, Renee Wikaire, and David Zang. Special thanks to his mom and dad; to his awesome brother Seth; to his best friend and partner Anne, for always being so kind and selfless; and to Rhys, for all the warm smiles and hearty laughs.

Michael also thanks his colleagues in the College of Media at the University of Illinois (his former home), especially Norman K. Denzin, CL Cole, Cameron McCarthy, and Peter Sheldon, and in the Department of Sport Management at Florida State University (his new home), especially Jeffrey James, chair of the department, and Marcy Driscoll, Dean of the College of Education, for continued support of his research endeavors. Special thanks to Andra K. Manczur, Michele K. Donnelly, and Jeremy H. Tate for conversations related to "flowcharts, Christmas trees, and baseball." Extra special thanks to his mom, for her love and support.

Finally, we thank the editors and publishers of the following editions for allowing us to reprint portions of our earlier work, which are interspersed throughout the book:

Newman, J. I. (2010). Full-throttle Jesus: Toward a critical pedagogy of stockcar racing in theocratic America. *Review of Education, Pedagogy, and Cultural Studies, 32*(3), 263–285.

Newman, J. I., & Beissel, A. S. (2009). The limits to "NASCAR Nation": Sport and the "recovery movement" in disjunctural times. *Sociology of Sport Journal, 26*(4), 517–539.

Newman, J. I., & Giardina, M. D. (2008). NASCAR and the "Southernization" of America: Spectatorship, subjectivity, and the confederation of identity. *Cultural Studies ⇔ Critical Methodologies, 8*(4), 479–506.

Newman, J. I., & Giardina, M. D. (2010). Neoliberalism's last lap? NASCAR, cultural politics, and the consuming mythologies of a failing empire. *American Behavioral Scientist, 53*(11), 1511–1529.

Also, parts of Chapter Six were presented on October 31, 2008 at the Annual Conference for the North American Society for the Sociology of Sport by Beissel, A. S. and Newman, J. I. as "Manufacturing America: Post-industrialism and the militarized stock car spectacle."

JOSHUA I. NEWMAN
MICHAEL D. GIARDINA
December 2010

INTRODUCTION

O n February 15, 2004, George W. Bush made the nineteenth visit of his presidency to the state of Florida, site of the contested 2000 election returns that eventually elevated him, by way of a controversial U.S. Supreme Court decision, to the highest office in the land. This visit would be like no other, however, as Bush was scheduled to attend the Daytona 500 race, which is generally accepted as the most important and prestigious event of the domestic automobile racing season. Like virtually all of his previous presidential appearances, this one was scripted like a Broadway show to timeless perfection: Bush arrived on the scene in grand fashion, his motorcade driving once around the 2.5 mile racetrack and creeping slowly past the main grandstand to the fanfare of the 180,000 cheering, clapping, and flag-waving fans in attendance (some flags of which were of the Confederate variety) (Benedetto, 2004). With each ostentatious left turn on the track, the president further forged a powerful symbolic relationship between stock car automobile culture and the conservative political agenda he had come to embody over the previous decade. Political scientist William Connolly (2005) described the scene of Bush emerging from his SUV "to an incredible roar of approval" in this manner:

> The crowd responded to the SUV as a symbol of disdain for womanly ecologists, safety advocates, supporters of fuel economy, weak-willed pluralists, and internationalists. Bush played upon the symbol and drew energy from the crowd's acclamation of it. Resentment against those who express an ethos of care for the world was never named: a message expressed without being articulated. (p. 879)

Wearing a black leather Daytona 500 jacket covered with stock car racing-themed insignias, Bush inspected cars and posed for pictures with the sport's most popular drivers (Benedetto, 2004). Country western singer Lee Greenwood entertained fans with his well-known rendition of "God Bless the USA," which had experienced something of a popular revival as a post-9/11 anthem of American patriotism. Adding military flavor to the spectacle of sport, machines, and politics, two F-15s streaked by overhead, followed by another flyover from a B-2 stealth bomber flanked by fighter jet escorts. Air Force One, stationed at nearby Daytona Beach International Airport, was clearly visible to fans in the grandstands.

By all accounts, Bush's wartime politics and nationalist rhetoric were welcome additions to the signature event of the National Association for Stock Car Auto Racing (NASCAR) calendar that year. Addressing the crowd prior to the start of the race, Bush praised the sport and thanked its drivers and fans for their unbridled support of the military, tacitly articulating the sport and its popularly perceived patriotic undertones with his own religious-inflected political agenda. He stated in part:

> Laura [Bush] and I are honored to be here for this fantastic spectacle. We ask God's blessings on the drivers, NASCAR fans, and on our great nation. Now it is my honor to start this race. Gentlemen, start your engines. (Bush, quoted in Allen, 2004, p. A1)

During an interview televised later during the race, Bush turned his focus to wars in Iraq and Afghanistan, explicitly pointing to the role the NASCAR fan had in supporting interventions that would soon become deeply unpopular amongst most self-identified Americans:

> [o]ne of the things about NASCAR and NASCAR fans is they support our military. We've got a lot of really good young men and women who are sacrificing for our country...I'm the Commander-in-Chief of a great group of people, and to know that citizens who support NASCAR support them makes me feel good. (Bush, quoted in Sanger, 2004, p. A17)

Rhetorically invoking the image of a wartime military leader instead of a run-of-the-mill politician leading a country during a time of relative peace, Bush then made the racing-war nexus even more explicit, stating: "I flew fighters when I was in the [national] guard, and I like speed" (ibid.).[1]

This active linking of sporting fervor, military enterprise, and nationalist zeal is, of course, not unique to George W. Bush, to the United States, or to NASCAR. From Spartakiad-era Soviet athletics fields to post-September 11, 2001, baseball diamonds in the United States, and across a vast panoply of national sporting spaces in between (think: Berlin 1936, Barcelona 1938, Melbourne 1956, Mexico City 1968, Munich 1972, or Argentina 1978), sport has been an incubator—if not in many nation-states the *crucible*—for popularizing the militarized nation. And make no mistake, George W. Bush did not hostilely invade NASCAR that early winter's morning in 2004. The appearance was a cooperative effort between the White House and the burgeoning racing league—each seeking to further their popularity within the realms of sport and political consumerism; they did so knowing that such a symbiotic endeavor *would work*. For, as political and sporting pundits alike were well aware, the millions of spectators either at the track or watching from home on television were generally some of the most satisfied constituents with Bush's otherwise controversial first term as president. Fans in attendance were quick to voice support for Bush; consider the following two comments overheard by the *Daily Telegraph*'s (London) Alec Russell (2004) while covering the Daytona 500:

> One of the best presidents we had. He wasn't handed his career on a silver platter. And just compare him to past presidents, like Clinton...That's embarrassing. (Candace, age 29, school secretary and mother of three).

> I'd still vote for him even if he didn't back NASCAR. He freed a lot of people in Iraq from what they were under. It's just a shame we didn't finish it off 10 years ago. (Steve, middle-aged father from Kentucky).[2]

*   *   *

In some ways, the 2004 Daytona 500 was a signpost. It was one of the highest-rated televised races of the decade. Dale Earnhardt, Jr., son of one the most revered racers of all-time, Dale Earnhardt, Sr., produced the most significant victory of his career at the same place where his daredevil father had perished four years earlier. In a scene that unfolded in ways a Hollywood scriptwriter could never conjure up, a throng of sunburned bodies looked down from Daytona's mammoth grandstands, weeping as the prodigal son of the sporting South exorcized the specters of his father's tragic passing. Moreover, the victory by "Junior," far and away the most popular driver on the circuit at that time, could be understood as a surrogate triumph for the legions of "Southern men" who largely identified with their auto-hero archetype. He was the embodiment of a new Southern man, and his triumph transcendent of the moment and the sport that brought it to life. And with George W. Bush—himself a media-constructed "Southern" man—in tow, and millions of adoring fans looking on, this moment seemingly reaffirmed the place of the imaginary

"South," its culture, and the labors of its high-profile luminaries in shaping both the sporting and national condition.

Here, at the heights of his presidential purview, George W. Bush basked in the protracted drone emanating from the sporting *carnivale* of his "American Empire"—at home in a sporting space awash with corporate logos celebrating capitalism's most successful global conglomerates, drowning in the murmur of national solidarity and roaring V-8 modernity, and amidst a sea of all-American bodies that seemed to be feverously endorsive of the political order that he had brought to bear. In this moment, the spectacle of NASCAR's "signature event" provided much more than an aesthetic backdrop for reveling in the cultural politics produced and embodied by this icon of "American masculinity." To borrow from Maurice Roche (2000), it was a "mega-event" that transcended its sporting confines and gave witness to the contextual specificities of its time. Or, put differently, it was at once *a sign of the times* and *a producer of those times.*

This revelry, if not synergy, between NASCAR, its fans, and Bush's Republican Party was not something that materialized out of thin air. Having spent the better part of the preceding two decades courting the fans of "America's fastest growing sport," conservative Republican figures had become seemingly natural fixtures at the weekly NASCAR events before, though especially during, that 2004 election season. Throughout the 2004 racing season—at what some might argue was the apex of the "Republican Revolution" that started more than a decade prior—the son of an oil magnate-turned-baseball bourgeoisie-turned President of the United States of America had successfully carved out an important cultural space from which to anchor, and indeed protract, his brand of free market conservative Republicanism. It was thus here, in, and through the NASCAR spectacle—*perhaps more than any other aspect of the national culture*—that Bush, Vice President Dick Cheney, Secretary of Defense Donald Rumsfeld, and a legion of Republican campaign hands had committed themselves to redefining the core precepts of their "America."[3]

At each stop, Republican hands took to NASCAR's grandstands, infields, and airwaves, consistently espousing rhetorical declarations of a return to Christian "fundamentals," a stripping-back of any regulatory measures that might flout the procession of the free market, the abolition of Affirmative Action, a retrenchment of "gay rights," a recentering of middle-class American "family values," a conjoining of faith and State, a "tougher approach" to stopping immigration in the wake of September 11, 2001, the demise of "big government," proposals to expand government subsidies for the wars in Iraq and

Afghanistan, and increased autonomy for "Homeland Security." Importantly, they were welcomed with open arms, as when Secretary Rumsfeld received a standing ovation during the prerace drivers' meeting during a Pepsi 400 race in Daytona on Independence Day weekend, where he served as the honorary Grand Marshal for the race; he was quoted as saying, "Everywhere I go around the world the troops talk about NASCAR and how much it reminds them of home" (Alvarez, 2005, p. 1). (Either, one would assume, because of NASCAR's widespread publicity, or the fact that so many servicemen and servicewomen hail from the working-class U.S. South.) At each stop, these political actors made use of the sporting spectacle to deploy their strategically orchestrated performances of "good ole boy" sportsmanship and Southern-inflected partisan nation-building.

And it worked! Within these stock car circles, the cultural, economic, and political promise of George W. Bush's "America" had caught on. What emulsified was "NASCAR Nation": an imagined spectator community of "rural, small-town, mostly white, Southern fans of America's fastest growing spectator sport" (Derbyshire, 2003, p. 29). In a sporting era defined by various forms of *faux* "Nationhood" (i.e., Boston's "Red Sox Nation," Florida State University's "Seminole Nation," etc.), NASCAR Nation was an ephemerally imagined formation that categorized the cohesive sporting-consuming and cultural-political community of North American stock car racing. However, unlike the other sporting "nations" of its time, especially from 2004 onward, NASCAR Nation came to signify much more than fans of fast cars and checkered flags. As it was deployed in print media journalism, multiplatform newspeak, Fox News Channel bylines, and "America First" satellite radio programming, NASCAR Nation played a large part in defining what Lauren Berlant (1997) refers to as a discursive articulation of *cultural citizenship* within the broader national imaginary.

In the 2004 election year, and with the sport garnering more national attention than ever before, NASCAR Nation as popular discursive element came to represent a *double entendre*: in sporting terms, it referenced the collective configurations of fan-consumers of North American stock car auto racing; in terms of national polity, it came to signify a palpable solidarity around an "American" nationalism grossly transcendent of its sporting origins. Newscasters, politicians, advertisers, and media pundits began to reference NASCAR Nation not only when speaking of the legions of fans that congregated at weekly NASCAR events, *but also* when evoking a more homogenized cultural politics they assumedly shared. When Republican political figures sought public mandate for a new initiative or piece of legislation, Washington politicos would almost intuitively make declarations such as "it is backed by NASCAR Nation" or "it is the will of NASCAR Nation" or "it will benefit NASCAR Dads everywhere." When Bush's domestic or foreign policy came under public scrutiny (such as when he gave the orders to invade Iraq), pundits across the political spectrum quickly pointed out that while it may indeed be a "tough" and perhaps "unpopular" decision amongst many voters, the NASCAR Nation bloc was "unwavering" in its support for "the cause."

Under these platitudes of partisan politics meets consumer culture, NASCAR Nation had become political shorthand for white, working-class, Christian fundamentalist, (Southern), conservatism. While on its face it alluded to an imagined community of America's newest favorite spectator sport,[4] it can be more critically understood as a linguistic and cultural strategy eliciting broader ideological capture, identity politics, and machinations of American nationalism under the George W. Bush presidency. Along the way, the latter meaning came to impose itself on the former, whereby to be a member of sporting NASCAR Nation became synonymous with adherence to the staunch ideological foundations upon which the Republican Party's platform was thrust into the national consciousness. In sum, NASCAR Nation was at once a subject position, an imagined community, a commercial invention, and a political identity all crystallized around one of—if not the most—public and dominant popular formations of American nationalism in recent history.

In turn, consumption of the sporting spectacle became more than a simple act of fandom, sporting allegiance, or stock car fetishism. It became an expression of loyalty *to the Nation*, and the direction it was heading under the reign of the man they called "Dubya." By the time voters went to the polls to determine the outcome of that year's presidential contest, the semiotic collision of sport and politics had become the foundation upon which Bush's successful reelection bid was popularly constructed. As many political analysts (rightly) predicted, fans of stock car auto racing played a significant role in determining the outcome of that year's race (the political one). While the Republican Party was able to tread water in nationwide congressional elections, Bush and other political figures who had strategically aligned themselves with the discursive iteration invoked by NASCAR Nation expanded their electoral "mandate." The consensus was clear: the Right's ability to connect with the imagined fan base of stock car racing had been instrumental in the victory. As one CNN analyst proclaimed, "Right now Republicans rule. They control the

White House, both houses of Congress and most state governments. The basis of the Republicans' ruling majority: NASCAR Nation" (Schneider, 2004).

WHY NASCAR? WHY NOW?

In *Sport, Spectacle, and NASCAR Nation*, we examine how the sport of stock car automobile racing was, and continues to be, an important site for "manufacturing consent" (Chomsky, 2003a) for the ideologies, identities, and policies that defined the George W. Bush presidency; and which continue to challenge and in some ways define the presidency of Barack Obama. While the contrived use of sport for political or economic purposes is neither new nor exclusive to the modern-day United States (we can think as far back as the bread-and-circuses maxim of Roman gladiatorial spectacles), what is worth further exploration are the ways in which NASCAR's spectacular spaces—both the mediated spaces we see on TV/online and the physical spaces where the events take place—have been mobilized over the past decade-plus to delineate the boundaries of a "national" critical mass that continues to perpetuate a dominant, sometimes exclusive, cultural, political, and economic agenda.

This book was conceived at the heights of the George W. Bush presidency, a historical moment when—despite early signals of a failing free market economy, increased national unemployment and poverty, heightened Wall Street corruption, the erosion of the nation's Social Security system, extensive outsourcing of the nation's skilled labor jobs, increased tensions around issues of immigration, abortion, and gay rights, an uptick in Patriot Act-led civil rights violations and human rights abuse (e.g., Guantanamo Bay, torture), and escalated (and increasingly unpopular) wars in Iraq and Afghanistan—the president was for the first time able to capture a majority of the popular vote in his 2004 reelection bid. As critical scholars, we found it increasingly difficult to turn away from the important role the sport of stock car racing was playing in the continued expansion of the Bush regime's autonomy over the judicial, military, pecuniary, moral, cultural, and legislative facets of American society. Given the rapid ascent of NASCAR as a popular sporting formation within the United States and beyond—and the peculiar relationship the racing league had forged with only *one side* of the U.S. political binary—we were both surprised and disappointed to find that stock car racing had garnered but very little critical attention within the pages of most academic and journalistic texts (sporting or otherwise).

In the few instances where the scholarly klieg light had theretofore been turned toward the sport (e.g., Hagstrom, 1998; Howell, 1997; Wright, 2002), NASCAR was curiously *celebrated* as the "idyllic" American sport: portrayed as a gas-guzzling sporting utopia of late modern *pax Americana*. As Jim Wright (2002) concluded in his year-long study of NASCAR, the sport had emerged as the sporting arche-type of "all that was good" about America: a celebration of "normal" American values and virtues. NASCAR racing, he wrote,

> is a festival of cars, a celebration of America, a metaphor for the American dream...[where] patriotic sentimentality hangs thick in the air...American flags streaming from the infield RVs...the singing of the National Anthem and the Blue Angels flyover, the benediction, the cars, the competition, the postrace fireworks, and just about every-thing else you encounter at the track drip with traditional America. (pp. 34–35)

Indeed, most contributions to the public discourse amounted to little more than this type of writer-fan hagiography—glossing over NASCAR's exclusively white racial identity politics, its underlying patriarchal gender politics, its overtly conservative political com-mitment, its hyper-Christian orthodoxy, and its omnipresent com-mercialism—or locating each as a "natural" product of NASCAR's Southern roots.

Surprisingly absent from and within the aforementioned texts, however, is any sort of prolonged, physical engagement with the NASCAR empirical and the contexts within which it is grounded.[5] By way of example, and although now somewhat dated, Mark Howell's (1997) *From Moonshine to Madison Avenue: A Cultural History of the NASCAR Winston Cup Series* provides a traditional, if perhaps overly fawning, historiography of NASCAR read primarily through the lens of automobile culture and history, and Robert Hagstrom's (1998) *The NASCAR Way: The Business that Drives the Sport* is a useful if business-oriented introductory text that limits its discussion to that of business practices and consumer behavior. In these texts, NASCAR is most often depicted as a sport league devoid of gender inequality and class determinacy, and which is in the process of sweeping the last residues of racism under its proverbial grandstands.

From the journalistic perspective, Jeff MacGregor's (2005) main-streamed *Sunday Money: Speed! Lust! Madness! Death! A Hot Lap Around America with NASCAR* vacillates between a serious journal-istic meditation on the sport and a literary exercise in watching auto racing for a year. Likewise, syndicated columnist Monte Dutton's

Postcards from Pit Road: Inside NASCAR's 2002 Season (2003) portends to be an insider's account of a "day at the races," but is nonetheless a predictable, by-the-numbers "roadtrip" account that does more to celebrate the drivers and their sport than challenge the official mediated pedagogies of the NASCAR spectacular. In addition, a number of journalists have added to this overly celebratory trend since we first set out to write this book. Liz Clarke's (2008) *One Helluva Ride: How NASCAR Swept the Nation*, which received advance praise from NASCAR celebrities such as Rusty Wallace, is a recent example of another uncritical foray into attempting to explain why NASCAR is "interesting."[6] Most recently, Mark Bechtel's (2010) *He Crashed Me So I Crashed Him Back* reads like a fisticuff novella—dramatizing through prose recklessness, bravado, and abandon—that looks back at the 1979 season and the legacies of NASCAR "good ole boys" Junior Johnson, Richard Petty, and the Allison brothers to retrace the emergence of stock car racing out of the U.S. South and into the U.S. mainstream.

Against this trajectory, *Sport, Spectacle, and NASCAR Nation* is a stark departure from this standard, overcelebratory fare. Instead, we map the sport of stock car racing as a significant cultural and, to borrow from French social theorist Louis Althusser (1971), "ideological," apparatus in the service of free market cultural and political economies. To this end, we connect two seemingly unrelated, yet politically incontrovertible, questions that many individuals—both those progressives within the United States and those onlookers abroad—have no doubt been asking themselves over the past few years: (1) "why (and how) has NASCAR become so popular?" and (2) "why would so many Americans consent to the seemingly antidemocratic policies of the so-called modern-day 'conservative movement'?" As such, we argue that at a contextually specific intersection of a *laissez-faire* economic revival, a resuscitation of the U.S. South's (neo-)Confederate cultural politics, and new moral projections of fundamentalist individualism—those organized around, and often for, the purposes of the free market, regimes of ecologically unsustainable corporate capitalism, and ethnocentric, heteronormative sectarianism—the "institutions, rituals, and subcultures" of NASCAR do indeed celebrate dominant social and political ideologies, but do so not in the service of what is "right" and "good" about America (as numerous mainstream commentators have suggested). Rather, we attempt to demonstrate how the cultural politics of "NASCAR Nation" have been co-opted in ways that stand in direct opposition to the rudiments of equality, democracy, and freedom.

In short, this is a study of the cultural politics of neoliberalism—of cultural politics as consumption—and how singular acts of consuming the sporting spectacle are complicated by cultural, political, and economic forces acting upon the seemingly banal sporting sphere. By way of this study, we pry these political regimes loose from both their discursive (sporting) veneer and stock car signifiers, and thereby illuminate and demystify the identities, practices, subjectivities, and hierarchies that are made "normal" or, as Wright (2002) suggests, "worshipped" through the spectacular machinations of NASCAR. Put more simply, we examine how, by entering into NASCAR spaces (mediated, physical, imaginary, etc.), the individual is subjected to the broader social, cultural, political, and economic imperatives of neoliberalism. We do so not to suggest that NASCAR fans, drivers, or administrators are cultural dupes or greed- or hate-mongering authoritarians, but rather we seek to map the sociopolitical architecture by which individual and group agency, freedom, and sovereignty is constrained by, and within, NASCAR Nation.

To get a better sense of what might be wrong and Right with the sport of stock car racing, we spent the better part of five years consuming all that NASCAR had to offer. We went to dozens of races around the United States, and watched even more on television. We loaded up the car for numerous road trips spanning the Northern-, Western-, and Southern-most reaches of NASCAR Nation; set up many weekend camps at NASCAR's most famous tracks (Talladega, Martinsville, Phoenix, Bristol, Darlington, Dover, Charlotte, etc.); spent many a late night cavorting with NASCAR faithful at the nearest overpopulated Motel Six or Red Roof Inn; and watched week-by-week as 43 automobiles completed thousands upon thousands of collision-crazed, adrenaline-filled, "hot laps." We joined fantasy NASCAR leagues,[7] bought souvenir race-themed kitsch, tailgated with NASCAR "diehards," swilled plenty of Budweiser beer, gorged ourselves on Bojangles biscuits, and attended everything from prerace concerts to post-race Bible study sessions. We watched live races on network television, blogged on fan websites, tuned in to NASCAR reality television programs, listened to stock car pundits on satellite radio, and read racks of auto-sport magazines to gain a better perspective of the complex, often contradictory, nature of the consumer cultures of the sport.

Along the way we established connections with fans, vendors, racing teams, members of the newsmedia, and corporate sponsors. However, as the reader will no doubt recognize early in the book, we avoided any direct or sanctioned research relationship with NASCAR. We did so for several reasons: First, in writing a book about "consuming NASCAR," we thought it best to consume NASCAR from the ground up, as much in the spectating arena as possible. Like most other fans, we never went behind the curtain to meet the Great and Mighty Oz, but rather lived within the sporting world he created. Thus, we focused on the consumer cultures and community practices of the sport's fan base. While others have solicited interviews or conducted field research with NASCAR officials, drivers, or sponsors, we thought it best to find out what the everyday NASCAR *consumer* had to say.[8]

Second, and perhaps more importantly, in order to most fairly represent the NASCAR spectacle, we did not want to *owe* NASCAR anything, and in so doing potentially subject our study to what MacGregor (2005) refers to as the "blithe revisionism of NASCAR and its reflexive hypersensitivity to any version of events other than its own" (p. A13). There was actually some precedence for our concerns: in an updated edition of *Sunday Money*, MacGregor points out that while developing his book, NASCAR had pressured him to avoid using terms like "moonshiners" and "traveling carnival," to selectively exaggerate the sport's popularity, to use NASCAR's internal research data in delimiting its "fan base," to remove all images of the Confederate flag, and to only use representations of fans the league deemed suitable. Rather than compromise our empirical method, and fall prey to such a systematic scheme of "we gave you access, now write a pro-NASCAR story," we decided from the outset that to better tell the story of NASCAR's consumer spectacle—and to do so in a dialectically committed and critically engaged way—we would be best served not to be indebted to the league office in any way.[9]

In sum, we cultivated an extensive critical ethnography of fan experiences, consumer behavior, producer codes, and media coverage active within NASCAR events. Through qualitative interviews and participant observations[10] conducted over the course of more than 300 hours spent at NASCAR races, we critically mapped the spatial, practical, and political dimensions of NASCAR Nation. We were consumer-researcher-*flâneurs* seeking to better understand how, and why, the spectating acts of NASCAR had become so politically malleable and commercially viable. And in what follows, we do our best to fairly and accurately represent what we saw and what we did along the way. Unlike many of our scholarly friends in the social sciences, we make no nomothetic claims and promise no metatheoretical ends. Rather, we seek to flesh out the finite, nuanced cultural practices upon which this sport-polity symbiosis was constructed. Furthermore, we offer no generalizable portrait of the "typical" NASCAR consumer or the citizen of NASCAR Nation, but instead try only to identify those intermediaries, organizations, and structures of power that intercede upon lived praxis within broader formations of this Nation.

Again, it should be noted that our intention here is *not* to dismiss or denigrate NASCAR, its fans, or even those most strident of "American patriots." Rather, our aim is to deconstruct the practices and processes by which cultural citizenship has been forged and articulated in and through the sport of stock car racing in hopes of writing toward a better NASCAR Nation—one less structured around economic exploitation, political manipulation, racial exclusivity, gender inequity, and religious proselytization. As we make clear in what follows, we found in contemporary NASCAR a sport, a collection of fans, and a set of traditions that have been besieged from all sides by political ideologues, religious fundamentalists, corporate capitalists, white supremacists, and mercenaries of militaristic conquest acting not in the best interests of the sport or its spectating masses, but in their own interests. In the process, the sport has been stripped of its pluralistic, democratic, and humanistic potentialities. And so through critique, we hope to also exfoliate a better, more humane, and more equitable NASCAR Nation.

THE CHAPTERS

In total, *Sport, Spectacle, and NASCAR Nation* offers a critical exploration into the role that the NASCAR organization, its celebrity-drivers, proprietors of race-themed wares, and the sport's ancillary cultural and moral intermediaries have played in expanding what the U.S. South's foremost critical pedagogue, the late Joe Kincheloe (2008), often referred to as the "recovery movement." This movement, Kincheloe tells us, involves the systematic reinvigoration of the conditions and mechanisms that have historically (re)produced power and unequal social relations within society—whether they be "colonial power resuscitated by new forms of colonialism"; "gender power by new forms of patriarchy"; "racial power by new forms of white supremacy"; or "class power by new forms of class elitism and globalized empire." It is a multimodal "movement" that manifests itself in economic reinvigorations of *laissez-faire* capitalism, in "bicultural" imaginings of the (neo)colonizer, in the "homophobic" stylings of Fundamentalist zealots, and so on. We argue that with Dubya as the figurehead, merchants of this domestic (and globally interconnected) "brand" of conservative cultural politics and liberalized political economy made use of sport, and in this case NASCAR, in their incessant efforts to *recover* the systems of power imbedded in the identity politics, market hegemony, and national morality from which NASCAR Nation was defined.

Our investigative and interpretive reflections on this sport-politics relationship are interwoven through a discussion on the broader implications of stock car spaces and spectacles—mesmerizing cultural features that give life, power, and privilege to a dominant "ideological blanket" (Baudrillard, 1989) and authorize a public pedagogy framed in the discourses of the recovery movement (Giroux, 2004b). Hence, our aim here is indeed a critically pedagogical one*: to politicize the seemingly innocuous sporting spaces and spectacles of NASCAR's contextually contrived "Git-R-Done" faux populism over and against the context of post-September 11, 2001, social relations in the United States.* Thus do we connect the dots: we bring into focus the problematic nature of this nonnatural, strategically orchestrated sporting spectacle. Drawing from an interdisciplinary breadth of theories relative to consumer culture, political and cultural economy, and identity politics, the interrelated studies of *Sport, Spectacle, and NASCAR Nation* articulate the relationship between NASCAR's dominant symbols (e.g., Confederate Flag and corporate logos), celebrities (e.g., Jeff Gordon or Dale Earnhardt, Jr.), practices (e.g., tailgating in the infield or praying before a race), spectacles (e.g., the Daytona 500), and commodities (e.g., themed merchandise or media products) to the rise of George W. Bush's brand of free market enterprise and its nonneutral economic, cultural, and political extensions. In so doing, we explicate NASCAR's recent ascendance as part of a broader shift in contemporary sport, whereby the act of "being a fan" has been subjected to the strategic co-optation of public (sport) culture by political ideologues and corporate actors.

Organizationally, the remainder of the book is divided into eight interrelated, yet topically distinct, chapters. In Chapter One, "Sporting Automobility," we begin by situating stock car auto racing within its broader historical and political contexts. Drawing upon theories of "automobility"—and that of John Urry, Raymond Williams, Jeremy Packer, and Donna Haraway in particular—we examine the automobile's ascendant place within the cultures of production and consumption in the United States during the twentieth century. As Mike Featherstone (2004) suggests, the American car, in both its productive and consumptive imaginings, evokes the "powerful cultural dreams of adventure and freedom: the capacity to go anywhere, to move and dwell without asking permission, the self-directed life free from the surveillance of the authorities" (p. 2). That freedom, Americans have been reminded for more than a century, comes through their dual places (producer/consumer) within industrial capitalism.

Thus in Chapter One do we meditate on stock car racing's role in producing these frames of "automobility"; whereby the control, manipulation, and acceleration of the automobile on the track became a central signifier and practice of human autonomy and a celebration of the logics of late-Fordist Era automobile production. We offer a brief genealogy of the sport of stock car racing, tracing it from the back roads of Southeastern Appalachia and the factory floors of Detroit through to Bill France's conglomeration of the sport's disparate rural competitions across the South to NASCAR's recent rise up the North American professional sporting hierarchy. As such, this chapter serves as a partner discourse to Paul Gilroy's (2010) recent book *Darker than Blue*, in that we seek to frame the role of the automobile in constructing forms of subjectivity, class politics, and whiteness—an attempt to answer Gilroy's (2010) call for analysis that encompasses "the alienated but nonetheless popular pleasures of auto-freedom (mobility, power, and speed) while appreciating their conspicuous interpersonal and civic...costs" (pp. 30–31). Finally, we explore the contradictions of "autonomy" and "mobility" that arise within a sport that at once gained its "hot rod" popularity for rejecting regulation (outlaws breaking speed laws) and yet became the nation's most-highly regulated sporting enterprise.

Chapter Two, "The Road and Serfdom," serves as a primer on the terms and conditions of neoliberalism operative within the United States during a specific conjuncture a late-capitalism, and against which we situated the NASCAR enterprise. As the final episodes of the twentieth century unveiled a plot twist toward the (eternal) return of a pure market society in most developed nation-states—and particularly in Reagan's United States, Thatcher's United Kingdom, and "Chicago Boy" South America—the United States became a major artery in the flows of polity, cultural, and capital across increasingly porous international boundaries. This, in turn, presented new challenges to the American worker in places like Detroit, Michigan, where thousands of automobile manufacturing jobs were outsourced to developing nations. We begin by discussing the influential work of Friedrich von Hayek as it relates to free market ideology. Next, we unpack the various strains of conservative dogma that have become entrenched within the United States over the past several decades. This entails examining both paleo-conservative and neo-conservative political rationalities, as well as the fusion of the two emerging out of the Reagan era. Finally, we move to define the terms of neoliberal empire (see Pieterse, 2006), and how it informs our study moving forward.

In this chapter we also explore how within this contextual paradox—and as the political economic structure of the nation seems to increasingly assume a natural free market status quo (in spite of a long, healthy, welfare state tradition)—the fast-moving car, both on the road and on the track, presents a metonymical site for understanding the movement and flows of capital, politics, and autonomy. In our analysis here, we draw especially on the work of French social theorist Paul Virilio as counterpoint to neoliberal orthodoxies of market freedom and sovereignty. Our aim is thus to "catch up" with the speed of capital, and in so doing examine how the automobile as a commercial and cultural formation accelerates the concentrated logics of what Ben Agger (1989) calls "fast capitalism"—a just-in-time system of capital accumulation, technological transference, communicative interconnectivity, and consumer intensity.

Chapters Three, Four, Five, and Six make up the core empirical and analytical thrust of the book, examining the spatial practices and empirical performances active within and about NASCAR Nation. In these chapters, we investigate how political economies of consumerism, identity politics of race, social class, and gender,[11] cultural politics of faith and religion, and the militarization of U.S. nationalism intersect within the spatial practices of the NASCAR spectacle. Starting with Chapter Three, "Consuming NASCAR Nation," we examine the corporate and commercial architectures of NASCAR—both on the balance sheets and in the grandstands. As most anyone who has ever attended a NASCAR event can attest, no other North American sport rivals stock car racing in terms of commercialization and saturation of corporate symbols. Hence, we offer a spatial forensic of the corporate-sporting body. Informed by Michel Foucault's (1988b) notion of "technologies of the self," we examine how expressions and performances of freedom and individualism—often situated within the core *epistemes* of "being an American"—often subject these laboring and consuming bodies to broader constructs of "consumer-citizenship."

In Chapter Four, "NASCAR and the 'Southernization' of Sporting America," we revisit John Egerton's notion of "the Southernization of America" and update his thesis for the southerly shift in contemporary social, cultural, political, moral, and popular discourse. Egerton (1974) suggested that the ascendance of a "Southern ethic"—and particularly the singular version bound to Old South politics of racism, sexism, and class privilege—not only signaled a change in the sociospatial configurations of the public sphere, but increasingly influenced ideals relative to American policy, economy, and culture. We thus examine stock car racing as an important fixture in this resurgent South. Written against the backdrop of a resurgence in Confederate remembering—vis-à-vis Confederate History celebrations recently reactivated in many Southern states—we report on a vast field of observation in what has been described as "the whitest sport on Earth" to better understand how the imaginary South, subjectivity, whiteness, and stock car racing coalesce around an amalgam of market-friendly "neo-Confederate" identity politics. We make the case that these identity politics of the "New Sporting South"—a distinctive formation whereby a localized form of sport culture stirs the specters of Old South racial hierarchies and gendered patriarchies, while simultaneously articulating new expressions of knowledge and old formations of power in the context of global/local pluralism—now act to reinforce the hypermasculine, hyperwhite center of power not only in the contemporary South, but in contemporary "America" more generally.

Chapter Five, "Racing for Jesus," offers an analysis of the dialectic interdependencies between Christian fundamentalism and NASCAR's spectating bodies, and how this peculiar convergence serves to territorialize race day grandstands as spaces of hyper-Christian proselytization. Through a vast array of observations and critical analyses, we interpret the *mélange* of those same bodily practices and moral discourses as powerful formations that consequently normalize conservative faith and neoliberal politics in NASCAR Nation. We bring into focus the assemblage of practices, signifiers, narratives, and ideologies that actively promulgate a spectacle of conservative Christianity within the sport and, as we contend, beyond. We further argue that the dialectics of performativity and spectacle within contemporary stock car culture (sporting consumption, sport and spiritual devotion, and performances of a politically-infused collective consciousness) have abetted what Kevin Phillips (2006) refers to as a new "American theocracy." In this way, religious and political intermediaries have not only seized the sport and its relative discursive formations—repackaging the hyperwhite, "Southernized" sporting spectacular as a central cultural apparatus in a Rightward-moving, theocratic American national imaginary—but also that the sport's newfound godliness has concomitantly recapitulated the capitalist imperatives of an increasingly deified neoliberal marketplace.

In the first part of Chapter Six, "NASCAR as/in Petrol Empire" we look into the sport's (spectacular) role in normalizing new paradigms of petrol dependency and "peak oil" politics. We argue that within the contemporary U.S. energy economy, NASCAR acts as a fulcrum of petrol excess. Against the backdrop of oil spill catastrophe and oligarchic megaprofits, these gas-guzzling race cars promote a culture of petrol euphoria. Then following on in the second part of Chapter Six, "Militarizing NASCAR Nation," we examine how this petrol emphasis is belied by, if not conjunctive of, NASCAR's pronounced militaristic nationalism. No other feature of the U.S. sportscape is as saturated with promilitary imagery and rhetoric as NASCAR. Which is to say, at a moment when U.S. forces move about the globe seeking to "stabilize" the nation's place atop the economic, moral, and political hierarchies of the "new world order" (amidst significant international backlash toward perceived political and cultural imperialism), stock car exponents look to the military to keep pumping Iraqi oil fields for the last drops of petrol needed to keep running the race—so that they might then beam footage thereof via satellite television back to new sport consumer markets in the Middle East.[12]

Prying loose the machinations of the military-industrial complex from the sporting spaces they inhabit, we deconstruct the synergy of hypermilitarized spaces and national identities within the sport of stock car racing and unravel NASCAR's "frames of war" (as Judith Butler [2010] might put it). Written while deep in a sporting empirical where pro-gun and anti-immigration bumper stickers adorn the sea of Ford and Chevy SUVs and trucks outside NASCAR tracks, this chapter especially focuses on the transformation of NASCAR tracks into prowar, militarized spaces of "hypermasculine American imperialism," a space in which the following signs and symbols were all-too-often visible: "Charlton Heston is my President"; "Osama Bin Laden's worst enemy" (with a picture of a red-white-and-blue-striped machine gun; and "Homeland Security" (illustrated by a caricature of a Confederate flag-emblazoned "Southern man" holding a shotgun), and proffer solutions to the "oil crisis" such as "send the illegal Mexicans over to Iraq and make them earn it."

In Chapter Seven, "Selling Out NASCAR Nation," we explain how NASCAR's international, if not global, corporate aspirations are consequentially, if not paradoxically, bound to its own cultural introversion within the interconnected free market. That is, the most localized of North American sports has built brand equity through the cultural politics of conservative, white, Judeo-Christian, masculine-militaristic, "Southern" exclusivity. In turn, we argue that while in the short term NASCAR was able to become "America's fastest growing sport" in North America by capitalizing on its popularity within the contextually hegemonic confluence of neoliberal political economy and a proliferated Bush-era politically conservative South, the expansionist impetuses have been limited by these contradictory logics of the isolated local and the free-flowing global. Given that the league has in recent years seen a significant downturn in ratings and race attendance, as well as merchandise sales and corporate sponsorship, we offer a few preliminary conclusions regarding NASCAR's struggles within the free market it has so closely aligned its business and cultural edicts.

Utilizing a late-2010 visits to Talladega, Alabama and Phoenix, Arizona as our narrative backdrop, we draw our book to a close with a brief conclusion that looks beyond the days of the Bush era to the Age of Obama, a time in which NASCAR seems to be at an impasse (low ratings, low attendance figures, etc.), and also when white male resentment has been growing nationwide (inflamed by the so-called Tea Party and their de facto figurehead, former Republican vice presidential nominee Sarah Palin, who herself has become a mainstay in NASCAR circles), the Republican Party has become evermore regionalized and marginalized, and the future prosperity of the NASCAR experiment is in question. We point to broader machinations of neoliberal subjectivity within these configurations of *stock car citizenship*—subjectivities that at once position members of NASCAR Nation within (false) pedagogies of freedom: freedom to choose their branded consumer-citizenship, to choose their neo-Confederate identities, to perform their faith, and to belong to the militarized nation.

1

Sporting Automobility:

Contextualizing NASCAR Nation

America dreams driving. In these dreams you are alone. Flying low and loud and fast down a long, straightrazor stretch of Nebraska interstate, perhaps in late autumn, headed west, sharp cold just coming on, the desolate geometry of those golden stubble fields strobing past you, the sun wobbling low and weak on the horizon, your windshield embroidered with the glare of it, and in your rearview mirror the sky behind you as blue and deep as a bruise. You are cupped in the heated seat. The earth spins beneath you. All the shining instrumentality of uncomplicated power falls easily to hand. Your body dissolves into the machine until you are no more and no less than acceleration itself. The brute music of the engine rises up through the floorboards and the soles of your feet and into your blood until your heart pounds with it, the world blurs and the vast web of human complication dissolves somewhere far behind you and there is no past and no future and nothing bad can ever catch you. Nothing can touch you. That's the American dream. That's freedom.

—Jeff MacGregor (2005, p. x)

Freedom. If the nation's *tableau vivant* of commercial imagery and political rhetoric—filled with patriotic slogans and All-American symbolism—has taught us anything over the years, it is that "freedom" is not *just another word* in the ongoing story of "America." Freedom from what, or to do what, is often glossed over in order to get more directly to the main storyline: that in the United States, hard work, self-determination, devotion to the country, perseverance, obedience, and above all else, *individualism*, are all made possible through, and rewarded by, this collective sense of freedom. And as the epigraph suggests, the automobile is often positioned as a central apparatus for achieving such freedom within that enduring story (Packer, 2008). Historically, the automobile has been viewed as a way to realize freedom from boredom, a rite of passage toward adulthood, an escape from bucolic isolation, a mechanism for usurping the law of the land, and even a way to emancipate oneself from the condition of poverty (through the exchange valued labors of industrialism).

We knew the automobile was different from its very inception. Unlike its transportive predecessors (rail, horse and carriage, etc.), the individual was fully in control once inside the car. "The auto in the term automobile," writes Mike Featherstone (2004), "initially referred to a self-propelled vehicle (a carriage without a horse)." He continues, suggesting that over time drivers realized "the autonomy was not just through the motor, but the capacity for independent motorized self-steering movement freed from the confines of a rail track" (p. 1). And as the "juggernaut of modernity" (Giddens, 1990) churned forward, the automobile and the mastery of its potential for speed and freedom of movement became a way for the individual consumer to connect with the tides of modern progress. Through the car, the driver could *make* himself or herself *modern*. Put another way,

> the entire gamut of practices that foster car culture, qualifies both as a product and producer of modernity. Its constitutive visual image is one of dignified convoys of individual cars, vehicles whose solitary drivers can remain separated from each other as they collectively pursue private goals on public highways. As such, this picture captures the salient features of cars in a post-enlightenment order: the experience of driving, identified by the quiet pleasures of the open road, speed, power and personal control, neatly compliments the functionality of covering distance, managing time and maintaining certain forms of individuation. One might thus portray an ontology of automobility that reinforces its teleology; together, they establish characteristically that which is *modern* and, by definition, permanently desirable. (Rajan, 2006, p. 113)

Perhaps more than any other social bond, we might surmise that the car-driver relationship evolved into one that "transformed the material environment and the nature of sociality in late modern societies" such as the United States (Dant, 2004, p. 75; see also Dant & Martin, 2001). In turn, the national story of the twentieth century featured tales of hypermasculine, hyper-American auto impresarios in high-speed pursuit of that freedom. We need only look at automobile advertising from the 1940s and 1950s to see how narratives of autonomy and freedom (often framed within Western modernity's patriarchal norms of provider-father, stay-at-home mother, adoring children, and a white picket-fenced house in the growing suburbs) were operationalized in the national imaginary (Bachmair, 1991).[1]

Within these mass-mediated auto literacies, fast cars have long been both a fixture of—as well as the mode of choice for chasing—the "American Dream." In terms of the material relations of production, and as numerous scholars have often suggested (Freund & Martin, 1993; Gartman, 1994; Kay, 1997; Luger, 2000; McShane, 1994; Shukin, 2006), the automobile played a contextually significant, economically and socially important position in shaping the U.S. economy as an early twentieth-century industrial "superpower." The automobile was instrumental in ushering in an age of streamlined production, vertical integration, interchangeable parts, transferable technologies, and economies of scale and scope (Allen, 1992, 1996; Doray, 1988). Moreover, the rise of the automobile industry brought with it a trickle-down stimulus to *other* industries. As James Stuart Olson (2002) writes,

> Demand for better-quality roads led to a boom in construction, engineering, and architecture, and satellite businesses sprouted—service stations, roadside hotels and fast-food restaurants, engine-repair and body shops, and vacation resorts. By 1925, the automobile industry had surpassed steel and petroleum, in terms of the annual gross value of its products, as the dominant sector of the [U.S.] economy. (p. 16)

The ancillary effects of the burgeoning automobile industry were further illustrated in the lucrative national derivatives of glass, rubber, paint, and leather (Olson, 2002). Looking back, social scientists have long suggested that the car played a double role in the formation of U.S. modernity: "first, as a commodity that exemplifies the development of production in industrial capitalism and, second, as a commodity that exemplifies the desired object that motivates consumers in late capitalism" (Dant, 2004, p. 61). Consequently, most of the major industrial sectors that came to define the late-industrial U.S. economy were either directly or indirectly connected to the U.S. automobile industry.

Henry Ford's systems of standardized production and streamlined efficiency have been well-documented elsewhere (Allen, 1992, 1996; Doray, 1988; Harvey, 1989). However, what often gets overlooked is the extent to which his systems of production *produced* new regimes of mass consumption. Symbolically, the automobile industry became the anchor of the U.S. industrial economy, employing over 7 percent of the U.S. manufacturing workforce prior to the Great Depression (Olson, 2002). The standard within that sector, as set forth by Ford, was to reward workers with relatively high wages and fringe benefits for their labor (Harvey, 1989). Ford described his philosophy this way: "There is one rule for the industrialist and that is: make the best quality of goods possible at the lowest cost possible, paying the highest wages possible" (quoted in Beaman, 2004, p. x). Out of Ford's factory model emerged a new generation of highly skilled laborers—machinists, metalworkers, painters, upholsterers, and chemists. These workers garnered higher wages than semiskilled laborers in other sectors of the U.S. economy, sought and achieved labor reform, and through trade unions attained better working conditions (Babson, 1991). And the auto bourgeoisie obliged, yielding to a union-friendly (or at least union-tolerant) regulated capitalist system out of which, between 1889 and 1929, real hourly earnings increased incrementally, as did labor productivity levels (Jaher, 1968).

Furthermore, economists often point to the relatively affordable prices of the Model-T as a significant stimulus for middle-class (one overpopulated by skilled factory laborers) mass consumption during the first half of that century. Where at one time possessing an automobile was limited to the conspicuous consumer cultures of social elites (Packer, 2008), Fordist manufacturing methods brought the Model-T to new consumer markets with a moderate price point of $950 by 1909;[2] and Ford's intensified marketing techniques ensured that middle-class America *knew that a Model-T was within their reach* (Olson, 2002). In turn, between 1908 and 1927 Americans bought 15 million Model T's, with the total number of automobiles on the road rising from 200,000 to 20 million (Packer, 2008).

The automobile's rise in popularity ushered in a new era of reciprocity between cultural and economic realms—with wage laborers reinvesting their wage labor capital into the very products they produced. More importantly, those products became the stuff of modern consumer fetish—the act of consumption at once signaled loyalty to the industrial labor structure, the corporate mechanism, the commodity brand, and the national narrative woven into that system of accumulation. Whereas in the factory space production relations produced social relations, on the open road, sociality was constructed in conspicuous auto-parlance; in this way, one might argue, the "car as a consumer item legitimized and naturalized consumption rather than participation in the social world" (Bachmair, 1991, p. 527). This early century "car culture" became a source of both connectivity and *dis*connectivity: connecting Americans from disparate agrarian spaces through a sophisticated network of roads and highways and connecting the isolated worker to the consuming masses through new consumer-based cultural experiences; but also creating isolated, pod-like mobilities for the now atomized consumer-driver. New life-style industries also boomed, with well-paid workers spending money on service economies that included entertainment, amusement, restaurants, clothing, shopping, doctors, and banking industries. According to Olson (2002), "Finally, the automobile redefined the meaning of the term freedom" (p. 18).

Much like its central apparatus, car culture took us places. By driving, watching, and being in and amongst cars, we were immersed in an *autocade of modernity*. In mid-twentieth century U.S. culture, the car became the iconic linkage between the working/consuming individual and the structuration of modern capitalist democracy (Milkman, 1997). Ford himself was an outspoken advocate of this project of modernity—and particularly of abandoning the old logics of society for new, consumer-driven, instant-gratification, live-for-the-moment, pleasure-seeking principles that had come to define the revolution he had played a large part in creating. He once famously declared: "History is more or less bunk. It's tradition. We don't want tradition. We want to live in the present, and the only history that is worth a tinker's damn is the history that we make today" (*Chicago Tribune*, 1916).

And his cars became a metallic symbol of this new logic. For the greater part of the twentieth century, Ford's private automobiles "constituted something of an index of hegemony," suggests Paul Gilroy (2010). In the modern United States, he continues, "the inadequacies of public transport confirmed and cemented the appeal of radically individualistic solutions and communicated the general defeat of the idea of public or common good" (p. 23). In the introduction to their edited book *Against Automobility*, Steffen Böhm and his colleagues (Böhm, Jones, Land, & Paterson, 2006) suggest that the discursive formations of the car came to tell us a series of seemingly "self-evident" truths about modern society and our places within it:

- They are efficient, both for individuals and in social or economic terms;
- They are convenient;
- They are cheap—the costs of journeys are lower than for alternatives such as the bus or the train;
- They are stylish—they enable the user to express elements of individuality through the car itself, but also to arrive looking smart, untroubled by close contact with others (as on the bus or train) or

the exertion of physical efforts and thus sweating (as with cycling or walking);

- They are modern or progressive; they represent the natural developments of society both to greater mobility and to greater individualization and thus associate their users, and their corollaries, roads, with modernity itself;
- They are democratic in the sense that they level people—all those on the road are equal;
- They are liberators; not only in the immediate but tautologous sense of embodying individual autonomy but also in that they have helped the development of a politics of freedom and equality. (p. 6)

Although we might take issue with a few of these observations, each point no doubt echoes a broader consensus shared by most twentieth-century American motorists. As a composite sketch, Böhm et al. (2006) and others (Dery, 2006; Latimer & Munro, 2006; Rajan, 2006; Shukin, 2006; Urry, 2004) argue that these defining social characteristics of the car present a newfound *mobility* for those consumer-drivers who can access an automobile.

On Automobility

In the sociology and critical theory literature, this perceived mobility enabled by the proliferation of the automobile has often been referred to as *automobility*. As the portmanteau implies, "automobility can be understood as a patterned system which is predicated in the most fundamental sense on a combination of notions of autonomy and mobility" (Böhm et al., 2006, p. 4). Drawing from the work of Donna Haraway (1991) and Nigel Thrift (1996), John Urry (2006)—perhaps the leading scholar on matters *auto-mobile*—explains the use of the prefix "auto" this way:

> On the one hand, "auto" refers to reflexivity to the humanist self, such as the meaning of "auto" in autobiography or autoerotic. On the other hand, "auto" refers to objects or machines that possess a capacity for movement, as expressed by automatic, automation and especially automobile. This double resonance of "auto" is suggestive of how the car-driver is a "hybrid" assemblage, not simply of autonomous humans but simultaneously of machines, roads, buildings, signs and entire cultures of mobility. (p. 18)

Thus through the automobile, consumer-drivers have been able to relocate themselves—repositioning the self as a consumer-subject within the systems of capital, movement, mobility, and modernity. Hence the notion of "automobility" suggests both the automobile's potential to create spatio-temporal autonomy and expand the human capacity for movement. Urry (2006) famously outlines the key characteristics of automobility as follows, which is worth quoting at length:

- the quintessential *manufactured object* produced by the leading industrial sectors and the iconic firms within twentieth-century capitalism (Ford, GM, Rolls-Royce, Mercedes, Toyota, VW, etc.); the industry from which Fordism and Post-Fordism have emerged;
- the major item of individual consumption after housing that provides status to its owner/user through its sign-values (such as speed, home, safety, sexual desire, career success, freedom, family, masculinity, genetic breeding); is easily anthropomorphized by being given names, having rebellious features, seen to age, and so on; and disproportionately preoccupies criminal justice systems;
- an extraordinarily powerful *machinic complex* constituted through its technical and social interlinkages with other industries, car parts, and accessories; petrol refining and distribution; road-building and maintenance; hotels, roadside service areas and motels; car sales and repair workshops; suburban house building; retailing and leisure complexes; advertising and marketing; urban design and planning;
- the predominant global form of "quasi-private" mobility that subordinates other "public mobilities" of walking, cycling, traveling by rail, and so on; and it reorganizes how people negotiate the opportunities for, and constraints upon, work, family life, leisure, and pleasure.
- the dominant *culture* that sustains major discourses of what constitutes the good life, what is necessary for an appropriate citizenship of mobility, and which provides potent literary and artistic images and symbols (ranging from E. M. Forster to Scott Fitzgerald, John Steinbeck, Daphne du Maurier, and J. G. Ballard);
- the single most important cause of environmental resource-use resulting from the range and scale of material, space and power used in the manufacture of cars, roads and car-only environments, and in coping with the material, air quality, medical, social, ozone, visual, aural, spatial, and temporal pollution of a more or less global automobility. (p. 18)

Urry (2006) goes on to argue that perhaps more than any other feature of modern American life (as well as elsewhere), the automobile has long stood as a symbol and mechanism for *advancement* through both time and space—for making flexible those systems and matrices of a national political and cultural economy. It requires a significant concentration of capital investment (both in its production and purchase) relative to other consumer goods as a symbol of social advancement. In this way, it signifies status, achievement, and belonging within middle-class consumer culture. It is generative, both in terms of the conquest of space and the sustained possession thereof. And perhaps more than any other material form, it symbolizes excess; the ability to mutate the natural world into the modern world of economic, cultural, and technological control. As Gilroy (2010) cleverly surmises, "envy, status, and class-based forms of conflict—between urban and rural, as well as between rich and poor—were important parts of the decisive impact cars made" (p. 14).

We return to the various tenets of Urry's description of automobility throughout the remainder of this book (and particularly the problems of automobility), but for our current purposes in situating the ascent of the stock car within twentieth-century American culture, we should emphasize here automobility's *modern* logics. For automobility is one of "the principal socio-technical institutions through which modernity is organized. It is a set of political institutions and practices that seek to organize, accelerate and shape the spatial movements and impacts of automobiles, whilst simultaneously regulating their many consequences" (Böhm et al., 2006, p. 3). Between these modalities of regulation and freedom lay the *architecture of a nation's modernizing project*. On the one hand, the twentieth century was defined in large part by massive outlays in roadway expansion;[3] major industries in steel, petroleum, and rubber came to the fore of American industry; highways such as Route 66 that connected the transcontinental, road-traveling *flâneur*; ballads and novels were written about the cultural significance of the car in American life; and goods were moved faster as old transportation technologies such as boat and rail gave way to efficiencies of the 18-wheeler. And the car, right there in the middle of these logics, offered the perfect combination of "consumer freedom with elective confinement" (Gilroy, 2010, p. 27).

At the same time, however, scads of new road safety laws were institutionalized, traffic-related deaths swelled dramatically over the course of the twentieth century, car workers and buyers alike became further entangled in auto-specific capital relations, and the social relations native to noncar transport (the subway chat or the walk to school with friends) withered away. What emerged instead, as Urry (2004) argues, was "a system that coerces people into an intense *flexibility*. It force[d] people to juggle fragments of time so as to deal with the temporal and spatial constraints that it itself generates" (p. 28). In short, driving became a spectacle of atomized mass (conspicuous) consumption, of modernity, and of individuality.[4]

In his various works, urbanist philosopher Paul Virilio argues that unlike the chaotic ideological contestations native to the battlefield or the proletarian malaise unique to the factory, the street—or in our case, the *racetrack*—has become modernity's foremost choreographed, dramaturgic public space. The perfect balance of structure and speed, the street offered a vascular and cultural canvas of such auto-modernity. It is public in its orientation and in its creation; in its access and in its passage. The street reconciles many of modernity's contradictory logics. It is a place of resistance and of conference. Regarding the street and capital relations, Virilio writes (1977/2006): "the revolutionary contingent attains its ideal form not in the place of production, but in the street, where for a moment it stops being a cog in the technical machine and itself becomes a motor (machine of attack), in other words a producer of speed" (p. 29). In Goebbels' Germany, or in Virilio's Paris a few decades later (think: 1968), or in the contested roadspaces of the late-twentieth century U.S. South (e.g., suffrage marches, Freedom Rides, bus boycotts, immigration, and Gay Rights protests), roadway movement offers the perfect paradox of freedom (of inhabitance, of occupation) and control (signified, automated, and practiced regulation). On the one hand, the State acts as fundamentally inhibitive convener of street autonomy: "the political control of the highway, aiming precisely at limiting the 'extraordinary power of assault' that motorization of the masses creates" (Virilio, 1977/2006). On the other, the superstructural apparatus is enabling, providing the asphalt canvas for physical and ideological mobility: "No more riots, no need for much repression; to empty the streets its enough to promise everyone the highway" (ibid., p. 49). In this way, the street occupies both an imaginary and physical political quality.[5]

Nowhere can the endless possibilities of consumer capitalism be performed and celebrated like in the street—it is a rich canvas of commuter and consumer identities. Virilio (1977/2006) once asked: "can asphalt be a political territory?" (p. 30). To which we respond: it can and most certainly is political. In the United States as elsewhere, the road offers the transcendental metonym for the free market. Indeed, nowhere in Western nation-states, and especially not in the United States, have these territorial impulses manifested themselves in more significant ways than on the road. In terms of basic capital relations, "the visibility and influence of the car as a key object of mass production (Fordism) and mass consumption, the impact on spatial organization through roads, city layout, suburban housing and shopping malls, are undisputed" (Featherstone, 2004, p. 1). The road, as well as the automobilites created therein, is both symbolically and materially generative of the core logics of the late-industrial market state. In one sense, the American roadway presents a great paradox:

> while automobility can usefully express the physical experience of freedom and equality, liberals are wary of validating that experience discursively because of the perils that lie in that direction. After all, it is well established that automobility implies not just the proliferation of cars but also the cultivation of an entire physical, social and regulatory infrastructure to support movement along prescribed routes and modes. It entails vast investments of capital and mammoth social and environmental costs (estimated at roughly $2–5 trillion per year in the U.S.). (Rajan, 2006, pp. 118–119)

And yet, in another sense, the road as a conduit for conquering both space and time have become inexorable fixtures within a market-based state (see Trumper & Tomic, 2009). The road system—once lauded as a spectacularized web of state-subsidized modernity—has in recent years been cordoned off by private firms and profit-seeking lawmakers who, by controlling space and access, hold possession over the terms by which goods are transported, automobile-autonomy can be wielded, and "mobility capital" (Dant, 2004) can be extracted.

In economic terms, capital flows on, and across, the roadway. Control over those flows, over how those movements are generated and conceived, has become a substantial feature of contemporary American life. As Virilio famously posited in a 2000 interview, "Whoever controls the territory possesses it. Possession of territory is not primarily about laws and contracts, but first and foremost a matter of movement and circulation" (see Virilio & Armitage, 2000, p. 2). Physically, then, the automobile-occupied road provides a trifurcated spectacle of market capitalism, featuring: spatial occupation (territorialism), possession (ownership of space), and conspicuous consumption. In cultural terms, the American road has come to signify liberty, freedom, and the visce(realities) of speed (or embodied emotional responses to automobility). While in the car, the individual is free to pursue their destination and the symbolic features its inhabitance evokes. The car becomes an "extension of the driver's body, creating new subjectivities organized around the extraordinary disciplined 'driving body'" (Hawkins, 1986) (Urry, 2006). In these *metabolic cells*, to use Virilio's *double entendre*, the body of the car provides an extension of the human body:

> surrounding the fragile, soft and vulnerable human skin with a new steel skin, albeit one that can scratch, crumple and rupture once it encounters other cars in a crash. The car is both all-powerful and simultaneously feeds into people's deepest anxieties and frustrations, ranging from the fear of accident and death to the intense frustration of being stuck behind a slow vehicle while trying to save precious fragments of time. Within the private cocoon of glass and metal intense emotions are released in forms that would otherwise be socially unacceptable. (Urry, 2006)

Hence, we might argue that when situated within the automobile, the body takes on an inhuman or super-human form (Haraway, 1991). It is one part artifice and one part crystalline edifice; flowing across space as a metabolic prosthesis while suturing the car-driver to the structural formations it entitles the body to disengage.

With its proximal links to the core thrusts of late capitalism (material production and mass consumption), the inhabited automobile (i.e., the car-driver) presents "a moving private-in-public space…involv[ing] punctuated movement "on the road" and produc[ing] new temporalities and spatialities" (Urry, 2006, p. 22). Its imminence has more broadly propelled what Meghan Morris calls a "transit-ion" (Morris, 1988a), connecting spaces of production to spaces of consumption, the public and the private, the atomized and the composite, and past iterations of modernity to future projections of limitless prosperity and freedom. Once inside the car, "the human driver is habitually embodied within the car as an assemblage that can achieve automobility" (Dant, 2004, p. 73). "The individualized form of locomotion," writes Bachmair, "makes the car the vehicle of display, self-determination and prosperity, which aristocratic self-determination makes possible, usable and generalizable, so linking itself with the *republican* need for an individual subject-formation" (Bachmair, 1991, p. 524)

As a "human subject of speed" (Schnapp, 1999), the car-driver acts in dual articulation; perceived to be autonomously (subjectively) controlling propulsion through time and space and yet subjected to the laws of consumer capitalism, the market conditions being accelerated within the driving act, and the ideological formations from which both are embodied and constituted within this car culture.[6] As such, the metabolic command over the car and its potential for speed are meaningfully practiced discursive formations; etched into the national psyche as both a means and medium of automobility, enterprise (within the frames of free-market capital), and the *conservation* of a national polity that accepts no alternatives to this synergistic arrangement. And it is here, within these psychographic configurations, where a sport like NASCAR—full-throttle in each of the aforementioned platitudes—not only merges into the cultural politics of contemporary America, but crashes headlong into the hasty market imaginings of a fast-track nation. As Mark Howell (1997) rightly observed more than a decade ago,

> The culture at the center of the Winston Cup Series is American culture. It embodies the traits and qualities that are essential to what we know as the American character: individualism, self-reliance, dedication to community, hard work, and common faith. NASCAR racing is essentially an all-American sport, from the cars to the drivers to the fans in the stands. From the patriotic rituals to the competition on the track, the Winston Cup Series celebrates the spirit of America. (Howell, 1997, p. 197)

AUTO-MOBILE SPORT

> Is this what is meant by the idea of automobility—a driving of society away from decorums governing the freedoms of speech into a celebration of the "freedoms of speed"?
> —Latimer and Munro (2006, p. 33)

Enter stock car racing: where organized sport meets these auto-imaginings of modern American freedom. Here, at the intersections of the "cults of speed and sport," writes Gilroy (2010), we find the "destructive automobile and its undoubted pleasures"; pleasures that should be understood "in a historical setting shaped by the flight, restlessness, and mobility that characterized American society in its transition to mass automotivity and the new conceptions of speed and space derived from it" (p. 20). According to most historians, the roots of this stock car viscereality can be traced back to a Thanksgiving Day race that took place along the shore of Lake Michigan in 1895 (e.g., Rybacki & Rybacki, 2002). In the decades that followed, a network of auto racing unsystematically proliferated across the nation. With very few regulations on the size or make-up of the race car, and even fewer codified rules regarding the structure of competition (track size, location, or shape), mechanic-daredevils would enter their modified cars into improvised competitions. Those earliest races bore little resemblance to the mass spectacles race fans have come to expect from the NASCAR of today. Nonetheless, they reflected a country's increasingly palpable interest in, if not fetish for, eight-cylinder modernity. And by the turn of the century, NASCAR had become synonymous with these machinations of Industrial era American automobility, a sentiment best captured in the following quote:

> No wonder stock-car racing—a fast, furious sport contended on a paved roadway with snarling, smelly machines operated by hand—is surging in popularity…Stock-car racing expresses the industrial age more than does any big sport in America. Even NASCAR's efforts to present itself as a sport built around god-fearing, family-oriented drivers who bring their own wives and kids to the track plays into this. Go to a Winston Cup race and get away from all the new revolutions wracking America. (Ronfeldt, 2000, p. 2)

Although car enthusiasts in the industrial North brandished a producer's fixation with testing the boundaries of speed—ultimately reconfiguring their race cars and race cultures to test the engineering possibilities of the machine land-speed conquest (most notably through the advent of open-wheel race cars)—it was the *consumer* cultures of the early century U.S. South that perhaps most instrumentally *produced* the building blocks for the brand of stock car racing that has become so popular today. Surprisingly, it was in those Southern communities rendered *least mobile* by industrial capitalism where this NASCAR fervor intensified.

In a context marked by the Southern elite's profitable cooperation "with northern industrial and financial titans in the exploitation of the southern labor force and the region's vast stockpiles of raw materials" (Hall, 2002, p. 635), the auto-mobile spaces of the South's working-class emerged as the *cultural prologue* upon which the early NASCAR story would be written. Despite being somewhat disconnected from the automobile industry's core design and manufacturing processes, Southern "speed-freaks" in many ways catalyzed the sport's early evolution from showroom floor commodity to welded steel sporting enterprise. During the Prohibition Era—when early NASCAR "moonshine runners" speedily navigated their "souped-up Hot Rods" through the winding dirt roads of rural Piedmont while being pursued by enforcers of prohibition law (Menzer, 2001)—stock car racing emerged as one of, if not *the*, definitively mythologized Southern sport. During this period, the winding roadways of the Bible Belt[7] were transformed into veritable testing grounds for a new generation of auto-obsessed late-industrial sport-outlaws. The "Hot

Rod," in turn, became both the metallic fulcrum of industrial fetish and resistance to judiciary confines of the modern state. Ownership of a Hot Rod meant power, agency, and status within the developing South. As social scientist Gene Balsley (1950) later wrote at the heights of the Hot Rod craze, "When a hot rodder rebuilds a Detroit car to his own design, he [*sic*] is aiming to create a car which is a magical and vibrant thing" (p. 355). Balsley's contemporary, David Riesman—a sociologist and author of *The Lonely Crowd*—further emphasized this point, stating that "As the hot rodder visibly breaks down the car as Detroit made it, and builds it up again with his [*sic*] own tools and energies, so the allegedly passive recipient . . . builds up his own amalgam . . . and in this, far from being manipulated, he is often the manipulator" (quoted in Balsley, 1950, p. 357).

This seemingly autarkic "Hot Rod culture," as Balsley (1950) described it, eventually took a turn toward codification in the form of organized exhibition and competition. As the legend goes, the sport of stock car racing took a significant leap forward during the Great Depression in part because the underground network of the illegal alcohol trade had expanded the social—and, in this case, commercial—relations of disparate Southern populations. However, in these early days, the "sport" usually materialized as little more than an intermittent enclave of informal roadside challenges between two competitors—often to determine who had the skills, the *machismo*, and the machine to most proficiently (and perhaps dangerously) circumnavigate winding dirt road moonshine routes.

In the age of industrial standardization, however, it would not be long before patchwork backcountry auto-amusement became big business. The South's first significant organized stock car competition took place on November 12, 1938, at Lakewood Speedway in the "Capitol of the New South," Atlanta, Georgia. That race was won by Lloyd Seay, an 18-year-old who outran a "gathering of hard-core renegades who spent most of their lives deliberately crusading on the wrong side of justice" (Fielden, 2004, p. 9). In the decades that followed, stock car racing was transformed from informal, small-town gatherings with "little publicity, virtually no organization, crooked promoters and a nonexistent rule book" (Fielden, 2004, p. 9) to beach- and mountain-side grandstanded spectacles that celebrated the extent to which auto-culture had taken over the mid-century fabric of rural American life. The spread of stock car racing into the South, however, was not simply incidental. In the region's warm climate, racing teams could compete year-round, and thus maximize prize earnings and sponsorship revenues. Most importantly, Southern race organizers and entrepreneurs held a competitive advantage over their race-sponsoring northern and western counterparts in that they could build new tracks and spectating structures at a fraction of the cost paid outside the region. As historian Alex Lichtenstein (1993) explains, this was a result of Jim Crow–era labor exploitation practices prevalent throughout the South, whereby the region's incarcerated workforce—grossly overrepresented by African Americans—was forced to build new roadway projects for, among other things, the purposes of stock car racing.

Amidst this Southerly momentum, racing organizers began to consolidate their enterprise. In December of 1947, a Maryland-based race promoter by the name of Bill France, Sr., convened a meeting of regional race organizers in Daytona Beach, Florida, with the intention of creating a single regulating body that would oversee all forms of stock car competition (Clarke, 2008; Hall, 2002). At that meeting, France was appointed as principal leader of the National Association for Stock Car Auto Racing (or, NASCAR). In the years that followed, France used the new racing league to implement and codify a rationally defined set of policies and standards that would govern every race it sanctioned thereafter (Branham, 2010). For example, unlike other national and international racing leagues of the era, NASCAR competitions were restricted to only "stock" cars—meaning the race cars had to conform to the standards and designs set forth by American automobile manufacturers (those cars effectively "in stock" at local dealerships).

Much like other professional leagues during what historian Allen Guttmann (1978) refers to as sports' "modern era," the earliest structure of NASCAR reflected the highly regulated and rationalized logics of the Industrial era. In the age of quantification, it was a sport that privileged statistical labors: number of laps in the lead, the engine's revolutions per minute, gear-ratios, hyper-Taylorized[8] pit stops, and prize money earned per season. The league's governing scheme included incentives for performance (point standings), mechanisms for dealing with disciplinary procedures (guidelines), and governance over the allocation of financial resources available to competing drivers (prize money) (Hagstrom, 1998; MacGregor, J. 2005).

In fact, historians have argued that during the middle part of the twentieth century, NASCAR was North American professional sport's most highly regulated conglomeration (Branham, 2010; Menzer, 2001; Thompson, 2006). Daniel Pierce (2001), for one, has suggested that, "NASCAR's management style was more typical of a cotton mill than a modern, professional sporting enterprise" (p. 8). From its very inception, NASCAR operated under an autocratic governance structure that mandated the codification of flexible, yet rigidly enforced rules—adjusted to penalize those stock car racing innovators who had gained an "unfair competitive advantage" by tweaking the configuration of their stock cars (Cokley, 2001). Bill France was notorious for "blackballing any dissenters" whose vision for the burgeoning league contradicted his own (Thompson, 2006, p. 8). Whereas most major North American sport leagues of the era were collectively governed by team owners (i.e., Major League Baseball or the National Football League), each sharing equal rights in decision- and profit-making, NASCAR's revenues and governance were streamed into a single entity, and then dispersed amongst individual teams through prize money (see Hagstrom, 1998).

NASCAR's heightened systems of control allowed stock car capitalists to not only control the means of production (production of the event, of the cultural brand, etc.), but also suppress wage labor and variable costs through oligarchic, if not fundamentally cartel-esque, forms of governance. The point of reference for such an argument can be found in the tribulations of early 1960s driver Chris Turner, who was suspended by "France the Master Organizer" from the circuit "for life" (which actually ended up lasting four years) after attempting to organize a drivers' union in 1961 (Menzer, 2001). Eight years later, NASCAR drivers boycotted a race at the newly opened Alabama International Speedway (later renamed Talladega Superspeedway) due to concerns over the safety of the track.[9] In September of that year, NASCAR's best-known drivers formed the Professional Drivers Association (PDA), an organization "they hoped would make their jobs safer, guarantee their futures and raise their paltry incomes" ("NASCAR's Failed Union," 2007, p. 1). A few weeks later, however, the PDA was disbanded by the "iron hand" of "Big Bill" France (ibid.). In ironic terms, North America's most (auto)mobile consumer sport was perhaps its least mobile for sporting laborers.

In stifling the drivers' attempts to unionize, the racing conglomerate was also successful in avoiding labor-empowered dynamics that threatened the profit-maximizing aspirations of their professional sport league contemporaries. At a time when other leagues were confronted with the emergence of free agency and union-directed labor strikes following Curt Flood's U.S. Supreme Court battle with Major League Baseball in 1969–1970, stock car racing's totalitarian governance structure cultivated the conditions for: (1) suppressing the market value(s) of NASCAR's next generation of wage laborers and (2) centralizing the regimes under which surplus capital could be extracted and maximized. In some ways, NASCAR's "benevolent dictatorship" (Hagstrom, 1998) harnessed the ability to wield full autonomy in addressing issues and regulating competition, and at the same time thrived as a cultural commodity within free-flowing (sporting) capital markets.

In cultural terms, these tight controls over the production of stock car commodities, spectacles, and business practices allowed the France family to promulgate an isolated, if not exclusionary, sporting enterprise. In suturing the realm of sport consumerism to the technologies that "drove" late-industrial *pax Americana*, stock car racing became the archetypical sport of blue-collar symbolism, American values, patriotism, cultural "heritage," and entrepreneurialism (Assael, 1999). Corporate sponsorship also took on a parochial feel, with the "quarter panels" of stock cars emblazoned with the names of local auto part stores and local auto repair shops, the logos of Winston cigarettes and Wrangler jeans, and the celebrity rhetoric of country music stars and Bible Belt fundamentalists (Patton, 2002). In a collective effort to showcase their products' power and performance on the race track, Detroit automakers poured millions of dollars into NASCAR, banking on the latter's cultural import as a "premium gateway" for building brand equity (Goldenbock, 1993).

TURNING SOUTHBOUND

> Ask any Southern "good old boy" to name three things which are irrefutably of the [Southern] region and he will likely list: grits, moonshine and stock car racing.
>
> —Pillsbury (1974)

NASCAR was in the business of selling (Southern-spun) "All-American" sporting automobility, and business was good. Team owners were strategically referred to as "independent campaigners" while mechanics in team repair shops stuffed oversized motors into family sedans to create a *spectacle of sporting modernity*—symbolically constructed of one part horsepower-driven racing masculinity and one part homage to localized American ingenuity (Fielden, 2004). A writer for the Galveston, Texas *Daily News* summarized this early NASCAR sponsorship system in the following way:

> Not only does the automobile race bring joy to thousands of temporarily deranged spectators, but, viewed from the angle at which the manufacturer stands, [it] is a huge commercial enterprise of tremendous sales-producing value. Since Galveston beach race gossip

began going the rounds in automobile circles several months ago, the sales departments of the automobile factories have drawn red rings around the figures [August] 8, 9 and 10 on their calendars and have been looking toward Galveston. Some of them have entered cars and some have not, but it is safe to say that a good many of them have instructed their Texas agents to be represented at the beach races; it is business that they be there, for great sales are made at automobile races. Those factories having cars entered in the beach races today, Friday and Saturday will await the result of their races with keen interest. If their car wins the race the money expended in financing the entry will expand a hundredfold through advertising channels. (quoted in Hall, 2002, p. 660)

Over the middle part of the twentieth century, NASCAR's competitions became more organized, more popular, and more closely illustrative of the region's shift away from agrarian parochialism and toward late-modern industrial capitalism. In turn, stock car events became a centrifugal *spectacle of Americana*, a phantasmagoric assemblage of flag-waving Americans who had come to "worship at the altar of automobilia" (Rybacki & Rybacki, 2002, p. 294). "It was as spectacle," writes historian Randall Hall (2002), "that the races functioned best, and alert business owners worked to nurture the embryonic culture of consumption underway in American cities" (p. 661).

However, while the engines of late-industrial American capital might have been forged in the factories of Detroit, it was in the rural American South—the region former vice-presidential candidate Sarah Palin rather atavistically referred to as "the real America" during the 2008 U.S. presidential election season—that the dominant sport cultures of automobility were promulgated, negotiated, and mythologized. As has been well-documented (and as we address in Chapter Four), "much of the basis for NASCAR's growing popularity [was] derived from its Southern roots, particularly the…myth of the Old South" (Rybacki & Rybacki, 2002, p. 296).

Although other forms of international motorsports, such as Formula One, were open to international owners, drivers, and automobile manufacturers (as well as featuring races across transnational borders), early NASCAR articulated a decidedly local sensibility by allowing only domestically manufactured race cars to compete on the circuit and limiting the influx of drivers to the likes of former moonshine runner Junior Johnson, Lee Petty, Fireball Roberts, and Red Byron—all of whom hailed from states south of the Mason-Dixon Line[10] (Pillsbury, 1974). On the one hand, notes Hall (2002), stock car racing "symbolized the reconciliation between the once antagonistic regions," as Southern fans "flocked to tracks to satisfy their curiosity about technology" (p. 635). On the other, as Neal Thompson (2006) captures in the following quote, NASCAR was uniquely positioned as a rural Southern sport:

> In the South, where the Great Depression infected deeper and festered longer than elsewhere, there were few escape routes. Folks couldn't venture into the city for a baseball game or a movie because there weren't enough cities, transportation was limited, and the smaller towns rarely had a theater. There were no big-time sports either (the Braves wouldn't settle in Atlanta until 1965, and the Falcons a year later). It was all cotton fields, unemployed farmers, and Depression-silenced mills, mines, and factories. But if you were lucky enough to have a nearby fairgrounds or an enterprising farmer who'd turned his barren field into a racetrack, maybe you'd have a chance to stand beside a chicken-wire fence and watch Lloyd Seay in his jacked-up Ford V-8 tearing around the oval, a symbol of power for the powerless. (p. 9)

It was an *assemblage* of (albeit limited) industrial capital and local sport culture. Crew member's attire on race days often resonated an Old South aesthetic: bib overalls, blue jeans, straw hats, and denim shirts were ubiquitously adorned by busy mechanics and race officials (Pierce, 2001). Not surprisingly, consumers reciprocated this local particularism. As Paul Hemphill (1998) has noted,

> fans were famously ornery and down-right close-minded about their racing preferences.... If a car didn't at least look like something they could drive away from a dealership, wasn't big and loud and fast, hadn't been built in an American plant and retooled by some salt-of-the-earth mechanic named Pete, or Mike, or Harry, wasn't driven by someone who had come up the hard way (better a Southerner named Bubba), and went around the track any other way than as a counter-clockwise circle...well, it hardly counted. (pp. 38–39)

NASCAR thus operated with a distinctly local *panache*: peddling and celebrating a bucolic brand around drivers who "worked with their hands," drank the occasional snip of moonshine, waved the Confederate flag, listened to country artists like Patsy Cline, Hank Williams, and Johnny Cash, and raced cars on Sunday that could be driven to the cotton mill on Monday (Pierce, 2001).[11]

By maintaining its localized *cachet*, stock car racing carved a successful niche among members of the working-class, White South—making it, as some commentators have suggested, "the most

Southern sport on earth" (Pierce, 2001). More importantly, long after the vaunted football teams of the University of Alabama and the University of Mississippi—as well as the heralded basketball squads of Adolph Rupp's University of Kentucky—had integrated, and professional sport leagues had similarly broken through racialized barriers during the Civil Rights era, NASCAR remained an exclusively white sport (sans the brief, and tumultuous, career of the sport's only black driver, Wendell Scott).

Whereas collective governing bodies such as the National Collegiate Athletic Association (NCAA) forced their member athletic programs to integrate, and the public demonstrations at the 1968 Olympics in Mexico City unsettled the dominant racial order(s) within other sporting and nonsporting realms in the United States, the NASCAR organization's sovereignty and isolationism permitted the France family and others inside the governing faction to perpetuate all-white participant, owner, and spectator exclusivity within their sport. Grafted onto a pervasive lynch mob vigilantism, Ku Klux Klan–led public spectacles, and spectacles of political racism of the 1960s South, NASCAR emerged as a distinctly conservative sporting and cultural space during the late civil rights era—one seemingly mobilized to maintain, if not *celebrate*, the white (supremacist) status quo and manufacture branded forms of symbolic value for the corporate body:

> NASCAR's home in the Solid South seemed exactly that…a solid, all one thing and indivisible. Opaque, impenetrable, indistinguishable from one part to the next, a monolith of cracker cult and culture. And all those firehoses and attack dogs on the news didn't help when it came to growing NASCAR's brand. (MacGregor, J. 2005, p. 141)

Perhaps most paramount to the growth of stock car racing as a social institution and commercial enterprise, NASCAR was careful in promulgating its moorings to the mythologized, racialized South. In turn, the modern sport of stock car racing "benefit[ted] from this myth of its rural roots among so-called southern good ole boys" (Hall, 2002, p. 630). Through the propagation of Old South conservative values and exclusionary practices, NASCAR races brought to life a contextually important, racially homogenous *exclusivity*. In selling the auto-mobile sporting South, NASCAR strategically positioned itself along the triple axes of American modernity, Old South parochialism, and New South racial politics.

But race-based identity politics were only part of NASCAR's entrenched parochialism. Unlike baseball, which has long been known as "America's pastime," NASCAR was a sport very much woven into the cultural fabric of the Industrial Era U.S. South. The sport's definitional equation was straightforward, writes MacGregor (2005): "fast cars + young men + physical courage + moonshine + the honored roll of Rebel dead = early NASCAR" (p. 31). This second striation of stock car's Southern allure evolved out of the region's protracted celebration of a regionally mythologized individualistic chicanery. It was the sport that best captured the "outlaw ethos" of the "moonshine tripper"—a social space where acolytes of the Rebel South could cathartically race with the specters of their Confederate calling (Rybacki & Rybacki, 2000). Thus, NASCAR became both the quintessential "Southern sport" (Wright, 2002) and the archetypal site of sporting individualism; "here," writes Tom Wolfe (1965/2010), "was a sport not using any abstract devices, and *bat* and *ball*, but the same automobile that was changing man's own life, his symbol of liberation...all that was required was a taste for speed, and guts" (n.p.). It became a celebration of white masculine courage, of capitalist ingenuity, and of Southern tradition (and particularly the traditions of patriarchy and racial exclusivity).

In summary, while most twentieth-century sport organizations in Europe, South America, and even North America[12] were undergoing transformational democratic shifts (both in the organizational and economic structures), this "golden era" of NASCAR was undergirded by twin "closed systems"—highly regulated commercial spheres productive of, and reproduced by, a social and political order very much filtered through the politics of autonomy and exclusivity. This allowed NASCAR to create a unique brand—one ensconced in articulations of Southern culture, technologic modernity, and (as we make clearer in the coming chapters) liberal individualization. As Hall (2002) illustrates in his well-researched account, in the intervening decades, "this one business-oriented organization dominate[d] the rapidly growing sport using a tight governing structure, while perpetuating the story of its freewheeling beginnings" (p. 630). Thus, NASCAR's ascent through regional nodes of consumer culture was dialectically bound to economic and cultural regulation that in turn created surplus value through the consumption of a branded local identity (which, in turn, one might argue, resurrected the banalities of the Old South). Through the affective mechanisms of the sporting spectacle, these identity politics and processes were commodified, congregated, and made real. NASCAR subculture had become more than a site of motorhead amusement—it had emerged as a powerful moral, political, and economic piece of the social mosaic of the modern-day American South. And it was soon to take its multidimensional import *nationwide*.

FAST-LANE POLITICS

By the late-1970s, NASCAR had become a dominant part of the Southern sporting landscape (if only a modest fixture within the broader North American sporting scene). The racing series gradually expanded its schedule, and by 1979 league officials had secured a network television contract for broadcasting that year's Daytona 500 race to a national audience. In that race, a final lap crash between drivers Cale Yarborough and Donnie Allison famously culminated in an infield brawl between the drivers. The incident would in turn—both to the sport's favor and detriment—leave an indelibly reprobate imprint on the North American sporting public (Fish, 2001; Menzer, 2001; Richardson & Darden, 1997). From that moment forward, NASCAR drivers were marked in televisual glory as good ole boys, as hard drivin', hard livin', rugged men—the die was irrevocably cast in our national imaginary.

It is of no coincidence that Ronald Reagan, who would ascend to the presidency the year following the infamous Yarborough-Allison brawl, would a few years later find himself aligned with the earliest inklings of a modern-day assemblage called NACAR Nation. Unlike most Republican presidents before him, Reagan was wildly popular in most regions of the U.S. South—a popularity that signaled a dramatic shift away from the Southern Democrat stronghold that defined much of the twentieth century—in part because of his ability to rebrand his version of populist "conservatism" to speak to the identity politics of Southern whiteness and court the so-called Reagan Democrat voters.

In 1983, Reagan—ever displaying the air of Hollywood actor-turned-common-man hero, and heading into a forthcoming election-year landslide victory over Walter Mondale—had burnished his image among auto-mobile Midwesterners with his protectionist actions to the favor of the Harley-Davidson motorcycle company (in which the Reagan administration moved to impose additional import tariffs on Japanese motorcycles, which at the time were greatly outselling Harley-Davidson and threatening to put the company out of business [see Holt, 2005]). The following year, Reagan majestically captured the imagination of the nationwide vox populi when, like Bush would 20 years later, he made a much-ballyhooed public appearance at a NASCAR event in Daytona Beach, Florida:

> It was a day that NASCAR fans will never forget. With the President in the press box and the immense tail of Air Force One visible from the airfield behind the Daytona International Speedway, Reagan watched

Richard Petty—the sport's most popular driver—win his unprecedented 200th race during the running of the July 4, 1984, Firecracker
400. (Yates, 2005)

Aside from delivering the customary, "Gentlemen, start your
engines!" invocation at the start of the race, Reagan also addressed
the NASCAR faithful at a picnic on the infield later that afternoon,
where he enjoyed a fastfood meal from Kentucky Fried Chicken with
Petty, Allison, and other NASCAR dignitaries. His words clearly
marked out the growing prominence of the sport, while also tacitly
articulating it to the historical legacies of automobility and "freedom"
in the United States. He stated in part:

> I think I can understand why stock car racing is so popular. Americans
> have always cherished mobility, and we greatly admire innovation.
> And by combining man and machine, stock car racing brings out the
> best of both of these American impulses. [...] [T]oday we're celebrat-
> ing our country's independence and freedom. Our Founding Fathers
> gave us a wonderful gift 208 years ago—a free country, a country
> where no one need live in fear and where everyone can speak and pray
> and live as he or she sees fit. As we commemorate our country's birth
> and its freedom, I hope we can take a little while today to breathe a
> little prayer of thanks for the great blessings that we enjoy in America.
> ("Remarks at a Picnic Following the Pepsi Firecracker 400 in Daytona
> Beach, Florida," 1984)

Often overlooked in the official record is that Reagan also made an
appearance during the radio broadcast of the event, at which time it
became clear that numerous drivers on the track that day had made
public expressions in favor of the president: Allison, for example, had
hung a "We love Ron" banner on the pit wall, and another driver,
Ken Ragan, put a sign on the back of his car that read "Ragan's for
Reagan." The broadcasters also made it a point to play up Reagan's
early career as a broadcaster, which allowed Reagan to deftly play off
his sports background in the booth and sound knowledgeable about
auto racing[13] (Woolley, 1984).

The courtship between NASCAR and the Republican Party would
not end there. Reagan begets Bush the First (George H. W. Bush),
who in his run for reelection in 1992, found himself standing in
Reagan's shoes at the very same race. This time the president honored
the retiring legacy of Richard Petty, and offered what was becoming
a now-normal peroration describing NASCAR: "I salute the spirit of
NASCAR, the spirit of racing. If there's ever a group of people that
stood for what we call family values, American traditional values, it's

this crowd I'm talking to right now" (quoted in Woolley, 1992). At a second campaign event held that day, Bush would add: "I can think of no better place to wish our Nation happy Independence Day, happy Fourth of July, than standing right here with this patriotic, wonderful turnout of people, all-American crowd" ("Remarks to the Pepsi 400 Drivers and Owners in Daytona Beach, Florida," 1992).

While Presidents Reagan and Bush were generally welcomed with open arms into the NASCAR family of fans throughout the 1980s and into the early years of the 1990s, Democrat Bill Clinton would find little favor.[14] In 1992, for example, while campaigning in South Carolina, then-governor Clinton visited the Darlington Speedway, drawing a "hostile response from the 75,000 fans" in attendance, and where "boos and anti-Clinton chants nearly drowned out the roaring engines," including those of "draft dodger!" and "We want Bush! We want Bush!" (Martin, 1992, p. 1). Several prominent drivers themselves went out of their way to offer Clinton a cold shoulder:[15] Dale Earnhardt, Sr., refused to meet with Clinton, stating "I'm a Republican. I won't show him around. They should find someone else," and Richard Petty was alleged to have called Clinton a "socialist" and refused to participate in any ceremonial events with him (ibid.).[16]

None of these politicos turned racing enthusiasts, however, had theretofore been able to graft a sport-specific *mandate* to the extent that George W. Bush was able to achieve a decade later during the 2004 election.[17] Ironically, Bush had never displayed any particular affinity for NASCAR or auto racing in general, only attending his first race in 1999 while governor of Texas (Aron, 1999). However, his appearance was widely reported on CNN, with reporter Jeanne Meserve (1999) stating: "Bush may have made some points with the sports crowd this weekend. Some 200,000 fans and a national TV audience saw the Republican presidential hopeful drop the green flag to start a NASCAR race. Bush says he took his duties yesterday very serious [*sic*]."[18] Bush would later make a campaign stop at a June 2000 NASCAR event in Daytona Beach, where he served as Grand Marshal and extolled its fans, racing crews, and drivers for being "very good Americans . . . people that work for a living" (quoted in Royse, 2000, p. 1). Yet the extent to which Bush directly courted NASCAR during his 2000 campaign was otherwise outwardly minimal, never gaining much traction or coverage; he even cancelled a scheduled appearance as grand marshal of a NASCAR event in New Hampshire in September 1999 (which was expected to draw 100,000 fans), and had to be replaced by another presidential aspirant, Elizabeth Dole (Woodruff, Karl, & Black, 2000).

How quickly times can change: by 2004, many in the punditoc-racy were (rightly) predicting that the members of NASCAR Nation would play a significant role in determining the outcome of that year's race (the political one). As we cataloged in the Introduction to this book (and as we explain in the chapters that follow), Bush and his high-profile farrago of advisers (Cheney, Rumsfeld, etc.) quickly became fixtures at the weekly racing series. In the media jostling leading up to the 2004 election, a "new" political constituency—the so-called NASCAR Dad—was reified into political shorthand for "blue-collar white men from rural and Southern parts, who tend to be conservative, live in "red" states and are drawn to the racial-gender politics of the Republican Party" (Pollitt, 2004). In the year-long run-up to the election, these NASCAR Dads were likely to have been hurt by the economy, witnessed manufacturing jobs outsourced to India or China, and may have had a family member serving in the military. The NASCAR Dad, the story went, goes to church, loves to hunt and fish, or participate in other such outdoor activities, and con-siders himself to be part of the cultural mainstream.[19] As Laurel Elder and Steven Greene (2007) later explained, these were patriarchs of the South whose father and grandfathers were Southern Democrats, but who were "leaning more and more toward the Republican Party as the result of their conservative positions on social and cultural issues, including gay marriage, abortion, and guns" (p. 6).

We should point out, however, that although most pundits in the media acted as if this was a new political constituency, Claibourne Darden (1992) effectively categorized this same group of voters—that is, "the NASCAR crowd"—as the "Bubba vote" back in 1992 (Karr, 1992, p. 1). As Darden defined, this segment comprised "the middle of the middle-class, the blue collar, the lower-white collar workers. They are the ones who elect the president"; a Bush (H. W.) campaign aid further added that NASCAR "is what basic America does for entertainment" (ibid.). "Basic America," we should note, was being linguistically deployed as a euphemism for *white* America, as the racial politics of NASCAR underpinned most analyses of the demographic.[20]

In turn, and as political and cultural analysts alike will attest, the generic NASCAR Dad became the face of a major voting bloc upon which George W. Bush's bid for a second term successfully gained momentum (Vavrus, 2007): NASCAR dads became depicted as "deeply patriotic" (McCade, 2004) *white men* who, as driver Bobby Labonte opined, are "loyal to their wives" and who "don't like their kids seeing a lot of blue material" ("Hardball with Chris Matthews

[February 13]," 2004). Or, as Mary Douglas Vavrus (2007) more critically surmised, "NASCAR dads have become a brand [and] NASCAR has become the literal and metaphoric vehicle for selling commodities, a political platform, and a specific masculine identity" (p. 246).

CODA

It is safe to say that throughout the course of the 2000s, perhaps more so than ever before, the politics of NASCAR *mattered*. It had become a politically important and culturally pervasive part of the American sportscape. In this moment, NASCAR:

> evolved from rural, workingman's domain into an attraction—often an obsession—for eighty million loyal fans. Today's NASCAR...is a phenomenon, a churning moneymaker—equal parts Disney, Vegas, and Ringling Brothers—and the second most popular sport in America, with races that regularly attract two hundred thousand spectators. (Thompson, 2006)

This dialectic relationship between stock car racing and the market forces that ushered in a new era of profitability emerged as a consequence of a brazenly triangulated synergy of sport spectatorship, consumerism, and political economy grafted by NASCAR, right-wing American politicians, and capitalism's corporate hegemons. It is to this space that we now turn.

2

THE ROAD AND SERFDOM:

THEORIZING THE CULTURAL
POLITICS OF NEOLIBERALISM

> A return to "free" competition means for the great mass of people a
> tyranny probably worse, because more irresponsible, than that of the
> state.
> —George Orwell, in his review of Hayek's *The Road to Serfdom*

When Friedrich von Hayek sat down at the heights of World War II to
write his seminal free market manifesto, *The Road to Serfdom*, he did so
seeking a political solution to the rise in state-based totalitarianism that
had come to cloak much of Europe (e.g., Hitler in Germany, Stalin in
the Soviet Union, Mussolini in Italy, and Franco in Spain). Writing at a
time when young Austrians from his homeland were engaged in combative slaughter with soldiers from his new home country of England,
Hayek labored to point out how the precepts of extensive state planning
would invariably result in the subordination of the individual to the
impulses of the state—and thus outlined a critique of planning, humanism, and collectivist utopics. Recounting the political and economic
progressions from feudalism, mercantilism, and industrial capitalism,
Hayek (1944) argued that centralized state-planned economies were
inherently susceptible to authoritarianism and totalitarianism, and that
the socialist "dream" was—and could only ever be—a mechanism for
reinstituting political hierarchies and thusly constraining individual
freedom. Updating earlier neoclassical doctrines such as that of Henry
Calvert Simons' (1934/1948) neoliberal treatise *Economic Policy for
a Free Society*, Hayek (1944) proposed that democracy and deeply
participative political systems would *always* produce bureaucracy and
expanded state control—and concurrently subjugate the individual to
subordinating forces thereof (toward "serfdom").

Hayek's alternative—a line of thinking that had been under development since the days of Ancient Rome—was a *pure* free market political economic structure; a (trans)national condition in which the individual was free to pursue his or her own ends with minimal state intervention. Much like his classical predecessors, namely Adam Smith, David Ricardo, and Thomas Malthus, Hayek's vision was largely guided by the assumption that people always act in their own self-interests, that social relations can and always will be fundamentally *capital* relations, and that the marketplace thus always presents a space where liberties can be accumulated and exchanged and the cumulative effects of unfettered individualism can be realized.

What, the reader will no doubt be asking, does a book written by a London-based, Austrian-born economist more 60 years ago have to do with stock car racing in America? To which we might respond: Hayek matters because context matters. Most economists agree that Hayek's book—alongside a few others we discuss later in this chapter—has served as a foundational text in guiding economic reform in the United States and around the world over the past half-century (Boettke, 2000; Macedo, 1999). For his work, Hayek was awarded the Nobel Prize for Economics in 1974 and the U.S. Presidential Medal of Freedom from George H. W. Bush in 1991. His partisans have likewise taken up important policymaking roles in the cabinets of every U.S. president since Jimmy Carter, in the finance ministerial roles in the United Kingdom, in every government in what is now the European Union, and in numerous other parliaments around the world (Vanberg, 1994; Zappia, 1999).

To such an end, Hayek's free market dream has become one of, if not *the* most celebrated and contentiously debated, features of the contemporary U.S. political economic context.[1] No industry—indeed no feature of American domestic or foreign economic policy—has evaded the influence of Hayek's market libertarianist dictums. Over the past 30 years, and in enacting Hayek's philosophies, policymakers from around the world have ravenously stripped away the infrastructural vestiges of the Keynesian welfare state; and in so doing introduced radically marketized transformations in the health care, educational, communication, transportation, agriculture, finance, entertainment, and energy sectors.

In this chapter, we revisit the core theses of Hayek's book—those concerned with the structural elements of society (market economies, democratic processes, and state constructs of freedom). To do this, we offer a brief contextual overview of the changing landscape of U.S. political economics and cultural politics. We outline two dominant, yet sometimes contradictory, political sensibilities that have shepherded in the Hayek-inflected neoliberal transformation of domestic and foreign economic policy: *paleo-conservatism* and *neo-conservatism*.[2] We then discuss how these two oft-dichotomized conservative paradigms found common ground through a shared "nuisance"—that of "Big Government" and its constitutive democratic processes—and how conservative politicians and corporate capitalists have in recent decades been able to *fuse together* prevailing imperialist maxims with fundamentalist, traditionalist logics in popularizing a new, individualistic U.S. nationalism. We make the case that the recent evolution of the American Right—from the Ronald Reagan presidency through to the first Middle East invasion, from the "Republican Revolution" to the "Moral Majority," from the "Bush Doctrine" to "Tea Party" nationalism—has largely been influenced by, and influential of, a broader shift toward neoliberalism. As a whole, this chapter serves as a primer of sorts. Through a cursory synthesis of the historical, political, and theoretical, we set the stage for the coming chapters' detailed engagement with NASCAR as a dialectically important cultural formation within these broader paleo-/neo-conservative/neoliberal conjunctures. In other words, if we aim to better understand why NASCAR has in recent decades become America's most "commercially saturated" and "politically conservative" sport franchise, then we must first map the commercial and political landscape from which it emerged as such.

THE RISE OF FUSION-ERA CONSERVATISM

When "conservatism" is spoken about in the United States, most folks often assume a singular, unified philosophical and political orientation shared by tens of millions of the country's Right-voting citizenry. This tendency, of course, is misleading in that political movements are contextually specific, eternally fractious, and multifariously fluid in scope and orientation.[3] That being said however, historically, and certainly over the past half-century, two dominant "schools" of conservative thought have emerged in the United States. Generally speaking, political scientists have distinguished the two strains of the conservative split in this way: on one side, there has been a resurgence, led by the voices of the U.S. "Moral Majority" (and more recently the agonistic "Tea Party Movement") in what is often referred to as "paleo-conservatism"; on the other side of the conservative bloc stand the more economically minded, state-supportive conservative ideologues, described in political discourse as "neo-conservatives."

On Paleo-conservatism

The former political sensibility, often described as the "Old Right," is typically focused on cultivating the nation's core social, moral, and cultural bedrocks—those rooted in traditionalist, European, Christian, patriarchal, heterofamilial, sometimes racist, anti-Federalist ideologies (Scotchie, 1999; Smant, 2003). This line of conservatism was famously summarized in Russell Kirk's six "canons of conservatism":

1. a belief in a transcendent order, based in tradition, divine revelation, or natural law;
2. an affection for the "variety and mystery" of human existence;
3. a conviction that society requires orders and classes that emphasize "natural distinctions";
4. a belief that property and freedom are closely linked;
5. a faith in custom, convention, and prescription; and
6. a recognition that innovation must be tied to existing traditions and customs, which is a respect for the political value of prudence. (see Russello, 2004, p. 109)

These precepts of "traditionalist conservatism" particularly gained traction in the public sphere in the years following World War II (Henrie, 2004). Through publications emanating from U.S.-based right-wing think tanks such as the *Heritage Foundation* and the *Intercollegiate Studies Institute*, these traditionalists generated volumes of heuristic writings that rejected notions of collectivism, social progressivism, and modernity and instead called for a revival of what T. S. Eliot referred to as "the permanent things" (those perennial institutions that ground society: the church, the family, the state, community life, etc.) (Smant, 2003).

From the early 1980s onward, those theories were thrust into the public sphere by a legion of paleo-conservative icons such as Kirk, Pat Buchanan, Thomas Fleming, Samuel Francis (Ashbee, 1998)—and most recently by Sarah Palin and Glenn Beck (see Hitchens, 2010). Making use of newsprint (i.e., *Chronicles: A Magazine of American Culture* or *The American Conservative*), AM talk radio, and television mediums, prominent paleo-conservatives (i.e., Francis, Fleming, Buchanan, etc.) popularized an anti-Federalist, anti-immigrant, Eurocentric revival of America's "rootedness." As Francis (2005) wrote in what later became the "Statement of Principles" for the Council of Conservative Citizens, paleo-conservatives,

> believe that the United States derives from and is an integral part of European civilization and the European people and that the American

people and government should remain European in their composition and character. We therefore oppose the massive immigration of non-European and non-Western peoples into the United States that threatens to transform our nation into a non-European majority in our lifetime. We believe that illegal immigration must be stopped, if necessary by military force and placing troops on our national borders; that illegal aliens must be returned to their own countries; and that legal immigration must be severely restricted or halted through appropriate changes in our laws and policies. (pp. 1–2)

Like Francis, most self-identified paleo-conservatives are vehemently opposed to feminist and social justice movements, to women's choice and same-sex partnerships, and to social welfare. Conversely, paleo-conservatives generally support strict and absolute constitutionalism, theocratic state intervention, handgun ownership, and the death penalty (Ashbee, 2000).

Generally speaking, paleo-conservative orthodoxy is guided by the fundamental idea that it is within the domain of *tradition*, rather than democracy, that society will best move forward. Kirk and self-described paleo-conservative and University of Dallas professor Mel Bradford wrote in the prologue to their updated edition of *A Better Guide than Reason*:

The only freedom which can last is a freedom embodied somewhere, rooted in a history, located in space, sanctioned by genealogy, and blessed by a religious establishment. The only equality which abstract rights, insisted upon outside the context of politics, are likely to provide is the equality of universal slavery. It is a lesson which Western man is only now beginning to learn. (Bradford & Kirk, 1994, p. xviii)

Correlatively, in their *Washington Post* article "The New Dixie Manifesto," Fleming and Michael Hill (1995) argued that local social institutions and legacies such as those that persist in the U.S. South provide the crucible of American life. As such, they argue that Southerners (and particularly *white* Southerners) have been stripped of their heritage and their history through postbellum reform, antisecessionist Federalism, protectionism, and the growing disquiet for the symbolic South (i.e., the Confederate flag and other symbols of the Old South). Fleming and Hill (1995) stridently contend that "After so many decades of strife, black and white Southerners of good will should be left alone to work out their destinies, avoiding, before it is too late, the urban hell that has been created by the lawyers, social engineers and imperial bureaucrats who have grown rich on programs that have done nothing to help anyone but themselves" (p. C3). In their work, the South emerges as a metabolic preserve for the heritage of (white) European, patriarchal America. They conclude, then, that the South is best situated to serve as an incubator for the preservation of European values, Christian proselytism, localized governance structures (e.g., "States' Rights"), nuclear domesticity, antiscientific thinking, nativism, and antimodernization and should be left alone to do just that.

During the 1980s and 1990s, this political ideology found its way into popular discourse through the media stylings of Alex Jones, Robert Novak, Paul Craig Roberts, Joseph Sobran, and Michael Hill. The movement further secured political power through the labors of North Carolina Congressman Walter B. Jones, Constitutional Party leader Chuck Baldwin, U.S. Senate nominee Bob Conley, Tennessee Congressman Jimmy Duncan, U.S. Congressman Virgil Goode, and most notably Texas Congressman Ron Paul, whose 2008 presidential campaign garnered significant attention and acclaim. Paleo-conservatives were also able to generate significant interest in the Bible Belt South through faith merchants such as Jesse Lee Peterson and Pat Robertson. In the academy, scholars like Paul Gottfried, Donald Livingston, Virginia Abernathy, Claes Ryn, Clyde Wilson, Roger Scruton, and the aforementioned Bradford all became outspoken torchbearers of the paleo-conservative impulse. Collectively, these intermediaries fashioned an effective network of paleo-conservatism, creating organizations—such as the League of the South, the Rockford Institute, and the Abbeville Institute—that galvanized a once-marginal political ethos into a formidable force in contemporary U.S. politics.

In the early stages of the Obama Presidency (c. 2009–2010), the paleo-conservative movement garnered even more mainstream attention, particularly through the media-spectacularized Tea Party "movement." Guided by the fundamental beliefs in social tradition, conservative Christianity, and "simpler," antiquated institutions and symbols—coupled with the penchant toward less government involvement in commercial and social relations—these self-proclaimed "Tea Partiers" regularly assembled in protest of what they perceive to be too much government involvement in their everyday lives (to the extent of protesting health-care reform with such illogical sign statements as "Keep the government's hands off my Medicare").

As evidenced in well-attended rallies throughout the U.S. South and Midwest during the Obama era, this (corporate-influenced and occasionally organized) groundswell of paleo-conservatism created a significant public space for reactionary traditionalism. Take, for instance, the events that took place in Washington, DC, on the anniversary of Martin Luther King, Jr.'s, famous 1963 "I Have Dream" speech on August 28, 2010. The event, themed around the idea of "Restoring America," was organized by right-wing (pseudo-) populist Fox News Channel personality Glenn Beck. As the event's self-appointed keynote speaker, and just as King 47 years before, Beck spoke from the steps of the Lincoln Memorial promising to restore not only the nation's honor, but "American values" too. While not often sharing Lincoln's apprehension for corporate capitalism, nor his penchant for governmental involvement in the processes of reconciliation and equality, Beck positioned both his soft white physicality and the rhetoric emanating therefrom firmly within a revisionist counterdemocratic positioning of his renewed "civil rights" project. Ian Buruma (2010), the Henry R. Luce Professor of Human Rights at Bard College, summarized the event, and its contradictory politics in relation to those of the King legacy, this way:

> there was something odd about the entire event, just as there is something odd about the Tea Party movement itself. This latest surge of American populism is financed by some extremely wealthy men, including a couple of oil billionaires named David and Charles Koch, who favor cutting taxes for the super-rich and abolishing government subsidies for the poor, such as Social Security and President Barack Obama's health-care plan. This agenda might seem selfish, though understandable from the point of view of an oil billionaire. But who are all those people wildly cheering for the billionaire's dream, on of all days the anniversary of Martin Luther King's speech? They are almost uniformly white, largely middle-aged and above, and for the most part far from wealthy.
>
> The majority have no college degree. Many say that they are afraid of losing their jobs. No doubt quite a few of them would have trouble paying the astronomical costs of American health-care bills without government assistance. In other words, they would benefit from the publicly financed programs that the Tea Party's sponsors wish to abolish. And yet, there they are, denouncing as "socialism" Obama's health-care legislation, or a slight tax increase for the richest 1 percent of the population. To them, "socialism" means "European," or simply "un-American." Unlike the movement's sponsors, the crowds chanting "USA! USA!" do not appear to be motivated by economic self-interest. (pp. 1–2)

But this was not an isolated event, nor was Beck the only figure to garner such attention. Other significant figures in the contemporary Tea Party movement also made waves in 2010 by becoming serious challengers for elected office; among them, newly elected Kentucky GOP Senator Rand Paul (son of "Tea Party Godfather" Ron Paul), Alaska GOP senatorial candidate Joe Miller (who successfully primaried but eventually lost to sitting GOP senator Lisa Murkowski via a contentious write-in campaign during the general election), and Minnesota congresswoman Michele Bachmann (MN-6), who has called President Obama "very anti-American" and publicly stated the need for McCarthyite investigations into members of Congress to "to find out if they are pro-America or anti-America" (Stein, 2008).[4]

Critics of the Tea Party movement argue that cloaked in the code words of economic populism (government "stealing" taxpayer money, government as "gangsters") and hyperreligious fundamentalism (if not outright biblical literalism), what Beck, Paul, Miller, and their cohort are perpetuating and profiting from is a form of white victimhood in the United States that is made meaningful against the backdrop of economic hardship, a dwindling racial majority, and the growing acceptance among the under-30 crowd of gay rights, abortion rights, and multicultural or ethnic identities. Leon Hadar (2009), a research fellow at the nonpartisan Cato Institute (a promarket, libertarian think tank), summed up the general tenor of these forces operative in mid-2009 thusly:

> These people believe that "their America" is being robbed from them by an African-American president who has just nominated an Hispanic woman [Sonya Sotomayor] to the Supreme Court and who, together with a cabal of secular multiculturalists and radical socialists, is going to "de-Christianize" America; force white Americans out of their jobs; provide reparations to African Americans to compensate them for slavery; nationalize the entire country under the control of bureaucrats in Washington; and open the country's gates to millions of Latin immigrants who are bound to demand that California and Texas be returned to Mexico. […] While this End-of-America scenario has nothing to do with reality, its popularity among the "birthers," "deathers," and the Republican Party's electoral base exposes genuine fears among those who find it difficult to adjust to the new political realities that are driven in part by dramatic demographic changes, including a growing non-White and non-Christian population and a more tolerant and secular generation of young Americans. (n.p.)

In particular, these fears approached an outward manifestation of genuine—through misdirected—anger, as Tea Partiers became aggressively involved in leading up to the 2010 midterm elections, spewing vitriol at both democrats and moderate republican candidates for office, bearing signs and T-shirts along the likes of "Obama = Hitler," and especially supporting candidates of the kind detailed above (Paul, Miller, etc.).[5]

Importantly, as Rich Benjamin's (2009) ethnographic account of America's "whitest communities," *Searching for Whitopia: An Improbable Journey to the Heart of White America*, makes clear, the current social, cultural, political, and economic climate—read over and against an emerging political majority rooted in communities of color and young people—has ultimately resulted in some whites retreating further *into* whiteness (as opposed to what Hua Hsu [2009] refers to as the "flight *from* whiteness," or the *eagerness* of young whites under 30 who were raised during an era of multiculturalism to divest themselves from their whiteness entirely). Benjamin (2009) deploys the term "Whitopia" to refer to racially homogenous Pleasantville small towns, gated 18-hole golf course communities, or boomtown exurbs that have posted more than 6 percent population growth since 2000, are comprised of 90 percent whites, and have what he terms "an ineffable social charm—a pleasant look and feel" (Coeur d'Alene, Idaho, being one such location Benjamin identifies). It is not a stretch to similarly include the physical sites of NASCAR racing as yet another Whitopia (more on this in Chapter Four).

In effect, such Whitopia's and their attendant political entrenchments are an effort to recreate an America—"their America," as Hadar (2009) puts it in the earlier quote—that never really existed in the first place, other than perhaps from the mid-1950s to early-1960s television fictions of *Father Knows Best*, *The Donna Reed Show*, *The Andy Griffith Show*, *Ozzie and Harriett*, and most notably *Leave It To Beaver*, which exemplified the idealized post–World War II suburban nuclear family in America. Put differently, while some of the louder voices on the right, such as Pat Buchanan (2009), continue to argue that "traditional Americans are losing their nation"—and by this he means an America once defined by its whiteness—it is a historically inaccurate view, one that survives only in narrative form, divorced from any empirical reality.[6]

On Neo-conservatism

Unlike its paleo-ideological sibling, neo-conservatism is typically associated with what critics have referred to as the state-fashioned "American empire building project" (see Johnson, 2004). The fundamental neo-conservative doctrines assume the United States' preeminence in establishing global democracy and in overseeing the proliferation of Western liberal market economics (Gerson, 1996). Like their paleo-conservative counterparts, neo-conservatives generally prefer limited government involvement in domestic social and economic activities. However, unlike paleo-conservatives, neo-conservatives often look for substantial public outlay to strengthen militaristic capacities, more rigorously expand and enforce immigration laws, stimulate the flows of commerce in and out of domestic borders, and glorify individuality (Kristol, 2003). Neo-conservatives further tend to be prowar (and war spending), against social welfare programs, and increasingly preoccupied with the Middle East and the threat to Israeli power in the region (Dorrien, 1993; Fukuyama, 2004).[7]

Historically borne out of a growing discontent among Washington elites toward Lyndon Johnson's *Great Society* initiatives—as well as fraught over a nation struggling to capture solidarity amidst the 1960s countercultural, feminist workers, and civil rights movements—this new political formulation advocated increased military expansion to both win the Cold War and as a vessel for spreading liberal Western democracy abroad (Offe, 1987). Neo-conservative influence quickly gained traction in the U.S. political sphere: By 1979, the neo-conservative movement's figurehead, Irving Kristol, was featured on the cover of *Esquire* magazine with the caption: "The godfather of the most powerful new political force in America—Neo-conservatism." As early as 1968, Kristol was making the case for the nation's manifest destiny with world power and presence, writing "Power breeds responsibilities, in international affairs as in domestic—or even private. To dodge or disclaim these responsibilities is one form of the abuse of power" (quoted in Kristol, 1983, p. 238). He called for the displacement of all heads of state working against the interests of Western liberal capitalism and the return to faith-based doctrines as moral guidelines for national development.

In his book *Two Cheers for Capitalism*, Kristol (1978) mapped the political economic foundations of neo-conservative polity; asserting that capitalism, and more specifically bourgeois capitalism, is worthy of "two cheers": One cheer because "it works, in a quite simple, material sense," by improving living conditions for people; And a second cheer because it is "congenial to a large measure of personal liberty" (pp. x–xii). Kristol (1978) further asserted that *only* capitalism had proved capable of providing these conditions for widespread improvement and personal liberty (Bell & Kristol, 1981). In the generations that followed, neo-conservative ideologues such as Elliott Abrams and Irving Kristol's son, William Kristol, publically campaigned for more U.S. involvement in Middle Eastern nations such as Kuwait, Iran, and Iraq, as well as the Philippines and later Bosnia and Croatia (Wolfson, 2004).

Through a vast network of privately funded initiatives, such as the *Project for a New American Century* (PNAC), the *Hudson Institute*, and the *Bradley Foundation*, these figures were able to influence the foreign policy agendas of Presidents Reagan, Bush I, Clinton, and Bush II (as well as, to varying degrees, Obama). For example, it was George W. Bush's chief speechwriter, self-proclaimed neo-conservative David Frum, who conjured up the now-infamous "Axis of Evil"—a conceptually aligned enemy-scape to American national security and well-being that became a newspeak staple prior to, and especially during, Bush's dual wars in Afghanistan and Iraq. After heavy lobbying from groups such as the American Israel Public Affairs Committee (AIPAC), and despite continued and fervent opposition from most of its international allies, Bush committed what would later amount to more than one trillion dollars to the war efforts in Iraq and Afghanistan in an effort to "secure the region" (and, in the case of Iraq, remove Weapons of Mass Destruction that, as we well know, *never existed in the first place*). At the same time, he inaugurated the Office of Homeland Security (and by association, the Transportation Security Administration), routinely aligned himself with popular expressions of military celebration in sport and entertainment, and took to wearing an aviator's flight jacket during his tenure as a (self-proclaimed) "war-time president." Most notably, Bush's foreign policy perspective—what would come to be called the "Bush Doctrine" within the contemporary mediascape—was paradigm-shifting in its alignment with the concept of *preemptive* war. Published as part of the September 17, 2002, *National Security Strategy of the United States of America*, the policy directive made "a long-building imperial tendency explicit and permanent" (Gitlin, 2003). As the noted communications scholar Todd Gitlin (2003) put it, the Doctrine was "a romantic justification for easy recourse to war whenever and wherever an American president chooses" (ibid.).[8]

This incursion into a state of perpetual "preemptive war" was generally praised in neo-conservative circles, with William Kristol lauding on the PBS program *Frontline*: "The world is a mess. And, I think, it's very much to Bush's credit that he's gotten serious about dealing with it...The danger is not that we're going to do too much. The danger is that we're going to do too little" ("The War behind Closed Doors," 2003). This mentality has carried forward into the Obama presidency, where *safety* (of the individual, of the nation, of the economic, and of the rights to prosperity) has become tantamount for the national agenda. Today, many within the government (and beyond) see the role of the state—often at implausible expense to the U.S. taxpayer—as an orchestrator of global political and economic affairs in the pursuit of a hierarchical world order of which the United States is positioned atop.

Of and In Fusion

Of course, the case has been made that while both forms of conservatism share common intention within the previously mentioned "recovery movement"—to hegemonically reproduce power for a dominant faction—the significant, seemingly irreconcilable discontinuities between the two schools of sociopolitical thought had left the Right disjointed and disempowered on a national scale (Bottum, 2004). However, with the emergence of Reagan-era conservatism and the "Republican Revolution" that soon followed, it has become increasingly difficult to distinguish between these two ideological formations in United States' recent political history. Through the Reagan years, and later the senior and junior Bush presidencies, paleo-conservative foundations of faith, tradition, and protectionism found consonance with neo-conservative dictums of American empire, expansionism, and market-first deregulation. Within the "Reagan coalition," the domestic protectionist social agenda was strangely reconciled with hypermilitaristic, expansionist, free marketization. Reagan was successfully able to popularize an agenda that at once promoted further class divisions, job outsourcing, and increased financial instability (namely in the medical, property, and finance sectors), while at the same time concretizing the fundamentalist canons of "traditional American values" and liberties. This fusionist conservatism named "both the defence of liberty against undue state intervention as well as the opposite doctrine, according to which state power should be deployed to ensure the conditions of equal liberty" (Barnett, 2005, p. 8).

This intersection, or more accurately worded "fusion," of paleo- and neo-conservative ideologies crystallized around the common ground of Cold War anti-Communist nationalism. In basic terms, what later came to be known as the conservative "fusionist strategy" (first proffered by *National Review* editor Frank Meyer in the late 1960s), called for disparate conservative ideologues (e.g., neo-, paleo-, fiscal conservatives, social conservatives) to "work together" to revive *traditional* norms of social conservatism, reestablish a free enterprise economy, refocus fundamentalist moral imperatives (such as abortion, creationism, and prayer in schools) into the national dialogue, grossly expand military spending and endeavor, and eradicate many of the "liberal" social welfare initiatives introduced during the New Deal and implemented throughout the civil rights era (Adler, 2004; Rothbard, 1998).

In spite of underlying contradictions between the various schools of conservative thought, these fusionists were successful in grafting a public iconography that appealed to a national coalition longing for recovery. Through Reagan in particular, Republican politicians were able make use of the paleo-conservative groundswell not in isolation of, or opposition to, neo-conservatism. Rather, as political philosopher Wendy Brown (2006)—reading through the work of Anne Norton, David Harvey, Grant Smith, and others—suggests, the schism between paleo-conservatism and neo-conservatism somewhat collapsed during the Reagan presidency. As conservative commentator Rich Lowry later wrote, Reagan capably wielded a fusionist "sweet spot" of both ideological flexibility and adherence to conservative principles (Phillips-Fein, 2009). This new conjunctural Right cultivated longstanding yearnings for traditional (if imaginary) American protectionism—which, many scholars argue, successfully forged a systematic "Southerly" shift within American cultural and political discourse (Denzin & Giardina, 2007; Giroux, 2004b; Hardt & Negri, 2000; Harvey, 2005; Kincheloe & Steinberg, 2006; McLaren, 2005)—with nationalistic, if not Zionistic, U.S. imperialism.

What followed was a multidecade-long volley of rhetoric, initiatives, and political performances siphoned through the rhetorical stylings and political mandates of the "Moral Majority," Republican Revolution, the Bible Belt, and the most recent "electoral mandates" of so-called Red State America. Right-wing luminaries as vastly oppositional in their political leanings as Paul Wolfowitz and Rush Limbaugh effectively coauthored the narratives and coordinated the cultural institutions through which the longitudinal effort to recenter American politics along this newly *mélanged* Right came to fruition. Their collective "plan" was quite simple: make use of media outlets, church pulpits, college lecterns, think-tank seminars, and Senate floors to popularize a new (Right) "revolution"—an amalgam of paleo- and neo-conservative agendas that played on the fears of immigration, welfare moms, overtaxation, "political correctness," state involvement, the demise of U.S. empire, and the passing of "traditional American values."

In his 1993 memoir *See, I Told You So*, Limbaugh (1993) himself explicitly explained this ideological strategy:

> In the early 1900s, an obscure Italian communist by the name of Antonio Gramsci theorized that it would take a "long march through the institutions" before socialism and relativism would be victorious...Gramsci theorized that by capturing these key institutions and using their power, cultural values would be changed, traditional morals would be broken down, and the stage would be set for the political and economic power of the West to fall...Gramsci succeeded in defining a strategy for waging cultural warfare...why don't we simply get in the game and start competing for control of these key institutions? In other words, why not fight back? (p. 87)

Limbaugh's selective misreading of the (not so obscure) Italian Marxist—who was imprisoned by Mussolini for his resistance to Fascism—offered a quasi-theoretical guiding light for the conservative "revolution" in the years that followed. In the truest sense of hegemony, these political ideologues were successfully able to naturalize Jesus-inflected, all-American sanctions and policies that ultimately widened class wealth gaps, promoted cultures of patriarchy, xenophobia, and racism, and heightened fears of the omnipresent enemy-Other (Communists, Cold War rivals, jihadists, Japanese auto makers, drug cartels, intranational nonbelievers, etc.).

What we might conclude then, at the risk of reviving the contentious Marxian claim of economic determinism, is that the most significant shift in American life brought forward by the Reagan-era fusion of conservative ideology came in the radical overhaul of the domestic (and global) economic structure. While in the first instance the ability of Reagan's fusionist Right to appeal to the voting masses momentarily bridged the gap between the cultural logics of paleo-conservatism (which in the U.S. context have historically empowered white, Christian, heteromasculine "citizens") and neo-conservative imperialism (which empowers those bourgeoisie elites who have large sums of capital to wield on the open market), in the second it coalesced around a vox populi bent on radically eradicating the embedded features of the American welfare state (Moore, 1991). Recurring themes of state simplification—found in declarations such as "No new taxes," "the death of Big Government," and "the age of free enterprise"—at once capitalized upon post-Goldwater national Cold War binaries (public = Communism, private = America) and framed the mythscapes of corporate capitalism and "trickle-down" economics.

ON NEOLIBERALISM

> The ascendancy of neoliberalism and corporate culture in every aspect
> of American life not only consolidates economic power in the hands
> of the few; it also aggressively attempts to break the power of unions,
> decouple income from productivity, subordinate the needs of society
> to the market, reduce civic education to job training, and render public
> services and amenities an unconscionable luxury.
> —Henry A. Giroux and Susan Searls Giroux (2004, p. 249)

History tells us that much like Ronald Reagan's conservative social
policies, which bore the specters of an old guard residual traditionalism, his liberal economic policies were by no means recent inven-
tions. From the failed *laissez-faire* market systems of ancient Rome
to the axiomatic early Industrial-era currencies of Smith, Malthus,
and Ricardo on through to today, the deified "invisible hand" has
maintained a cyclical grip over many "developed" economies for quite
some time (Lal, 2006). As famed world-system theorist Immanuel
Wallerstein (2008) suggests, these macroeconomic structures (or lack
thereof) have historically acted as counterpoints to what geographer
David Harvey (2003, 2007) refers to as an "embedded liberalism"
within market-based economies:

> Neoliberal globalization will be written about ten years from now as a
> cyclical swing in the history of the capitalist world-economy. The real
> question is not whether this phase is over but whether the swing back
> will be able, as in the past, to restore a state of relative equilibrium in
> the world-system. Or has too much damage been done? And are we
> now in for more violent chaos in the world-economy and therefore in
> the world-system as a whole? (n.p.)

In other words, the expansion of state planning, programs, and intervention in capitalist economies such as those in Europe and North
America tends to be cyclically undermined by short-term capitalization of those otherwise publically owned entities. In simpler terms,
when the market failures (late 1880s, 1930s, 2000s) lead to expanded
state spending and development (more realistic trickle-down spending, if you will) and limited profit maximization for the capitalist
class, there has been a tendency to *swing back* toward "freer" market
conditions.

In Western capitalist economies, the deregulated *laissez-faire*
market has resurfaced as the contextually redundant alternative for
stagnating iterations of the social welfare state.[9] In these economies,
as well as many other "developed" nation-states, that embedded

economic model was framed by the influential theories of John Maynard Keynes. Under Keynesianism, the United States in particular established a series of economic policies that regulated growth, attended to the social needs of its people, controlled the import and export of capital and goods, operated by way of moderately high taxation (weighted in favor of the working poor), and stimulated growth through investments in the public sector (Adamson, 1990; Leeson, 2000; Skocpol, 1985).[10] However, by the later part of the twentieth century, the "embedded" Keynesian protocols that had ushered in an era of *pax Americana* languished under the recourses of the 1973 OPEC oil crisis, the accumulating fiscal and social debt of the Vietnam War, the stagnation of the worker-empowered domestic manufacturing sector, and the revolt of the global capitalist class (whose profits had failed to grow at a rate investors had forecasted a decade earlier) (Hetzel, 2007).

At the impasse of this late-Keynesian malaise—the end of the "cycle," if you will—an influential faction of bourgeois elites began to repopularize a hybrid of Adam Smith's theory of the "invisible hand" (Palley, 2005). "When the Fordist-Keynesian configuration that had been formed in response to the 1930s crisis of capitalism...itself ran into difficulty in the 1970s as economic stagflation and rising inflation took hold," writes Barry Smart (2010), "political administrators in the USA, the UK, and New Zealand...(re)turned to neo-classical policies and associated assumptions about social and economic life" (p. 34). This neoliberal revolution was in large part guided by the theories of highly influential University of Chicago economics professor Milton Friedman. Drawing on the rudiments of Adam Smith's classical, self-regulating, "invisible hand" doctrine and building upon the work of Hayek and other exponents of a market-first social order, Friedman and his adherents[11] implemented a series of measures intended to eliminate the regulatory mechanisms of the Keynesian "welfare state" (Hetzel, 2007). Friedman's neoclassical theory advocated for a pure capitalist order; whereby only by giving oneself over to the market—to the logics of surplus value and accumulation—can the individual ever truly be free.

Rooted in classical liberal economic theory, Friedman's interpretation also signaled a significant break from classical liberal forbearers in that while his predecessors saw *some value* in regulation and state intervention into economic activity, by the latter part of his career (and despite his own welfare under New Deal economic reform), Friedman advocated for a near complete abolition of economic regulation and planning activities. In his 1962 treatise, *Capitalism and Freedom*,

Friedman outlined a complete overhaul of the public sector, calling for floating exchange rates, the privatization of public works, educational vouchers, and increased "monetarism" (inflation as money supply problem) as a solution to stagflation. Friedman assumed the potential and limitless prosperity for all through their engagement with unshackled market relations.[12]

Fellow Nobel Prize–winning economist Paul Krugman (2007) points out that unlike his classical forbearers, Freidman's philosophy was based on two simple assumptions: "that markets always work and that only markets work" (p. 6). The core impulsion of this "correction" was the principle that individual liberty and freedom are the "high point of civilization" and that such an "individual freedom" can be ascertained and preserved only by fostering private property rights, free markets, and free trade and by abolishing corporate tax and minimum wage (Friedman, 1962/2002, 1993).[13]

In cultural and political terms, writes Wallerstein (2008), the neoliberal "counteroffensive" was led by the Reagan and Thatcher governments in the United States and Great Britain, respectively, working hand in hand with the International Monetary Fund and the World Bank, which together "jointly created and enforced what came to be called the Washington Consensus" (p. 1) and restructured the rudiments of democratic polity to use its power to preserve private property rights, nurture the institutions of the free market competition, privilege corporate sustenance and growth over social welfare, and promote each on both the local and the global stages (see also Garrett, 1993; Newman, 2007b; Podobnik & Riefer, 2005). Wallerstein (2008) continues:

> The slogan of this global joint policy was coined by Mrs. Thatcher: TINA, or There is No Alternative. The slogan was intended to convey to all governments that they had to fall in line with the policy recommendations, or they would be punished by slow growth and the refusal of international assistance in any difficulties they might face. (p. 1)

By the end of the twentieth century, Friedman's political, military, and cultural "mercenaries" had transformed large sectors of the global economy into an interconnected network of flexible, cheap labor (and free of any trade union "interference"), government support of top-heavy economic growth, elimination of social programs, and a madeover marketplace that empowered corporate growth over human or environmental well-being (MacGregor, S. 2005; Nelson, 2007).

By the time the last few pieces of the Berlin Wall were being carved into souvenir kitsch, a *new world order* of deregulated, unfettered capital interdependencies had emerged—giving rise to an ephemeral boon for a global capitalist class and particularly for those bourgeoisie with investments in the crude oil, biotechnology, digital communication, and mass entertainment sectors (Harvey, 2005, 2006). Around the world, and within the frames of "TINA" discourse, capitalism evolved from one way of organizing an economy (juxtaposed against socialistic alternatives) to *the way*; and debates once focused on weighing up the merits of state socialist democracy versus market republicanism turned into discussions of how free a market-based economy should be.[14]

Back in the United States, Right-wing politicians (re)popularized the idea that if the State could extricate its involvement in the economy, wealth would soon "trickle down" to the working masses.[15] "No New Taxes" became a rallying counterpoint to the expanded state-based programs of the New Deal, and gained traction amongst the majority voting bloc to ensure Republican control of the White House throughout the 1980s. In summary, neoliberal ideologues

> advocated for unbridled entrepreneurial freedom, free markets, free trade, and a radically reduced state, and vigorously promoted consumerism. Deregulation, privatization, market forces, and consumer choice became the watchwords of neo-liberal states as they extolled the virtues of economic globalization and sought to provide the appropriate institutional setting within which economic growth could be maintained and corporations could significantly increase rates of profit by generating increasing consumption of goods and services. (Smart, 2010, p. 19)

Under this new paradigm, "corporate America" emerged as the dominant teleology of the now global late-century economy. It was, as Henry Giroux (2004b; 2006a, 2006b) has repeatedly made clear, a materially consequential confluence of unfettered profitability for the private sector and antigovernment governmentalities; *a realigned democracy at the service of global commerce*. When Friedman died in late 2006, *National Review* columnist Larry Kudlow (2006) declared: "Milton's mantra of free markets, free prices, consumer choice and economic liberty is responsible for the global prosperity we enjoy today" (p. 1). And by every measure, Friedman's apprentices in the fields of banking, biotechnology, military and aerospace engineering, and (homeland) security had prospered from his profit-first regime of "globetrotting" accumulation. In the short term, markets soared, shares blossomed, and surplus value flowed freely through the global veins of capital exchange. By containing expenditures through wage labor suppression and opening up "emerging" producer and global consumer markets, Friedman and his policymaking acolytes had resuscitated a struggling domestic and global economy.

Looking back, we can see that while offering very few innovations or sustainable "corrections," Milton and his "mantra"—and the intensified global interconnectivities both brought to life—did ephemerally *speed up* international capital relations (and surplus value extracted therefrom). While a considerable amount of political economic scholarship has been devoted to this late, or global, capitalist order (Appadurai, 1996; Bauman, 1998; Beck, 2000; Castells, 2000; Featherstone; Held, 2000; Jameson, 1991; Jameson & Miyoshi, 1998; Lechner & Boli, 2000; Mandel, 1975; Ritzer, 2004; Robertson, 1992; Sassen, 1998; Scholte, 2000; Tomlinson, 1999), the temporal aspects of this reconfiguration is perhaps best theorized in the work of the aforementioned Paul Virilio, whose understanding of *dromology* (taken quite literally from the Greek word *dromos*, meaning "to race") offers a conceptual framework for problematizing the governance of *speed* and its power relations. In general terms, Virilio (1977/2006) argues that the speed at which something happens likely changes its essential nature, and that those forces of society that move with great speed come to dominate those that are slower.[16]

This dromological theory provides a useful heuristic for understanding the movement of capital (both real and imagined in form) within the context of Hayek- and Friedman-prescribed neoliberalism. For Virilio (1977/2006), power and "progress" are not necessarily consequences of spatial arrangement or geometric conquest—as many scholars have suggested (e.g., colonization, globalization, empire)—but rather are more incontrovertibly produced by, and productive of, control over movement and circulation. He writes, "there is no 'industrial revolution' but only a 'dromocratic revolution'; there is not democracy, only dromocracy; there is not strategy, only dromology" (Virilio, 1977/2006, p. 69). Put differently, power created through surplus value accumulation is first a matter of speed; of the immediacy of transfer, transport, exchange, volume, signification, hypermediation, and proliferation. As was the case with other means of power and accumulation (warfare, colonization, serfdom, etc.) in previous epochs, autonomy is produced through the transference and mobility of capital in the contemporary global economy.

As neoliberal formations enlivened market interdependencies (both domestic and global), they also sped up the circulation of goods, commodity flows, and the *dromos* to command both. With the alignment of late-twentieth century contextual forces—namely, the advent of a worldwide Internet, the explosion of satellite communications technologies, increased dependence on digital surveillance technologies, and an exponential increase in personal digital assistants (PDAs) and, later, smartphones (i.e., iPhones, Blackberries, etc.)—the production of surplus value hastened and expanded, and collapsed the old industrial networks of limited material transfer. As we now know, this acceleration of the modes of accumulation held with it both material and ideological consequences—new *phenomena of speculative excess* if you will.[17] Materially, the "new global marketplace" introduced a variety of new supply-chain distortions. In this context, Industrial-era manufacturing technologies gave way to "just-in-time" instantaneity, national Fordist production strategies withered in the global post-Fordist factory-scape, speculators scavenged the globe to extract and capitalize upon the planet's last remaining natural resources, producers became consumers of the "global popular" (Kellner, 1995), and the international bourgeoisie scrambled to gain control of the circuits of what Virilio refers to as "habitable circulation" (Virilio, 1977/2006). Capital flowing across national borders quickened and expanded, so much so that global capital flows increased almost tenfold from Reagan's inauguration to George W. Bush's second term.

Ideologically as materially, TINA accumulation paradigms brought forth a new age of hyperconsumerism, media spectacularization, and market fetishism. Geographic dimensions (terrain, distance, the nation, etc.) collapsed inward and onto the circuits of the commodity. States, such as the United States, abandoned social welfarism and its bottom-up democratic stratagems for the effervescent logistics of *laissez fairism*. Rather than an inhibitor or regulator of speed, the State opened the motorways of commerce like an autobahn. These new logistics came to interpenetrate the domestic psyche; a collective consciousness inundated with signs of the nation's manifest market destiny. Put another way, "governance by speed (by states or otherwise) is logistics, and logistics, like the oceanic vectors from which it is born, is omnidirectional" (Bratton, 2006, p. 12). The State, once an overdetermining force within economic life, yielded to this fast-tracked free market hegemony. And perhaps most consequentially, the state democracy emerged in the popular discourse as a nuisance or impediment to dromocratic economic process. Or as Virilio put it, the two forces are often framed in diametric parlance in terms of *dictatorship of movement* versus the *freedom of movement*.

In this *"the war of Time,"* as Virilio calls it, *"speed* guarantees the secret and thus the *value* of all information" (Virilio, 1995, p. 53). Commanding the longitudinal spectacles of modernity, "progress," and "freedom," the dialectics of speed and neoliberal hegemony have become normal if not tantamount. In short, conspicuous movements, and the moveable systems of capital, now hold sway over contemporary social life. These neoliberal turns moved us away from the more materially defined "solid phase of modernity" (Bauman, 2007) and a shift from what Smart (2010) describes as "the solid, stable, more secure and, by implication, 'heavy' and slower society of producers" to a "lighter, more mobile and flexible, and faster pace 'society of consumers'" (p. 12). The consumer-citizen, then, becomes an edifice of speed—pronouncing through the conspicuous consumptive act the social relations of production within the unfettered marketplace. Neoliberalism has allowed, both through polity and practice, capital and its logics to flow in and through the citizen-consumer in newly unobstructed ways.

CODA: TOWARD A DROMOLOGIC NASCAR

Although the term neoliberalism might not flow freely from the mouths of NASCAR Nation, the sport is both implicitly and explicitly bound to the fate of Hayek's and Friedman's free market utopics. A sport that has historically been marginalized in the mainstream American media and popular sporting imaginary as a local, Southern, "small-time," "redneck," Southern pastime, NASCAR and its parent corporate umbrella, International Speedway Corporation (ISC), have emerged as a significant force in the highly competitive North American sport marketplace.

In perfecting the "NASCAR Way," as Robert Hagstrom (1998) observed more than a decade ago, NASCAR officials have perhaps been more successful than those of any other professional North American sport in promoting, and seizing, the dominant market ethos pervaded by soothsaying, NASCAR-touring policymakers. However, we argue in the coming chapters that the rise of the NASCAR enterprise is more than an emerging cultural destination in Friedman's free market utopia. The sport that best represents the conservative cultural politics of the neoliberal turn has prospered precisely because it is directly constituent, and constitutive of, this dominant economic order. This dialectic relationship between stock car racing and the market forces that have ushered in a new era of profitability is a consequence of a brazenly triangulated synergy of sport spectatorship, consumerism, and political economy grafted by top-ranking NASCAR officials, right-wing American politicians, and neoliberal corporate hegemons.

As we detail in the next chapter, NASCAR Nation is squarely embedded within—in fact implicated in—the political and cultural economic formations outlined above. In point of fact, NASCAR has positioned itself as a seemingly *natural* platform for advancing what Ben Agger (1989, 2004) refers to as "fast capitalism": It organizes its spaces—mediated, practiced, spectacularized, and imagined, and the practices thereof—in ways that propagandize, authorize, and normalize the conjunctural market conservatism we have described thus far. In NASCAR, the banal becomes sensational and the sensational becomes marketable; all organized around the thrust of the road (and its politics), speed, and marketized sport. For "speed is the medium that ensures that the conjunction between human and mechanical individuals will engender not relaxation and tedium, but bigger living: quickened senses, aroused faculties, expanded powers of vision; acts of heroism, improvisation, and innovation; spectacular crashes and catastrophes" (Schnapp, 1999, p. 34).

3

CONSUMING NASCAR NATION:

SPACE, SPECTACLE, AND CONSUMER-CITIZENSHIP

> NASCAR creates an emotional bond which connects fans to the brand and connects fans to one another.
> —NASCAR Internal Marketing Documents (2009)

Each NASCAR race is a unique spectacle. Usually starting around Friday afternoon, a convoy of literally thousands of race car-symbolized, American flag-adorning recreation vehicles, SUVs, and automobiles cut through race-specific traffic patterns (put in place and administered by dozens if not hundreds of local police officers). Serpentine trails of taillights circumnavigate winding mountain roads, the glow of the local metropolis (whether Norfolk, Charlotte, Phoenix, Chicago, Birmingham, or Atlanta) shimmering off a thousand rearview mirrors. Descending in droves upon the racetrack, these auto-mobile transporters of domesticity—and the humans that create it—buzz down back roads, highways, and interstates—each converging on an assemblage of specially marked parking lots and campgrounds that will serve as micro-neighborhoods over the coming weekend. Fans from around the country make the pilgrimage to each race, anxious to see their favorite drivers—as well as good friends/"NASCAR neighbors" they have made over the years—in these semiregular get-togethers. In the same document from which the epigraph to this chapter is drawn, NASCAR promotes such a mass race-gathering in this way:

> Our fans' journeys to our racetracks are an emotional expression of their lifestyle:
>
> The heart of the fans' passion;

Average of nearly 120,000 spectators at each NASCAR Sprint Cup Series race;

Some racetracks can hold nearly 200,000 or more spectators;

NASCAR fans see race attendance as a rite of passage. ("This Is Our NASCAR," 2009)

Upon arrival, whether morning or night, Friday, Saturday, or Sunday, Dover or Martinsville, Daytona or Talladega, attendees will notice two things, things that NASCAR "die-hards" have come to expect and indeed relish: First, NASCAR races have a very distinctive smell. The air is filled with a strange aromatic cocktail of burnt firewood and burnt rubber, the ratios of which, interestingly, are directly related to how close to the track one is located, and thus how much money someone is willing/able to spend for that location. Second, attendees will be welcomed by the inevitable hum of literally tens of thousands of gas-powered generators—rhythmically purring in simpatico with the collective coffee sip remedies for the previous night's hangover. This nomadic power grid is important, as it provides the gross wattage necessary to regenerate today's modern (mobile) homespace(s)—replete with satellite dishes, televisions, full-range kitchenettes, and so forth—that sprawl across the otherwise rural spaces both inside and outside the racetracks.

Perhaps a third definitive, and for our purposes more pertinent, atmospheric of the NASCAR experience are its collective assemblage of sights, signs, and symbols. NASCAR organizers have long held that "Racetracks are a living embodiment of our fans' lifestyles, with attendance often becoming an annual tradition" ("This Is Our NASCAR," 2009). While most high-profile, professional sports share a visible energy—made of both homologous competitive fervor and conspicuous collectivism—that transcends the routines of everyday life, the NASCAR spectacle is unique in the extent to which the symbolic and practiced evoke a particular allegiance to corporate commercialism: In NASCAR Nation, corporate sponsorship is more than just capitalistic paternalism (think: the sponsor of a school baseball team) or civic responsibility; *it is identity politics, it is belonging.* From the cacophony of commercial signifiers that blanket the racetrack to the hypercommercialized trans-active exchange praxes undertaken by corporate-emblazoned bodies therein, NASCAR *oozes business.*

In this chapter, we explore the symbolic and corporeal architectures of NASCAR's corporatized consumer spaces and places. In so doing, we offer partial answers to two central interrogatives put forward by David Harvey (2005) in *A Brief History of Neoliberalism*: (1) in what ways are "average" Americans "being subjected to" the dictums and ethics of the free market?; and (2) "how was sufficient popular consent generated to legitimize the neoliberal turn?" (pp. 40, 60). Using ethnographic observation and descriptive statistics, we contemplate the ways in which "consent" (or its perhaps equally powerful myth) has been manufactured from, articulated through, and internalized within the identity politics and atomizing practices germane to NASCAR's spaces of consumption.[1] Our key focus, then, is on the commercially intonated public pedagogies unique to NASCAR spaces, and especially on the consuming bodies of NASCAR Nation within these spectacular(ized) racing spaces.

By way of illustration, we examine how the NASCAR spectacle generates dominant body pedagogies and collective corporeal praxes while at the same time reproducing neoliberalism's economies of individualism, alienation, and mass consumerism. We identify the cultural and consumer politics of NASCAR's "kinematic subject" (Schnapp, 1999), and in so doing return to Michel Foucault's double meaning of the term "subjectivity." Informed by Foucault's (1977, 1982, 1983, 1984) work on subjected bodies, we thus explore how the subject of the sporting spectacle is *subjected to* broader power relations and structures of neoliberalism, but also how out of that subjectivity the spectator is at the same time *made into* a subject (as opposed to an object) that is afforded a sense of control over his or her existence therein.

We further argue that within NASCAR spaces such as those described above and below, the body becomes a site of this identity performance—an enfleshed, kinetic, mobile expression of the social order of things. As an amalgamation of competing corporealities, we suggest that the body cultures of the NASCAR racing weekend constitute a theater of the spectating masses. As Paul Virilio (1995) once wrote, "since movement creates the event, the real is kinedramatic" (p. 23). Thus do we explore the production of kinedramatic realit(ies) within spaces of the stock car spectacular. We make the case that the *conjunctural* sporting spectacle, wrought with paradoxes of inclusivity and exclusivity, is not only projected onto the sporting masses, but also *consumed* (through them) as a technology of identity, subjectivity, and power in neoliberal times. That is, we suggest that in the age of market individualism, consuming NASCAR and its spectacularized commodity forms connects the individual to the collective machinations of NASCAR Nation, while concurrently disconnecting, or alienating, that same person from what Marx referred to as *Gattungswesen*, or the connective aspects of her/his "human nature." In sum, this chapter explores the spaces within and between the dual definitions of the "subject"—as both a seemingly autarkic, or self-sufficient, free-spending extension of consumer culture, and at the same time a human agent always already subjected to, and arguably subordinated by, the logics of the market.

PRODUCING THE CONJUNCTURE

Most observers could hardly argue against the notion that NASCAR is, and has for many years been, a deeply commercialized and corporatized enterprise. Some might argue, in fact, that NASCAR operates as the archetypal corporate sport, with revenues coming primarily in the forms of (1) television rights fees from broadcasters eager to acquire highly sought-after racing content; (2) corporate sponsorship deals; (3) ticket sales to live events; and (4) merchandising of stock car-related intellectual properties. By the 2000 season, International Speedway Corporation reported $440 million in revenues—a number that came as a shock to analysts—and gradually increased to a reported high-point of $814 million in earnings for the 2007 season ("International Speedway Reports Record Revenues for the 2007 Fourth Quarter and Full Year," 2008).[2] When combined with profits generated by the individual teams that compete under the sanctioning body's circuit, American stock car racing organizations reported a record $3 billion profit for the 2007 fiscal year (Tuggle, 2008).

As we noted in Chapter One, automobile manufacturers, tire and oil companies, banks, insurance providers, and cigarette and alcohol brands have infused billions of research, development, marketing, and sponsorship dollars into NASCAR over the years.[3] To wit, it has been argued that NASCAR's corporate-sport synergy is unmatched in professional sport (Hagstrom, 1998), even with television viewership numbers steadily declining over the past four years (Ourand & Mickle, 2010). By the end of the millennium, for instance, it was estimated that General Motors was spending upward of $100 million per year in motorsports, while Ford and Dodge were spending $75 million and $50 million, respectively (Margolis, 2008). Moreover, the 2006 arrival of Japanese automaker Toyota, whose estimated auto racing investments exceeded $200 million annually, forced U.S. automakers to drastically increase their funding (Margolis, 2008).[4] This philosophy stretched across various industrial sectors, as marketers representing a wide range of business interests tied their growth aspirations to the circuit. Corporations such as longtime circuit sponsor Winston cigarettes, and more recently telecommunications multinationals NEXTEL and Sprint, have injected billions of dollars into the racing league, its subsidiaries, teams, and drivers (not to mention the lucrative eight-year, $4.8 billion broadcast agreements with ESPN/ABC, Fox/Speed, and TNT).

The NASCAR enterprise is also made profitable by lucrative admission prices and merchandising arms that dwarf their competitors who make up professional sport's "Big Four" (Major League Baseball, the National Football League, the National Basketball Association, and the National Hockey League). NASCAR races average more than 120,000 spectators per event (e.g., 17 of the top-20 highest attended sporting events in North America in 2007 were NASCAR races) and command an average of more than $90 per ticket to the Sprint Cup events (Lemasters, 2008). In total, NASCAR generated $253 million in admission-based revenues for the 2007 season alone, its most successful season of gate receipts in the league's history (almost 10 percent higher than the previous season) ("International Speedway Reports Record Revenues for the 2007 Fourth Quarter and Full Year," 2008).[5] Most significantly, in late 2004 (i.e., during the high water years of NASCAR's recent popularity), marketing firms Landor Associates and Penn, Schoen, & Berland were predicting that NASCAR would end the decade as

The NASCAR Spectacle (Phoenix, AZ, November 2010)

the *"second most important brand"* in the American marketplace—
trumping Apple, Wal-Mart, and Google (McCarthy, 2004).[6] In
short, during the heyday of the fusion conservative-neoliberal conjuncture, the stock car racing business was good, real good.

BRAND LOYALTY

On par, most spectators would likely agree that the overt corporate
presence at NASCAR races is necessary and essential for the sus-
tenance/growth of the sport. As one Ryan Newman fan we spoke
with near the racetrack in Bristol, Tennessee, put it quite bluntly, for
her, these corporate underwriters "make the races happen, and we're
grateful for them." Another fan with whom we spoke in 2007 lauded
her commitment to her favorite driver's sponsor, stating: "Hell yeah
I buy Bud [Budweiser beer]...I love Junior [Dale Earnhardt Jr.] and
I wouldn't drink anything else!" Yet another racing fan from suburban Charlotte, North Carolina, who supported both Carl Edwards
and Tony Stewart "equally," offered a more lengthy and poignant
explanation:

> Look, American companies are already getting a bum rap these days.
> With the bailouts and whatnot, and the overseas jobs, the American
> economy is in rough shape....It's the same for these NASCAR teams.
> Hell, they can barely find 43 cars each week to run the races! These
> fellas gotta find a way to pay the bills, and we should just consider
> ourselves lucky that there are enough companies out there doing well
> enough to step-up and support our sport.[7]

These interview excerpts echo a more universal sentiment among
NASCAR fans during the early part of the past decade. A study conducted for NASCAR by the market research firm of Edgar, Dunn,
& Company in 2000–2001 reported that a staggering 92 percent
of "hardcore fans" and 89 percent of "casual fans" believed that
"NASCAR drivers could not run their cars without sponsors' support" (*NASCAR brand study*, 2001, p. 24). According to that same
report, 93 percent of NASCAR's hardcore fans and 87 percent of
casual fans agreed that stock car racing "is the kind of sport that
needs corporate sponsorship" (*NASCAR brand study*, 2001, p. 24).
As NASCAR internal communication reports made clear, stock car
racing fans are three times more likely to buy sponsors' goods or services than fans from other North American sport leagues (*Irwindale
Speedway: NASCAR Dodge Weekly Series 2004 Report*, 2004, p. 25).
And, as noted in a more recent NASCAR report, "Sponsor brands

hold a special place in our sport—everyone understands their importance and embraces them" ("This Is Our NASCAR," 2009).

NASCAR fans' exceptionally strong attitude toward corporate
involvement has become career-making stuff for both academics and
sport marketers—as NASCAR is seen to be the archetypal sport for
nurturing "brand loyalty" amongst its consumership. The intense
"brand loyalty" of NASCAR fans is evidenced by the fact that the
above-mentioned 2004 report noted that NASCAR fans were 94 percent more likely to have "positive feelings" about sponsors than fans
from other leagues (*Irwindale Speedway: NASCAR Dodge Weekly
Series 2004 Report*, 2004, p. 25). Various sport business scholars and
"industry insiders" have similarly concluded that NASCAR fans are
much more likely to purchase goods or services from their team's corporate sponsors than are fans in other North American sports (Levin,
Beasley, & Gamble, 2004; Levin, Joiner, & Cameron, 2001). And in
their internal documents, NASCAR administrators themselves have
identified and promoted the notion that "Fans understand sponsorship is the ultimate enabler of our sport" and that they "support their
favorite race teams, and the sport as a whole, by actively purchasing brands involved in the sport" ("This Is Our NASCAR," 2009).
"NASCAR fans are tremendously loyal, so when they're going to
buy a new vehicle, they're going to buy a vehicle that is racing in
NASCAR," said Dick Berggren, Executive Director of *Speedway
Illustrated* magazine and himself a racing fan. A middle-aged racing fan confirmed this notion, saying in the same article: "The only
vehicles I buy are vehicles whose manufacturers race in NASCAR. I
won't buy anything else" (quoted in Gomstyn, 2008, p. 1). *This is a
common declaration among NASCAR fans.*[8]

Event and series sponsors are similarly rewarded with positive "purchase intent," as marketers like to call it. Researchers have concluded
that companies like NEXTEL, Nationwide, and Sprint have also
seen increased profit margins and consumership as a consequence of
their relationships with NASCAR in recent years (Sirgy, Lee, Johar,
& Tidwell, 2008). What this effectively means is that to a greater
extent than any other professional sport entity, NASCAR can assure
its "corporate partners" a successful translation of its fans' sporting
fervor into an intense exposure to, and more importantly *consumer
action* toward, their commodity brand. In other words, the league
can effectively promise advertisers and sponsors that NASCAR fans,
in spite of their already established consumer behavior patterns and
tendencies, are the most malleable—yet in an odd paradox, simultaneously *loyal*—consumer-spectators in professional sport.

To get a better sense of how and why this corporate-sport reciprocity had become such a defining feature of the NASCAR experience, we thought it best to go to races and see how race fans experience, or consume, both the products and sign values associated with the sport's prominent corporate sponsors. As we detail below, what we found were distinctive patterns of corporeal contact, whereby consuming bodies interface with a complex universe of signs, symbols, and practices of consumer culture.

CONSUMING THE CONJUNCTURE

Throughout our research at NASCAR events—conducted over the course of five years and hundreds of hours on the ground—it became evident that corporate capitalism was not only a prevailing fixture within these spaces of the corporate spectacular and of the fan/spectator praxis, but a seemingly *naturalized* one. Commercial transactions proliferate throughout the NASCAR racing space. In symbolic terms, NASCAR bodies flow across a tapestry of overtly signified *automobilia*—both as 150-mile-per-hour billboards of late-modern consumer culture and as leather jacketed, T-shirt emblazoned, or tattooed markers of enfleshed sporting allegiance—weaving together a sign-space of corporate logos, commercial signifiers, and symbols of commerce. In NASCAR Nation, drivers and teams are most commonly identified not by color schemes, mascots, or team logos, but rather by the limitless universe of corporate intellectual properties that dominate the sport's bodies, automobiles, and stadia. Through this "mobile self-display" (Schnapp, 1999), spectators stitch themselves into and across a mosaic of symbolic corporatism unlike any in the highly commercialized North American sporting landscape. Fans communicate their identities, indeed their very *place-ness*, through a visual language of corporate signifiers—Jeff Gordon fans adorn jackets swathed with his primary sponsor, Dupont (through 2010); Dale Earnhardt, Jr.'s, supporters brandish either U.S. National Guard or Amp Energy Drink insignias; Tony Stewart = Old Spice; Kyle Busch = M&Ms candy; Carl Edwards = Aflac; and so on.[9]

These symbolic gestures correlate with multidimensional strata of status within the spectacle. A newly purchased Tony Stewart T-shirt might suggest a change in allegiance or an update of sponsor, but if worn in tandem with too many other new pieces of garb (a hat or jacket, for instance), then one is likely to be read as a conspicuous-consuming neophyte. Conversely, if one were to bring merchandise from home—perhaps purchased at a hometown Wal-Mart or online purveyor—such as radio scanner or a race-themed seat cushion, then that would be suggestive of a more longstanding, and indeed genuine, consumer relationship with NASCAR. In this way, the commodity-toting, corporate-inscripted body is a moving symbolic vessel—transmitting both the (social) location of the individual and the embeddedness of the brand within the social formation.

In this spectacle of sporting corporatism, the physical is symbolic (and vice versa), and thus bodies are limited in that they constitute a means of recognition, rather than critical awareness, for those who have inherited them (Berlant, 1997). Such spectacles of the corpora-tized auto-mobile body form closed universes "where everything is a sign; collections of codes to which only some hold the key but whose existence everyone accepts; totalities which are partially fictional but effective" (Augé, 1995, p. 33). Which is to say, the corporate sig-nifiers of NASCAR necessitate *spectatorship*, rather than authorship. Throughout our observations at NASCAR events—observations that resonate in most journalistic forays in the realm of stock car racing (Hinton, 2007; Hofstetter, 2006; Patton, 2002; Rushin, 1999)—it is safe to conclude that the most die-hard race fans were those who donned only the logo of their favorite driver's *corporate endorser.* Thus, "real" Matt Kenseth, Kasey Kahne, or Denny Hamlin (and so on) fans show their deep-seated loyalties by abandoning conven-tional NASCAR garb—likely saturated with Kenseth's, Kahne's, or Hamlin's image, their cars' silhouette, or their team's respective num-bers—and instead adorn merchandise that identifies their allegiance only through singular, transcendental corporate signifiers: that of Crown Royal (or DeWalt before that); or of Budweiser (or Dodge before that); or FedEx.

SPACES OF THE CONJUNCTURE

The spaces of NASCAR are similarly shrouded with corporate insignias and an explicit commercialism. At Phoenix International Raceway, for instance, the grandstands are crowned by an interesting mixture of American flags interdispersed amongst hundreds of ban-ners decorated with corporate sponsors such as Coca Cola, Kobalt, Bashas, Chevy, O'Reilly's Auto Parts, Budweiser, Gatorade, and Sprint (the racing series' current title sponsor). Charlotte, Dover, Bristol, and most other tracks are similarly fashioned with a multitude of cor-porate banners. At Talladega, giant Toyota flags thrusting in excess of 100 feet into the air flap above the main grandstand. In fact, most rac-ing spaces—from the grass infield, to the asphalt on the track, to the signage in and around the pit areas—bear some explicitly corporate imprint.

In material terms, officials are very strategic in organizing how bodies flow through, and engage with, the assorted spaces of commercial and corporate encounters.[10] To wit, racing fans line up hours before the event to purchase tickets, merchandise, and other NASCAR-vended commodities. Some observers have alleged that racing fans are likely to spend almost $500 per race weekend on tickets, accommodation, travel costs, food and beverages, and merchandise. A racing insider, using the "unscientific" example of a story told to him by a waitress in a rest stop near Daytona Beach, conjectured that most of the people "visit Daytona with at least $1,000 in their pockets and intend to go home with zero." He continued by suggesting that race fans get "bragging rights" by making the trip to a major NASCAR event "and coming home with empty pockets" (quoted in Auerswald, 2002). Hyperconsumption is thus prefigured as an *integral*—rather than *ancillary*—part of the fan experience. And, in doing its part, NASCAR (and its corporate partners) configure the racing spaces to maximize these *commercial* encounters: There are literally hundreds of beer and hot dog stands, merchandising tents/trailers, and restaurants at each race. There is even a portable Sam's Club (Wal-Mart's wholesale-to-the-public superstore) in the Talladega infield (as at many tracks), where fans can outfit their campsites and RVs with food and beverages, cooking supplies, lawn chairs, and various other accoutrements.

Indeed, each NASCAR race creates an economy unto itself, with tens of thousands to hundreds of thousands of people (depending on the race location) temporarily inhabiting a transportable, hyperconsumptive sporting village. While at a NASCAR race in Richmond, Virginia in the fall of 2006, we noted:

> The presence of corporate logos, corporate hospitality tents, and corporate merchandise—ranging from Skoal to Crown Royal to the latest HDTV technologies—is staggering. The commercial spaces span the perimeter of the track, which is nearly one mile in circumference. Interestingly, NASCAR fans and spectators engage these highly commercialized spaces as if they are part of the sporting event, arriving at the track hours before the race to take in the temporary shopping mall of NASCAR sponsoring wares and experiences. Even more interesting is the considerable diffusion of corporate signifiers through the ornamentation of the spectating body with these same symbols. In a procession of the commodified corporeal, these spectators parade toward the NASCAR spectacle and its mesmerizing qualities.

Newer racetracks, and particularly those run by International Speedway Corporation, are laid out such that the major parking areas all siphon attendees into one (and sometimes two) major traffic arteries. Take, for instance, Phoenix International Raceway or Kansas Speedway, where spectators must make their way through an inescapable labyrinth of "corporate villages," "hospitality tents," and merchandising tailors in order to enter the raceway. At older tracks such as Martinsville or Darlington, these commercial spaces are configured in a more anfractuous or circuitous fashion, capturing spectators as they enter from various positions around the track. These pathways are lined on both sides with merchandising and vendor tailors and apparatuses, guiding the flow of traffic.

In the first instance, the bodies flowing in and around these events are strategically subjected to, if not herded through, what Henri Lefebvre (1991) would identify as NASCAR's highly commercialized "representations of space." In the most generic sense, the notion of representations of space refers to conceptualized space, the "space constructed by assorted professionals and technocrats" (Merrifield, 2000, p. 174). These representations of space, or "conceptualized

Spatial Arrangements of Consumption in the "NASCAR Arcades" (Martinsville, VA, October 2006)

spaces," are "tied to the relations of production and to the order which those relations impose, and hence to knowledge, to signs, to codes, and to 'frontal' relations" (Lefebvre, 1991, p. 33). Active consumerism and the adornment of corporatized "badges" of citizenship represent not only the convergence of spectator-consumer identity, NASCAR driver-celebrity, and corporate sponsors benevolence, but also the exaltation of prevailing hegemonic economic structures of neoliberal corporate capitalism. Here in the spectacular, on the visible plane of what Jean Baudrillard (1983b) might refer to as the "frontal" representations of NASCAR space, the complex assemblage of artificial signifiers and human movement—from the preponderance of corporate logos to the layout of buildings and pathways to the flow and deportment of bodies therein—is manufactured to reproduce the dominant ideological fanaticism of a neoliberal/paleo-/neo-conservative conjuncture to which each is equally bound.

We have seen such spatial arrangement practices before. In his seminal work on the physical spaces of the Industrial-era Parisian arcades, Walter Benjamin (1999) situated the blurred dyadic of commercial and ideological spaces within the notion of "phantasmagoria." For Benjamin (1999), this type of phantasmagoria was an archipelago of "rapidly shifting scenes of real or imagined things" (p. 9), forever swarming, constantly charming, always seducing the consumer-subject. Within what we might call the "NASCAR Arcades," the hyperconsumerist impetuses of neoliberalism are layered onto and through the visceral geography, forging an inseparable bond that beckons the consumerist *flâneur* into a corporate sport phantasmagoria, an enchanted capitalist dreamworld that stimulates both reflexes of alienation (and the opportunity to escape that alienation and connect to the imagined NASCAR collective through the consuming and signifying act) and the (restrictive) exclusivity of citizenship (see Benjamin, 1969). Stated simply, NASCAR's racetrack spaces offer fans more than a natural or neutral spectator venue (indeed, no such space exists in the Disney-fied, commercialized sporting contemporary). Instead, a sociopolitical matrix of images, experiences, geometric order(s), and social relations mediate the nodes of engagement by which spectator identities are formulated; and through which the mechanisms of consumer capital are made powerful and the identity politics of paleo-conservatism's moral-political rationality are made meaningful (more on this later).

In these so-called central business districts of NASCAR Nation, then, the flow of human bodies and human interaction is organized around, if not made cohesive by, the logics of conspicuous consumerism (see Soja, 1989). Our fieldnotes taken at a race in Martinsville, Virginia, speak to the engineering principles of these stock car pseudo-cities:

> There is a plethora of entry points into the expansive commercial village surrounding the track....Fans are not required to show credentials or tickets to gain access to the activities or merchandising tents that encompass the track. Once in these areas, tens of thousands of people weave through the maze of merchandising trailers, interactive games, and "NASCAR experiences." While the rows of merchandising trailers snake around the hills outside the track, creating a uni-directional path leading to the gates of the track, VIP tents and "Hot pass" areas are restricted to those subjected to corporate entertainment or those who paid large sums of money to gain access. Signs stating *Entry Prohibited* and *Not Open to the Public* meet those who deviate from the preconfigured course of movement.

In these conceived NASCAR spaces, physical space is structured so that fans and spectators are allowed open access to the various sites of normalized consumption (merchandise, media technologies, concessions, etc.) and restricted from other spaces requiring "credentials" (advanced acts of consumption) to gain access. Indeed, one security guard with whom we spoke to at the Talladega Superspeedway referred to an area on the infield reserved for high-paying spectators and their high-end motor homes, as the "gated community" of the track, a direct reference to the kind of gated communities dominating the suburban landscape, especially throughout the past several decades in the United States.

It is important to point out that on race days, the NASCAR track and the bodies flowing through its surrounding physical spaces are not only transformed into spaces of commodification, but are indeed *themselves* commodified—a material world that gives way to consumer-driven material culture. In this way, representations of NASCAR space create a spatiality conceived in the mold of a decidedly structured asphalt shopping mall; one where, "invariably ideology, power and knowledge are embedded in this representation" (Merrifield, 2000, p. 174). Meaningfulness through praxis within this playground of consumerism is organized through a series of concentric circles of capital; starting at the epicenter: a circular track filled with fast-moving "billboards" and jam-packed with consumer-revelers of the highest devotion (those willing to pay up to $20,000 at some races for the "opportunity" to be "in the pits"); surrounded by a grandstand packed with corporate embossed bodies and undergirded by a phantasmagoria of concession-based foodstuffs and merchandised wares; and ultimately encircled by an outer-crust of encircling spectator bodies encircling the cylindrical arcade filled with Dupont embroidered leather jackets, Dale Earnhardt T-shirts, and corporate sponsored banners.

THEATER OF THE "ATOMIZED MASSES"

The performances of embodied corporate (identity) politics are in some ways highly regulated (both internally and externally), over-determined as they are by the monosemic order of corporate capitalism (see Jameson, 1999). Those spectators not adorning logoed merchandise—and thus failing to engage in the signifying processes of allegiance to both driver/team and to the market logics that allow them to "do their thing"—are considered by many to be, as one fan proclaimed, "outsiders." Or, as another Dale Jarrett fan from Arizona put it, "they must be new to the sport or lost." In NASCAR, the *Fortune* 500 provinces the *lingua franca* of embodied identity, in that the act of brand purchase, not unlike that seen in a shopping mall or department store, symbolically locates the consumer within the lexicon of consumer capitalism. What makes the brand-bearing NASCAR consumer unique, one might argue, is that while the Gucci-toting, Burberry-adorned mall consumer is subjected to what Gilles Lipovetsky (1994) refers to as the "empire of fashion," in NASCAR Nation, the brand yields to cultural economies of consumption (and cultures thereof), production (of meaning, of identity, and of those same cultures of consumption), *and* the conspicuous endorsement of the political economy upon which each is constituted by and constitutive of.[11] Put another way, while postmodern fashion tends to obscure the process of material production, or popular media commodities often appear without history, NASCAR wares—both symbolic and material—bear the imprint of the logics upon which they have come to *be* commodities.

In short, to adorn a Sunoco racing jacket within NASCAR Nation (or to drink a Coors beer, etc.) is to do so *knowingly*, and with a purpose. It is to have an awareness not necessarily of the processes of alienation, exploitation, and subjectification at work within the commodity exchange, but rather to know the commodity as a political form within the throws of consumer culture: thus, "Real Men" don't wear GoDaddy.com gear, for instance, because despite its overtly sexualized advertisements featuring race car-driver Danica Patrick, many fans see the sponsor's place within NASCAR—yet alone the broader

U.S. economy—as fleeting; an unstable vestige of the Clinton-era silicon technology boom. Conversely, Budweiser, once the iconic "good ole boy" brand du jour (largely due to its sponsorship of Dale Earnhardt, Jr.), now sponsors "pretty boy" Kasey Kahne—oft-derided as the antithesis of the Southern hard man (who was emblematic of Reagan-era hard body politics of the kind Susan Jeffords [1993] has written about)—and thus their intoxicant no longer rests inside most race-day beer coozies. Moreover, based on the majority of fireside conservations we had, we can conclude that "Real" NASCAR fans don't buy DuPont products (Jeff Gordon's sponsor), don't drink Crown Royal, and don't drive Toyota automobiles. Instead, they support the Army, drive Ford trucks, and drink Jack Daniels or Miller Genuine Draft.

In this way, consumption within the NASCAR spectacle is a *national* act; it is *political* act; it is *individual* act; it is an expression of identity; and perhaps most importantly, it is an act of *citizenship*. Within NASCAR Nation, then, there exists a "politics of product" (Micheletti, 2003), the result of what Nikolas Rose (1999) described as the conduct of consumerism:

> These fuse the aim of manufacturers to sell products and increase market share with the identity experiments of consumers. They are mediated by highly developed techniques of market research and finely calibrated attempts to segment and target specific consumer markets. Advertising images and television programmes interpenetrate in the promulgation of images of lifestyle, narratives of identity choice and the highlighting of the ethical aspects of adopting one or other way of conducting one's life. (p. 178)

Under the throws of this neoliberal hegemony, the corporatization of the consuming body in and around NASCAR events seems a natural extension of liberal democratic society, whereby the individual laborer *earns* the right to consume as she or he sees fit, but not under conditions of his or her choosing. Paradigmatically, the *tabula rasa* of belonging within commercialized stock car spaces protracts the myths of unlimited freedom (through consumption) while simultaneously reinforcing the very structures by which the individual's freedom is in fact limited.

To reappropriate Ben Bachmair (1991), this seductive quality of the spatialized, performed, and embodied NASCAR consumer spectacle is brought to life by, and in so doing enlivens, a series of seemingly contradictory, yet mutually reinforcing neoliberal processes: mass *individualization*; *equalization* (or a false sense of equality); and *spectacular automobility.* In the chapter's final sections, we turn to a discussion of these processes, and then move to reconsider how this convergence *produces* consumer-subjects and subjectivities complicit in the neoliberal order of things.

Producing NASCAR's Consuming-Subject

Following Guy Debord (1967/1994), we would argue that the above-defined compulsion of individuals within NASCAR's spectacular spaces to actively consume fetishized material and nonmaterial commodities "perceptibly" connects them to the broader spectacle of neoliberalism (see also Kellner, 2007).[12] As Debord (1967/1994) posits,

> Here we have the principle of commodity fetishism, the domination of society by things whose qualities are "at the same time perceptible and imperceptible by the senses." This principle is absolutely fulfilled in the spectacle, where the perceptible world is replaced by a set of images that are superior to that world yet at the same time impose themselves as eminently perceptible. (p. 26)

The "perceptible world" of NASCAR, much like Lefebvre's (1991) notion of "representation of space," presents the "atomized" spectator with a conduit to broader configurations of social and cultural "belonging." NASCAR's own internal marketing programs note that the sport's fans are unique in their "shared sense of belonging" and have indentified that as a potentially fertile pillar upon which to build brand awareness and commercial activity ("This Is Our NASCAR," 2009). As a consumer-driven *phalanstère*—a self-contained utopian communal space through which form and function unite (Benjamin, 1999)—NASCAR tracks forge the prevailing logics of the market with the act of "being" within the geometric spaces of the hypercommercial spectacle.

To be a part of the NASCAR spectacle thus in some ways means to be part of the society of the (neoliberal) spectacle; and thus the formation of new identities, and the creation of new possibilities to indulge oneself *through* the spectacle (Best & Kellner, 1999). The spectator systematically becomes part of the spectacle, incessantly consuming and engaging the modalities of the spectacle to locate him- or herself within the popular discourses of networks of representation, signification, and ultimately subjectivization (Debord, 1981a, 1981b). In the age of hyperconsumption, Debord (1967/1994) suggests, "In form as in content the spectacle serves as the total justification for the conditions and aims of the existing system" (p. 13). The semiotic dialectics assigned to commercial goods and social practice, and the broader social forces that inform the consumer sensibilities toward consumption, are the core interrelationship within Debord's society of the spectacle (Best & Kellner, 1999). But these neoliberal consumers—or more accurately, consumer-*citizens*—are at the same time located in the discursive landscape of the spectacular—carving their identity(ies) out of the commodified pluralities of corporate signifiers (Debord, 1990).

Such is the allure of the spectacle of neoliberalism. The individual is drawn into, indeed seduced by, a plethora of signifiers and experiences promising a sense of collective belonging within the broader formations of consumer culture. Each NASCAR race presents but one of many loci of "individualized collective action" (Micheletti, 2003), a space in which an otherwise disconnected body of individuals can come together to celebrate NASCAR's (a particular version of) "America," and the perceived freedoms each provides the individual to graft technologies of the consuming self. The sport and its spectacularized racetracks at once present the willing consumer with what Ulrich Beck and Elizabeth Beck-Gernsheim (2002) famously refer to as "*Individualisierung*," or institutionalized individualism; and at the same time—by way of praxis and performance—the individual becomes institutionalized.

Strangely, the collective spectacle is perhaps the definitive social space through which neoliberal individuality can be realized. An underdeveloped theme from Beck's (1998) seminal text, *Risk Society*, the notion of individualization suggests that the market society has been successful in forming a new social paradigm in which the individual is increasingly seen to be a *market-based* project; that is, to be actualized outside of history, outside of the material dialectics of race, gender, social class, and so on, and outside of the platitudes of determinacy. This form of individualization, which has become a defining feature of the neoliberal turn, is perhaps best described by Zygmunt Bauman (2002a) in this way:

> To put it in a nutshell, "individualization" consists in transforming human "identity" from a "given" into a "task"—and charging the actors with the responsibility for performing that task and for the consequences (also the side-effects) of their performance: in other words, it consists in establishing a *de jure* autonomy (although not necessarily a *de facto* one). No more are human beings "born into" their identities...Needing to *become* what one *is* is the hallmark of modern living—and of this living alone. (p. xv, emphases in original)

NASCAR's neoliberal consuming masses are located within spaces of consumption in ways that remind them that through capital relations—and particularly those that give meaning to bodies and practices of the NASCAR spectacle—they are free to pursue individual (consumer) identities, interests, and politics.[13] Symbolic contact with the various corporatized markers of status—from racing apparel to RV size to campsite location to brand of beer chugged—locates the individual, her or his (consumer) politics, and the agency to locate oneself within this phantasmagoria of neoliberal commerce. And thus within the current market society, the NASCAR-spectating body emerges as both *a consumer project* and as *a projection of individual achievement.*

Through the commodity, the broader social networks and power configurations of neoliberalism are at once celebrated and obscured. By way of purchase and performance (and the recognition thereof), corporate NASCAR effectively promises "a shift from governing through society to governing through individuals' capacities for self-realization" (Barnett, Clarke, Cloke, & Malpass, 2008, p. 626). To realize the Self, as a meaningful sociopolitical organism within these spaces, means to come to terms *with* corporate capital *through* corporate capital. It is here where the neoliberal individual(-as)-self is seemingly actualized, or at least made normal.

In this "lonely crowd" (Riesman, Glazer, & Denney, 1950/2001) of atomized masses, one is both one and the sum of many. Individuals travel across intersecting "lines of flight" (Hardt & Negri, 2000), baring in the practices and identities precarious movements toward and away from capital. NASCAR spaces provide the discursive canvas upon which the neoliberal *homo clausus* is thus constructed, reproduced, and contested. As the figurational sociologist Norbert Elias (2001) explained, this notion of *homo clausus* suggests a Self-ness that can be actualized only through individual (false) consciousness:

> The conception of the individual as *homo clausus*, a little world in himself [*sic*] who ultimately exists quite independently of the great world outside, determines the image of man [*sic*] in general. Every other human being is likewise seen as *homo clausus*; his core, his being, his true self appears likewise as something divided within him by an invisible wall from everything outside, including every other human being. (p. 204)[14]

Hence, connection creates a false sense of *disconnection*. The individual consumer, cloaked in a mosaic of corporate symbols, undertakes her or his individual fan-identity project, and is disciplined by the cumulative spectacle of individual consumer projects she/he encounters. All the while, they are becoming one with the imperatives that both bring them together and separate them. "This implicit individuation of society," write Joanna Latimer and Roland Munro (2006), is "an individuation that is visualized as growing apace, to the exclusion of other possible ways of being and relating" (Latimer & Munro, 2006, p. 33). The individual learns through the public pedagogy of the NASCAR spectacle that to belong is to belong *corporately* and *individually*.

Paradoxically, then, these mostly working-class NASCAR consumers, who (as we discuss later) are among those most marginalized by neoliberal reform, actually find in the interconnected spectacle a social reality *sans* connectivity. They are both disconnected from the lives of those producers of the spectacle *and* of their own productive experiences. Regarding the former, this "individualization and fragmentation of growing inequalities into separate biographies [becomes] a collective experience" (Beck & Beck-Gernsheim, 2002, pp. xxiii–xxiv). The imprint of Exxon-Mobile or Sunoco comes to signify NASCAR, its legacy, and the role of corporations is fueling the sport that so many people love. On the other hand, and within the NASCAR spectacle, these imprints do *not* come to represent ecological disaster (such as in the Gulf of Mexico during 2010) or air pollution, nor do these symbols mean bailouts, higher taxation or national debt, laid-off factory workers in Detroit, or the failings of U.S. economic stalwarts.[15]

Also lost in the logocentrism of the spectacle are the social realities of those workers in developing nations who stitch the very images on the merchandised fabric that makes the spectacle.[16] The image appears as atemporal and without a geopolitical legacy, and in so doing reminds the consumer of a corporate literacy whereby: "The promotion of 'free trade' and the formation of a global marketplace has served to further increase the distances between producers and consumers" (Smart, 2010, p. 19). The individual consumer, by way of symbolic association, is thus subjected to a neoliberal pedagogy in which "workers must know little of the marketed lives of the products they produce and consumers must remained sheltered from the production lives of the brands they buy" (Klein, 1999, p. 347).

Just as spectacularized individualization loosens the shackles of the interconnective imagination—chains that can be burdensome to consumer conscience in the age of fast capitalism—it also promotes a sense of false egalitarianism amongst many consumers. Through these cultural (public) pedagogies we "learn" that individuals are free to make their own consumer choices (both within NASCAR and beyond), and that in the marketplace these choices are equally accessible to everyone (a false promise if ever there was one). By practicing good corporate citizenship (which has been affectively realized as a form of *ethical* citizenship in the contemporary moment [King, 2008]), the producer of consumption/architect of the self-building consumer project is made responsible (or *ir*responsible) for her or his own well-being within the spectacle of neoliberalism. This "responsibilization of the consumer" (Barnett et al., 2008, p. 626) appeals to the idea that while the political species-being is limited (by government, by social norms, by history), the entrepreneurial subject is seen to be a free-wheeling, free-spending autarkic agent—able to graft both experience and identity as one wishes through the infinite offerings of the market.

CARNIVALS OF SELF-BUILDING CAPITAL

For political philosopher Wendy Brown, the collectivity of these neoliberal spectacles (as well as the broader spectacle of neoliberalism) entails a massive de-democratization, as terms such as the public good, rights, and debate no longer have any meaning. "The model neoliberal citizen," writes Brown (2005), "is one who strategizes for her or himself among various social, political, and economic options, not one who strives with others to alter or organize these options" (p. 43). This is the power of not only NASCAR's metonymic spectacle of neoliberalism, but of the cultural and political economies of neoliberalism more generally—the *promise of empowerment*. As Nikolas Rose (1999) duly notes,

> Advanced liberal forms of government thus rest, in new ways, upon the activation of the power of the citizen. Citizenship is no longer primarily realized in a relation with the state, or in a single "public sphere," but in a variety of private, corporate and quasi-public practices from working to shopping. (p. 166)

Like other cultural industries, then, one might argue that NASCAR is *fundamentally* in the business of producing "citizen-consumers" (Micheletti, 2003). In this way, to belong within NASCAR Nation is to be first a good *consumer*; that is, a good consumer of goods, images, and experiences. As Colleen O'Manique and Ronald Labonte (2008) would have it, "the seemingly just *consumer*" has supplanted the seeming just "*citizen*" (p. 1562, emphases original)—social activism replaced by social consumerism, the active promotion of corporate capitalism over grassroots participation (see Giardina, 2010, p. 133). But all this consumption has to be conducted in ways that glorify both the act—and perhaps more importantly, the logics—of consumerism.

Such is the condition of neoliberalism. Pierre Bourdieu (1998b) understood this: "the undivided reign of the market and consumer, the commercial substitute for the citizen" (Bourdieu, 1998a, p. 25). The citizen-consumer within NASCAR Nation, by way of performance and praxis, emerges as a reaffirmation of the social conditions of late-capitalist production. Moving about corporatized space and awash with corporate symbols, the citizen-consumer acts out citizenship, belonging, and authority of existence through market pathos—at once conferring upon the spectacle *through* the spectacle:

> The companies, which offer no security to their employees and contribute to instituting a consumerist vision of the world, herald an economic reality akin to the social philosophy inherent in neo-classical theory. It is as if the ... individualistic, ultra-subjectivist philosophy of neo-classical economics had found in neo-liberal policy the means of its own realization ... the conditions for its own verification. (Bourdieu, 2003, p. 30)

Related to our earlier discussions of neoliberalism, individualism, and perceived autarkic sovereignty, one might argue, then, that NASCAR's spaces of consumption perpetuate, and indeed authorize, what John Kenneth Galbraith (1969) once referred to as "a presumption of consumer sovereignty" (p. 216). In this way, consuming NASCAR could be understood by the masses as an empowering fiction. That is, for those workers otherwise disenchanted by the social means of production, or disenfranchised by a political machine, NASCAR Nation presents itself as an important, vibrant, and deeply performative space for forging an individualized self-identity (especially around issues of race and class).

Foucault (2008) once poignantly noted that this project of self-building is belied by the basic assumption that "we should think of consumption as an enterprise activity by which the individual, precisely on the basis of the capital he [*sic*] has at his disposal, will produce something that will be his own satisfaction" (p. 226). This is the neoliberal subject, always represented as being "in ultimate command" (Galbraith, 1975, p. 29) of her or his own *Self-building* agenda. In building the Self through the NASCAR experience, the neoliberal corporation as social and economic being is reified, through organizing the bodies, spaces, and pedagogical interplay thereof—at once naturalizing and spectacularizing its place of authority, and indeed benevolence, within the contemporary market sensibility. The Brazilian critical educator Paulo Freire (2006), as if writing from an Italian prison cell circa 1932, once posited that such an economy of ideas promotes the illusion of "free action." The NASCAR mystification is this: the consensus among the members of NASCAR Nation is that they are free to choose whom to cheer for, whose merchandise to buy, when and where to attend races, and that "less-government-is-better" political dictums are working to secure those freedoms, all the while being subjected to a spectacular system that subjugates their human experience and experiences to the impulses of maximized surplus value (see Giroux, 2004; Harvey, 2005; Kincheloe, 2002).

This, of course, leads to a disconcerting "paradox": All the quantifications of "brand loyalty" and "purchase intent" aside, the devotion to the munificent neoliberal corporation and its consumer culture has brought with it the mass colonization of spectating physicalities in a *carnival of capital.* In these weekly spectacles of corporate capital, allegiances to driver, team, sport, and the intense corporate presence "needed to make it all happen" are blurred—infused with, and within, the hegemonic structures working against the individuals they always-already hail. As such, the commercial precepts of NASCAR present a twisted contradiction, whereby the enchantments of this NASCAR superstructure separate the individual as spectator from individual as laborer, all the while guaranteeing their complicity to what Ferdinand Tönnies (1887/2002) might call a consumer-driven *gesellschaft.* Such is commercial life in NASCAR Nation: where the individual worker labors within a local outpost of multinational corporate capitalism (which likely replaced the local, "small-business" predecessor) and becomes more and more nestled into neoliberal systems of accumulation (where your benefits are being cut back, your skills becoming increasingly devalued, and your employment stability all the more tenuous); exchanges her or his time and labor for a diminishing wage; reinvests that wage in the signifying acts of fan loyalty (i.e., a cap, leather jacket, or T-shirt); spends significant portions of the remainder of that wage on access to the race track as to best display those forms of corporate allegiance; and is reminded throughout the race weekend that they should be grateful for the (albeit tenuous) working and consuming conditions that the corporate organism has provided them.

In the interplay of signifiers, embodiment, and praxis, NASCAR's spectator-fans come to celebrate the free market behemoths while being disenfranchised by the same processes and institutions they are applauding (Denzin & Giardina, 2007; Giroux, 2004; Harvey, 2005; Kincheloe, 2004). While a significant number of NASCAR fans draw employment from the expanding universe of low-paying, dehumanizing, no-benefit American service jobs—what George Ritzer (1998) refers to as "McJobs"—and increase their credit card debt on holidays spent in NASCAR Nation, they in the same gesture applaud the architects of neoliberalism as they eternally round the circuits of capital accumulation. Just as the stability of their working lives is put under duress—as the captains of capital move jobs off-shore and politicians increase the taxpayer burden for public services whilst simultaneously siphoning public funds off to the corporate sector—these working fans are in no uncertain terms reminded of the essential role the corporation plays in reproducing their own livelihoods (and in this case sense of self).[17]

In some ways, the corporate pedagogies that proliferate the NASCAR space serve to further these double interests of insecurity and gratitude. As fans suffer through the global market's trend toward "a deterritorialization of the company," NASCAR—as it has done in years past—teaches us that these are natural patterns of capital progression. The messy social relations created by a fractured labor climate, a toiling domestic economy, and a new order of working-class economic survivalism are all smoothed over through the NASCAR spectacle.

CODA

In sum, NASCAR produces a unique consumer habitus, which normalizes, and is normalized through, spectacular bodily encounters with neoliberalism. These corporate goliaths, which many have argued are the most "anti-humane" social technologies of our time (Bakan, 2004; Klein, 2002; Lasn, 1999; Pierce, 2003), alienate and oppress contemporary wage laborers through the uneven distribution of capital, discontinued access to health care, "fat-trimming" layoffs, fraudulent accounting practices, deskilling and unsafe working environments, the further toxification of the planet, and antidemocratic political lobbying in favor of "progress" and greater surplus value (Albert, 2003; Giroux, 2004b; Hardt & Negri, 2004; Negri, 2003). It makes normal the core tenets of Ronald Reagan-Milton Friedman's lasting "gift" to the American people:[18]

> The practical instituting of a Darwinian world in which the springs of commitment to the job and the company are found in insecurity, suffering and stress would undoubtedly not succeed so completely

if it did not benefit from the complicity of the destabilized habitus produced by insecurity and the existence—at all levels of the hierarchy, even the highest, especially among executives—of a reserve army of labour made docile by insecure unemployment. The ultimate basis of this economic order placed under the banner of individual freedom is indeed the *structural violence* of unemployment, of insecure employment and of the fear provoked by the threat of losing employment. (Bourdieu, 1998a, p. 98)

At the most micro-consumer level, even the level of the flesh, the spectacle reaffirms a neoliberal orthodoxy that "States, corporations, individuals are all governed by the same logic, that of interest and competition" (Read, 2009, p. 35). Thus politics, in both the macro and micro sense, is always a win-loss proposition, often rendering a condition of noncompromise/stasis/inertia.[19]

Ultimately, performances of NASCAR fandom authorize a public pedagogy intended to evade public contemplation, whereby spectators engage what Raymond Williams (1981) might refer to as a *preferred* knowledge of the corporation as facilitator but fail to make the connection between the neoliberal economic structure and the disproportionate capital accumulation afforded these corporations at the expense of workers' human capital. But these enchantments of mass marketization are neither a product of circumstance nor happenstance. Those spectacles, in turn, produce the discursive formations of which the subject is only one part.[20]

We have argued throughout this chapter that by existing within the spaces of the NASCAR spectacular, those spectating bodies are in some ways subjected to the preferred, or dominant, free market(ized) public pedagogies. Following Foucault (1988a, 1994), we have endeavored to illustrate how the experiences of these sporting subjects are rationally polyvalent: First, the subject cannot create her or his identity outside this pedagogical terrain and, therefore, each spectator is the subject of market discourse (those of the market, its brands, and the corporation that produce those conditions). Second, the spectator becomes subject to the discourses of neoliberalism if she/he puts her-/himself at the position from which this discourse makes most "sense" (as a member of the atomized masses of the working-class "Nation"). Thus, the consumer—through the interplay of spectacularization and individualization—occupies a place within a "new habitat of subjectification." As such, the neoliberal self is constructed through consumption choices, choices that in total reaffirm the conditions by which those very consumer's livelihoods are destabilized.

Of course, we are not suggesting that NASCAR's spatialized neoliberalism is necessarily new to the realm of professional sport (or that commercialism is an exclusively neoliberal phenomenon). However, as we aim to make clear in the flowing chapters, we are arguing that spectatorship and consumerism within the spaces of neo-liberal NASCAR Nation coalesce—often with other cultural-political axes (gender, race, sexuality, morality, etc.)—to produce important, contextually specific power relations. As such, the following three chapters turn toward an analysis of the ways in which these cultural/political intersections "recover" formations of power embedded in formations of white, (neo-)Confederate, paleo- and neo-conservative, Evangelical, militaristic U.S. nationalism.

4

NASCAR AND THE "SOUTHERNIZATION" OF SPORTING AMERICA

NASCAR is a breakout sports sensation. It is also—let's just come right out and say it—the Whitest sport in America. The drivers are White, the pit crews are White, and it has become a cliché to note that at most races, Confederate flags outnumber African American fans. For good or bad...at a time when professional sports seems to be embracing hip-hop culture, NASCAR is heading in precisely the opposite direction.

—C. W. Nevius (2003, p. CM12)

In his bestselling sojourn, *Confederates in the Attic: Dispatches From the Unfinished Civil War*, Pulitzer Prize–winning author Tony Horwitz[1] (1999) offers a timely journalistic anthropology of a contemporary U.S. South still wrestling with the last vestiges of an antebellum-borne, Jim Crow–era-refined, and segregationist-practiced cultural and racial history. Making use of sharp prose and an exhaustive sociological fascination, Horwitz guides his readers through the negotiations and contestations of everyday life within the region—stopping along the way to meditate on both the enchantments of a charming regional vernacularism and the specters of recalcitrant racism and (hyper)patriarchy that still haunt the life experiences of many Southerners. Perhaps most importantly, *Confederates in the Attic* offers inspection—and to some degree, introspection—of the ways in which the spaces (many of which remain segregated), symbols (such as the Confederate flag), identities (located in the discursive disgorges of terms such as "redneck," "nigger," "hillbilly," and the like), and histories (both recovered collective memory and revised traditionalism) of the Old South incontrovertibly constitute the region's current cultural and political economies.

The principal objective of Horwitz's book, since followed by a growing quantity of like-themed manuscripts that have made their way to press in recent years (cf. Blight, 2001; Goldfield, 2002; McPherson, 2007), seems to be fixed on illuminating the "meaning-fulness" of Southern identity and the reemergence of what the author refers to as a "neo-Confederate" Southern eth(n)ic. This strand of neo-Confederate recalcitrance is thrust forward it two parts: (1) as a reclamation of masculine white privilege resuscitated in imaginar-ies of a modern-day supremacist Southern faction; and (2) as a much softer romanticization of Southern "tradition," the gentility of plan-tation life, and, to quote from the slave minstrel "Dixie," "old times there not forgotten."

Although it may seem that the parochial nature of such an intel-lectual project reaches its limits in the explanatory theses of local identities and traditions, in light of a recent upsurge of all things "Southern" in the North American popular, this striation of inquiry paints a much wider brushstroke across a contextually specific con-servative conjuncture that has come to increasingly inhabit the spaces of everyday life beyond the (fictionalized) "heart of Dixie." Indeed, the "conservative values" of a Christian "moral majority" (Diamond, 1995; Giroux, 2004b; Goldberg, 2007; Hedges, 2007; Kaplan, 2005) the "Red State" polity of cowboy politicians (i.e., George W. Bush; cf. Phillips, 2006), the "redneck" balladry of country western crooners (i.e., Gretchen Wilson or early Dixie Chicks), the "blue collar" humor of Southern comedians (i.e., Jeff Foxworthy, Larry the Cable Guy, or Rodney Carrington), and the hyperwhite physicalities of the ideal-ized Southern sporting Man(ning) (i.e., NFL Super Bowl–winning quarterbacks Peyton and Eli Manning) dominated the public sphere throughout the 2000s. Thus, it would be hard to argue against the notion that in the contemporary United States, the South (or, at least, a particular discursive iteration thereof) had indeed, at least in some discursive form, "risen again."

Considering the contextually specific import of all things Southern, a more meaningful theme emerges in Horwitz's (1999) contempla-tions (as well as those of his contemporaries): the current populariza-tion of the South has been used to suture the political and economic imperatives of free market capitalism to broader contortions of the fusionist "conservative movement" (and vice versa). And follow-ing Horwitz's conclusions, it could be posited that the sociogeo-graphic dimensions of the South—those of white supremacist biker bars in Kentucky, of Confederate flag rallies in South Carolina, and the sprawling plantations of many of Dixie's "genteel elite" spread throughout the region—have provided a cultural seedling from which national (and indeed global) hyperwhite, hypermasculine, (paleo-)conservative mediated identities have been sowed, nurtured, and, in terms of political and cultural capital, harvested. As this imaginary, emergent South has expanded and become reified through the multiplatform, hypermediated dealings of Hollywood film houses, Fox News Channel, Comedy Central, incendiary diatribes of popular conservative writers, and other media machinations, it has brought with it new pedagogies of "what it means to be a Southerner" (Cash, 1941/1991; Faust, 1988; Foster, 1987; Hale, 1999; Hoelscher, 2003; Hufford, 2002; McPherson, 2003; Williamson, 1984). We also find this dual aestheticization and politicization of the South in recently invented Confederate History Month ceremonies, at Dixie-themed amusement parks, and in a host of other cultural spaces.

This imaginary South—as an accumulation of physical, social, and cultural spaces—has been transformed into a highly commercialized, deeply politicized place of identity and identification, one that is inextricably linked to a broader paleo-conservative ideology currently saturating the North American popular political sphere (McPherson, 2003; Reed, 1986; Wagner, 2002). In contemporary discursive formations of U.S. conservatism, where policies and rhetoric are created to stimulate economic growth under free market regimes of (corporate) capital accumulation, the symbolic South has been transformed into cultural tender for *reproducing the conditions of production and consumption*. That is, the South, in its numerous discursive iterations, has been refinanced as the acculturated currency of corporate capitalism by way of the identity politics of a "White masculine global patriarchy" (Kusz, 2007, p. 79). The dominant neoliberal-(neo-/paleo-) conservative order now extracts political and economic capital out of these Southern-identity politics (through album sales, pickup truck brands, campaign fundraising, Wal-Mart merchandising, the collection plate on Sunday, and so forth). In short, Southerners (and non-Southerners alike) now more than ever buy their local identities back from (non- Southern) corporations and politicians.

The more time we spent in NASCAR Nation, the more apparent it became that the sport's corporate architects have successfully translated its provincial, if not seemingly bucolic, nuances into the preeminent mass produced, highly consumable (and consumed) Southern sport commodity. As *USA Today* writer Seth Livingstone (2007a) plainly proclaimed, "As much as any sport in America, NASCAR has roots tied to a certain culture: White Southerners" (p. 1). Indeed, NASCAR is made important, and simultaneously problematic, by its Southern dialects and dialectics. Stepping outside the benevolent musings of most who contribute popular commentaries on the subject, syndicated *San Francisco Chronicle* writer, C. W. Nevius (2003), suggested that this seemingly natural synergy of NASCAR, the contemporary U.S. South, and the sport's (nearly) exclusively white spectatorship has not only advanced the sport's popularity but made for a more lucrative enterprise:

> Could there be an undercurrent of racism to NASCAR's popularity? Consider, 4 out of 5 NBA players are African American, 67 percent of NFL players are minorities, and last season, 23 percent of Major League Baseball players were born in Spanish-speaking countries (an increase of 40 percent from 1989). All of those sports, except football, are experiencing a dip in popularity. Meanwhile, the conspicuously white NASCAR is on an unprecedented run up the profit chart. (p. CM12)

In this chapter, we follow Nevius in arguing that NASCAR has been, and continues to be, a significant cultural technology in framing the processes of signification through which new, paleo-conservative Southern identities are constructed. We make the case that modern day stock car spectacles legislate a *lingua franca* of racialism (and racism) and white privilege under the auspices of a seemingly natural "heritage culture." In more succinct terms, we surmise that in NASCAR, "the South" *stands for something*: It symbolizes and represents the confluence of a romanticized history of White privilege and a localized (re)mediation of neoliberal conservatism, linking the Confederate cause of old to the same banners inscribed with "NNN," or "No Niggers in NASCAR" that have been stretched across many a NASCAR-visiting RV over the past few decades.

These re-articulations of an imaginary South resurrect the "mystic chords" of a collective memory (Kammen, 1993), a new "Southernness" that is constituted by a *mélange* of time (new identities and old power structures) and space (local subjectivity and global plurality), and whereby the burgeoning sport of stock car racing currently articulates an *Old* South cultural vernacular and racialized power structure with more recently popularized paleo-conservative identity politics. As the epigraph to this chapter suggests, then, the sport's almost exclusively white fan base[2]—both as product and producer of this particular, discursively constituted (while at the same time imagined and performed), overtly white U.S. South aesthetic—has positioned NASCAR as the preferred sporting fare for an overrepresentative faction of many white paleo-conservative Americans. And under the auspices of a George W. Bush-, and later Tea Party-inspired, post-9/11, anti-Affirmative Action backlash, "the South's national pastime" at once gives license to the resurgent regimes of the most vigilant factions of the ethnocentric (American) white Right while simultaneously profiting off of the race-based identity politics embedded therein.

Within these frames of Tea Party nationalism, NASCAR offers an important social, political, and economic space through which the Nation's cultural politics and corporate logics can coalesce. In his article for *Rolling Stone* magazine, Matt Taibbi (2010), in rather harsh terms, explains this rise of this paleo-conservative/neoliberal hegemony in this lengthy quote:

> So how does a group of billionaire businessmen and corporations get a bunch of broke Middle American white people to lobby for lower taxes for the rich and deregulation of Wall Street? That turns out to be easy. Beneath the surface, the Tea Party is little more than a weird and disorderly mob, a federation of distinct and often competing strains of conservatism that have been unable to coalesce around a leader of their own choosing. Its rallies include not only hardcore libertarians left over from the original Ron Paul "Tea Parties," but gun-rights advocates, fundamentalist Christians, pseudomilitia types like the Oath Keepers (a group of law-enforcement and military professionals who have vowed to disobey "unconstitutional" orders) and mainstream Republicans who have simply lost faith in their party. It's a mistake to cast the Tea Party as anything like a unified, cohesive movement— which makes them easy prey for the very people they should be aiming their pitchforks at. A loose definition of the Tea Party might be millions of pissed-off white people sent chasing after Mexicans on Medicaid by the handful of banks and investment firms who advertise on Fox and CNBC.[3]

Under such polarizing political conditions, we explore the cultural and sporting fulcrum of this (neo-Confederate) paleo-conservatism and two interrelated (Southern) banalities exigent within: the cultural veneer glossed over apoliticized renditions of the South and the ostensibly ludic qualities of regionalized (and racialized) sport spectatorship. Correlatively, in both the NASCAR Nation of Brian France (the current chairman and CEO of NASCAR) and the mediated public sphere of Southernized America, subjectivity is (re)configured around the normative amalgamation of masculinity, whiteness, and neo-Confederate nationalism. In the following, we unsettle those shared values, identities, commodities, and experiences constructed in and through the spaces and spectacles of NASCAR Nation. More important, we formulate an analysis of the ways in which those ideologies, commodity symbols, and subjective practices that dominate NASCAR Nation are both *shared* and *performed*.

ON WHITENESS

In the discursive, pedagogical, and practiced formations of "America," whiteness often coalesces with other forms of power such as masculinity and heterosexuality to produce conditions for the reign of the "oppressive, invisible center" (Giroux, 2003, 1997b, p. 376). Peter McLaren (1998) outlines the context thusly:

> Whiteness in the United States can be understood largely through the social consequences it provides for those who are considered to be non-white. Such consequences can be seen in the criminal justice system, in prisons, in schools, and in the boardrooms of corporations such as Texaco. It can be defined in relation to immigration practices and social policies and practices of sexism, racism, and nationalism. It can be seen historically in widespread acts of imperialism and genocide and linked to an erotic economy of "excess." (p. 66)

With whiteness as norm, racial difference is encoded with the power dynamics of the oppressive center. Nonwhite spectators, of sport and of the social order of things more generally, are thus "Othered" (a process Stuart Hall [1997] suggests establishes order, and, therefore, power, around the established identity politics of those in power).

In the U.S. South, these formations of a Southern (white) identity were transformed into highly commercialized, politicized, and reified technologies of twentieth-century subjectivity. The imposition of whiteness was a powerful political process for the segregationist electorate; a powerful moral strategy for antimiscegenation Evangelicals; a powerful scientific discourse for oppressive pedagogues; and powerful enterprise for the merchants of twentieth-century commodity racism. And it is through the spectacles of whiteness, in the arenas of morality, governance, education, commerce, and culture (such as sport), that congregations of white bodies engaged in historically white practices become all the more *productive in reproducing the conditions* upon which whiteness is made powerful. Again, the work of McLaren (1998) captures the power relations forged under the dominion of whiteness:

> Whiteness is not only mythopoetical in the sense that it constructs a totality of illusions formed around the ontological superiority of the Euro-American an subject; it is also metastructural in that it connects whiteness across specific differences; it soldiers fugitive, breakaway discourses and rehegemonizes them. Consumer utopias

and global capital flows re-articulate whiteness by means of relational differences. (p. 67)

Here, we make the case that the NASCAR spectacle is one such "consumer utopia" (or Whitopia, to hearken back to Rich Benjamin's formulation): a physical, imaginary, and contextually ephemeral space upon which whiteness is thrust, through which whiteness is negotiated, and by which the power dynamics of the Old South are brought back to life in unifying consumer praxis. Through the sporting spectacular, whiteness was, and continues to be, "deployed" as seeming natural—"normal" within the discursive regimes of the reimagined U.S. South (Kincheloe & Steinberg, 1998).

For in NASCAR, whiteness as process often starts from an unspoken, clandestine center of power. And while the centrality of a Southern power/knowledge dynamic is pervasively located within a white center, the *conspicuous* response of (and from) empowered white identity politics has brought about a more noticeably pronounced, *visible* center.[4] Unlike Eric Lott's (2001) postulations of whiteness and the "vital center," in which the author imagines a subversive, yet all-encompassing center of power, or Henry Giroux's (1997b) "invisible" whiteness, in NASCAR Nation we often found whiteness to emerge as conspicuous performance—whereby an overt *theater of white power* is brought to life in and through the practices, places, and people of the sporting spectacular (see also Giroux, 1997a).

LOGOCENTRIC SPORTING WHITENESS

The consumptive spatial orientation of capitalist relations at NASCAR events outlined in the previous chapter become all the more critical when we consider that, more than any other North American professional sport entity, there is an *equally* powerful (hypercommercialized) spectacle of racialism and racism[5] at work in these spaces (Wetzel, 2006). In other words, just as bodies flowing through the spaces of NASCAR Nation act as vessels of the neoliberal cultural economy, so too do the flags, symbols, and gestures that cloak the sea of mobile homes at any given NASCAR race mark the territorial and cultural boundaries of those spaces. Most pervasive among these symbols is the flag of the Confederate States of America—the wartime emblem of the secessionist faction during the U.S. Civil War.

NASCAR Nation, more than any other contemporary U.S. sporting enclave, is widely seen to be the most Confederate-allied professional sport. Reporting on his observations from the infamous

2001 Daytona 500 race (more on this in Chapter Five), Jeff MacGregor (2005) paints a vivid picture of the omnipresence of the flag at a NASCAR race:

> Here's the motorhome protocol for flag display as per this morning's unscientific survey of our campground neighbors. The flagpole, 15 to 20 feet, fiberglass (think pole vault), is mounted vertically to a fitting on the rear bumper. The poles fly the following flags, in descending order (both in their arrangement and their rate of occurrence): United States of America, Dale Earnhardt #3 (white numeral, red shadow on black field), Confederate States of America, Dale Earnhardt Jr. #8 (white numeral, black drop-shadow on red field)....Variation: CSA flag appears on top, USA just below, rate of occurrence, plus or minus 10 percent. CSA flown below, plus or minus 10 percent. (p. 62)

In the nine years since MacGregor's initial 2001 observations, not much has changed in the hierarchy of infield flags at Daytona (and many if not most other race venues, for that matter). The Dale Earnhardt, Sr., signifier is still a fixture at every race. His son's emblem, now in the form of a green #88, can be spotted throughout any given NASCAR infield. Tony Stewart, Jeff Gordon, and Jimmy Johnson maintain a strong presence as well. And just as in decades prior—whether you are in Talladega, Martinsville, Dover, or Phoenix—the Confederate battle flag is rivaled only by the American flag as the dominant (national) symbol within these spaces.

In the first instance, the Confederate symbol, much like the corporate insignias that cloak NASCAR's celebrity-drivers, extracts "sign value" as a socially profitable marker of citizenship. In the same way as iconic logos of corporate sponsors operate as extensions of neoliberal corporate capitalism, the symbols of the (neo-)Confederacy that are adorned, consumed, and mediated by spectating bodies at NASCAR races act as extensions of paleo-conservative whiteness.[6] As such, the flag has evolved into a culturally powerful signifier with both a dominant, or preferred, reading and a resistive, or oppositional, reading. The preferred reading for those tens of thousands of *always* white, flag-waving consumers of the Confederacy is hence encoded in the discourses of power, racial hierarchy, and neo-Confederate traditionalism. In this way, consumption, signification (of body and space), and the all-consuming presence of the flag at most NASCAR events discursively reinforces the dominant meaning of the symbol as marker of a white Southern pride and heritage and the "preferred" place of white identities within these spaces.[7]

Of course, not all NASCAR fans read or experience the Confederate flag—nor the antiquated or contemporary causes it represents—in the same way. However, as Theodor Adorno (1991) suggested, what any given cultural product means to any individual matters less than the overall organization of power created by these forms of public culture. As such, the cultural power of the flag as a representative symbol of NASCAR Nation lies in its effectiveness as a *marker of territories*—the territories of race and the imaginary citizenships of a dominant ethnic (NASCAR) nationalism that has historically acted on social relations in the region (and beyond).[8] And, as most NASCAR fans would attest, if the number of Confederate symbols at each race is any indicator, NASCAR Nation *is a (neo-)Confederate state*. Our observations from a race in the fall of 2006 at a Southern racetrack echo those of sports journalist Dan Wetzel (2006), who wrote after attending a race in Talladega, Alabama, "In America...a NASCAR race is the last major sporting event where the Stars and Bars is still so prevalent, still so prominent" (p. 1). As we described the scene at the time,

> The Confederate flag is incontrovertibly imbedded in the socio-spatial fabric of NASCAR. Looking out over the vast expanse of temporal domiciles congregated for the race, a considerable number (literally thousands, in total) are adorned by some semblance of the "Stars and Bars." There are renditions of the Old South signifier flying all around, often (ironically) situated next to the American flag, in the vast expanse of NASCAR symbols, and often incorporating sport and non-sport icons of today in evoking a distinctively Southernized, if not racially-encoded, phantasmagoria.

In this instance, the congruity in meaning between white bodies' performed identity within NASCAR Nation and the Confederate symbolic authorizes a dominant neo-Confederate accord between this brand of signified and practiced paleo-conservative white-ness. It creates a "sense of belonging to an imagined community" (Coombe, 1998, p. 33); uniting the collective configuration of idealized Southern whiteness under the banner of historical domi-nance. This racialization of space and spatialization of racist, nepotis-tic entrepreneurialism (the inheritance industries of white privilege) is given currency by symbolic knowledge, nostalgia, and power; a cultural currency through which journalists, political officials, reli-gious leaders, and governing bodies have intervened in attempts to either reconnect, or disconnect, the flag's representational politics from the South's incendiary material history. In turn, this symbolic territorialization of NASCAR tracks and their ancillary spaces as an exclusively white, neo-Confederate place gives a geometric power to the prevailing idioms of whiteness (and white supremacy). In other words, within these neo-Confederate spaces of NASCAR Nation, meaning is not produced through the free play of signifiers alone. The sign aligns power, based on the artificial link made between the individual and the racialized, commodified (we will return to this later) symbol. The "Rebel flag" thus authorizes an antiquated power structure and re-articulates the normative discourses of identity and ownership within this U.S. South region and beyond, while simultaneously reinscribing the regimes of symbolic violence that alienated and oppressed Southern brown- and black-bodied "Others" under its dominion (Bonner, 2002; Coski, 2005).

In the same way that the Confederate flag resurfaced in the South during the Civil Rights era—and particularly in spaces of white privilege—the meaningfulness of the flag is sutured to the context in which it is being evoked. Kristen Ross (1988) suggests that signified space such as that found at NASCAR tracks "is not an immutable thing. It is made, it is remade, every day" (p. 91) through social practice. The interactions of the body—or embodied practice—and anthropological space converge to create an *aura* of "place," a sense of representational location grounded in the logics of white-bodied collectivity, the (naturalized) nonexistence of nonwhite spectator-subjects, and the iniquitous antiquities that give a discursive palate to these logics. At many NASCAR events, we observed signifying practice and practices of signification manifesting themselves in both form and function. To give but one example, spectators had pasted a number of topical Confederate- and Southern-themed signifiers on the personal spaces they inhabited—from their automobiles, to their temporary quarters in NASCAR's many campgrounds and RV parks to their (performance-based) physicalities.

But NASCAR's symbolic, hyperwhite paleo-conservatism goes beyond the Confederate flag itself. Throughout our travels across NASCAR Nation, we encountered a proliferation of what Roland Barthes (1967) might refer to as "logotechniques" of a conspicuous reclamation of productive power embedded in neo-Confederate whiteness. As researcher-*flâneurs* wandering about the spaces surrounding NASCAR tracks (in the spirit of a Situationist *derivé*), we encountered temporal, domestic, and corporeal spaces emblazoned with a vast array of white reclamation intonations and narratives—namely, in the form of bumper stickers, T-shirt script, banners, and other artifacts of visual culture. Consider the following declarations we encountered on T-shirts and automobile bumpers over the years:

- "Stop Southern cultural cleansing";
- "It's not racial, it's regional" (accompanied by an outline of the states of the Confederacy);
- "I'm offended that you're offended" (set against a Confederate flag backdrop);
- "Politically correct is another way of sayin' anti-Southern";
- "I love the flag and car racin'";
- "Heritage not hate";
- "My ancestors fought the first terrorists" (suggestive of the "War of Northern Aggression");
- "Pride not prejudice";
- "We may be politically incorrect, but we vote too";
- "You've got your 'X,' We've got ours" (alluding to Malcolm X versus the Confederate flag); and
- "Hey y'all, remember, racin' is a Southern sport."

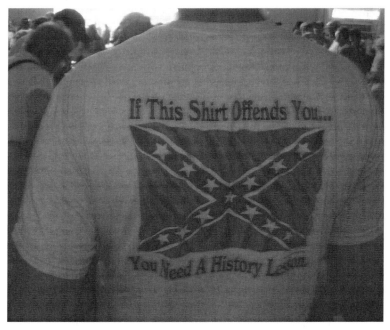

History, Fashion, and Neo-Confederate Cultural Politics on Display (Richmond, VA, September 2006)

These signifying acts, each of which was conjoined in illustrative form to some element of the Confederate symbolic, speak to a prevailing logic in contemporary NASCAR Nation: *White bodies* in almost exclusively *white spaces* are "under attack" and are calling upon the socio-political magazine of post-9/11 reactionary rhetoric in the fight to maintain their entitlement. These discursive formations frame white (working- and middle-class, heterosexual, males) "as the real victims of antiracist excess (of leftist antiracist racism, of political correctness, of liberal soft-headedness, of the ideology of egalitarianism)" (Goldberg, 2009, p. 92).

As floating signifiers of a contextually specific passage of both paleo-conservative moral-politics and neoliberal political economy (embodied though the spectacularized practices of Southern whiteness), these neo-Confederate markers also act as "signatures of authenticity"; registering "a real contact, a making, a moment of imprinting" (Coombe, 1998, p. 169). As one of the authors concluded in fieldnotes from a spring 2007 race at "the track too tough to tame" (in Darlington, South Carolina),

> The Confederate flag seems to symbolically locate *every* fan or spectator within the boundaries of Southern heritage. By way of its omnipresence, it simultaneously offers an imaginary space through which the track and its surrounding areas can be connected to popular constructions of Southern Whiteness. The flag is everywhere—on tents and trailers, on spectating bodies (both by way of adornment of T-shirts and ball caps and literally tattooed onto the flesh). Today's race featured an aircraft flying high above the track, pulling behind it a large banner that read: "Don't Forget Your Roots." The few "bodies of difference" at the race avoid spaces where the Confederate symbol is most intense. As the flag canvases both the geometric spaces outside the track and the corporeal spaces within, it infuses race and privilege into those spaces. In these spaces, White privilege reigns supreme.

Importantly, these geometric features and signifying acts bind the dominant subject position (Southern, white) to a collective sense of place activated by the discursive stylings (symbols, narratives, spatial configurations) and cognitive reflexes (collective memory of the Old South romantic) of performative spectatorship.[9]

This *corporeal spatialization* is problematic when those symbols of "Dixie South Whiteness" (Newman, 2007a, 2007c) and those conspicuous practices of racial exclusivity organize the signified constellation under which this unity in spatial discourse is constructed. As Lefebvre (1991) postulated, "Every social space is the outcome of a process with many aspects and many contributing currents, signifying and non-signifying, perceived and directly experienced, practical and theoretical. In short, every social space has a history" (p. 110). The spatial imaginations of NASCAR spectator-subjects are dialectically intertwined in the perceived and experienced possibilities of the paleo-conservative, post-9/11 signifying system from which the track and its ancillary geography (as place) are immersed.

To such an end, the exclusionary racialized performances of many of NASCAR's neo-Confederate subjects come into sharp relief by way of ephemeral spectacles of white supremacy in and around the track space. For example, when shopping for the "hottest merchandise" in one of the NASCAR-sanctioned retail spaces outside the track, we encountered the "Top Ten" apparel vendor. One of the T-shirts on offer from the vendor at the 2007 Darlington race was imprinted with the following racist mockery:

"TOP TEN REASONS There's No Black Race Car Drivers"

10. Have to sit UPRIGHT when driving.
9. PISTOL won't stay under front seat.
8. Engine drowns out the RAP MUSIC.
7. Pit crew can't work on car while HOLDING PANTS up at the same time.
6. They keep trying to CARJACK Dale Jr.
5. POLICE CARS on track interfere with race.
4.No passenger seat for the HO.
3. There are no sponsors for CADILLAC.
2. Can't wear HELMET SIDEWAYS.
and #1 Reason why BLACKS can't be Race Car Drivers.
1. When they crash their car, they can't BAIL OUT and RUN.

Although our empirical encounters would suggest that many within NASCAR Nation would cringe at this callous, racist imprint, the shirt (as well as numerous other garments of an equally detestable bent) nevertheless maintained a conspicuous, uncontested presence at the Darlington race. It was, as the vendor proclaimed, "one of [his] bestsellers." More to the point, symbolic wares of this nature are commonplace, *almost normalized*, markers of identity within most events in NASCAR Nation (and particularly those in Darlington, SC; Bristol, TN; and Talladega, AL). To wit, this same brand, indeed this very same T-shirt design, was a popularly adorned fixture at races throughout the entirety of our ethnographic journey—fashioned by race-goers as recently as the fall 2010 Talladega race.[10]

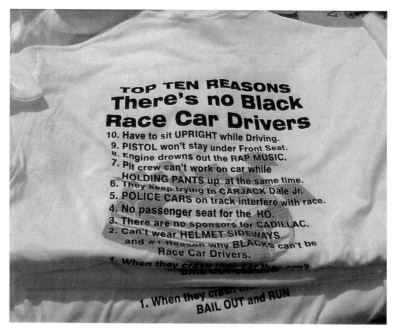

"Top 10 Reasons There's No Black Race Car-Drivers" (Darlington, SC, May 2007)

In the imaginary and geometric realms of "Sweet Home Alabama," these types of costumes—often sutured to the Confederate banner in its endless iconic permutations—have come to signify both the centrality of whiteness and the control over "embodied otherness" (Bishop, 2001, p. 32). Moreover, NASCAR fans are commonly subjected to (and consume) "bestselling" neo-Confederate brand accoutrements such as "If the South woulda won, we would have had it made!" and the number "88" (Dale Earnhardt, Jr.'s, number) or the number "3" (his father's number) positioned in the center of the "Southern Cross." As signified commodities, these goods affix the authority of neo-Confederate whiteness squarely in the politics of race and exclusion in NASCAR Nation. Furthermore, they reify the central position of the Confederate flag and other symbols of white supremacy, and particularly those that mark the spectating bodies of NASCAR Nation, in a discursive conjoining of the sign, the social institutions of race and racism, and the hegemonic social construction of signified white privilege.

Most significantly, (neo-)Confederated NASCAR space authorizes what Giroux (2004a) might refer to as public pedagogies of Old South racial politics. Much like their predecessors did

(Ross Barnett, George Wallace, and Orval Faubus), many (white) Southern politicians of today have galvanized a vitriolic vox populi around these and other spectacles of neo-Confederate racism. At a historical juncture when spectacles of the South such as Confederate Memorial Day parades and state-sponsored Confederate History Month activities—seen to be imprudent in most Southern states following Reconstruction[11]—have suddenly been reinvented and remobilized in the pursuit of white backlash-infused political capital (see Rich, 2010), NASCAR has provided an important public space for paleo-conservative politicians and ideologues to promote their polities (Sarah Palin, George Allen, Rand Paul, etc.).

A CLOSED SYSTEM

Interestingly, although these and numerous other symbolic iterations of the Confederacy swirl about the spaces of NASCAR Nation, most fans seem to have amended or reconciled the race- and slavery-based impetuses for which the Confederate-symbolic stands. Those who would actively use the NASCAR spectacle for their neo-Confederated ends performatively and emphatically reject the general consensus among most Civil War historians that slavery indeed held primacy for the "Lost Cause," and instead place the burden of "ignorance" squarely on the side of "bleeding heart," "Yankee," politically correct "femi-Nazi" liberals (Fieldnotes). In field interviews we conducted over the years, fans consistently postulated that the "Confederate cause was all about States' Rights" or "the South's interests in limiting the role of the Federal government." Indeed, not a single interviewee with whom we spoke suggested that race or racism had anything to do with the "War Between the States."

As the neo-Confederated super speedway space is transformed into a discursive formation evoking a normalized postplantation aesthetic, in the same instance it operationalizes signifying action therein to create a quasi-sterilized, strategically intermediated cosmos of solidarity under the arches of Southern whiteness. Indeed, this partial reading of the history of the South, and of the Confederacy in particular, creates power. Discursive formations within the social world, these public pedagogies are bound not only to the manipulation of time, but perhaps more so to the resituation of space therein. Maurice Mandelbaum (2001) reminds us of a core precept of Marx's historical materialism, that history is not a series of sequentially absolute moments, but rather a collection of dialectic passages that are diachronically interwoven into the conceptions of time: "a relationship of part to whole, not a relationship of antecedent to consequent" (p. 56).

In metaphysical *and* ontological terms, and following Marx and Mandelbaum, these new memories of the old Confederacy do not simply evolve through linear patterns from antebellum to postbellum times (and thus the future), but rather *histories* are mobilized by intermediaries of the present to protract, contest, or remake the hegemonic readings of collective memories of the past.

As such, cultural memories of the imagined community are always-already political in that they arouse and reify dominant positionalities.[12] In the case of the pedagogical stylings of neo-Confederate NASCAR Nation, the past is made political through its "normative qualities"—socially constructed readings of the past mobilized to reify, and glorify, the racial banalities of "the Cause." Whereas history "represents and reflects the past," writes Louise Weissberg (1999), memory in this way is "'a perpetually actual phenomenon' that can capture the present eternally. It is absolute, while history is relative; it claims objects, images, and space for itself, while history insists on the passing of time" (p. 17). Through remembering (and forgetting) the consuming-subject selectively mobilizes the past, linking historical events while separating others; privileging select individuals, events, and narratives and marginalizing or erasing others. In such times, we are reminded that those "who *posses history*," as Guy Debord (1967/1994, emphasis in the original) suggests, "give it an orientation—a direction, and also a meaning" (p. 96). Hence, the architecture of the Confederate mythscape becomes an important mechanism for transecting the spaces of uncertain neoliberal times.

In the case of neo-Confederate NASCAR, the Janus face of the mythscaped Confederacy both reconstructs old politics of race onto the cotemporary South, and projects that past onto social and economic relations of NASCAR Nation's present-future. As Debord (1967/1994) suggests, "to reflect upon history is to reflect upon power" (p. 98). In this way, and following David Theo Goldberg (2009), this form of selective racial memorialization promotes a culture of "*born again racism*" without the burdens of racialism—a refutation of history in a "post-racist" society (p. 23). The flag and its assorted bodily and spatial permutations mediates a "racism gone private"; at once an individualizing consumer technology and a systematic forward-fusion of racist logics—all the while ensuring the simultaneous abstraction (or denial) of the social conditions and histories of racism that give the neo-Confederate symbol meaning.[13]

By consuming the Confederate aesthetic, subjectivities of NASCAR Nation—and particularly those of a hyper-Southern resolve—both produce and are produced by a phantasmagoria of "heritage, not hate" and "pride, not prejudice"; (re)mediating the meaning of the flag in the order of a dominant, Southern, white (often masculine) cultural history and silencing that history and its critics by taking ownership of the spatialized discursive formation through which such a knowledge/power dynamic is forged. This resuscitation of the Old South, or what many scholars have referred to as a cultural "revisionism" (Ayers, 1993; Barrett, 2005; Bonner, 2002; Bontemps, 2001; Cowden, 2001; Egerton, 1974; Faust, 1988; Foster, 1987; Goldfield, 2002; McPherson, 2003; Rubin, 2002), colonizes both *collective memory* and *the process of remembering* under the dominant position of white subjectivity. Ann Stoler (1997) refers to this as a form of "motility"—where the meaning and significance of history shift for the political purposes. Moreover, this solidarity in the absolution of the signifier from the signified, or the liquefaction of the "preferred reading" of the sign, has turned the revisionist simulacrum into historical reality for many members of NASCAR Nation. In turn, and while for the (white) majority, the neo-Confederate symbolic spaces of NASCAR harmlessly connect the referee (the modern-day "Southerner"—always white, almost always a man) to the referent (Old South politics), they equally enact spaces of oppression for those subjectivities that have long suffered under its banner.

A recent Chevrolet advertisement illustrates this pseudo-absolution: In the ad, two of NASCAR's most popular drivers, Dale Earnhardt, Jr., and Tony Stewart, are tailgating in the infield of a NASCAR track, with the famous Lynyrd Skynyrd anthem, "Sweet Home Alabama," serving as the sonic backdrop. In what becomes a strange interjection, Southern rap artist TI drives through the crowd (and the song immediately takes on a hip-hop beat accompanied by rap lyrics) in what is assumed to be a "tricked-out" Chevrolet coupe. In an awkward gesture, Earnhardt, Jr., takes the key from TI, as though accepting the auto-mobile culture of the interloper, and drives away from the scene. The second assumption that the viewer is expected to make, and one that would contradict the exclusively white experiences of NASCAR spectators, is that TI is giving up his car so that he might join the NASCAR party (both the infield fête featured in the commercial and the bigger spectacle of NASCAR Nation). Amid an overrepresentative throng of women and multiethnic fans, the convergence of "traditional" stock car culture and "the new NASCAR" is meant to redefine the boundaries of consumerism and identity in

NASCAR Nation. As a consequence, this new media literacy offers a suspension of disbelief in decoding Chevy's multicultural stock car subterfuge.[14]

This commercialized signifying system actively transforms the praxis and symbols of NASCAR Nation into what Umberto Eco (1976) refers to as "a lie," or, as Mark Gottdiener (1994) prefers, "something that stands for something else" (p. 156). Problematically, the commercial "liquidates the real" (Bishop, 2001), becoming Southern simulacra of the racially divisive material realities of NASCAR Nation. Moreover, this dream world featuring (1) a multicultural fanscape; (2) a Confederate-flag-free celebration of *all* Southerners (and non-Southerners); and (3) a veneer of opportunistic egalitarianism—in other words, an inclusive NASCAR Nation—surgically grafts the myth of "a new NASCAR" while simultaneously reinforcing the hierarchical desires of this form of ethnic nationalism or "neo-tribalism" (Cova, 1997; Maffesoli, 1995). Selective correspondence of "encoding" and "decoding" (Hall, 1980) of these NASCAR signifiers is thus two degrees separated from slavery, segregation, the Confederacy, and so on, creating a false dimension of the NASCAR empirical, all the while situating heteronormative white masculinity at the center of power within its "Nation." Indeed, the mediated and material realities of NASCAR Nation, and particularly those we observed over the past few years, are devoid of an oppositional or alternative subjectivity—this is a "closed system," as Joe Bageant (2007) might say.

Driving for Diversity

Despite these and other efforts to mediate an alternative reality, NASCAR's "diversity problem" has been the stuff of considerable media scrutiny over the years (see Bernstein, 2006). This "problem" was exemplified by the significant overrepresentation of white fans in the grandstands, white drivers in the cars, white owners in the luxury boxes, and white administrators at NASCAR's corporate headquarters—as well as the league's perceived failure to embrace "diversity" in a moment when most other North American professional sports leagues were *seen to be* bending toward cultural plurality (Bernstein, 2006). Furthermore, NASCAR's diversity problem was exacerbated by two drawn-out, high-profile racial discrimination lawsuits. The first lawsuit was filed by an African American crew member who formerly worked on NASCAR's top circuit. At a race in 1999, and while working as a motorcoach driver for one of the racing teams, David Scott was (allegedly) harassed by two white crewmembers from a rival team. According to the complaint, Scott was confronted by the pair during the event, where they yelled racial slurs such as "nigger" and approached him wearing a white pillowcase over their heads (imitating a Ku Klux Klansman). The incident was frequently cited in the media during the intervening years as an example of NASCAR's ongoing "race problem," until when in 2006 NASCAR and Scott eventually reached an out-of-court settlement (Long, 2008).

The second high-profile lawsuit against NASCAR came a few years later, when in 2008 a former official sued the racing league, citing racial and sexual discrimination, sexual harassment, and wrongful termination. Mauricia Grant, a self-identified black woman, started working for NASCAR's second-tier Nationwide Series in January 2005 as a technical inspector responsible for certifying cars until her (wrongful) dismissal in October 2007. In her $225 million lawsuit, Grant alleged that during her tenure she was referred to as "Nappy Headed Mo" and "Queen Sheba" by white co-workers. She also claimed that she was told she worked on "colored people time" and was frightened by one official who routinely made references to the Ku Klux Klan. Later, the two officials named in the racial discrimination and sexual harassment lawsuit were placed on administrative leave for "violating company policy." It was later revealed that these employees had been suspended for (allegedly) exposing their genitalia to their former co-worker (Zirin, 2008). Prior to reaching an undisclosed settlement with Grant, NASCAR's public defense (at least that on offer to the court of public opinion) was that Grant had been negligent in reporting these offenses to Human Resources.[15]

NASCAR's already tarnished reputation, at least in terms of its history of racial exclusivity, certainly was not bolstered by these two highly mediated incidents. In response to a perceived "crisis of diversity," NASCAR had previously established the Drive for Diversity (D4D) program in 2004. D4D draws upon corporate sponsorship dollars to fund an annual educational, training, and competitive program in which prospective drivers and pit crew members from racially diverse backgrounds learn about, and eventually compete, for spots on one of NASCAR's various circuits. The program's administering organization, Revolution Racing, oversees D4D's Charlotte, N.C.-based operations. During the program, participants spend about 20 hours a week working on their cars in the shop, undergo various forms of physical training, and compete in weekly races. The goal is to have these minority and women drivers and pit crew members (some as young as 17) spend about 2 years learning the trade and competing for a place on one of NASCAR's lower circuits. This initiative was intended first to create new opportunities for aspirant stock car professionals who might otherwise not get the opportunity to enter NASCAR's corporate-sport pantheon (which, on the face of it, would seem laudable in some fashion). Second, it was meant to offer a sort of *trickle-down diversity*; whereby NASCAR strategists hoped that by putting minority and women drivers on the track, more otherwise "untapped" market segments would identify with these celebrities and in turn become stock car consumers. NASCAR officials even cited Tiger Woods' impact on professional golf consumerism as a catalyst for their intervention (which, as most marketing and consumer behavior data suggests, is more myth than reality).

Fast forward to 2010. Not a single driver from the D4D program has made it as a full-time racer on the Sprint Cup series. Indeed, other than a few pit crew members who have passed through the top ranks, the D4D program has yielded virtually no major success stories. And yet, in that same year NASCAR sanctioned and produced (in a joint-initiative with cable channel BET [Black Entertainment Television]) a "docu-reality" television series titled *Changing Lanes* (Bernstein, 2010). The show features the trials and tribulations of Drive for Diversity participants as they "struggle to make it" in the competitive world of NASCAR. Over the eight-week series, women and ethnic minority drivers perform for NASCAR's (overly white) competition and corporate brass, trying to "impress" NASCAR hierarchs while along the way being given "guidance" from (white) "racing pros." In an awkward amalgam of corporate and racial paternalism, these otherwise sport-disenfranchised individuals are made to spectacularly "battle it out" for the "opportunity" to ply their labors on one of NASCAR's low-paying minor circuits. As any critical race scholar would surely agree, the reality TV fare of *Changing Lanes* aggrandizes a particularly problematic racial neoliberalism. Or perhaps more fittingly, it promotes the cultures of *neoliberal racing*—a *double entendre* suggestive of both the individualistic, hypercompetitive platitudes of free market sporting subjectivity and the ways in which NASCAR's performing bodies (both in the grandstands and behind the wheel) are *raced*. *Changing Lanes* reminds us of NASCAR's dominant whiteness, and more consequentially of the hierarchical place that whiteness holds over the sport's nonwhite subjects. While on the ground NASCAR's corporate imperatives are served by a promulgated neo-Confederate eth(n)nic, by way of the media-spectacularized

D4D project, NASCAR seeks absolution from the racial politics upon which its brand rests (more on this in the conclusion of this chapter).[16] In some ways, by marking the racialized Other as *different*—and as an *outsider* seeking to come *inside*—this and other mediations reinscribe the normalcy of whiteness and the power relations it conjures up.

In some ways, then, neoliberal NASCAR offers the false promise of racial transcendence through corporate capitalism. The lesson is simple: if an individual works hard, plays by the rules, and doesn't challenge the status quo then they can make it in NASCAR Nation (sporting or otherwise). This "stress on individualized merit and ability" in the name of racelessness (Goldberg, 2009) promotes a public pedagogy of deracialized entrepreneurship. For the foremost lesson of this neoliberal sporting literacy—whereby commercial responsibility is the new civic responsibility—we need look no further than the tribulations of longtime lower NASCAR circuit and "minority" driver Bill Lester. Lester, who was depicted as the "face of NASCAR's new diversity" throughout the 2000s, has struggled throughout his career to sustain spectator and corporate support needed to compete at the highest levels (he participated in two Cup races in 2006). When asked about his lack of support, Lester chided: "I criticize corporate America for not putting their money where their mouth is … It's disappointing that these … companies that preach diversity wouldn't come on board" (Alleyne & Witcher, 2004, pp. 1–2). His wife and business partner, Cheryl, elaborated on the uncomfortable place an African American driver holds within the NASCAR-corporate paleo-conservative/neoliberal nexus:

> Potential sponsors look at him and go, "Well my audience isn't African American." Or they'll say, "I do target African Americans, but they're not watching racing." Then Bill responds that they're not watching racing because there's no one in the sport to identify with—the chicken and the egg problem. And most sponsors are not willing to be a pioneer. It's quite an uphill battle. (quoted in Alleyne & Witcher, 2004, p. 2)

As we make clear later in this book (see Chapter Seven), any alterations to the twinning of whiteness as consumable commodity with the entrenched consumer logics of NASCAR Nation can pose significant problems within and among its imagined fan base. This becomes especially clear when interrogating the imposition of Toyota into the NASCAR marketplace, as well as that of driver Juan Pablo Montoyo and his attendant celebrity iconicity.

CODA: NASCAR'S COMMODIFIED WHITENESS

This brings us back to the opening question posed by C. W. Nevius. For many, NASCAR Nation (and its so-called Southern cultural forms more generally) can be seen as selling its consumer-spectators "a set of values that are simple, down-home, and pleasurable—for both the producer and the consumer" (Smith & Wilson, 2004, p. 182). Put differently, as George Lipsitz's (2005) reading of Ronald Reagan's emotion-laden rhetorical skill for celebrating personal feelings and family ties over the realities of politics, war, and freedom reveals, it is NASCAR's spatial, spectacular, and popular discursive formations that renarrate a Confederated "nostalgia for the Whiteness of the pre-civil rights era with the affective power of nationalist narratives rooted in private family obligations and the responsibilities of paternal protection" (p. 99).[17] In short, NASCAR's increased import—and the (Southern) cultural qualities it features and on which its rival professional sport goliaths have yet failed to capitalize—is incontrovertibly bound to its seductiveness as a *consumer-based expression and market-oriented extension of (paleo-) conservative white paranoia.*

As *Washington Post* writer Warren Brown (2004) made clear a few years ago, NASCAR and its corporate partners already know all this. In his scathing article titled "NASCAR Diversity Dearth May Be Sponsor Driven," he wrote that the sport's diversity problem is a product of the sport's "exclusionary athletic enterprise in terms of race and sex" (p. G02). Brown (2004) argued that NASCAR's own marketing research has illustrated that the sport's fans "see their drivers as 'people like me'…They see them [the drivers] as having 'regular physiques,' and being 'regular guys' and 'role models'" (p. G02). Brown (2004) posited that the commercial pursuits of NASCAR have led to an exclusionary condition whereby the equilibrium between drivers, sponsors, and spectators has necessitated an overreliance on a "traditionalists" view of NASCAR subjectivity. He concludes that NASCAR has failed to put minority drivers behind the wheel as a result of sponsors' "fear of alienating" their predominately white-market segment. Brown (2004) cited Randi Payton, president and chief executive of On Wheels Inc., which publishes *African Americans on Wheels*, who explained that "'people like me' bias generally leads to the exclusion of 'people like us'…Sponsors don't want to take a chance on black drivers because they believe they won't be accepted by the larger fan base…And in the capital-intensive auto racing business, teams won't look at drivers who don't attract sponsors" (quoted in Brown, 2004, p. G02). In other words, Payton and Brown argue that (neo-Confederate) whiteness is part of NASCAR's business plan. In simple terms, they, along with their sponsors, have created a *niche* market whereby keeping black folks out of the sport has made for a solid, lucrative market segmentation.

Throughout this chapter, we have tried to elucidate the notion that although NASCAR Nation acts as a social destination or cultural conduit, it forms the boundaries of an important—if not emergent—intensely white subjectivity. In this way, and following Gilles Deleuze and Felix Guattari (1987), the rhizomatic multiplicities of consumer-based identities within NASCAR Nation collapse under the auspices of a unified regime of identity politics—that of an anti-immigrant, antiblack, antigay, exclusively conservative, fearful, "Southern" whiteness. This adhesive quality, or defining unifying feature (what Deleuze and Guttari have referred to as *unité*) of NASCAR fandom is reiteratively performed in and through the spaces of NASCAR Nation. When assembled at these races, NASCAR fans act as semiotic organisms of spatialized norms and normalizing space: subjected to the laws of what de Certeau (1984) refers to as a cultural "strategy" and thus subjects that reproduce the "imposition of power through the disciplining and organizing of space" (Crang, 2000, p. 137). As "space is fundamental in any exercise of power" (Foucault, 1984, p. 252), the proliferation of these hegemonic, white Southern identities and aesthetics within NASCAR spaces have been used to authorize paleo-conservative identity politics (and those subject positions authored around such politics). The conjoining of spaces of the imagination with the physical spaces of NASCAR spectacles has brought to life the collective thrusts of "normalizing judgments" ordered around Southern whiteness.

Although these formations of power may seem to be natural extensions of the sociopolitical traditions of the region, they are neither natural nor neutral. Within the collective imaginary of NASCAR Nation, geometric discourse is reconfigured into an illusory space of unification. That unity of discourse is a transferable source of cultural capital accumulation. The articulated solidarities of citizenship, space, and the semiotics of whiteness (as a locus of representation) comprise the knowledge-power basis that transposes the ideological onto the physical—grafting imagined collective configurations of white privilege onto the geometric layers and social fabric of stock car spectacles. In other words, performing one's whiteness (in effect, *being White*) in NASCAR Nation means belonging to the collective articulations of a particularized "we." In this way, corporeal iconicity is a linkage to sentimental belonging, to a seemingly banal citizenship in a singular ethnic nationalism.

By no means are all NASCAR fans seething arbiters of white supremacy—far from it. Rather, we are suggesting that to exist in the spectacularized spaces of NASCAR Nation means to be subjected to the strategically deployed strands of sign-valued Confederate symbols, neo-Confederate identities, and racial neoliberalism. Returning to Foucault's (1982) double interpretation of the "subject"—"subject to someone else by control and dependence, and tied to his [sic] own identity by a conscience or self-knowledge. Both meanings suggest a form of power which subjugates and makes subject to" (p. 212)—it can be argued that within the spaces of NASCAR Nation, that "self-knowledge" and the discursive formations from which it is constituted are indeed "free-floating" (Andrews, 1996). Both are pushed and pulled in multiple, often contradictory, directions—some political, some economic, many cultural. They are contemplated, contested, and manipulated by cultural intermediaries, the "citizenry" of an imagined sporting community, and dissidents and hegemons who seek to make the sport meaningful. They are brought to life in the physical spaces surrounding NASCAR tracks (the geometric circuits that give order to NASCAR Nation), the identity-based symbols of subjectivity (fluttering Confederate and American flags), and the spectacular practices (the act of making both identity and subjectivity *visible*). In short, NASCAR becomes an important technological space through which paleo-conservative/neoliberal systems "form, fashion, make, and mold—in short, how they manage—their heterogeneous populations" (Goldberg, 2009, p. 328).

What we are suggesting then is that in the spaces of NASCAR Nation, consumerist fandom as a "new technology of the self" (Foucault, 1988) fails its emancipatory potential and instead is delimited by the cultural physicalities of Southern whiteness (and particularly whiteness as an extension of the "theater of power" active throughout the region's configurations of identity); a series of "structural phases" (Baudrillard, 1983a) that operated in and were (re)productive of pronounced systems of sameness and "difference."[18] As such, we offer a further rationale for NASCAR's "diversity dearth," one that lies in the commodity logics of maintaining an "Other." If "outsiders" are to become "insiders," it might cloud an otherwise unified market segment. Rooted in the language of "brand loyalty," "marketing strategies," "target market," "diversity," and "demographics" and cleansed of its racist, sexist, and elitist cultural polity, the marketing vernacular of NASCAR Nation thus not only blurs the regimes of corporate capitalism and neo-Confederate racism, it also in some ways creates an amalgamated celebration of oppression at the vices of each. Under such a consumer-driven, neo-Confederate, late-capitalist condition, NASCAR fuels its bottom-line by renting out vendor space to companies such as "Top Ten" racing and portending to be merely "giving the fans what they want."

Hence, NASCAR Nation reveals itself as a productive space for authorizing *neoliberal whiteness as American standard*. In the domain of the sporting banal, rephrasing McLaren (1998), capital's regimes of desire are linked with the fantasies of omnipotence in a stable utopia constructed out of the longings for "old times there not forgotten." In simple terms, exclusively white bodies, cloaked by Old South commercial signifiers, and congregating to watch exclusively white drivers, were, and continue to be, both powerful and lucrative enterprise for many within the South's conservative faction. The corporate logics of neo-Confederate/paleo-conservative NASCAR are perhaps best described this way:

> This narrative of NASCAR's colorful background means a lot to the sport. NASCAR could hope for nothing more during its current success than to be indentified with the authenticity of the newly virtuous, rural South. As one corporate sponsor recently recounted the heroic journey for promotional literature, "Both Hardee's and stock car racing grew from rural southern roots to become a strong national presence, and we make an excellent team." Myths and profits go together. (Hall, 2002, p. 633)

Neoliberalism tends to "exacerbate inequality, further privileging the already privileged" (Goldberg, 2009, p. 332), and in the age of fusionist individualization, these myths of the South often serve to enhance the social profits and economic motives of such sporting enterprise. For many "racial Americanists," the NASCAR brand and its spectacular spaces act as counterpoints to state-based interventions toward equality.

In some ways, then, this form and function of Southern sporting whiteness seduces—and indeed is made powerful—because it reinscribes *old* identities and *old* subjectivities in the *new language* of corporate sport and "the South." Thus does the individual create her or his identity through subjected consumption of subjective privilege. At the crossroads of a contextually specific order of neoliberal corporate capitalism and neo-Confederate hyperwhite (Southern) nationalism, NASCAR Nation may be more parallax than paradox: seen by some as a burgeoning, yet innocuous, celebration of the norms and values that "make America great" and by others as a site for reproducing the "terrors of neoliberalism" through the social currency of an anti-immigration, veneer multiculturalist, post-9/11 "ethnocentric monoculturalism" (Sue, 2004, p. 761).

In this way, NASCAR has evolved into an important cultural playground of riches amidst the current paleo-conservative revival. It provides a consumer-driven, performative space for promoting a paleo-conservatism encapsulated by a Tea Party movement made of an angry white voting bloc who "overwhelmingly reject the notion that economic disparities between blacks and whites are mainly the result of discrimination" while simultaneously holding fast to the notion that "blacks lag in jobs, income and housing 'because most African Americans just don't have the motivation or willpower to pull themselves up out of poverty'" (Page & Jagoda, 2010, p. 2). By way of the pervasive (dehistoricized) Confederate signifier, a proliferated bumper-sticker jingoism, the paternalistic Drive for Diversity program, white market segmentation, Bill Lester's struggles, and Hollywood antiracialism, NASCAR authorizes a racial neoliberalism in which "homogenized apartness is taken as a deracialized norm, the assumed, the natural, the given. Integration, or at least desegregation, comes over as unnatural, literally absurd and irrational in the prevailing order of things, requiring intervention by the state at the cost of individual liberty" (Goldberg, 2009, p. 92); the liberties to capitalize upon exclusion, upon the technologies of the white self, and thus upon the spatialized territories of Tea Party–inflected neo-Confederations of sporting whiteness.

5

RACING FOR JESUS:

SPORT IN THEOCRATIC AMERICA

> There's a logic to evangelical Christianity and big-time sport having
> this kind of cozy relationship. In many ways, they're similar. Both are
> win-loss mentalities. In evangelical Christianity you are either saved or
> lost. You've gone to heaven or you've gone to hell, you win or you lose,
> and that's what this sport is all about.
>
> —William J. Baker (2007)

God is watching over the super speedway. Or at least it can be
surmised by both believer and nonbeliever alike that, within the
imagined community of NASCAR Nation, there exists a pervasive, if
not inveterate, devotion to Christian orthodoxy—as well as a steadfast belief in the ideological precepts that give material "credence"
to such biblicized public pedagogies. "Nowhere in sports," observed
PBS anchor Bob Abernethy, "is there more unself-conscious expression of religion as there is at NASCAR races" (quoted in "NASCAR
and Religion," 2001). Indeed, as numerous commentators have
suggested (see Hagstrom, 1998; Menzer, 2001; MacGregor, 2005;
Rhee, 2007; Lipsyte, 2006; Thompson, 2006; Clarke, 2008), the
120,000 or more spectators who flock to weekly NASCAR events
are regularly greeted by a palpable, omnipresent faith-based revival,
which has come to permeate all aspects of the sporting spectacle: the
bevy of trackside crucifix-emblazoned revival tents, the multitude of
Jesus-endorsed stock car insignias, to conspicuous performances of
"sharing the gospel," and the panoply of symbolically christened RVs
and SUVs packing the race track infields on race days being three
major examples. Likewise, consumers of NASCAR's print, television,
and cyberspatial texts are equally subjected to a vast universe of con-
fessional blogs, sanctimonious declarations, and baptismal-sporting
performances. Perhaps most importantly, stock car racing's principal

institution has been "unapologetic" (Newberry, 2004, p. 1) about this sport-orthodoxy symbiosis.

In a special report for *ABC News*, correspondent Dan Harris (2005) connected NASCAR's prevailing religiosity to the sport's (neo-)Confederate regionalism, explaining "because NASCAR grew up here in the Bible Belt, it's probably the most openly-religious of all sports."[1] Journalist Zane Ecklund (2007) similarly argued that this religious order of NASCAR

> appeals to people by offering salvation and a perspective of the world....In the Church of NASCAR the deity most worthy of followers would be racing legend Richard Petty. The pope is Jeff Gordon, as he is the face of the "sport." Finally, there is the messiah, the patron saint of hillbillies, Dale Earnhardt. (p. 2)

Perhaps crude in its assumptions and delivery (e.g., "hillbilly"), Ecklund's (2007) rumination speaks to a contextually important conjuncture of Southern identities, sport spectacle, and religious fundamentalism that (1) extends beyond typically pedestrian "opiate of the masses" rhetoric often afforded both religion and sport; and (2) highlights the extent to which the sport has become a crucifixture in the construction of identity and consent in contemporary American life.

In addition, and although Christianity and U.S. race car culture have shared a mutually sacrosanct—if understated—bond since the first green flag waved on the sandy beaches of Daytona, these articulations of Jesus Christ and stock cars have in recent years been made more significant by their dialectic interdependencies with, and to, a contextually specific "conjuncture" of neoliberalism (see Pieterse, 2006) and faith-based, GOP-dominated paleo-conservatism. As numerous scholars and journalists have suggested (Connolly, 2005; Denzin & Giardina, 2006; Kusz, 2007; J. MacGregor, 2005), this strange intersection becomes even more significant when articulated with post-1994 Republican Revolution neoliberal/(paleo-)conservative "Red State" hegemony—one that is both a product, as well as a producer, of the cultural and pedagogical technologies (i.e., the practices, spaces, narratives, and discourses) active in what is commonly referred to as the "stock car congregation."[2]

In what follows, we illustrate how stock car and political intermediaries have (re)ordered the material and symbolic sign value of racing iconicity to the "surplus value of rapture" (Hedges, 2007) to reproduce the iniquitous conditions of production (and consumption) within broader formations of NASCAR Nation and beyond. We point to the ways in which NASCAR's mediated and performative spaces promote proselytizing public pedagogies bound to dominant logics of "end-times" fellowship, patriarchal Christianity, missionary Evangelism, and perhaps most notably commercialized piety. Moreover, we make the case that NASCAR has been a key ingredient in the sociopolitical adhesive that sutures neoliberal market regimes to paleo-conservative identities and ideologies within contemporary "Tea Party" *Americana*.

NASCAR NATION, AD

From the outset of the chapter, it is important to note that NASCAR's promotional synergy of the holy and the speedy is a relatively recent avowal. In the early days of stock car racing, the sport's import among its dominant, if not decidedly local, consumer-subjects was in part indebted to its "rebellious" cultural imprint. For many of these stock car racing fans, a night at the races was a way to attend to their hedonistic proclivities; a social space where spectators could imbibe the spirits of late-Prohibitionist inebriation, escape the constraints of the domestic sphere, and, as many historians have noted, flee the specters of an intensifying mid-century Bible Belt asceticism (Huff, 1997; Menzer, 2001). As stock car racing grew in popularity during the middle part of the twentieth century, the tendency among Southern evangelical preachers was to denounce the sport as an "unholy institution" rife with "corn-liquor fumes and hog-wallow anarchy" (Miles, 2005, p. 4). In turn, God-fearing Southerners generally associated the sport with the region's "miscreant" working-class faction.

During the sport's formative years, a period stock car historians often refer to as the "modern era" (roughly beginning in 1970; see Chapter One), this cacophony of Southern morality and stock car rebelliousness reared itself in the performative politics of "bad boy" drivers such as Junior Johnson, Richard Petty, the Allison brothers (Donny and Bobby), Darrell Waltrip, and Cale Yarborough—an ensemble of Southern identity politics, "good ole boy" masculinity, and parochial working-class ruggedness. Strangely, in the years that followed, these sporting ruffians came to define a new type of lionized "Southern man," one whose penchant for winning was often tempered (or staged as such) by an unbending conviction to execute the "Lord's Will" ("In NASCAR, Racing and Religion Intertwine," 2004). These novel mediations of stock car celebrity and the rise of the sport's popularity resulted in the emergence of a new catalogue of NASCAR's Southern men (e.g., Bill Elliott, Darrell Waltrip,

Dale Earnhardt, Sr., and Mark Martin). More consequently, the narrative and performative politics popularized by these racing icons cemented this paradoxical follower (of Christ)/leader-at-all-costs iconicity within the popular discourse. As such, the NASCAR that thrust its way into the North American mainstream was constructed out of this Budweiser-drinking, Winston-smoking, God-fearing, "ass-kicking," tire-rubbin' conjuncture of sacrosanct Southern and sporting identities. Indeed, the burgeoning NASCAR brand of the 1970s and 1980s was mediated as a "deep-fried spectacle . . . with its schizo mix of beery loutishness and Promise Keeper piety" (Miles, 2005, p. 1).

While erstwhile NASCAR parishioner-"bad boys" such as Bill Elliott, Junior Johnson, and Darrell Waltrip each played their meaningful part in promoting stock car racing's paradoxical iconography, no celebrity captured the adoration of racing fans to the extent of Dale Earnhardt, Sr. (Miles, 2005; Montville, 2001; Wright, 2002). On race days, NASCAR tracks were cloaked with the Earnhardt's mythologized black color scheme and accompanied by various iterations of his signature #3.[3] Earnhardt was, as a host of biographers and sportswriters will attest, the "face of NASCAR" throughout much of the 1980s and 1990s (Montville, 2001). Country music artists recorded ballads about his racing exploits, and shopping mall concourses throughout America were canvassed by his oft-reproduced image. With Ronald Reagan's political "revolution" and the rise of Jerry Falwell's "moral majority" as sociopolitical backdrop, Dale Earnhardt, Sr., surfaced as NASCAR's archetypal, neoliberal "Southern Man." In a late-Reagan American media technocracy dominated by anxieties of Japanization, Fidel Castro, the Iron Curtain, and later Clarence Thomas, Willie Horton, and NAFTA—and a changing sport lexicon now informed by the "controversial exploits" of national sporting outliers such as Charles Barkley, Dennis Rodman, and OJ Simpson—Earnhardt emerged as a dominant sporting embodiment of Reagan's (recalcitrant, virile, hypermasculine, white, Southernized, conservative) bootstrap-pulling "America" (Amato, Peters, & Shao, 2005). And in turn, the soft-spoken "Intimidator" became the most popular driver in the nation's "most Southern," White, "unapologetically" conservative sport.

Out of such a material and mediated history, NASCAR took a hard right turn toward emphasized godliness when, in 2001, the circuit's most beloved Southern "rebel" catalyzed the sport's coming evangelical Christian revival during that year's Daytona 500. On the final lap of the February 18 race, "The Intimidator" found himself positioned in third place and closing fast on the race leader, Michael Waltrip. (It would be prudent to note here that Dale Earnhardt, Jr., was in second place, between the leader and his father.) On the final lap of the contest—as he approached the infamous "turn four at Daytona"—Earnhardt, Sr., crashed his much-ballyhooed GM Goodwrench-sponsored black Chevrolet Monte Carlo into the outside retaining wall while trying to "hold off" encroaching rivals. In that instant, and as more than 150,000 startled fans in the Daytona grandstands and an estimated 10 million television viewers watching the Fox Network's debut NASCAR telecast looked on in disbelief, the sport's most visible icon, most-beloved "last Confederate Soldier" (Rybacki & Rybacki, 2002) and most-marketed brand pitchman passed on to the "big racetrack the sky'" (Spitzer, 2001).[4]

In the days and weeks that followed, the NASCAR organization, driver-rivals, media commentators, and millions of racing fans transformed stock car spaces into a veritable living cenotaph. NASCAR distributed black Dale Earnhardt, Sr., T-shirts to every fan who attended the following week's race (Montville, 2001). A number of enraged fans reacted by sending death threats to stock car-driver Sterling Marlin (the fourth-place driver Earnhardt was holding off); more solemn mourners constructed memorials around more than two dozen NASCAR tracks nationwide (Montville, 2001). Earnhardt's fatality brought about Southern-spun candlelight vigils of the scale theretofore afforded the likes of John Lennon, Martin Luther King, Jr., and John F. Kennedy (Rybacki & Rybacki, 2002). These tributes typically featured Earnhardt's image, or that of his #3 Chevrolet, amid a sea of Confederate flags, Christ-like insignias, enlarged scripture-referencing text, and a constellation of NASCAR themed merchandise (both on bereaved bodies and trackside memorials).

The passing of Earnhardt, Sr., brought about two important shifts in stock car culture. First, as the post-Earnhardt, Sr., NASCAR "congregation" reassembled in the weeks and months that followed (a period that came to be known in stock car circles as "AD": "after Dale"), they reinvigorated a number of public discourses related to the "danger" associated with racing stock cars, the allure of "death-defying" speed fetishism, and the "imminence" of the afterlife. NASCAR Nation's faith was, in effect, born again. Second, this posthumous memorialization of Dale Earnhardt, Sr., through ceremonial praxis and popular discursive formation(s) effectively relocated the driver of the famous #3 car as a representative embodiment of Christian faith, American principle, capitalist prudence, and heteronormative steadfastness. As Robert Lipsyte (2006), writing for *The Nation*, would later put it,

> The beatification of Dale Earnhardt, Sr. as a man's man who sacrificed himself to shepherd his flock to the finish line, a hero who in death evoked both John Wayne and Jesus, presented America with its biggest joint jolt of sports and evangelical Christianity since Billy Sunday left the Philadelphia Phillies outfield more than a century ago to become a superstar preacher. (p. 4)

The cornerstone of these convictions, by way of the "majority voice," continually bore itself in the rudiments of an evangelical Christian faith. Faith-based events before and after NASCAR racing increased, the Fellowship of Raceway Ministries expanded its efforts at NASCAR's super speedways (more on this conglomerate of Christian-based missionaries later), and driver-celebrities began to more ardently publicize their place in NASCAR Nation, AD's newly minted Christian fellowship (Menzer, 2001). In the wake of the Earnhardt tragedy, his most-reviled adversary, Jeff Gordon, put the Christian revival of NASCAR Nation into perspective: "Because our sport is so dangerous, it strengthens all our faiths in God." Gordon continued, "I think I've been put on a platform to show other people what God has done for me in my life and I think God wants all of us to spread that word and be able to influence others so they can live a better life" (quoted in "NASCAR and Religion," 2001). Indeed, the notion of membership within such a "nation" was reformulated— re-articulated with the dialectic, if not teleological, resonance of an intensifying Red State Evangelism.

In the years that followed, the linkages between the "people" and the "Word" to which Gordon referred came to be more deeply interwoven into the sport's mass-mediated, spatially practiced spectacles. Through those spectacles, a didactic, pervasive *gospel according to NASCAR* emerged; a doctrine guided by the pillars of 150-mile-per-hour divine masculinity, the spoils of a heightened (post-9/11) end-times paranoia, and a contradictory conflation of Bible Belt–stumping and commodity secularism. However, as we learned during our detour through what many fans refer to as "the church of NASCAR," this rise of Christian hegemony in NASCAR Nation, AD, is not something that evolved organically. Rather, in the current stock car spectacular, drivers are carefully trained to be modern-day soothsayers, Right-leaning politicians are afforded a mass-mediated platform from which to discursively re-articulate sporting enthusiasm as political capital, and spectators are incessantly subjected to the omnipresent twin public pedagogies of paleo-conservative orthodoxy and neoliberal deification. In the sections that remain, we connect two dominant paleo-conservative public pedagogies of the post-Earnhardt NASCAR spectacular to the market-based neoliberal imperatives they serve: pedagogies of the apocryphal Bush-era "values-based" (Christian) family and pedagogies of post-9/11 end-times fellowship.

PATRIARCHS OF SPORTING FUNDAMENTALISM

In his suggestively titled biography *At the Altar of Speed: The Fast Life and Tragic Death of Dale Earnhardt, Sr.*, Leigh Montville (2001) echoes Lypsite by depicting stock car racing's archetypal hero as a "man's man," a nurturing father to his soon-to-be superstar racing son, a loyal husband, a neo-Confederate patriot (a strange combination of "South will rise again" parochial *doxa* and assiduous American nationalism), and a servant to the Lord and Savior Jesus Christ. Montville (2001) makes the case that in some ways, and perhaps more so in death than in life, Dale Earnhardt, Sr., was the iconic torchbearer of a unique brand of stock car Christian masculinity: a contradictory blend of Southern drawl-inspired local identities rooted in the vernacular of working-class whiteness and a working-man-by-day/hedonist-by-night/church- and race-guzzling-on-the-weekend patriarchy. His predecessor in that role, racing legend Richard Petty, had lived to see his own similar repositioning in the reshuffled field of *récemment créé* driver-celebrities. Often referred to as "The King," Petty resurfaced as a born-again Christian in the years following his retirement from competitive racing, a gilded repersonification as bad-boy-turned-believer and carouser-turned-family man (Rybacki & Rybacki, 2002).

Molded in the image of The King and The Intimidator, NASCAR's celebrity-driver AD, as Jeff MacGregor (2005) suggests, is a peculiar Renaissance man who is well-versed in how to all-at-once be "a salesman and a matinee idol and a motivational speaker and a casino greeter and a role model and a stand-up comic and a humble, right-thinking crusader for the American Way." As a cursory survey of the media constructions of driver-celebrities suggests, these stock car men are *empowered*. These "full-throttle" impresarios are fueled— both on the track and in the home—by the centrifugal synergy of Christian values, familial insularity, and fan adoration. As is common practice in the mediated iconoclastic lexicon of NASCAR Nation, driver-celebrities use pre- and post-race television interviews, website blog-diary musings, and Victory Lane pedestals to "praise the Lord," thank their "nurturing, supportive" wives, and cite the nuclear family structure that keeps them "grounded." Drawing upon recent "values"-based paleo-conservative narratives—which locate Jesus Christ as the authority over faith and family (Domke & Coe, 2008)—drivers are incessantly professing the priorities in a hierarchical order of "God, family, and racin'" (Miller, 2002; Rhee, 2005).

So exaggeratedly ensconced in NASCAR's media texts, this hackneyed heteronormative religiodomesticity became the fodder of ridicule in the aforementioned cinematic satire *Talladega Nights: The Ballad of Ricky Bobby* (mentioned earlier in Chapter Four). In the film's most celebrated scene, the protagonist-patriarch Ricky Bobby offers this blessing prior to a family meal:

> Dear Lord Baby Jesus, or as our brothers to the south call you, *Jesús*, we thank you so much for this bountiful harvest of Dominos, KFC, and the always delicious Taco Bell. I just want to take time to say thank you for my family. My two beautiful, beautiful, handsome, striking sons, Walker, and Texas Ranger, or TR as we call him. And of course my red hot smokin' wife Carley, who is a stone cold fox.

The scene climaxes by way of the ensuing sequence: (1) Ricky Bobby declares his gratitude for the Higher Power's intervention in his racing success; (2) the protagonist delightfully affirms his adolescent sons' threat to "go ape-shit" on their elderly grandfather, who had scolded the boys for acting up at the dinner table (Ricky Bobby: "I love the way they're talking to you"; Carley: "If we wanted us some wussies, we'd 'uv named 'em Dr. Quinn and Medicine Woman"); and (3) Carley, as if overcome by her husband-champion's expression of Dixie-paternal *machismo*, lustfully embraces Ricky Bobby while he wrestles her onto the dinner table in what is to assumed to be the beginnings of a family-watched sexual conquest of the mother.

While this Hollywood-inspired depiction mockingly caricaturizes the pervasive convergence of masculinity, consumption, family, and Christian faith on stock car culture, it nonetheless highlights the overt celebration of a fundamentalist hegemonic patriarchy that viewers have no doubt become accustomed to in mediated NASCAR Nation (see Talley & Casper, 2007). The celebrity stylings of popular drivers such as five-time defending champion Jimmie Johnson, Jeff Gordon, Mark Martin, Matt Kenseth, Bill Elliott, Jeff Burton, and Tony Stewart become important not only in NASCAR's *lingua franca* of Christian orthodoxy, but also (as both direct and indirect consequence) in the construction and reaffirmation of a mass fundamentalist, patriarchal pedagogy of "what it means to be a man" in the domesticized spaces of NASCAR Nation. These representative embodiments and the narrative technologies they deploy on a weekly basis have come to constitute a contextually specific, multithematic theocratic masculinity. One such theme that emerges in the NASCAR empirical is that all men—drivers and fans alike—are the patriarchs of a distorted, new-age biblical domesticity: firm disciplinarians, caretakers of "family values," god-fearing Christians, monogamous conquerors of their "trophy-wives," and watchdogs over their accumulating estates.

If the ubiquitous bumper sticker declarations of "I Love My Wife" that dominate super speedway parking lots offer any indication, many of these "NASCAR Dads" are loosely aligned (philosophically if not materially) with patriarchal fundamentalist sects such as Bill McCartney's Promise Keeper group; self-described as "a Christ-centered organization dedicated to introducing men to Jesus Christ as their Savior and Lord, helping them to grow as Christians" ("Promise Keepers: Men of Integrity," 2006). The organization, which is exclusive to men of the Christian faith and most noted for its *Stand in the Gap: A Sacred Assembly of Men* gathering of (reportedly) more than 1 million men at the National Mall in late 1997 (a proverbial rewriting, if not "whiting out," of the "Million Man March"), is one of many such conglomerations that function to further mark the boundaries of the domestic sphere under the dominion of Christian patriarchy.[5]

But this patriarchal, evangelical positionality is not exclusive to Promise Keepers (or Fellowship of Christian Athletes, Athletes in Action, or other sport-oriented ministries). Republican politicians such as Sarah Palin (more on her below) and Mike Huckabee, former governor of Arkansas (and, as of this writing, a leading contender for the 2012 Republican presidential nomination), have similarly expressed a desire for the reinscription of so-called traditional male roles within a marriage. In 1998, Huckabee (who was still governor at the time) was one of 131 signatories on a full-page ad in *USA Today* who declared: "I affirm the statement on the family issued by the 1998 Southern Baptist Convention." The statement on family, which Huckabee was endorsing, is impossible to misread: "A wife is to submit herself graciously to the servant leadership of her husband even as the church willingly submits to the headship of Christ."[6] (Strode, 1998). While many if not most "NASCAR men" might not explicitly identify themselves as part of the Promise Keeper group or likewise align themselves with Huckabee's specific views on marriage and family, from travels through various regions and numerous venues in

NASCAR Nation, we consistently noted that such a hypermasculine, patriarchal Christian orthodoxy is at the least most certainly *not* out of place in these racing spaces.

Indeed, these pedagogical instruments of NASCAR patriarchy are "made normal" by the spectacular machinations of popular discourse through television series such as *NASCAR in Primetime*, *NASCAR Now*, and a plethora of shows featured on the Speed Channel. Likewise, NASCAR fans draw inspiration from the shared stories of hope and inspiration, faith and family as narrated in texts such as the *New York Times* best-selling *Chicken Soup for the NASCAR Fan's Soul* series (e.g., Canfield, Hansen, Adams, Autio, & Aubery, 2003). This sentimentality is echoed in the writing of university lecturer-turned-NASCAR-hagiographer L. D. Russell's (2007) *Godspeed: Racing Is My Religion*. In the tradition of most (uncritical) popular U.S. sports writing and sport-related commentary, Russell—a self-described "evangelist for NASCAR" (Russell writes: "I spread the gospel of racing every chance I get")—wields a dotingly anticritical, antidialectic rendition of a sport in which God-speak becomes a means of translating race car fetish to broader contemplations of life, morality, and the spirit world. Drawing upon biblical epigraphs and autobiographical testimonials, these intertextual declarations echo the ideals shared by many within the dominant faction of NASCAR Nation—a shared endorsement for the patriarchal hegemony of evangelical Christianity and the return to "traditional American family values."

For this growing faction, such popular rhetoric offers salvation from the "unsavory," or 'unholy," elements that burden society, those that have come to be framed around the imaginary and material longings of a post-1960s-era Bible Belt that has often demonized changes to the moralist status quo (e.g., the feminist movement, antiwar protests, human rights campaigns in the context of uneven free market development, queer activism, and the civil rights movement). Along these lines, one forthright race fan from Alabama with whom we spoke explained:

> God made men for sport and made women to support. I mean, it's right there in the Bible. If He wanted women to be in charge, He would have said so.... But that's not the way it is; there's a reason all the folks you see here ain't on welfare, ain't begging for money, ain't on drugs, and there ain't no hookers running around. Because we all believe in what's right.

The logic of this fan's argument, as well as many like-themed interjections we incurred at NASCAR events, is that the institutionalized

Fundamentalist patriarchy maintained by members of conservative Christian sects has given order to American social life. While the liberatory and healing pedagogies of the Bible call for humanitarianism, tolerance, and welfare for rich and poor, such a calling is often glossed over or rejected in paleo-conservative articulations of contemporary Christian Fundamentalism. Failing to consider the contemporary sociocultural condition's multiple histories of oppression—many of which were brought about by persecution of those outside the dominant Christian mold—in a vast range of mediations, conversations, and discourses we engaged with the *moral majority of NASCAR Nation*, a series of similarly entertained, equally recurring contradistinctions emerged.

First, there seems to be an equally resonant populism that disease, suffering, and inequality are all part of, as fans we met often explained, "God's Plan." And while many NASCAR fans whom we interacted with during this project explained that "homosexual" relations and relationships are "unnatural" or "some kind of curable disease," they unequivocally lambasted the "queers," "lesbos," and "fags" who are engaged in same-sex relations. Echoing the paleo-conservative paranoia that has dominated national mediations on the subject in recent years, the prevailing sentiment in NASCAR Nation seems to be that the government should neither condone nor support these various "deviant sinners." In many ways, these prevailing idioms within NASCAR Nation echo those proffered in the broader national discourse, such as the silage recently offered up by Oklahoma State Senator Sally Kern:

> The homosexual agenda is destroying this nation, okay, it's just a fact. Studies show that no society that has totally embraced homosexuality has lasted more than, you know, a few decades. So it's the death knell of this country. I honestly think it's the biggest threat our nation has, even more so than terrorism or Islam—which I think is a big threat, okay? Cause what's happening now is they are going after, in schools, two-year olds…And this stuff is deadly, and it's spreading, and it will destroy our young people, it will destroy this nation. ("Politician's 'Anti-gay' Speech Sparks Outrage," 2008)

As public debates surrounding same-sex marriage and civil unions dominated U.S. media and political discourses throughout much of the decade, the heteronormative intolerance of Kern, Ann Coulter, and Bill O'Reilly seemed to hold sway over the ideascape of NASCAR Nation. To such an end, many of the racing spaces we inhabited were awash with anti-civil-union/gay marriage literature and symbols

"Marriage: One Man, One Woman" (Martinsville, VA, October 2006)

(such as pamphlets distributed by the American Family Association, a prominent right-wing nonprofit organization that opposes same-sex marriage, abortion, and government regulation of industry, and is classified as an "active anti-gay hate group" by the Southern Poverty Law Center [Schlatter, 2010]).

In Martinsville, Virginia, for example, local church groups invested thousands of communion dollars and volunteer hours on their "Marriage: One Man, One Woman" campaign to build support for an upcoming state proposition to define marriage in (heteronormative) legal parlance as a "bond between one man and one woman."

Most roadways and walkways leading to the isolated Darlington racetrack featured large billboards and lower-lying signs with the message. Throughout the weekend of the race we attended in 2007, Christian advocacy groups held demonstrations (such as the well-attended "Christian Marriage Rally") and a series of sermons and concerts similarly themed around the preservation of the "traditional" family structure. Performers called on NASCAR fans to "come together in the name of the Lord" in support of those politicians and policymakers who were "confronted by an age old sin with new fangled spin." The hundreds of attendees to the prerace concert were encouraged to pray for salvation and for the leaders of "this great nation" to "honor the Lord's Will and do what's right for the future of our children."

Second, and relatedly, many men with whom we spoke unequivocally and forthrightly described their role in the domestic sphere as "provider," "bread-winner," and "head of the household." As one self-described NASCAR Dad with whom we shared a beer at a prerace tailgate in Martinsville, Virginia explained:

> I look after my boys as best as I can. Look, these are tough times and I grew up learning that you have to look after your own first and foremost. If I can provide my kids with the best schooling which helps them get into college, then I'll do it. I put away money every month to make sure my young uns' will have that chance. Hell, the missus looks after them while often I work [the late shift], it's the least I can do.

Much like the "nepotistic" inclinations of driver-heroes who had provided for their sons both a legacy and advantageous scripts of cultural and economic capital (e.g., Dale Earnhardt, Jr., Casey Mears, Kyle Petty [or his son Adam or father Richard for that matter], Davey Allison, or Justin Labonte) (Groothuis & Groothuis, 2008), this and other self-identified NASCAR Dads seem to share a common belief in positionality: that in the hoarding (processes) of neoliberal capital, the father must provide the platform (financial, social, or otherwise) for stratification within capital's cultures of accumulation and promotion.[7] While none of these or similarly themed responses is alarming when considering the climate of contemporary gendered neoliberalism, the unanimity of these attitudes among the self-proclaimed NASCAR Dads we interviewed illustrates the heteronormative patriarchy prevalent within NASCAR Nation. In almost every one of our field interviews on the matter, the participants referenced the "natural" or "predestined" order of, as one fan put it, "the man's place in the family." Many men cited scriptures such as Genesis 3:16 ("I will greatly multiply thy sorrow and thy conception; in sorrow thou shalt bring forth children; and thy desire shall be to thy husband, and he shall rule over thee") and 1 Timothy 2:11–14 ("Let the woman learn in silence with all subjection. But I suffer not a woman to teach, nor to usurp authority over the man, but to be in silence. For Adam was first formed, then Eve. And Adam was not deceived, but the woman being deceived was in the transgression") in claiming license to a heteronormative, Fundamentalist, virile, patriarchal order of things. The common belief in NASCAR Nation, or at least among

an overrepresentative faction we interviewed, echoes the biblical doctrine that it is God's Will for a man to act as the shepherd and "watch
over" his/her nuclear family.

Moreover, the majority of self-described "NASCAR women"
with whom we spoke shared this unvarying vision of perpetuating
established roles within the domestic sphere. In "Mama Grizzly"
parlance—the odd contortion of antifeminist rhetoric with postfemi-
nist empowerment heralded by Sarah Palin,[8] in which to be a "modern feminist" means to celebrate "traditional" gender roles and to
be, among other things, antichoice and antigay—one mother of four
young Dale Earnhardt, Jr., fans attending a race in Dover, Delaware,
described her views on the family in this way:

> all this political correctness and feminazi stuff has ruined the American
> family. The Bible tells us that women's role is to raise the young 'uns
> and look after the house. I'm happy my husband takes care of us,
> workin' and all, and I do my part just the same.

Another young mother and Matt Kenseth fan made the point even
more concisely: "this is the way it is, and the way it's always been . . . why
change a good thing?" Synthesizing the work of Judith Butler, Julia
Kristeva (often seen to be oppositional feminist thinkers) and Henri
Lefebvre, Jenny Robinson (2000) suggests such a religio-patriarchal
"spatial vocabulary" shapes our collective "sense of political possibilities and hence our political choices" (p. 286). And as Butler (1990,
1993) herself makes clear in her seminal feminist doctrines of the
early 1990s, the pluralistic inferences extracted from this and other
forms of speech-action are perhaps less important than the collective
imprint (and power/knowledge dynamic) activated by their uncontested reign within these and other social spaces.

Consider the rhetoric of Palin, the leading feminine figure of
the contemporary conservative movement and a notable attendee
of NASCAR races—she has been at the forefront of pushing this
twinned narrative of traditional gender roles and religion read over
and against what she sees as an ever-encroaching secularism destined
to "destroy" the traditional family structure (i.e., via gay marriage,
the empowerment of women, the repeal of Don't Ask, Don't Tell,
etc.). In her most recent (pre-2012 election campaign) book, *America
by Heart: Reflections on Family, Faith, and Flag* (2010), Palin goes
to great lengths to advocate for breaking down the barrier of separation of church and state, at once attacking John F. Kennedy for not
"embracing" his Catholicism in his famous 1960 speech on religion
(an absurd misreading of history to begin with [see Townsend, 2010])

while simultaneously praising Mitt Romney for publicly embracing his Mormon faith (essentially positing that only an outwardly religious individual is fit to hold elected office). In the same breath, Palin announces that that she is a *"new* feminist" (emphasis in original), because, as she writes, "somewhere along the line feminism went from being pro-woman to effectively anti-woman." But as Michelle Goldberg (2010) makes clear, Palin "mischaracterizes the views of nearly every historical feminist she mentions.... Indeed, [*America by Heart*] is an object lesson in the power of right-wing propaganda to create imaginary history" (p. 1).

This moralistic trajectory, notes cognitive linguist George Lakoff (2004), evokes a rehistoricized, fundamentalist binary—what he refers to as backlash-prompted "conservative rhetoric to redress the cataclysmic assaults on white male identity in the 1960s." As it became clear to us throughout our travels, these identity politics offer empowerment—at once an escape from the perceived impending socialist State; and the specters of feminism, Affirmative Action, and taxation for the public good that it will (supposedly) bring. In turn, the NASCAR collective space offers sanctuary under the guise of a "natural" order of white privilege, subordination of the (feminine, matriarchal, queer, non-American/non-Southern) Other, and Christian orthodoxy.

In essence, NASCAR Nation, its drivers, fans, and owners comprise but one node in the globally invasive, reenchanted Fundamentalist discursive formation crafted by faith merchants such as Jerry Falwell, Jim and Tammy Faye Baker, Stu Weber, Bill McCartney, and Joel Osteen and recited by millions of parishioners around the world. Theirs is detritus of the separation of church and state, as evidenced by Falwell's on-air declarations that the terrorist attacks of September 11, 2001, were a result of God's judgment on the secularization of America:

> I really believe that the pagans, and the abortionists, and the feminists, and the gays and lesbians, the ACLU, People for the American Way—all of them who have tried to secularize America—I point the finger in their face and say, "You helped this happen." (quoted in "NOW with Bill Moyers," 2003)[9]

As many commentators have suggested, biblical injunction and paleoconservative religiosity offer reprieve for those "angry white male" and "Mama Grizzly" faction(s) who, failing to connect the reshaped domestic sphere to the postindustrial two-worker family, envisage—and labor to make real—a utopian, male-dominated, Christ-approved

American domesticity (Ferber, 1998). This bloc, "fed up with liberal handouts to the 'undeserving,' eager to regain and restore their rightful inheritance" (Kimmel, 2006), is able to mobilize those collective frustrations through these empowering, seductive, contextually important sporting subjectivities.

In and through this (imaginary) NASCAR Nation, as we aim to make clear in the section that follows, the religio-Fundamentalist performativities and politics of this movement arrive not naturally but in cadence with a series of contrived, strategically ordered interventions onto the sport's spatial practices and spaces of representation (to borrow Lefebvrean parlance). Further, they arrive not by historical accident, but rather are entangled in politically important, contextually specific cultural politics (and articulative power relations thereof).

THEOCRATIZING NASCAR SPACE

NASCAR's hyperreligiosity benefits not only from the public, "top-down" pedagogies proffered by its most visible "missionaries," but also from grassroots Envangelism as performed by a wondering multitude of church-bound pedagogues inhabiting super speedway spaces on race days. As is the case with most forms of faith, the flesh cultures of stock car Christianity's holy trinity—race car kings, track-wondering NASCAR Dads, and "gift-bearing" sponsors—are indeed empowered by the meaningful signifying processes of the material world. Throughout our travels across the material world of NASCAR Nation, we came to surmise that the omnipresence of Christianity is constituted by a strategically orchestrated theocratization of NASCAR spaces. These are *pedagogical* spaces; they comprise a meaningful social geometry where, as Linda Kintz (2005) instructively deduces,

> the Right, while claiming that Judeo-Christianity is inherent in the very nature of the cosmos and of human nature, in fact spends inordinate time, money, and grassroots work to construct that naturalness and to make sure it is thought as felt as real in the daily lives of people. Their success in doing so has eliminated the space of critical analysis for many Americans. (p. 50)

Kintz's reading of the constructed "naturalness" of religious space is echoed in Bernard-Henri Levy's (2006) Tocquevillian musings on megachurches in the United States, and the affective work that goes into making them thusly. Writing of his encounters at Willow

Creek Community Church—an interdenominational, intergenerational megachurch in the wealthy Chicago, Illinois, suburb of South Barrington[10]—Levy remarks:

> The banks in America look like churches. But here is a church that looks like a bank. It has the coldness of a bank. Its futuristic, somber architecture. No cross, stained-glass windows, no religious symbols at all. It is ten o'clock in the morning. The faithful are beginning to pour in. Or perhaps one should say "the public." Video screens light up pretty much everywhere. A curtain rises to the side of the stage, revealing a picture window that opens onto a landscape of lakes and greenery. And now the bank begins to resemble a congress. On the stage a man and a child in shorts, under a tent, discuss the origin of the world, eating popcorn. (p. 43)

Attending a handful of services there,[11] the experience of Willow Creek consists of more stadium-seating than wooden pews, more Christian rock concert than organ music recital, more amusement park than gothic cathedral, more shopping mall than place of worship. As Witold Rybcynski (2005) describes it,

> The sprawling complex, on an attractively landscaped 155-acre site, includes not only two sanctuaries but also a gymnasium that serves as an activity center, a bookstore, a food court, and a cappuccino bar.... It doesn't look like a place of worship, but what does it look like? A performing-arts center, a community college, a corporate headquarters? (p. 3)

Yet therein lies its affective sway; parishioners are engulfed in a self-contained megamall of Christian commerce, consuming not only "accessible" religious doctrine (sermons, as well as DVDs and books, which are for sale in the bookstore) but also memberships in youth groups, sports groups, men's clubs, women's clubs, seniors' clubs, international clubs, financial advisement seminar, conflict mediation workshops (e.g., relationship counseling), recovery programs (e.g., alcohol, chemical, or other addictions), disability ministry, and so forth, all underpinned by some form of biblical or theological engagement.[12] On this point, Michelle Goldberg (2006) strikes a critical tone:

> Because most exurbs are so new, none of the residents grew up in them; everyone is from somewhere else and there are few places for them to meet. In such locales, megachurches fill the spiritual *and* social void, providing atomized residents instant community.... While megachurches *look* like everything else in the newly developing parts

of America...they provide an outlet for energies that aren't rationale, productive, or acquisitive, for furies and ecstasies that don't otherwise fit in suburban life. Spiritual marketplaces, they are both the apotheosis of the prefab suburban lifestyle and the antidote to its dissatisfactions. (pp. 58–59)

In many ways, the scene Goldberg describes above relates closely to what David Harvey (2003), writing about the "spectacular" modernization of Paris in the mid-1800s, explained as "[t]he symbiotic relation between commercial and public spaces and their private appropriation through consumption" (p. 217). However, Goldberg (2006) further complicates the banality of megachurches in the present moment when she later writes:

> Walk into a megachurch during the height of Sunday service and you'll see staid suburbanites bouncing and swaying as strobe lights strafe the air and bombastic anthems crescendo...The preacher usually tells everyone to greet their neighbors, and worshippers of every race and age turn toward one another and exchange blessings with radiant smiles. Nowhere else in America is so indiscriminately welcoming. It can be beautiful, and to those wary of Christian nationalism, terrifying. Because megachurches *don't just serve as exurban versions of town squares and community centers. In many case they're also tightly organized right-wing political machines.* (p. 59, emphasis added)

This, we find, is quite similar in orientation to *NASCAR* spaces, where an extensive network of religious intermediaries relentlessly endeavors to mold the visceral sport-adoring experiences of (rural and suburban) spectators into meaningful faith-based praxis and conversion into evangelical homogeneity. As a NASCAR beat writer for the *Houston Chronicle* more aptly put it, "raceways are fertile ground for Christ-centered outreach" (Goodrich, 2006, p. 2). While this coalition of Christian corporeal narratives and spectating bodies serves to colonize NASCAR grandstands as natural(ized) spaces of orthodoxy, the crystalline convergences of those same bodily and spoken discourses more consequently normalize paleo-conservative faith and cultural politics in an increasingly theocratic, Ten Commandment–governed NASCAR Nation.

Indeed, the ether of Bible-inflected paleo-conservatism so saturates these sporting spaces that some have referred to the circuit's fans as the NASCAR *congregation* (Rhee, 2007). In these spectacularized spaces, cars are emblazoned with religious signifiers (such as those featured by Morgan Shepherd's "Victory in Jesus" team),[13] the Lord's Prayer is evoked before each race (more on this later), and drivers praise the Lord during their victory speeches (see Newman & Giardina, 2009); all the while, Christian orthodoxy peters out the public display of any alternative value systems.

On the ground, agents of the Lord engage in a series of unique proselytizing spatial practices. At each race we attended, and indeed almost every race on the annual NASCAR schedule in recent years, representatives from the National Fellowship of Raceway Ministries (a Christian advocacy group) actively moved about the crowd in an attempt to challenge or reaffirm NASCAR spectators' faith:

> Evangelical Christian preachers follow Nascar [sic] like old-time circuit riders. They have their own double-wide trailers parked in the garage area, conducting prayer meetings and operating with the full cooperation and encouragement of the tracks. They minister in cases of death and injury, counsel couples, and offer drivers and crewmembers a place to talk about stress, addiction, and depression. Like cops and soldiers, Nascarites would prefer talking to the chaplain than to a shrink. (Lipsyte 2006, p. 7)

Unlike most other North American professional sports, legions of ministers and field workers meander about NASCAR spaces, proffering insight into God's plan, and engaging in a practice commonly referred to as "making friends." Prior to offering the prerace 2008 Daytona 500 invocation, Rev. Bobby Welch, former pastor of the First Baptist Church of Daytona Beach, explained the faith-peddling strategy this way: "What better opening for a conversation about eternal things than after a crash at the speedway, while sitting knee-to-knee with someone who may not have that assurance of heaven and eternal life," he said. "What an opportunity to share the joy and peace and purpose you have in life because of Christ, during casual conversations" (quoted in Pinsky, 2008).

As we learned, this form of first-person Evangelism entails approaching potential converts and converted alike to discuss faith, racing, and in some cases even the rapture. These missionaries methodically advance toward NASCAR-loving consumer-*flâneurs* and launch into rehearsed race-related phatic banter, such as "Who do you think'll win the race today?", to more banal conversation starters such as "Beautiful day for a race today, ain't it?", to more pointed entrées such as "Hello friend, have you accepted Jesus Christ as your Lord and Savior?" (Fieldnotes). When speaking with a member of the Fellowship of Raceway Ministries in Bristol, Tennessee, we found that various features of cultural and "political politics" are not off limits in these conversations, but racing and Jesus are often the common "starting and ending points" in these missionaries' dialogical tactics. And those conversations, or at least those undertaken at places like Bristol Motor Speedway, Lowe's Motor Speedway (Charlotte), or Richmond International Speedway, "always" swayed in the direction of biblical Christianity. These were the "Right-wing Christian Zionists" Peter McLaren and Nathalia Jaramillo (2005) describe for whom, as Robert Jensen (2003) suggests, "there is only one religion—Christianity, which is truth. All others are cults." He continues by suggesting that these folks "can believe in freedom of religion and feel bad when [they] offend a person with another religion, yet still be convinced that all those other religions are, in fact, false."

Consider our observations from Talladega Superspeedway in 2010, where on the official raceway grounds we encountered no fewer than three separate physical locations given over to religious literacy, outreach, or amusement in the immediate shadow of the grandstands

Walking down the main public artery toward the speedway entrance, the first "information tent" we come across is for raceway ministry. Rectangular buffet-style tables are heaped with promotional items, including ones for Joe Gibbs' "Game Plan for Life Ministry" (see below). Middle-aged and gray-haired volunteers alike sit behind the tables on steel folding chairs, handing out brochures and trinkets (in our case, a penny with a cross stamped through it, like the kind you would receive from Cross Penny Ministries) to those who inquire within. Under the small tent to the rear, some attendees in racing- or corporate-logoed attire read from Bibles or converse with other assumedly like-minded folks. Interestingly, the volunteers at this particular station are not actively proselytizing or attempting to draw fans in; in fact, they are quite passive, not engaging anyone who doesn't engage with them first.

As we move deeper into the winding array of merchandise trucks, food stands, and corporate vendors, we come across another ministry venue. In the midst of the swirling mass of humanity moving to and fro, the two twentysomething representatives actively if not aggressively distribute their ideological wares, pushing brochures into and toward the hands of any and all who pass them by. At first glance, the pair initially seem out of place, positioned as they are in close proximity to a remote-controlled race car demonstration/point of sale, a Dodge "Chase to Win" promotional venue ("Enter for your Chance to Win a 2010 Dodge Challenger R/T"), and an R/E ("Racing Electronics") booth renting headphones and scanners for that day's race. Yet as Toby Miller (2001) might argue, this spatial arrangement is "utterly syntagmatic" given the biopolitical technologies operative within NASCAR Nation.

Winding our way south around the massive grandstand structure passed the Sam's Club Trackside Tailgating Center (essentially a small, plain, warehouse-type structure selling bulk items like cases of soda, bottled water, bags of ice, potato chips, hot dog buns, etc.) brings us to a less congested grassy area set up with a large stage, speakers, and so forth—performers or road crew, it's difficult to tell at this distance, relax on stage. Presumably organized in relation to the Alabama Raceway Ministries (given the location of the stage to a 50-odd foot long trailer baring such markings), the stage is festooned with a large banner proclaiming: "LIVIN' LOUD † LIVIN' FREE" in bold white script separated by a light blue cross splashed against a dark blue background, and book-ended by two American flag graphics. Performatively conjoined, it is impossible to collectively read these three sites—in the moment—as anything other than the overt normalization and naturalization of religion, commerce, and politics within the spectacle of NASCAR Nation.

*   *   *

In keeping with the extract above, consider that another naturalizing technology in growing the ranks of the faithful within NASCAR Nation is the utilization of mass-effect prerace sermons conducted by evangelical Christian groups. Prior to the start of each race, Motor Racing Outreach (MRO), a nonprofit 501(c)(3) evangelical Christian ministry founded in 1988 by Baptist preacher Max Helton (see Horton, 2008), facilitates prayer meetings and Bible readings that include fans, NASCAR officials, and members of the racing teams ("NASCAR and Religion" 2001). In addition, the group convenes a kind of "traveling Sunday School" for children and conducts Bible study groups that are widely attended by drivers and crew members before each Sunday's race (MacGregor 2005); Sunday morning services are also provided for merchants, vendors, and members of the media. Dale Beaver, former assistant director of MRO, explained that these public displays of theological devotion act as public pedagogies that "teach" NASCAR celebrities how to expand their roles in the public promotion of a belief in a Christian manifest destiny: "God is using these people in high profile positions whether they are the drivers or the ones that make it happen. God is using them to say 'I'm still here, I'm not silent, and I still care for you'" (quoted in Fotta 2004, 6).

One notable avatar of this public promotion and celebrity advancement of the Word is found in the organization of Joe Gibbs Racing.

Gibbs, the former legendary head football coach of the NFL's Washington Redskins, has been involved in NASCAR team ownership since 1991, winning three Sprint Cup championships since 2000. Of relevance to this chapter is not his racing team's on-track success but rather the overt Christian orthodoxy embedded in his team's organizationally hierarchy. Says Bob Dyar, chaplain for Joe Gibbs Racing:

> Our executive team are all committed Christian guys. We really feel like God has called us together to race and to win races and championships, but do it for the glory of God, not for the glory of man.... We believe that prayer changes things because God is at work. God answers prayers all the time: He either answers yes, no, or not now. He always answers. We don't tell God what to do because He's God. But we believe we try to be faithful to follow God's leading and as a result of that, God has chosen to bless, and some of those biggest blessings are years we didn't do very well. We want to win, and we think God wants us to win. He wants us to do our absolute best, but He's more concerned about our faithfulness, about whether we are utilizing the gifts He has given us, than the performance. (quoted in Horton, 2008, p. 1)[14]

Moreover, each of the prerace events we attended during this project, ministers and performers drew upon a number of nationally imperative Christian themes; imploring spectators to thank the Lord for this great nation and its leadership, stating that, as Americans, they "belonged to the greatest country on Earth."[15]

One flurry of such spectacular discourse at a late-summer race in 2006 illustrates this strange (pro)fusion of stock car culture and Bush-era paleo-conservative values:

> In the opening moments of today's race, a local minister evoked the "Lord's Prayer," through which he called on "Jesus is our savior" to "protect our American way of life." Then, a "special guest," Republican Senator George Allen took the microphone. Allen applauded the sea of "patriots" present at the event, and called on those same NASCAR fans to hold fast to their "patriotism" by "supporting our troops, staying together, and fighting the war of terrorism." Senator Allen then turned the focus of his stumping to his own political future, and rallied "his people" by saying "If the folks voting in the election were the folks at this race, I'd be in great shape!"[16]

Through these linguistic stylings within the spectacle of NASCAR Nation, religious language and performative politics create order, and that order is largely confirmed through the corporeal responses of

Freedom and Family Prerace Concert (Darlington, SC, May 2007)

race fans. There was uniformity and unanimity in spectators' reaction
to practices of prayer. A seemingly taken-for-granted—as if written
law in some informal guide to NASCAR fandom—response among
fans at every race (or at least those races that became part of this study)
was to stand, bow, offer a collective amen, and cheer in communal
sequence as directed by the prerace faith merchants. Immediately
prior to the commencement of each weekend's main event—and to
the vocal approval of the 120,000 or so race fans in attendance—
(nearly) every driver, pit crew member, team owner, and available
NASCAR official spectacularly congregate along pit road to take part
in the traditional prerace invocation. In turn, fans stand at attention
en masse to hear the Lord's prayer—a discursive praxis that is almost
always evoked by "men of the Christian faith" (Russell, 2007; see also
Newman & Giardina, 2009, p. 57).

It is important to note that this practice is unique in North
American professional sport, as such a mandatory religious appraisal
cannot be found in the spectacular machinations of major ballparks,
football stadia, hockey rinks, or basketball arenas.[17] In this way, loyalties to faith and nation become conjoined (if not conflated), and
the performative politics of intermediary (producer) and consumer

are blurred in what becomes a phantasmagoria—to evoke Walter Benjamin (1999)—of consent and consensus. Tens of thousands of teary-eyed, white-bodied, American flag-waving, corporate logo-emblazoned congregants praying in unison for things such as presidential penance, success of the military in Iraq, and an expansion of God's Will over the State; and in so doing bestir an amalgam that extends beyond the trite "sport as a mirror of society" thesis, and rather create a spectacle that produces the sociopolitical hegemony under which the nation is narrated, imagined, and indeed conceived.

On the surface, to be subjected to this unwritten code of conduct signifies the individual's membership in a much larger congregation of NASCAR Nation. More importantly, however, there is little space for bodily practices that contest, resist, or reject this confederation of God and country. Failure to stand, pledge, pray, or praise would signify heresy to the Christian faith and disloyalty to NASCAR Nation, as well as symbolic sedition toward its dominant political advocates (and thus allegiance to "the enemy"). (In much the same way that failing to stand at attention for the National Anthem or not applauding war-machine flyovers would be interpreted under the logos of "if you're not with us, you're against us.") In a signified space awash with the images of a *White American Jesus*, those spectating (in a Debordian sense) cannot avoid an uncontested spatial relationship with the Savior—and the Fundamentalist pedagogues "waging a campaign to ban same-sex marriage, serve up creationism instead of science, privatize Social Security, eliminate embryonic stem-cell research, and overturn Roe v. Wade" (Giroux, 2008, p. 31). Through bodily praxis as signifying act, it can be argued, all spectators in attendance (regardless of political or religious affiliation) are semiotically transformed into representative embodiments of paleo-conservative Christian solidarity and their complicit deportment becomes a meaningful performance of loyalty to a theocratizing State.

In these times, those neoliberal hegemons who have been forced to enact a proliferation of such de-democratic measures in order to ensure growing rates of accumulation, as Thomas Frank (2004) pointed out in *What's the Matter with Kansas*, "talk Christ but walk corporate." And as we have argued heretofore, in no other sport is this Jesus-speak more pronounced than in NASCAR. All this talk of fear, liberty, freedom, and God's will becomes more important in light of the dialectics of commercialization and theocratization. In the first instance, these broader contortions of market and theocracy are animated and made meaningful through a number of mutually beneficial partnerships between NASCAR's commodity leviathans and the discursive interpellation of Christianity—each of which simultaneously reconditions the social landscape of the sport and reinscribes the capitalist power structure that it serves. Through prerace performances or "Faith Night" themed events, Jesus gives NASCAR further brand identity—and in return NASCAR provides a fertile space for spreading His word. Or, to put it more simply, "God" has been good for NASCAR's business.

SPORT, THEOCRATIC AMERICA, AND THE ALMIGHTY MARKET

So what is at stake here? And why are the merchants of faith so focused on converting the NASCAR faithful? First, *NASCAR matters* because it is no longer a parochial—and never was an isolated—cultural formation. Under the auspices of Tea Party nationalism, NASCAR Nation offers a productive national signpost to what Kevin Phillips (2006) refers to as a new "American theocracy." Under the reign of this American theocracy, Phillips (2006) argues, "blatant business cronyism" now adjudicates both state interests and the moral referents from which polity is constructed. Moreover, spectacles of (Southern) paleo-conservative culture, the author maintains, have carved out a domineering space in the public discourse from which these "mainstream values and culture" are configured. Through these evangelicized spectacles of the nation, frequent NASCAR attendees George W. Bush or Sarah Palin transcend from political mouthpieces of American imperialism/corporate capitalism to "servants of God." In turn, the antidemocratic, polarizing politics of the man who in 2004 proclaimed, "I believe that God wants me to be President" (quoted in Aronson, 2004) becomes secularized in the popular discourse as material expressions of a sanctimonious "moral majority" (Palin herself reiterated a similar theme in 2010; others of the right-wing fringe such as Michele Bachmann have expressed comparable appraisals regarding their reason for being in or running for public office).

As the overarching politico-religious order of NASCAR Nation, evangelical Christianity has become the quasi-moralist lodestone upon which a number of prevailing paleo-conservative/neoliberal ideologies are drawn to and accumulate credence: from those of the Strong Father State (as opposed to Obama's Maternal Welfare State), to the taken-for-granted, virile, never "cut-and-run" military-industrial-complex(ities), to the heteronormative politics of "the sacred institution of marriage," to the hegemony of legacy capital in the age of free market dominion (the legacies of "Dale Junior's" inheritance of the Dale Earnhardt legacy or the inheritance of a Christian manifest destiny as embodied by Bush, Sr., and, Jr.). In short: the microreligious spectacles of a sporting NASCAR Nation now inform, frame, and indeed produce macrospectacular (Right, conservative, neoliberal) NASCAR Nation hegemony.

As NASCAR moved from the margins (parochial, "redneck," South) to the center of U.S. sport and popular culture, what became increasingly evident was how the sporting NASCAR Nation articulated with these broader machinations of cultural citizenship. In some ways, NASCAR became ground zero for sermonizing public pedagogies that privilege a specific set of religious values, ideologies, and identity politics. *New York Times* columnist Jonathan Miles (2005) sums up this point thusly:

> For a certain segment of the population, NASCAR's raid on American culture—its logo festoons everything from cellphones to honey jars to post office walls to panties; race coverage, it can seem, has bumped everything else off television; and, most piercingly, NASCAR dads now get to pick our presidents—triggers the kind of fearful trembling the citizens of Gaul felt as the Huns came thundering over the hills. To these people, stock-car racing represents all that's unsavory about red-state America: fossil-fuel bingeing; lust for violence; racial segregation; run-away Republicanism; anti-intellectualism (how much brain matter is required to go fast and turn left, ad infinitum?); the corn-pone memes of God and guns and guts; crass corporatization; Toby Keith anthems; and, of course, exquisitely bad fashion sense. What's more, they simply don't get it. What's the appeal of watching…traffic? It's as if "Hee Haw" reruns were dominating prime time, and the Republic was slapping its collective knee at Grandpa Jones's "What's for supper?" routine. (p. 1)

At the heights of what Stuart Hall (1979) often referred to as the "Great Moving Right Show"—or what the corpora-centrist Democratic economic policies of Barack Obama have more clearly revealed as a paradigm of "Left is the new Right"—the synthesis of sport, State, and secularism emerges as an important *assemblage* of texts, sociocultural practices, and bodily procedures that not only promote collective notions of theocratic nationalism, but also produce a particular brand of post-"9/11" paleo-conservative citizenship in controlled ways.

Inasmuch as NASCAR Nation is a living, thriving moral-political fulcrum within such a sociopolitical context, and erring to the side of presentism, we briefly conclude this chapter by turning to the work of Daniel Schipani (1997). Schipani's writings are instructive in deconstructing the relationship between "the dominant values of contemporary U.S. life such as achievement, affluence, individualism, competition, consumption, and militarism" and "church practices of patriarchy, moralism, legalism, and lack of compassion...domestication [i.e.]...compliance, indifference, or complicity with structures of injustice, oppression, and neglect" (p. 28). Informed by, and eventually developed in collaboration with, foremost critical pedagogue Paulo Freire, Schipani (1988) argues that mediated social environs such as NASCAR Nation, discourses of "family values," and the collective configurations of fatherhood, family, and conservative identity politics not only gain traction in the public sphere, but also authorize a distorted biblicalism that rejects the ecclesial imperatives of interdependence, equality, humanism, and a belief that "all human beings are called to be active, creative agents who participate with God in the ongoing liberation and re-creation of the whole world" (p. 47). Instead, it is in and through these collective configurations—and the encounters of Bible-wielding bodies—that NASCAR's faithful and faithfulness collide in pedagogically meaningful ways; ways that authorize biblical singularity and capitalize upon the collective longings for purpose, fellowship, and devotion.

NASCAR fans—who in their neoliberal working lives have become all the more alienated from the social relations of production (as the logics of the free market infiltrate the postnational, post-Fordist factory, the hypermediated, lifestyle-consuming shopping mall, and the disenfranchising lines leading to the voting booth)—are interpellated by, and reproductive of, the moral platitudes upon which a nation's paradoxical Exxon-dominated, Ford-failing, Winston-inhaling political economy is buttressed. NASCAR nationalists are thusly subjected to the mystifying pedagogies of market sanctimony; whereby *new literacies of (in)tolerance* are rationalized through the dual narratives of the Lord's blessing (or punishment) and an economic conviction bound to the moral economic entanglements of Cadillac Escalades, increased joblessness, eight-figure Evangelism, and ever-growing poverty rates. In his well-researched book *God Willing? Political Fundamentalism in the White House, the "War on Terror," and the Echoing Press*, David Domke (2004) posits that such mass cultural technologies constitute a means of individual *empowerment*—where religious conservatism holds for those economically dispossessed adherents a means for "recovering" social power.[18]

Herein lies the import of a racing Jesus. Capitalizing on what Chris Hedges (2007) refers to as the "surplus value of rapture," political intermediaries have successfully grafted a new language of theocratic citizenship by layering the gospel onto race consuming praxis. To paraphrase Hedges (2007), the principal commodity within this marketized religious order is "freedom": freedom from fear of the lesbian or gay interloper, from the fear of the welfare mother, from anxieties reserved for the brown-bodied "Other," from jihadist insurgents, and from an imminent afterlife where one's sins lay in waiting. This Christian fundamentalist bent is juxtaposed against the Jihad/insurgent in the currency of most stock car narratives:

> America is the land of the free and home of the brave. Its military might be hard at work, preserving freedom around the world but soldiers are dying. Iraqi insurgents don't play by the rules, they kill themselves while killing freedom fighters and innocents alike....America was founded on religious freedom....[NASCAR] espouses all things American, patriotic, religious, and competitive. (Miron 2004, p. 1)

In other words, the rise of corporatist neoliberalism, an imperialist military-industrial-complex (see the chapters that follow), a dehumanizing biotechnocracy, a resource-stripping regime of "footloose" accumulation, the reign of vast systems of what David Harvey (2005, 2007) refers to as "accumulation by dispossession," and ethnocentric, heteronormative sectarianism are not only abetted by the "institutions, rituals, and subculture" (Wright, 2002) of NASCAR, but are the reconfigured soothsaying pedagogies of a Falwell-inspired (LeHay-driven, Osteen-esque, etc.) stock car nomenclature grants authority and consent to now-normative North American conjunctural social and political knowledges.

CODA

Interestingly, both the Christianity proffered by NASCAR Nation's merchants of faith and the market logics imposed upon the American faithful by ideologue-policymakers of the Milton Friedman and Freidrich Hayek proscribed neoliberal order rely on the same infallible design: that of faith. As capitalists-turned-politicos siphon trillions of tax dollars away from the public good and into private enterprise, Americans are reminded that only through "faith" in the market can the collective body overcome these seemingly ordained downturns and deficits. Thus we are reminded of influential U.S. economist John Kenneth Galbraith's derision of such market deification (the failings of neoliberalism hide in the shadows of devotion and the "freedoms" [as Friedman puts it] of self-interest): "The modern conservative is engaged in one of man's oldest exercises in moral philosophy; that is, the search for a superior moral justification for selfishness." Moreover, these moralist literacies teach us new lessons on democracy, morality, and freedom. Writing at the heights of the Bush presidency, McLaren and Jaramillo (2005) use sharp prose in fleshing out the problematics of this new paradigm:

> The hawks around Bush genuflect at the intellectual altar of the late philosopher-king and University of Chicago classicist Leo Strauss, who imperturbably assumed the conviction that only an elite few in the government warrant the sacred custodianship of the truth, and are thereby charged with using "noble lies" to keep the truth from the unwashed masses by preoccupying everyday citizens not only with real or perceived external threats to the nation but also with the task of developing nationalist or militantly religious sentiments fanatical enough to ensure their willingness to die for the nation. (p. 263)

In a moment when most self-identified Christian, flag-waving, Tea Party American nationalist—faced with fractionally higher personal income tax burden (and in support of the death penalty)—decry the possibilities of public health care for all the nation's citizens, the gospel of NASCAR makes sense. Among the thousands of flag-waving adherents of surge warfare and George Allen-infused faith-race politics, George W. Bush makes sense. Sarah Palin makes sense. Creationist science makes sense. Xenophobic nationalism makes sense. Loyalty to capitalism makes sense. And so on, such that in a sport that spews exhaust from over 7 million liters of leaded petrol into the atmosphere each year (just on the race track) and is known for its collective derision for the faiths and peoples of oil producing regions of the world, is unparalleled in its corporate signifier saturation and working-class loyalties, and is inundated with religiosity and death-defying masochism, the contradictions of a society under siege—to borrow from Zigmunt Bauman (2002b)—*make sense.*

In the most basic sense of pedagogy, then, members of NASCAR Nation are being subjected to what Jacques Derrida (1987) refers to as "the logics of parergonality," whereby knowledges of citizenship are produced, shared, contested, and made meaningful within a contextually specific plasticity of conservative/neoliberal conjuncture. The NASCAR spectacle thus offers pedagogical legitimacy: legitimacy to be white (and guilt-free) in "Obama's America"; legitimacy to stand against equal marital rights for all U.S. citizens; legitimacy for "white man falling" paranoia; legitimacy to clog the roadways with planet-destroying sport utility vehicles (God's gift of safety and conspicuous consumption); legitimacy to believe in rapture capitalism; and legitimacy to trust that—much like a stock car-driver racing headlong into a cacophony of flesh and metal at 150 miles per hour—the Lord will see us through.

As we have written previously (see Newman & Giardina, 2009),[19] there is an ever-creeping symbiosis between commercial ventures and religious sites articulated along lines of political ideology: From Starbucks and McDonald's located inside the heartland's mega-churches to the hateful political invective spewed forth from their pulpits, and from the crass deployment of end-times fear-mongering to the hyperpontifical proclamations of NASCAR's cruciform-wielding drivers, a new holy trinity of commodified market logics dominating the American consumer-subject in the post-9/11 epoch has most certainly emerged: evangelical fundamentalism, hyperaggressive paleo-conservatism, and predatory neoliberal capitalism. Together and in isolation, these three conditions operate as "technologies of enchantment" (Cole, 2007, p. 153) that "activate, confirm, and extend" the normative power of such a discursive iteration. In effect, NASCAR Nation has risen from the proverbial ashes and ascended into triumphal glory at the right hand of the Once-Mighty Dollar: It has been transmogrified from its early days as a regional sporting venture into a complex system of signs, images, and practices that both adheres to the capitalist imperatives of its neoliberal overlords while simultaneously (and paradoxically) promoting a seemingly oppositional rationality as the answer to all that is "wrong" with the world.

And it is here in the hypercommodified spaces of the NASCAR spectacle that Christian nationalism—which, as Goldberg (2007) reminds us, "can exist only in opposition to something" (p. 69)—has been fomented most persistently: a *visible moral center* of anti-immigrant, antiblack, antigay, antichoice, antienvironment, anti-Other rhetoric prepackaged and sold hand-in-hand alongside (an equally commodified) restorative religious fervor delivered on high by celebrity-driver and (right-wing) politician alike. Specific to NASCAR Nation, its ruling class is selling a spectacle of fables: the fable of infinite growth under neoliberalism, the fable of an endless "American Century," the fable of a commitment to (Southern) cultural heritage, the fable of NASCAR Dad social conservatism and religious fundamentalism, the fable of Mitt Romney's "conservative" economy, and the fable of the free market's individual freedoms. But this "call" to national redemption and personal salvation is nothing but a false hall of mirrors, an untenable position, another example of the predatory logics of capitalism unleashed. Religion: yet another vehicle for shepherding untold dollars to the Wal-Marts, Exxon-Mobils, and Home Depots of the world—the selling *out* of the soul through the selling *of* the soul.

6

PART I

NASCAR NATION AS/IN PETROL EMPIRE

The U.S. Military is being used more and more for the protection of overseas oil fields and the supply routes that connect them to the United States and its allies. Such endeavors, once largely confined to the [Persian] Gulf area, are now being extended to unstable oil regions in other parts of the world. Slowly but surely, the U.S. military is being converted into a global oil-protection service.

—Michael Klare (2004)

If automobility and its attendant location within the field of the NASCAR enterprise reveals anything about the nation's political and economic trajectory over the past decade-plus, it is that the "domestic" infrastructure of an increasingly interconnected global economy—mined by Exxon-Mobil in the Gulf of Mexico, overlain with miles of criss-crossing interstate pavement, forged in Detroit factories and Pennsylvania mines, and speculated upon in Wall Street trading halls—is crumbling at its foundations. In the United States, "foreign" automobile manufacturers such as Toyota and Honda now outsell American stalwarts General Motors and Ford in the domestic market-place (for more, see Chapter Seven). Moreover, as concerns over fleeting energy resources and environmental catastrophe abound, hybrid fuel-cell cars (e.g., Toyota Prius, Nissan Leaf, Chevy Volt), tighter fuel emission standards, and green thumbprints have made strong headway in challenging—if not in some quarters supplanting—fetishes for V-8s and roaring engines in the popular imaginary. At the same time, the current trajectory of U.S. congressional political discourse, especially over the past five years (c. 2005–2010), remains pre-occupied with resuscitative promises for "off-shore drilling," "energy independence," "emissions control," and contentious wars to secure enough oil to "keep America running." As a result, the American car—and the resources that make it run—has, to many, become as much a national burden as a symbol of the nation's industrial proclivity.

In general terms, it can be argued that this auto-petrol crisis has become a metonym of a modern U.S. economic infrastructure not suited for the global free market it had a large part in creating. And yet, politicians, investors, and cultural citizens alike remain steadfast in their commitment to this auto-petrol modernity. As the national manufacturing sector is continually being made obsolescent (as Detroit industrialists reconcile the imperfect storm of increased domestic regulation and heightened competition from *laissez-faire*-empowered transnationals, needing in fact to be "bailed out" by the Obama administration), the thinking and rhetoric surrounding the national economy further reproduces an old national conviction in (1) protracted twentieth-century Fordist manufacturing and (2) an over-burdened, outdated, petrol-saturated, and oil-lubricated commercial infrastructure. As these "engines" that "drove twentieth-century America" increasingly prove outmoded for today's global market-place, the United States has simultaneously expanded its military-industrial dealings in the Middle East and elsewhere in order to at once (1) secure fleeting resources (and thereby sustain a failing imperialist project), stimulate national spending, and (2) stifle competition from nonaligned national outliers (such as Russia and Venezuela). At the same time, this heightened military fervor—contextually bound up in a discourse of the so-called War on Terror—has permeated throughout the cultural landscape as a whole, as military jet flyovers, themed package-reports, and calls to "support the troops" have become commonplace across the national media landscape (see King, 2008).

In this two-part chapter, we present a series of ethnographic vignettes that offer critical insights into how NASCAR (and sport more generally) has become an important cultural technology for not only "manufacturing consent" for, but ritualistically celebrating, the last movements of this ill-fated U.S. "petrol-empire." In the first part, we explore how, as David Campbell (2005) puts it, the United States' "'unbounded' consumption of automobility" produces both an unprecedented petrol-energy dependency and an "'unbordered' sense of state in which security interests extend beyond the national homeland" (p. 945). That is, we make the case that this assemblage of war machines, war games, vessels of a petrol empire, and militarized spectating/spectacularized bodies produces both the means of surplus value and national fervor, and also reproduces the conditions upon which the contextually important militarization of identity and ideology are forged within these sporting spaces and fan experiences.

We bring into focus the politics of a sport cloaked with signifiers from "disaster capital's" (Klein, 2007) most successful entrepreneurial mercenaries (Force Protection and Blackwater [later renamed Xe following numerous public relations debacles concerning the firm]), populated with youth-hailing military recruitment centers disguised as everyday amusements (such as the popular "Army Experience," discussed below), flanked by legions of tanks, fighter jets, flight simulators, sniper rifles, and other various military equipment, all hastened by racer-icons who openly proclaim their support for "the cause," and inhabited by vendors peddling unabashedly patriotic, politicized, and promilitary merchandise.

THE U.S. ENERGY ECONOMY

Few natural resources have been as fundamental to the formation and advancement of the modern U.S. economy as petroleum. Following Edwin Drake's nineteenth-century crude oil discovery in the Western Pennsylvania hills (Yergin, 1991), erstwhile energy mainstays such as coal and timber succumbed to the superiority of petroleum—a highly efficient, easily transferable, and readily available commodity.[1] Petroleum quickly became the foremost stimulant in mobilizing late-nineteenth/early-twentieth century U.S. industrialism, spurring on what Ernest Mandel (1975) classifies as capitalism's "second phase" of technological production. Kerosene heated homes and businesses, oil lamps extended production hours in manufacturing facilities, and oil-lubed transportation networks facilitated an expedient and reliable product lifecycle. Other large-scale industries—steel, agriculture, textiles, transportation, and communication—arose largely in conjunction with technological advances and refining capabilities of petroleum. Gas alleviated many of the temporal and spatial limits of capitalism, along the way transforming the United States from a rural society formed around, and sustained by, agricultural production to one of mass manufacturing, industrialization, and material production in urban hubs. From petroleum's incorporation in early U.S. industrialism, the sustainable trajectory of the U.S. economy has been inextricably linked with, and cyclically bound to, the continuous supply of petroleum energy. As Paul Roberts (2004) explains, "First in mining, then in textile manufacturing, and then in the production of steel, the pattern became clear ... the more you produced, the more energy you needed. And conversely, the more energy you used, the more things you produced" (p. 29).

We all know the story as it unfolded thereafter: the introduction of the internal combustion engine at the dawn of the twentieth century, and the emergence of the "Big Three" Detroit auto conglomerates and an abundance of automotive industries therein crystallized the foundations of the U.S. industrial boom. Today, the indivisible bond between petroleum and economic sustainability has intensified, and many have posited that the "fortunes" of U.S.-based multinationals are constructed around, and dependent upon, the continued (and relatively cheap) availability of petroleum (Klare, 2004; Klein, 2007; Roberts, 2004; Yergin, 1991). Petroleum and its refined byproducts are fundamental elements in plastics, synthetic fibers, synthetic rubbers, detergents, and chemical fertilizers. And the list of petroleum-based end-products is extensive: clothing, medicines, buildings, furniture, cosmetics, shampoo, contact lenses, eyeglasses, household cleaners, sneakers, televisions, and electronics (Moore, 2003). Petroleum thus holds a twofold position in the modern U.S. economy: as a key driver in the *material production of goods* and as a major *output of the production process.* With more than 40 percent of the nation's total energy supply coming from petroleum (Leeb & Leeb, 2004) and oil fueling more than 97 percent of America's transportation fleet (Klare, 2004)—not to mention the proliferation of products containing crude oil—"petroleum has proven to be the most versatile fuel source ever discovered, [and is] situated at the core of the modern industrial economy" (Klare, 2004, p. 7).

Clearly, oil is a critical commodity to the U.S. economy and of continually growing importance because, as its exponents would have it, "we cannot get by without oil, we cannot grow our economy without oil, and moreover, if you extrapolate from recent history, we can't grow our economy without ever-increasing amounts of oil" (Leeb & Leeb, 2004, p. 5). Many economists (e.g., Brown & Yucel, 2002; Jimenez-Rodriguez & Sanchez, 2005; Jones, Leiby, & Paik, 2004; Mork, 1989) have argued that the price of oil is one of the most important economic indicators in determining growth models, price indexes, market futures, and corporate stock valuations—and thus profitability of U.S.-based multinationals correlate to the current estimations and future projections of a barrel of oil's price.[2]

It is at this point that a fundamental problem arises: U.S. petroleum *consumption* outpaces domestic crude oil *production.* At present, the United States—with an estimated world population of less than 5 percent—consumes 25 percent of the world's total supply of oil, and it is expected that from 2001 to 2025 oil consumption will increase by 44 percent, while domestic production will decrease by 20 percent

(Klare, 2004). This disjuncture forges the *crisis of supply and demand* whereby the U.S. economy reconciles increasingly imbalanced levels of proliferating corporate consumption and fleeting domestic quantities of petroleum.[3]

Having exhausted almost all of its domestic oil supplies in the early 1970s (Itzkoff, 2008), the United States has increasingly become dependant upon global petrol markets to overcome supply/demand disparities. But with increased competition from rapidly industrializing nations like China and India, (inexpensive) global oil pools are being drained at an alarming rate. As a result, the recent decades have witnessed a growing concern forged around the idea of a global *peak oil crisis* looming on the energy horizon; that is, the critical apogee where the maximum rate of global oilfield extraction becomes insufficient for worldwide demand (Deffeyes, 2001, 2005; Heinberg, 2003; Itzkoff, 2008; Klare, 2004; Roberts, 2004; Simmons, 2005). Paul Roberts (2004) explains the *peak oil crisis* as follows: "Oil is a finite substance, and at some point...all the oil being discovered around the world will no longer replace the oil that has been produced, and global production will peak. Oil companies and oil states will find it harder and harder to maintain current production levels, much less keep up with rising consumption" (p. 46). Seymour Itzkoff (2008) goes further: "We will have entered a period of history when demand exceeds supply of this critical resource and the reserves available will either be of secondary quality, found at such unheard depths in the seas, all but guaranteeing to geometrically increase the price of the commodity" (p. 20).

In other words, new petroleum discoveries will be harder to locate, smaller in size, and be taxingly extracted from desolate regions throughout the world—meaning pipelines to many global markets will be costly and/or not possible. Which is to say (and this is a critical if esoteric point), as Greg Palast (2006) stresses, there is a difference between "an *economist's* conception of 'running out' [of oil] and a *scientist's*" conception of running out of oil (p. 336, emphases original). As he explains,

> The number one theorem of economics is that we are running out of everything and yet we can have as much as we want of anything. Again, there's no contradiction. All commodities are scarce and abundant at the same time. The difference between scarcity and abundance is price. You can get anything, in any amount, if you are willing to pay any price. (p. 336)

Thus, and while the peak oil Shell game has been effectively realized as a crafty public relations effort,[4] we *are* "running out of a certain kind of oil nevertheless: *cheap* oil. That is, we are coming to the end of the stuff we can pump at a low cost, the easy oil that practically jumps out of the ground...[but] as prices rise, so does supply" (ibid., emphasis added).

The definitional ambiguity of the "peak" is not our concern here. What warrants greater consideration, especially among those who see the capitalization of natural resources as anything but a natural process, is the notion that some form of oil-related limitation constitutes a contradiction in a capitalist mode of production; principally, that the coming oil crisis points to a capitalist regime of accumulation that is crisis-prone—with barriers to overcome in the first instance—and crisis-dependant—as a powerful and necessary disciplinary mechanism in the second.[5]

One locus of crisis formation, as David Harvey (2007) makes clear in *Limits to Capital*, is a crisis of natural resource exhaustion and environmental destruction.[6] Harvey (2007) writes: "It is, many on the Left now argue, the environmental crisis that defines the crisis of our times and our politics should evolve accordingly" (p. xxii). Although Harvey disagrees with the assessment that the environmental crisis merits primacy over all other contradictions of capital, ecological Marxists such as John Bellamy Foster and James O'Connor suggest that it is hard to differentiate the two. As O'Connor (1998) writes in *Natural Causes*, "An ecological Marxist account of capitalism as a crisis-ridden system focuses on the way that the combined power of capitalist production relations and productive forces self-destruct by impairing or destroying rather than reproducing their own conditions" (p. 165).

Where Marx believed that capitalist production (farming, for instance) ruined soil and destroyed the environment, ecological Marxists complete the reciprocal arrangement Marx left unfinished by pronouncing that nature itself will threaten economic crisis through shortage, exploitation, and destruction, leading to a crisis of *under*production. The dialectic of economic crisis and ecological crisis is a twofold contradiction. Economic crises, according to O'Connor (1998), cause ecological crises through emphasizing improvements in efficiency and cost-cutting measures (increasing the rate of exploitation) that instigate new forms of ecological degradation, environmental hazards, high-tech pollution, through the generalized externalization on costs. The obverse reading is that economic crises are responses to ecological crises, often triggered by shortages of raw materials that arise from market forces that squeeze profits and reduces surplus value (O'Connor, 1998). Such an ecological Marxist analysis is instructive in framing the impending *peak oil crisis* (however broadly or narrowly it is defined). On one side of the coin, the so-called peak oil crisis can be seen as an internal contradiction of capitalist *production relations and productive forces* and on the other side a crisis of the *conditions of production*.

Correlatively, a "peak oil" crisis (of whichever manifestation you subscribe) signifies an external contradiction in that "production relations and production forces self-destruct by impairing or destroying, rather than reproducing, their own conditions" (O'Connor, 1998, p. 165). The systematic pollution of the environment through the burning of fossil fuels manifests when burning circulates the carbon embers back into its natural habitat with deleterious effects—global warming, acid rain, and ozone depletion reflect the residual effects of this process. In short, beyond being nonrenewable, capital accumulation may also entail the destruction of the *conditions of production*.

This crisis of capital, which at its core is accelerated not only by a petrol-reliance that defined the modern U.S. industrial project but perhaps more importantly by new anxieties about American exceptionalism, is compounded when we consider (1) the fate of a faltering national economy and, perhaps more importantly, (2) the extent to which those collective longings for *pax Americana* are entangled in the imagined, mediated, and real predictions of petrol demise. In other words, these national-petrol linkages—between the cultural meanings and attitudes toward the ostensibly inexpensive and abundant natural resource as inextricably linked to the fate of the nation—now weigh heavy of the minds of ideologues, politicos, capitalists, and consumers alike.

For us, there are few, if any, cultural formations that authorize the *petrol excess* of postindustrial U.S. popular culture than that of stock car auto racing. In fact, as we argue in what follows, there are very few, if any, cultural domains that typify the underlying energy contradictions through a *twofold paradox within the internal forces (and relations) of production* and *external conditions of production* more than NASCAR.

A CELEBRATION OF PETROL EXCESS

Set within and against this context, witnesses to the NASCAR spectacle are subject not only to the litany of consumer brands mentioned in Chapter Three, but also to ubiquitous visuals of gasoline, petroleum, and crude oil, including such prominent commercial sponsors as Texaco, Havoline, Mobile 1, Quaker State, Pennzoil, Shell, Sunoco,

Marathon, Lucas Oil, STP, Valvoline, and Unocal 76. These petrol intensities were recorded prior to an event in Richmond, Virginia, very early on in our research:

> Entering a NASCAR space, we are taken aback by the widespread corporate logos and trademarks of petrol multinationals. As we pass through the commercial tents outside of the racetrack, merchandisers are constantly appealing to our consumerist impulses by the distribution of marketing pamphlets and the peddling of petrol-logoed merchandise

From the very outset of our field research, we were struck by the sheer quantity of petrol signifiers and rituals in these locales: Senses are overpowered by the sounds, smells, and visuals within the stock car spectacle: the thunder of forty-three 750-horsepower vessels speeding full-throttle at over 150 miles per hour; the distinct scent of burning rubber as race cars slip 'n slide along the pavement, and the stinging odor of 110-octane Sunoco gasoline particles expended out of the exhaust pipes of gas-guzzling internal combustion engines. Many interviewees frequently cited their affinity for these "pleasurable" sounds and smells they experienced when attending a NASCAR race—many shared with us their intent to purposefully select racetrack seats *closer* to the smells of burning tires and gas despite limited viewpoints.

Navigating the commercial and performative grounds that encircle the racetrack, one encounters instances of NASCAR spectator/consumers actively practicing fueling techniques/technologies through the corporeal experiences of "pit crew" simulations. Members of NASCAR Nation compete head-to-head against one another hoping to replace Goodyear tires, quick-pump a steel tire jack, and replicate the "refueling" process with two (empty) 11-gallon Sunoco-logoed gas cans faster than their fellow participants. On display are the latest excessive fuel technologies: V-14 high performance engines, diesel-powered off-road race trucks, and personal entertainment crafts: ATVs, motorcycles, and personal recreational crafts. At the Chevy Rock-n-Roll 400 in Richmond, Virginia, Chevrolet—and its parent company General Motors—leveraged its race sponsorship agreement by offering a unique fan experience in which spectators could sample the latest SUVs, oversized "pick-up" trucks, and sports cars that Chevrolet had to offer.[7] The Chevrolet Racing exhibition featured the technological capabilities and high-performance function of petroleum-thirsty classic "hot rods," top-fuel dragsters, pro-stock cars and bikes, and off-road rally trucks.[8]

The links between race teams/drivers and the motor oil industry are inseparable; these bonds extend beyond elite, on-track performance and commercial sponsorship symmetries and into the consumer marketplace. Citizens of NASCAR Nation can purchase Joe Gibbs Driven Racing Oil and lube their own hot rods with the identical high-performance motor oil that three-time NASCAR Sprint Cup Series championship–winning team Joe Gibbs' Racing uses on the racetrack (Perez, 2008). As Joe Gibbs himself puts it, "We know NASCAR fans love cars, specifically, muscle cars and hot rods...Now there's a product specifically designed by our team that millions of NASCAR fans can use in their hot rods and street rods" (quoted in Perez, 2008, p. 1).

Touring the merchandise venues that encase the racetrack grounds, spectators are confronted with endless queues of spectator/consumers eager to purchase the latest petroleum and motor oil-branded merchandise, clothing, and die-cast collectibles. Spectator bodies are adorned with the corporate logos and commercial signifiers of the most "crude" petrol multinational corporations without reluctance and reference. As we observed, individual race team and driver retail centers that are sponsored and financed by popular commercial petrol and motor oil conglomerates stood among the longest lines of the entire shopping "district." In an effort to identify stock car racer Kevin Harvick as their favorite celebrity-driver, NASCAR supporters frequently, and enthusiastically, purchase petrol-laden memorabilia, and wearable commodities to drape themselves in the commercial logos and slogans of his primary sponsors (at that time): Shell petroleum and Pennzoil motor oil. We observed the "sponsor integrated identity" (Gill, 2008) as follows:

> NASCAR fans identify race team and driver allegiances through the endorsements of their corporate sponsors. Embodying the petrol and motor oil brands that adorn race cars and team uniforms communicates a commitment to drivers and race team, such as: Ryan Newman (Mobile 1 motor oil), Kyle Petty (Marathon gasoline stations), Scott Riggs (Valvoline), and Juan Pablo Montoya (Havoline/Texaco).[9]

There is, here, another instance of a breakdown between the signifier and the signified (Jameson, 1991), in which logos, trademarks, and brand names appear disjointed from the referent; leaving only an assemblage of images with no rational meaning or understanding. To unravel these integuments, we must then return ourselves to the referent and contextually map the meanings concealed within these discursive practices and material realities.

Inside the racetrack gates such as those in Phoenix or Dover, NASCAR constituents exist under the corporate monolith of a conspicuous Sunoco neon-sign looming large in the racetrack's infield.[10] The beacon illuminates an authority that disciplines consumptive practices. It is difficult not to gaze upon this fixture during the race as its strategic location interrupts your following of cars circling the track lap after lap. At this track in particular, our view of some of the racetrack is actually obstructed by the enormous Sunoco logo. The effectiveness of this commercial authority is everywhere apparent in the purchasing practices of NASCAR patrons. There is much research regarding the highly correlative consumptive allegiances between NASCAR sponsors and subjects (Levin, Beasley, & Gilson, 2008), and we discuss elsewhere the surplus value impetus of the NASCAR sponsorship-matchup process (Braunstein, Newman, & Beissel, 2008). Cynthia Archer, Sunoco's vice president of Marketing and Development, confirms the corporation's purchase-driven intentions, "Racing is our core business, fuel is one of the components of what we do and Sunoco is a recognized leader in providing racing fuel. NASCAR fans will go out of their way to patronize companies that sponsor the sport. This is a particularly important sponsorship because it's a persuasive sponsorship. It's a terrific position to be in" (quoted in Mathis, 2004, p. 2).

We found the presence of Sunoco decals on spectator vehicles to be extensive as we toured tailgating locales and campervan zones on racetrack grounds. It soon came to our attention that these stickers were part of Sunoco's *market activation* strategy where supporters emblazoned the tow bars of their Ford F-150s with Sunoco's logos at the fortuitous prospect of a cash prize. The corporate power prescribed in a *petrol disciplinarity* contributes further to framing stock car auto racing as a social, cultural, and material solemnity. The holistic saturation of petrol logos, trademarks, and signifiers in NASCAR domains, a sporting (sub)cultural experience dependent on an abundance of petrol, and the *conspicuous consumption of petrol*—and the unequivocal consumerist loyalties therein—coalesce in forming a *stock car racing culture of petrol euphoria*.

The material (cultural) production of stock car surplus value elicits a twofold contradiction between the forces of production and productive relation on the one hand, and conditions of production commodity relation, on the other. In the former, the production of commodities (racing spectacle) requires an endless abundance of raw materials (petroleum, motor oil, fuel additives) for advancement in the commodity process. Though the exact amount of on-track petroleum consumption in NASCAR's highest touring series is concealed by Sunoco and NASCAR executives, it is estimated that the sum exceeds 200 million gallons per annum (Gerard, 2005).[11] Missing from these calculations are the millions of gallons of jet fuel used to transport drivers, teams, owners, and administrators on private planes and the excess of petroleum utilized by fleets of diesel-powered, 18-wheel stock car transporters to deliver the transportable NASCAR spectacle to its weekly destination. Moreover, this does not include the amount of fuel required to bring tens of thousands of large SUVs, pick-up trucks, pop-up campers, and mobile homes to each race.[12]

The forces of production and productive relations (fan euphoria of petrol excess) that exist internal to the (re)production of NASCAR capital accumulation thus objectify what Karl Polanyi (1944/2001) identified as a *limit to growth*, where the very act of (re)production destroys or impairs its own means of production in the compounding of resource scarcity. Which is to say, high-profile stock car auto racing cannibalizes its own circulation of capital, and, more importantly, hastens an impending global petroleum shortage for wider systems of capitalist production. Paradoxically, this internal contradiction is contrasted with its dialectic reciprocal—the external conditions of capitalist production. The pollution of the natural environment and contamination of the Earth's atmosphere threaten the productive conditions (natural features yet to be appropriated for commodity production, but treated as such) that allow for capital accumulation.[13] NASCAR's history in this disjuncture is compounded by a near 50-year commitment to environmentally toxic lead-based gasoline products.[14] This deep-rooted devotion to poisoning the greater environment damages not only its own ecological sustainability, but as the Environmental Protection Agency (EPA) notes, proliferates airborne particles of leaded gasoline that can cause neurological damage and mood swings, especially in children. This places drivers, pit crew members, the hundreds of thousands of supporters attending, and the residents nearby (who may or may not even be supporters of stock care racing) at substantial risk (Gerard, 2005).

It can, therefore, be asserted that stock car auto racing impairs or destroys at one and the same time its own *(future) conditions of production* and *the health of capital's productive labor power*. More critically, the *celebration of petrol excess* subverts the reproductive qualities of the conditions of production. Insofar as NASCAR is (1) inextricably linked with, and reliant-upon, a petroleum surplus for its own production, and (2) a cultural domain for the ritualistic celebration of petrol consumerism, NASCAR will eventually enter into its own crisis of capital—if it hasn't already.[15]

Part II

MILITARIZING NASCAR NATION

> NASCAR has draped itself even more in the American flag since the tragedies of 9/11 and the outbreak of war in Iraq in March 2003. At racetracks today, during the prerace rituals there are always multiple representatives of the American armed services on display, always a military color guard carrying the flag, and a military fly-over during the national anthem. Patriotism is one of the values NASCAR tries to emulate for its fans and arouse in its fans—those in person, those listening on the radio, and those watching the race on television.
>
> —Hugenberg & Hugenberg (2008, p. 648)

The history of petroleum overdependence (as a resource fueling broader systems of capital accumulation) and widespread anxieties over its global scarcity foregrounds both concerns for the state of twenty-first century American empire and the geopolitical militarism *it necessitates*. The "Global War on Terror" espoused by George W. Bush and his acolytes obscures the commercial and corporate interests that lie in part behind these movements: the tactical procurement of world oil reserves; the protection of existing domestic capital markets; and the establishment of global capital markets through acts of privatization and deregulation (Harvey, 2003, 2005; Klein, 2007; Phillips, 2006; Rutledge, 2005).

The sobering events of 9/11 jolted an already alarming (global) capital market recession and economic downturn that began earlier that year (Chernick, 2005; Langdon, McMenamin, & Krolik, 2002). U.S. financial systems were already experiencing many of the telltale signs of economic crisis: rising rates of unemployment; corporate scandals; accounting failures; spiraling international debts; Wall Street contraction; and escalating fears of economic insecurity and uncertainty (Harvey, 2005). And, quite obviously, the terror attacks further compounded these problems. When the U.S. stock market reopened on September 18, 2001, the Dow Jones Industrial Average fell 684 points (or 7.1 percent) amidst panics of global security, financial market instabilities, and downward-spiraling consumer confidence; the then-largest one-day point-loss in history and the worst trading week since the Great Depression (Garcia, 2001).[16]

In order to resuscitate the failing economy, the Federal Reserve issued interest rate cuts four times in a span of three months (Wesbury, 2006) and injected over $100 billion per day to protect financial markets. $15 billion of public funds was funneled directly to private enterprise—the airline industry (Makinen, 2002). Soon after the attacks, *homeland security* and *terror industries* (Giroux, 2004b) were formed, opening up trillions of dollars in taxpayer funds to corporate arms of the military-industrial-complex. The American public was encouraged by the commander in chief to do its part; they could best confront the enemy by arming themselves with their most dependable weapon: credit cards. These consumerist mobilizations, specifically involving the airline and travel/tourism industry, were best reflected in George W. Bush's consumption-laden post-September 11 declaration: "[O]ne of the great goals of this nation's war [against terrorism] is to restore public confidence in the airline industry. It's to tell the traveling public: Get on board. Do your business around the country. Fly and enjoy America's great destination spots. Get down to Disney World in Florida. Take your families and enjoy life, the way we want it to be enjoyed" (see "Bush Urges American to Fly," 2001).

While steadying domestic markets involved taxpayer subsidies and consumer (over)spending, foreign policy was directed toward protecting vulnerable petrol markets and energy resources (Phillips, 2006). That turn, which was predictable based on the nation's "intense interest to [Dick] Cheney and the Bush Administration" (Engdahl, 2004, p. 249), was toward Iraq—a country long-fixated upon by neo-conservatives seeking to "stabilize" its theocratic and political systems and in so doing better manage its petroleum resources as they made their way to market. And, as Noam Chomsky (2007) notes, "the 9/11 atrocities provided an opportunity and pretext to implement long-standing plans to take control of Iraq's immense oil wealth, a central component of the Persian Gulf resources that the State Department, in 1945, described as a 'stupendous source of strategic power, and one of the greatest material prizes in world history'" (p. 8).[17]

Even prior to the 2000 election, the soon-to-be cabinet members in the Bush's administration were entrenched in oil and energy issues like no other administration that had come before it (Briody, 2004; Engdahl, 2004; Miller, 2006; Phillips, 2006).[18] Soon after taking office, one of Vice President Cheney's first tasks was to conduct a comprehensive review of U.S. energy policy in which he sought the assistance of The Baker Institute, a powerful (neo)conservative think tank whose board members included high-ranking oil executives at Shell, British Petroleum, ChevronTexaco, and importantly, fierce activists for peak oil, such as Michael Simmons (Engdahl, 2004; Kellner, 2003).[19] As early as the spring of 2001, well before the War in Iraq and the terror attacks of 9/11, Cheney's group combed maps of Iraqi oil fields to estimate exactly how much oil could reach markets through privatizing Iraqi oil fields that would in turn persuade other OPEC countries to open up their reserves to Western Oil Companies (Roberts, 2004). As Kevin Phillips (2006) notes, "Iraq became the prize piece needed to complete three interrelated Washington jigsaw puzzles: the rebuilding of Anglo-American oil-company reserves, transformation of Iraq into an oil protectorate-cum-military base, and reinforcement of the global hegemony of the U.S. dollar" (p. 76). In geopolitical terms, Iraq mattered because "whomever controlled the Middle East controlled the global oil spigot and whomever controlled the global oil spigot, controlled the global economy, at least for the near future" (Harvey, 2003, p. 19).[20] So not long after the events of September 11, 2001, provided an impetus, Iraq again found itself in conflict among a long line of military wars, political-conflicts and economic crises in the Middle East rooted in petroleum: Musaddeq in 1951, Suez in 1956, the Arab-Israeli wars of 1967 and 1973, the Iranian Revolution in 1979, the Iran-Iraq War of 1980–1988, the Iraqi invasion of Kuwait in 1990 (Kubursi, 2006).[21]

While U.S. petrol-military interventionism in the Middle East has an extensive history, what distinguishes the imperialist project of the new millennium is its execution under the precepts of neoliberalism. While in the first instance the *oil-national security complex* (Phillips, 2006) sat at the core of the invasion of Iraq, the conflict presented a green light for "liberating" markets around the world. In *The Shock Doctrine*, Naomi Klein (2007) suggests that intervention in Iraq is the geopolitical capstone of a nearly 50-year crusade to systematically privatize (and colonize) nation-state economies through what she terms *disaster capitalism*. She sees Freidman's utopian model as imposed through *shock therapy* programs allowing corporate sectors to handsomely profit off of large-scale privatization of previously public assets, removal of currency controls, and the liberalization of trade restrictions. Although often extolled by supporters (Ronald Reagan, George W. Bush, Margaret Thatcher) as a peaceful deliverance of personal freedom, liberty, and prosperity, Klein (2007) argues the contrary. In her view, the spreading of democracy and deregulated capitalism relies on tactics of propaganda, coercion, torture, bloodshed, and genocide.

In the case of Iraq, Klein (2007) explains that "amid the weapons trade, the private soldiers, for-profit reconstruction and the homeland security industry, what has emerged as a result of the Bush administration's particular brand of post-September 11 'shock therapy' is a fully articulated new economy" (p. 14). Rather than repairing and rebuilding what once was, reconstruction in Iraq would, on the one hand, generate massive profits through the selling off of Iraqi property and infrastructures (power plants, oil facilities, and water treatment stations), and, on the other hand, afford a "clean slate" for commercial firms to access previously untapped Middle Eastern consumer markets. The chief architect for reconstruction in Iraq was former diplomat-turned-politico L. Paul Bremer, who oversaw the privatization and deregulation of virtually every state enterprise, opened up domestic industries to foreign firms and Iraqi banks to foreign control, and implemented a new corporate-friendly national flat tax (Harvey, 2005). The Bush administration's brand of reconstruction has been termed by Klein (2007) and Miller (2006) as an *Anti-Marshall Plan*—a complete inversion of the post–World War II plan for war recovery, whereby Iraqi assets were "sold-off" to U.S.-based multinationals while U.S. taxpayers simultaneously subsidized the reconstruction of Iraq's infrastructure (with most of the profits of course going to U.S. based multinationals).[22]

Although military outsourcing is nothing new (Briody, 2004), new millennium disaster capitalism cements a military-industrial-[Congressional-]complex that sustains the commercial interests of defense systems and weapons manufacturers (Lockheed Martin, Raytheon, Boeing, Northrop Grumman, Honeywell); private security companies (DynCorp, Blackwater/Xe); oil behemoths (Halliburton, British Petroleum, ExxonMobile); communication firms (Titan Corp; Hill & Knowlton); insurance conglomerates (AIG); and engineering firms (Bechtel Corporation, KBR, Inc.). With a surprising number of Department of Defense policymakers either board members, chairmen, trustees, or outright lobbyists in several of the above-mentioned corporations (Hossein-zadeh, 2006), "U.S. corporations like Halliburton and Bechtel were the recipients of no-bid—and therefore non-competitive—government contracts worth hundreds of millions of dollars with guaranteed profits" (Miller, 2006).[23] Expanding the contemporary military-industrial-complex thus became the Bush administration's cardinal function in mobilizing post-9/11 economic recovery through direct government spending on the military—to the tune of 44 percent of the fiscal year budget in 2004 (Hossein-zadeh, 2006)—and indirectly through privatizing and "liberating" nation-state economies and advancing profits of the war-dependant industries.[24]

PROBLEMATIZING MILITARISTIC CAPITAL

With these compulsions and political alignments in mind, we return here to theories on crisis formation to interpret the *new imperialism* and the surfacing of the military-industrial-complex as a consequence of neoliberalism's *crisis of capital (over)accumulation;* that which is inevitable, and can never be eliminated, in a capitalist mode of production. Following Harvey (1989, 2001b, 2007) as well as Paul Virilio (1977/2006), we have come to understand post-9/11 U.S.-sponsored military conflicts as a consequence of capitalism and the contradictions and crises that underpin it (see also Kellner, 1999; Luke & Tuathail, 2000). The logic is as follows: At the end of any circulation of capital, the capitalist is left with surplus capital relative to opportunities to employ that capital. A critical incongruence arises concerning the utility of this excess: How will this surplus be *profitably* "expressed, contained, absorbed, or managed in ways not to threaten capitalist social order" (Harvey, 1989, p. 181). Formations of surplus capital include an excess of commodities in the marketplace stemming from lack of effective demand; a surplus of funds available in the credit system marked by a monetary crisis or periods of inflation; and/or idle capacity in factories reflecting excessive productive capacity (Harvey, 2007). Crisis is thus a phase of devaluation and destruction of the capital surpluses that cannot be profitably absorbed (ibid.).[25]

In *Limits to Capital*, Harvey (2007) suggests that surplus capital is absorbed through spatial-temporal displacement—"the creation of the world market, foreign direct and portfolio investment, capital and commodity exports, and more brutally, the deepening and widening of *colonialism, imperialism and neo-colonialism*" (p. xxiv, emphases added). The (neo-conservative) U.S. Imperialism project and its "creative destruction" across geographical contexts is thus seen as an ephemeral, spatio-temporal "fix" to a crisis of (domestic) capital markets. As he explains "there is a deep and profound history of nations solving their domestic problems by foreign conquests or manufacturing foreign threats to consolidate solidarities at home" (p. 12). What gives Friedman-inspired *new imperialism* distinction from that in other epochs is the unique blend of "politics of state and empire" on the one hand and "the molecular process of capital accumulation in space and time" on the other (Harvey, 2005). This fusion, which Harvey (2003) terms *capitalist imperialism* and Jan Nederveen Pieterse (2006) deems *neoliberal empire* (as distinct from neoliberal globalization due to the *necessary* involvement of military armatures and functionaries), is fundamentally about the restoration and reconstruction of class power for the capitalist elite.

In *The Terror of Neoliberalism*, Henry Giroux (2004b) exposes the implicit power relations in neoliberal empire by arguing "neoliberal ideology, on the one hand pushes for the privatization of all non-commodified public spheres and the upward distribution of wealth. On the other hand, it supports policies that increasingly militarize facets of public space in order to secure the privileges and benefits of the corporate elite and ultra-rich" (p. xxiv). The widespread militarization of public spaces and social order is a central element to what Giroux (2004b) calls *proto-fascism*, or the growing authoritarianism in (post)modern American culture (p. 32). Viewing life as a permanent form of warfare (again, see Virilio's [1977/2006] work on this), *proto-fascism* is a reconstitution of old fascist elements that are produced and legitimated under the unique conditions of neoliberalism.[26] And while "old fascism's" overt militarization of public space usually meant that public action was subjugated by military surveillance and control, today's military-market fascism is more subtle and nuanced, but no less problematic (as we illustrate in the following section). The effects of proto-fascism are very much the same as those of its antecedent: militarization of public spaces in the post-9/11 context narrows community, suppresses dissent, and concentrates political power that challenges democracy and leads to a rise of a national security state (Giroux, 2004b). The distinction, perhaps, lies in the formation of subjectivities; whereby explicit subjectification has been replaced by technologies of subjectivity—often seen as the freedom to choose militarized encounters.

Giroux (2004b) sees militarization as a "powerful cultural politics that works its way through everyday life spawning particular notions of masculinity, sanctioning war as spectacle, and using fear as a central formative component in mobilizing an effective investment in militarization" (p. 33). A constant military presence is circulated through a "military-industrial-entertainment-complex" in which militarized values, symbols, and images underpin social institutions, the media, corporations, commercial goods and services, and popular forms of entertainment (ibid.). Such a dynamic has lead Arundhati Roy (2003) to state that America's entertainment industry is becoming not just more violent, but more warlike; an unsurprising turn, in her view, given that "The news and entertainment system in America is almost entirely controlled by a few major corporations: AOL-Time Warner, Disney, Viacom, News Corporation." Such a militarization of the entertainment economy effectively "functions as a mode of public pedagogy, instilling the values and the aesthetic of militarization through a variety of pedagogical sites and cultural venues" (Giroux, 2003, p. 40). In what follows we explore this militarization of sport-entertainment experiences and spaces.

THE MILITARY STATE (OF NASCAR NATION)

We have thus far argued that militarizing mass culture and entertainment industries relies on the use of cultural signs, spaces, and celebrities to solidify and advance *neoliberal empire* (Hardt & Negri, 2000; Wood, 2003). To this end, we now point to the ways in which the stock car spectacle has become inundated with petrol-thirsty, hyper-militaristic, neocon-imperialist cultural politics as delivered through the experiences and discourses of stock car auto racing. Specifically, we explore the cultural symbols, normative practices, and social discourses that mobilize consent for *petrol imperialism* and the *military-industrial-entertainment-complex* at home and abroad.

Just as with evangelical Christianity and with political conservatism, perhaps no other North American sport rivals NASCAR in its explicit ties to the military. Nearly half a dozen race teams are financed to some degree by the Department of Defense (c. 2010); that is, all five branches of the military and the Army National Guard sponsor NASCAR teams (even the U.S. Border Patrol has a sponsorship agreement).[27] In addition, military institutions such as the Veterans of Foreign Wars, American Legion, and Paralyzed Veterans of America have at one time or another had their signs and symbols located on the bumpers of stock cars (Hillhouse, 2007). Sponsors such as the U.S. Army spend an estimated $16 million per annum on NASCAR-related promotions—justifying such expenditures as a profitable investment based on the quantity of television exposure Mark Martin's car yielded at the time, and the exposure generated by Ryan Newman's car around 2010 (Bernstein, 2005). With the total annual marketing and recruiting budget for the five branches of the military surpassing $7 billion (Vogel, 2009), such a yearly, multimillion dollar investment into NASCAR is a low-risk, high-reward corporate agreement. Army National Guard Lt. General Clyde A. Vaughn testifies to the symmetries between NASCAR and the Army's core consumer bloc:

> We have to recruit some 70,000 Army Guard soldiers a year. The active Army has to recruit 80,000. This is big business... It just so happens that the strong point of recruiting the force happens to be

exactly where the "NASCAR Nation" is. You don't have to put two and two together too many times to figure this out. (quoted in Pate, 2008, p. 2)[28]

Prowar sponsorships extend far beyond the individual branches of the military. For example, several NASCAR teams have in recent years been financed by disaster capitalism's most profitable companies, including Blackwater Inc. (now known as Xe), Force Protection, and BMAR and Associates (Bernstein, 2005).

At the 2007 Dodge Avenger 500 in Darlington, South Carolina, we noted the prominence of one particular private contractor, Force Protection. Making their debut as a primary sponsor on the #11 CJM Motorsports Chevrolet in NASCAR's second division on the track, the Iraq War specialist-firm featured prominently off the track as they (1) plastered their logo and slogan "Racing to protect our troops today and tomorrow" on a conspicuous billboard adjoining to the speedway; (2) hosted a "Ground Zero Museum" to exhibit (and commodify!) powerful images and photographs of the September 11 terror attacks; and (3) showcased their ballistic- and blast-protected armored vehicles that the corporation proudly dubs an "SUV on Steroids" (Forceprotection.net, 2007). And as we noted, spectators patiently waited in long queues to snap a photograph of the massive six-wheeled camouflaged war machines that were positioned in their strategic, "can't miss" location guarding the entrance to the racetrack.[29]

As if these ubiquitous military sponsorships are not enough, themes of armed service are inscribed in the deportmental realm—as NASCAR drivers are leveraged as representative embodiments of military soldiers and recruiters. Hero-drivers such as Mark Martin (former driver of the #01, Army-sponsored car) or Dale Earnhardt, Jr., (current driver of the #88 Army National Guard car) are often used in promotional and recruiting materials. Martin described his Army sponsorship this way:

> Our team, myself included, we put great value on things like mental, physical and emotional toughness...and the values that our soldiers have and that the Army instils in our soldiers, like dignity and honesty, are values that are very important for me as well. So it has been one of the highlights of my career to be part of the U.S. Army team. (quoted in Pedley, 2008, p. 1)

As Martin attenuates, drivers become representative embodiments of soldiers as they refer to themselves as warriors and adopt a rugged militarized mindset, and use their celebrity and powerful brand star-power to influence young, white, Christian males to consider a career in the American armed forces. They "play the part" by wearing camouflaged uniforms representing military fatigues covered in the corporate logos of America's core defense groups. Their celebrity images appear in commercials, print advertising, and music videos aimed at targeting young men and women for enlistment.

Furthermore, the Army uses sponsorships of celebrity-drivers for more than just publicity; drivers like Mark Martina and Ryan Newman are expected not only to bring "future soldiers" to NASCAR races, but also to actually get these recruits to enlist in active duty (Bernstein, 2005). Whereas traditional military recruiters spend approximately 30 hours per successful recruit (Kitfield, 2007), NASCAR drivers have become a more effective and efficient means of recruitment (and particularly as the protracted Iraq and Afghanistan wars exhaust reserves). With the localness derived from their "good ole southern boy" representations in the media, drivers are a much more culturally effective means to attract potential. In the final years of the George W. Bush presidency, for example, NASCAR's most currently beloved icon, Dale Earnhardt, Jr., had a working agreement with the Navy in which he had quotas for the total enlistments he himself could generate (Faram, 2008a): For a $6.5 million race team sponsorship and $800,000 of personal endorsements for Earnhardt, NASCAR's well-paid "military recruiter" was obligated to solicit military training recruits to "enlist" in the "Dale Earnhardt Jr. Navy Division" and report for Recruit Training Command in Great Lakes, Illinois (Cragg, 2008; Faram, 2008b).

In 2007, when responding to a NASCAR fan's question of whether Earnhardt holds a moral responsibility to "speak out" about military issues—specifically the deployment of the National Guard or quality of care issues at Walter Reed Medical Center—"Junior" responded:

> I'm not in a position to blast opinions on anything like that. I mean, certainly when it comes to knowledge of those various and specific situations that you just spoke of, I'm not intelligent enough about them independently to be able to sit here and think that I would be able to tell a cameraman or a print reporter what I thought should be done. (Transcript, 2007)[30]

Echoing similar evasions like those by athletes from Charles Barkley ("I am not a role model") to Michael Jordan, Junior effectively positioned himself as an empty-vessel whose convictions were aligned not by careful consideration of an issue (or even brand) but of the almighty dollar. In fact, Douglas Kellner's critique of Jordan rings true of Junior in that he has effectively "abrograted his political and social responsibilities in favor of...a mega-stock portfolio" of sponsorship agreements. However, while many athletes and entertainers certainly may endorse various brands based on the highest bidder[31]—and do so without regard to the personal or the political—the danger of Junior's position is that supporting Coca-Cola over Pepsi or PowerAde over Gatorade *isn't a life-and-death decision.*

Just as the umbrella of Confederate flags and corporate logos cloaks most stock car spaces, these same spectacularized sporting spaces are well protected "on-the-ground" by a mantle of war machines and war-ready bodies. The latest military technologies—from camouflaged tanks, to stealth bombers, to military choppers, and armored humvees—are omnipresent in veritable warzones of NASCAR Nation. Once inside the track gates, fans are confronted by military processions honoring military servicemen, the infield conduction of *faux* combat training exercises, military fighter-jet flyovers, and a company of tanks, machine guns, and missile launchers (yes!), which are strategically interdispersed throughout the superspeedway spaces. These politically charged NASCAR spectacles became a fertile environment from which Bush II, Dick Cheney, Donald Rumsfeld, and other government functionaries manufactured consent for military intervention in Iraq and its attendant petrol desires. To further elucidate this point, we offer the following critical investigation of the everyday NASCAR experience. In so doing, we rely heavily on our field journal to direct us through a hypermilitarized public space and cultural experience.

Vignette I: "Now Hiring"

Earlier in the book we detailed the mobile commerce villages that enclose race venues. Passing through this territory, one is immediately confronted with a preponderance of militarized amusements, combat spectacles, war rituals, and corporate signifiers. In the mobile commerce centers, the military's presence is ubiquitous; it is hard to escape the tanks, planes, humvees, and newest warfare machinery. As our experiences at the Talladega Superspeedway in October 2010, illustrate,

> Amidst the clamoring throngs of bodies winding their ways among team/driver merchandise trailers and corporate partner sites organized by such entities as Sprint, Camel, Aaron's, and AMP Energy, stands the U.S. Army's interactive "Strength in Action" experience/venue. Arranged in a U-shape layout, there are not only informational tents

staffed by Army personnel (representing "Army Health Care," ROTC, etc.), but also a 30-foot tall wall-climb "victory tower," a physical training station with pull-up bar and push-up mat (complete with requisite drill instructors dispensing T-shirts for meeting certain performance indicators), a station with numerous pieces of weaponry and body armor laid out to be "played" with (see Figure 7 below) and two large-scale interactive venues: a group-oriented "Army Team Challenge" station (think: laser tag), and a helicopter-based flight simulator. Ryan Newman's "U.S. Army"-sponsored car is stationed in the center of the space, replete with corporate logos for Coors Light, DirecTV, Goodyear, Tissot, Sunoco, and others. The theme of this particular venue, judging by the electronic signs in the area, is "U.S. Army: Now Hiring," implying that while the U.S. economy, and in particular its employment opportunities, has been at a veritable stand-still, the Army (and the Armed Forces in general) remains a viable career choice.

In order for spectators to participate in the "experience," they must first go through a faux "recruiting" process at a check-in point staffed by young men and women attired in black GoArmy.com T-shirts. Upon providing a driver's license or other form of identification, a question-and-answer process takes place wherein the new recruit is asked questions about age, health, education level, and whether or not

"The Army Experience," Now Hiring (Talladega, AL, October 2010)

he or she is interested in receiving additional information from the Army regarding any of its programs. Of note, a laminated placard behind the check-in counter (which we were able to photograph—it was in plain sight) outlines "ID Badge Priority Indicators," breaking them down into "HOT: Priority 1, Priority 2, Priority 3, AMEDD, and ROTC," and providing direction for the "recruiters."[32] At the point of giving details about my education, the woman behind the desk says "good for you" and proceeds to skip over several sections; she clicks the "not interested in receiving information" radio button on her screen without even asking; clearly, she is following a demographic profile script.[33]

In line to experience what the flight simulator has to offer, the crowd of participants is diverse in both age and gender, as well as outward signifiers of differing levels of class privilege: The two men in front of me are late-thirties/early-forties, clean cut, wearing upscale name-branded buttoned-down shirts, blue jeans, and loafers. They intermittently engage in conversation about their work at a downtown Birmingham, Alabama, law firm, between individual calls taken on their cell phones. In front of them is a couple with two teen-aged daughters, both of whom are eager to "go for a ride" on the flight simulator. Behind me is a father-son combination wearing faded NASCAR shirts and denim shorts; the man has leathery skin and chiseled forearms, features suggestive of a career spent working with his hands in the outdoor sun (possibly in construction).

When my turn in the simulator comes after about a 30-minute wait in line, it's a rather straightforward experience lasting approximately 2 minutes. The visual imagery consists of two helicopter attack runs; one on a merchant ship located on an inland body of water surrounded by drab desert dunes, the other on a warehouse; both utilize gunfire and explosions. Although no faces are visible, nor are there any identifying markers for country of origin on any objects viewed, the implication is quite clear: at best, this is a simulated "training" mission for completing similar tasks on the battlefield, or it is supposed to be an *actual* battlefield, in which case living human beings are likely to be on board the ship or in the warehouse that is fired upon and destroyed. And this in the name of military recruiting, fun, or both?[34]

* * *

The promilitary activities, coupled with the overwhelming dominance of neo-conservative republicanism throughout the NASCAR spectacle, parallel quite nicely with Debord's (2002) notion that

> The spectacle, like modern society itself, is at once united and divided. The unity of each is based on violent divisions. But when this contradiction emerges in the spectacle, it is itself contradicted by a reversal

of its meaning: the division it presents is unitary, while the unity it presents is divided (thesis #54).

In other words, the militarized sporting spectacles of NASCAR give iconographic licensure to spectacularized ideologies while concurrently offering only one reprieve from alienation therein—that of the collective, war-endorsing experiences of acting out membership in NASCAR Nation. The inescapable prowar, pro-Republican simulacrum of NASCAR space thus colonizes its inhabitants and offers the rites to a militaristic citizenship in "NASCAR Nation" (and thus an escape from isolation, or alienation), and thereby institutionalizes a division of real consequences and unreal sporting and warring imaginaries. Below we detail a series of spatial activities located in the raceway proper before, during, and after the event.

Once inside the superspeedway arena, the spectacle becomes even more combative. Most on-track prerace processions consist of the latest in warfare machinery, combat artillery, and frontline battle technologies circling the racetrack in front of hundreds of thousands of military nationalists. Heavily armored tanks and combat fighting vehicles with large caliber machine guns, rotating turrets, and secondary machine guns "log laps" around high-banked military cathedrals. Steel reinforced Humvees and military supply trucks transport troops and military cargo before the citizens of NASCAR Nation. Low-flying airplanes, jets, and helicopters are integral to prerace ceremonies, stimulating emotional fervor for the military's power and precision. For many NASCAR spectators, the prerace fighter-jet flyover is the most powerful and memorable moment of a NASCAR race—perhaps even more than the waving of the checkered flag (to signify the race winner). As we noted,

> The F-16 jets fly so low that we can practically see the pilots themselves and the jet engines are so loud that we go deaf temporarily. There is a split second that paralyzes you from head-to-toe as a sensation of fear overcomes you. One nationalist sitting behind us, who it appears took particular joy in this encounter, exclaimed "Git-R-Done!"[35]

Before many races, the military bodies of the "few and the proud" are paraded around the racetrack in their battle fatigues and warring garb often patronizing their civic duty as they participate in the presentation of colors, conduct rifle drill exercises, serve as honorary "grand marshals," and frequently sing the national anthem. Attending a stock car race in Charlotte, North Carolina, what many insiders consider to be the hometown of NASCAR, we witnessed an armed military battalion marching past the front-stretch grandstand to the adulation and cheers of spectator/consumers. It was soon announced over the racetrack sound system that these soldiers represented the highest caliber rifleman in the Army and proceeded to conduct their "award-winning" rifle drill exercise for NASCAR fans in attendance.

Similarly, at a 2008 event in Richmond, Virginia, NASCAR held the Army Reserve Centennial Commemoration at their Chevy Rock & Roll 400 where the Army Reserve Drill Sergeant of the Year and Major General's from the Army Reserve were paraded around the short-track ("Army Reserve Centennial Commemoration at NASCAR's Chevy Rock & Roll 400," 2008). The same venue a few years earlier held a memorial for the youngest casualty in the War on Terror as state representatives presented the mother of the deceased hometown soldier with an honorable resolution in front of 100,000 sympathetic spectators (Thurmond, 2005). At the Pennsylvania 500 in 2007, NASCAR held a swearing-in ceremony for recruits from multiple military branches and donated 10,000 tickets to wounded service members and their families (Kruzel, 2007).

The France family and other members of the militarized NASCAR faction have often been praised for this type of commitment to honoring and celebrating the sacrifices of military personnel (Branham, 2010; Fielden, 2004; Smith, 2002).[36] Expounding on these stock car racing/military synergies, organization president Mike Helton said: "The NASCAR fan, the NASCAR competitor and the industry in general is *Americana*, and I don't know anything more American than American soldiers...Whenever we have the opportunity to be associated with and honor the military, we take advantage of it" (quoted in Bernstein, 2005, p. 1). More critically though, it becomes clear that NASCAR's motives are for economic capitalization; the intent to "stimulate consumption" by exploiting soldiers and other military personnel for their profitable symbolic value among the stridently conservative consumer base.

Consider a prerace event in Topeka, Kansas: the event organizers directed a simulated aerial assault mission on Kansas Speedway's infield grass, which culminated with the event's "pace car" being delivered to the track by a massive MH-47 Chinook helicopter (Pedley, 2008). This, however, was not the first time in which NASCAR ritualistically celebrated the "shock and awe" of America's armed forces. "Humpy" Wheeler, longtime corporate sales and promotional czar of Lowe's Motorspeedway in Charlotte, North Carolina—commonly referenced as the "P.T. Barnum of NASCAR" for his boundary pushing promotions—conducted on-track promotions where he produced a reenactment of the U.S. military's 1983 invasion of Grenada and certain aspects of the first Gulf War, which featured soldiers rappelling from helicopters and launching howitzers loaded with blanks at 200,000 spectators on Memorial Day Weekend (Rodman, 2008). And "according to media members who were privy to the plan that never saw the light of day was a proposed promotion whereby Wheeler would have announced that the late Saddam Hussein had been captured and was located somewhere in Lowe's Motor Speedway's infield—where his capture would result in a sizeable bounty for some fan" (Rodman, 2008).[37]

Through these militarized NASCAR armatures, young bodies are both located within the spatial discourses of "the cause" and serve to bring the *"spectacle of war" to life* (see Debord, 2002). Yet when confronted with this strange paradox of spectacle, interpellation, and "service/sacrifice," a critical awareness eludes many within NASCAR Nation. As one NASCAR fan put it, "I think it's great how NASCAR honors the military and its servicemen [*sic*]. Soldiers are appreciated here more than anywhere else in America." We might surmise that these "logistics of perception," as Virilio (2005) would have it, normalize not only the spectacle of war, but its co-present place within the commercialized spectacles of the sporting nation. Most problematically, these logistics of perception within the militarized NASCAR spectacle reauthorize dominant public pedagogies, if not *public ontologies*, of how we come to define the value(s) and precariousness of life.

Vignette II: "The Induction"

The Veterans Day prerace ceremonies held in conjunction with the 2010 Kobalt Tools 500 at Phoenix International Raceway is one such example of the public pedagogies of war at play in NASCAR Nation. Our fieldnotes from that sun-soaked late-autumn day reveal the ways in which the spectacle of war and the frames by which NASCAR Nation comes to understand the precariousness of life collide on the racetrack:

> Today's race is of considerable importance, as the Chase for this year's Sprint Cup is the "closest" ever. Three drivers, Jimmie Johnson, Kevin Harvick, and points-leader Denny Hamlin, all have a legitimate chance to win the championship—a topic of considerable discussion in surrounding campgrounds and RV parks prior to the race. Just as we've taken our seats for today's race, the event's emcee announces that "today's race will be preceded by a special military induction

ceremony." A few minutes later, and approximately 30 minutes prior to the start of the race, NASCAR officials and military commanders assemble on a stage positioned within the infield, just below the track's finish line. One-by-one, dozens of new Army enlistees—many of whom had agreed to join only earlier today [at one of the "Army Experience" enrollment centers described above]—are processed across the stage. The event's chief narrator reminds the audience that these soon-to-be-soldiers are "following in the footsteps of the great veterans who are in attendance at today's race." The name of each young man (all of today's enlistees are men) is announced over a sound system that can be heard from miles away. Each announcement is followed by the individual's hometown and favorite driver. The emcee makes a point to acknowledge the courage and age of a seventeen year-old who had just enlisted today. The emcee then briefly interviews a young Army man and Kyle Bush fan, concluding with the declaration that "Kyle's able to do what he does because you do what you do!" (to which the tens of thousands of spectators rousingly applaud).

After each young man makes his way across the stage, taking the proverbial steps from adolescence to the (battlefield) proving grounds

Armed Forces at NASCAR (Talladega, AL, October 2010)

of contemporary American manhood, the emcee introduces a number of special guests who will witness today's induction. First, we are introduced to a veteran soldier whose efforts in "protecting the sensitive desert environment by disarming 4,000 field weapons (land mines) and the recycling of 500 tons of metal" resulted in a "Global War on Terrorism" Ribbon award. Another soldier present at the event was lauded for his efforts in "The Battle of Fallujah." We are finally introduced to a current military man and local football stand-out, who will be "fighting for freedom" but also will be playing in the U.S. Army All-American Bowl later in the year—and we are encouraged to support him by watching the game.

After the men were sworn into active duty (a surprisingly brief and modest one minute passage), NASCAR legend Richard Petty was invited to the microphone to say a few words. Petty noted his own racing team's partnership with the Paralyzed Veterans of America, and then implored race fans to "stand up during the [upcoming] national anthem, and wave your flags, and really get patriotic!" His team's driver, Elliott Sadler, followed 'the King' and offered a brief message, saying "thanks to the people who have sacrificed so that we can do what we're doing here today." Following Petty and Sadler, and to great ovation, U.S. Senator John Kyl, who in the weeks following the race would become the face of resistance toward the U.S.-Russia START treaty (meant to curb the proliferation of nuclear weapons) and a chief antagonist of Federal aid to support 9/11 First Responders' health care, then offered a few words of encouragement for the drivers and urged fans to support the military, explaining that we owe them "a debt of gratitude."

Following the out-procession of the military inductees and the introduction of the drivers, a local group performed the national anthem for nearly 100,000 flag-waving NASCAR fans. The conclusion of the anthem, as with most races, was capped off by a military flyover to the delights of the vociferously approving spectators. Then, somewhat strangely, the loudspeakers began to play the song "Let's Get It Started" by the Black Eyed Peas (whose politics and demographics tend to sit outside the norms of this NASCAR space) and then oddly followed that song up with Los Angeles-based Rage Against the Machine's "Guerilla Radio"—both the song and the band unquestionably standing in opposition to dominant cultural and racial politics of NASCAR Nation. (We can't help wondering what would come if this song were to somehow bring together 100,000 NASCAR fans and 100,000 Zapatista-supporting Rage Against the Machine fans into the same physical space.)

*   *   *

This spectacle, wrought with its many and wide-reaching contradictions, brings us to our key point: Through its militarized spectacle—spatially and phantasmagorically dislocated from the human suffering created by war and the surplus value-combativeness of global neoliberalism—NASCAR presents what Judith Butler (2009) might refer to as a "new body ontology" (of sporting fandom); one that obscures, or reframes, the "precariousness, vulnerability, injurability, interdependency, exposure, bodily persistence, desire, work, and the claims to language and social belonging" (p. 2). Within the national narratives pervading both NASCAR spaces and the broader national landscape from which they are carved, these mediated, almost prosthetic bodies of the national cause (and their soon-to-be increased precariousness), are positioned as Right in the pursuits of a fusionist construction of manifest destiny. In her moral polemic, *Frames of War,* Butler (2009) argues that these national imaginings "work" in part by

> producing and sustaining a certain version of the subject.... what gives power to their version of the subject is precisely the way in which they are able to render the subject's own destructiveness *righteous* and its own destructibility *unthinkable.* (p. 47, emphases original)

It could thus be argued that, following Butler, NASCAR authorizes a particular understanding of the nature of human life (as it relates to war and accumulation), popularized through spectacularized pedagogies that aggrandize a posthuman simulacrum (Baudrillard, 1995); which is to say, a 17-year-old Dale Earnhardt, Jr.,-supporting body is not conceived as a body that might produce death (or become dead), but of an extension of naturalized (militarized) national sporting *epistemes.* These young men come to represent American nationalism and (neo-conservative) exceptionalism, but not the flesh processes by which these imaginary formations are made *real.* Moreover, we are made to think about the sustainability of human life not in terms of preventing ecological disaster or military ceasefire, but in ways where the military features largely in sustaining a particular version of human life—one defined by occupation, accumulation, and imperialism.

Through the processional of inducted bodies, we learn permanent war's *new bioethics* (Zylinska, 2007), one that normalizes war as a permanent state of the nation and does so without publically weighing its corporeal capital expenditures against the surplus capital and geopolitical gains being sought. To do so would be to pause, to take notice of the intersecting spectacles of capital, corporality, and war. And as Virilio (1991) cleverly surmises in *The Aesthetics of Disappearance,* there is a "social and political role to stopping." *In both the market and in war* speed is violence, speed is power, and in technical terms, speed is the transfer of energy. Regarding the former, Virilio states:

> Speed is violence. The most obvious example is my fist. I have never weighed my fist, but it's about four hundred grams. I can make this fist into the slightest caress. But if I project it at great speed, I can give you a bloody nose. You can easily see that it's the distribution of mass in space that makes all the difference. (Virilio & Lotringer, 1983, p. 45)

We can surmise from the dromological "epistemo-techniques" (Virilio & Lotringer, 1983, p. 47) at work within the NASCAR spectacle that to bring the proverbial fist to a halt, even in the seemingly innocuous domestic sporting space, would be to abandon the impetuses from which the fist is thrust. To pause and think about death, or to publically contemplate the reasons for war, or even to offer counterpedagogies such as those perfectly articulated in the lyrics to "Guerilla Radio" would interrupt the visceral, emotive, and public *dromos* and *dramaturgy* that military officials, corporate capitalists, and NASCAR officials had essentially "conspired" to orchestrate. At that moment, with flags aflutter and anthemic echoes in the air, there was *beauty* in war (and in its articulations to the liberty-seeking projections of a nation and its hero-mercenaries).

Yet had intermediaries not stopped the aforementioned Rage Against the Machine song just before its lyrics were introduced, the mood would have likely changed. In its lyrics, the song speaks to the construction of a false reality through the spectacle, one that serves the interests of oil-seeking monopoly capitalists and the military-industrial-complex. "Guerilla Radio," then, is an alternative to the mediums through which the "masses" engage the spectacles of war, or petrol empire, and global neoliberalism. In his words, Rage Against the Machine lyricist Zac de la Rocha complicates the spectacles of mass culture. While not naming NASCAR specifically, he would surely see the sport as an important platform through which these spectacular pedagogies are "transmitted." He describes a spectacle where the "fistagons" (a portmanteau descriptive of the military's, or U.S. Pentagon's, rule with an iron fist) have successfully usurped democratic process by gaining consent through various forms of cultural transmission—transmissions that naturalize war and the surplus value extracted from it.

But, of course, the song *was* stopped prior to its aural demonstration. This lyrical censorship is telling both in the order of simulacrum and in the aesthetics of militaristic pedagogy; a "hard hitting" song used to prolong the energy of an already-impassioned spectatorship, translating nationalistic and military fervor into a richer brand experience. Within this strategically orchestrated, highly militarized body ontology/pedagogy, the body persists within the social and economic conditions in which it is articulated (those that frame it), and produces those frames of subjectivity from which the bodily other is conceived, imagined, and detected. All the while, notions of security, prosperity, and freedom are leveraged onto the precarious human body, but not in ways that protect it, but rather in ways that reproduce the power relations acting upon it (relations of social class, of neoliberal biopolitics, etc.).

CODA

> Imperial democracy is state-sponsored violence masquerading as democracy.
> — Norman K. Denzin (2005, p. 274)

We have argued throughout this chapter that in the case of the United States, its military is being (partially) converted into a global oil-protection service leading to what Klare (2004) terms "energo-fascism"—the militarization of the global struggle over ever-diminishing supplies of energy.[38] In addition to leading to a transformation of the U.S. military into a global protectorate, energo-fascism consists, in part, of the "ruthless scramble among the great powers for the remaining oil, natural gas, and uranium reserves in Africa, Latin America, the Middle East and Asia accompanied by recurring military interventions" and "increased state intrusion into, and surveillance of, public and private life" in order to prevent destruction and sabotage of the pipelines fueling the U.S. petrol-driven economy.

We have also argued that the spaces and practices of NASCAR—revealed most notably by the location and promotion of the U.S. Army Experience on NASCAR grounds and the various other military armatures and processional spectacles performed throughout—are *necessarily* implicated in the militarization of sporting fandom, popular culture, and, by extension, everyday life. In other words, the use of popular NASCAR driver-celebrities in the recruitment of young men and women typifies—if not outright *promotes*—a condition whereby youth culture(s) experience the representational ecstasy of a militarized lifestyle (without the concomitant personal sacrifice) through a plurality of popular cultural commodities which include: children's toys (*G.I. Joes*); video games and combat simulators (*Call of Duty, Medal of Honor*, etc.); militarized fashion and patriotic clothing (camouflaged T-shirts, Armed Forces apparel, American flag-logoed hats, etc.); and Hollywood films and television programming (*Redacted, Generation Kill, Letters from Iwo Jima, Flags of our Fathers, 24, NCIS*, etc.). The implicit (or perhaps even explicit) military values that underpin these popular wares are "disseminated through a pedagogical force of popular culture itself, which has become a major tool used by the armed forces to educate young people about the ideology and social relations that inform military life—minus a few of the unpleasantries" (Giroux, 2004b, p. 42).

It is against this future-present that Giroux (2003) makes the case that "unless militarization is systematically exposed and resisted at every place where it appears in culture, it will undermine the meaning of critical citizenship and do great harm to those institutions that are central to a democratic society" (p. 44). Thus must we as critical readers and educators of history be vigilant against the forces of corporate fascism and state-sponsored violence and surveillance done in the name of freedom. As the distinguished American historian Howard Zinn (1997) once wrote, "There is no flag large enough to cover the shame of killing innocent people for a purpose which is unattainable" (p. 362). Furthermore, as Denzin and Giardina (2007) wrote, "we must question jingoistic, flag-waving displays of patriotic nationalism: Whose flag is being waved? What does it mean? How do we celebrate patriotism in this new war, when the war is taking away the very freedoms and ideals the flag stands for?" (p. 6). These are the kinds of questions pop culture satirist Sarah Vowell (2003) references in her missive about living in New York City in the aftermath of 9/11 when she writes:

> Immediately after the attack, seeing the flag all over the place was moving, endearing. So, when the newspaper I subscribe to published a full-page, full color flag to clip out and hang in the window, how come I couldn't? . . . [Because] once we went to war, once the president announced that we were going to retaliate against the "evildoers," then the flag again represented what it usually represents, the government. I think that's when the flags started making me nervous. (p. 158)

But in NASCAR Nation, this type of flag-waving seems to make no one nervous; indeed, in the post-9/11 condition, as Susan Willis (2002) points out, "By far the most preferred site for flag display is the automobile. Taped to the inside rear window, tattooed into the paint, or streaming from tailgate or antenna, the auto flag makes every roadway into a Fourth of July parade route" (p. 379). And, by extension, every NASCAR raceway and superspeedway as well. But they are parades without history, without critical memory; a place where gas-guzzling SUVs don American flag bumper stickers and gas-guzzling stock cars careen 'round tracks sporting U.S. Army-sponsored insignia emblazoned on their hoods. The irony is staggering.

Yet the center does not hold, and hasn't for a while. In the next chapter, we turn to the limits of NASCAR Nation, looking ahead to the future-present of the sport and, by extension, the context within which it is located, performed, and contested.

Selling Out NASCAR Nation

We have heretofore outlined that, on the balance sheet, NASCAR's salient place within the cultural politics of the (paleo-/neo-)conservative/neoliberal conjuncture produced tremendously lucrative brand equity during the Bush vicissitude. By the of the 2007 season, NASCAR's publically traded International Speedway Corporation reported revenues of $816.6 million, an increase of 2.3 percent from the previous year ("ISC Annual Report 2008," 2008). To sustain the rate of growth, NASCAR realized during the first eight years of the 2000s ($440m in revenues in 2000)—a rate that, at the time, would have left investors looking for approximately $2 billion in revenues from stock car-related organizations by 2020—NASCAR executives have in recent years actively sought new ways to enhance existing commodity streams and develop new forms of surplus value. Beyond most predictable twenty-first century techniques for enhancing sport-based accumulation (e.g., raising ticket prices, increasing commercial saturation in the form of new niche advertising and sponsorship, continuing the expansion of venue spaces), NASCAR executives have begun to more radically diversify their commodity wares and experiences. Under the direction of Brian France, the "new look" NASCAR has sought to expand its consumer markets both in the United States and abroad by opening new tracks, creating new events, expanding their international media coverage, and incorporating international celebrity-drivers into the stock car icon universe. In short, the sport that was once ridiculed as a bucolic, "redneck," "deep-fried" Southern pastime, has "gone mainstream" (if not global).

In the realm of popular media, celebrity-drivers such as Dale Earnhardt, Jr., have featured in music videos, on MTV's popular show *Cribs*, and in cameo roles on primetime network television programs.[1] The sport has also raised its nationwide brand profile through television series such as *NASCAR in Primetime* and *NASCAR Now*. And it has further increased its multiplatform exposure through a satellite radio channel dedicated solely to racing content, a plethora of stock car-related shows featured on the Speed Channel, and an expansive network of sport-related Internet sources.[2] On the ground, NASCAR has expanded the geographic reach of its sporting spectacles, advancing its Busch Series (the lower level of competition the organization also administers) events into Mexico City and Montreal as recently as 2008 (Perez, 2007; Stubbs, 2006).[3]

The latest "on-the-ground" development strategies employed by NASCAR, following their counterparts in North America's "Big Four" sport leagues, have focused on leveraging the sport's cultural import and mythologies of economic development[4] to subsidize the corporation's efforts to sustain its growth. In an attempt to penetrate the highly sought-after New York metropolitan marketplace, for example, NASCAR spent nearly five years (unsuccessfully) trying to obtain approval to build a new, semipublic-funded, 1.25-mile speedway oval on New York's Staten Island.[5] More recently, its officials have partnered with commercial real estate leviathan The Cordish Company to develop new commercial sites on existing ISC properties. Using the "Cordish model" of private property development through government subsidization, this new partnership enables NASCAR to redevelop existing brand armatures such as the NASCAR Café and NASCAR Sports Grille restaurants, enhance the consumer spaces at existing tracks by building new themed retailed spaces, casinos, and hotels in and around existing ISC tracks, and build new NASCAR-themed "entertainment" spaces with the help of taxpayer funding. Using a formula similar to that guiding the business operations of many of NASCAR's most prominent sponsors, NASCAR has sought to minimize both fixed and variable costs (through wage suppression and taxpayer subsidies) while simultaneously expanding its share of the North American sport marketplace. And much like its professional sport-league contemporaries (the NBA in China, the NFL in London, etc.), it has concurrently initiated a number of new initiatives to grow the NASCAR brand globally.

GOIN' GLOBAL

To achieve these expansionary ends, the racing league first opened up the narrowly defined and carefully articulated parameters of NASCAR Nation to broader (trans)national flows of capital and culture. For instance, when longtime title sponsor (and Southern business bastion) R. J. Reynolds chose to end its over 30-year title sponsorship, the most logical successor would have been a corporation whose values and mission would more explicitly overlap with the message of the distinctly American (South) sporting league. But in this case, telecommunications multinational NEXTEL (later supplanted as titular sponsor by Sprint following a merger between the two giants) took over the aforementioned title sponsorship of NASCAR's premier division; a $700 million exchange for 10 years' worth of sponsorship rights (Spencer & Grant, 2005).

As further illustration, between 1956 and 1980, every Winston Cup Champion was born in North Carolina, South Carolina, or Virginia (Alderman, Preston, Mitchell, Webb, & Hanak, 2001). However, none of the past 10 champions of NASCAR's top division hailed from a state inside the physical boundaries of the U.S. South. Moreover, 2007 marked the first time that a driver born in North Carolina, long considered the birthplace of NASCAR, failed to record a single victory on NASCAR's premier circuit (Mondaca, 2007). For the 2010 season, just 10 out of 42 full-time drivers in NASCAR's Sprint Cup Series claimed hometowns in states lying in the U.S. South (Nascar.com, 2010). Further, the current five-time defending champion (2006 through 2010 seasons) of NASCAR's most-prized Sprint Cup—Jimmie Johnson—comes from the farthest cultural place away from the ideological and geographic South: the "Left Coast" of California. In fact, California now has more drivers represented in NASCAR's top circuit than any other state.

Despite being well-behind the North American professional sport curve in terms of international diversity of participants (if not fans), NASCAR has recently sought to peddle its galaxy of celebrity- and spectacle-based commodity forms in markets both within the North American popular and beyond. While such sporting entrepreneurialism "has always been about the overcoming of spatial constraints as a means of improving the flow of goods from producer to consumer" (Silk & Andrews, 2001, p. 187), NASCAR has been unique in its attempt to broaden its consumer base by generating a polyvalent commodity-*communitas* that at once anchors the brand to its "auto-American" (Southern) roots while concurrently re-articulating its commercial phantasms across more pluralistic formations of consumer-citizenship (Silk & Andrews, 2001, p. 187).

What we have seen in recent years, then, is a paradigm shift. In order to expand, NASCAR intermediaries have begun the process of redefining the boundaries of NASCAR Nation by engaging and producing inward and outward flows of what some scholars have referred to as "glocalized" sport culture (Reich, 1991; Robertson, 1995; Robins, 1990); a hybridized (see Pietersee, 1995) stock car local and market-driven global constituted by (1) a strategic attempt by the racing circuit to *interpellate the burgeoning Latina/o consumer market* within the United States (in the context of heightened domestic backlash immigration politics, debates around the construction of border control walls, and the demonization of the ethnic "Other" under the guise of post-9/11 antiterrorist "Homeland Security"); (2) internationalization of NASCAR celebrity and the rise of what we refer to as *"redneck" cosmopolitanism*; (3) attempts to introduce "foreign" automobile manufacturers (namely Toyota) into the racing series while negotiating the dual fears of the *Japanization of "NASCAR Nation"* and what Michael Silk and David Andrews (2001) might refer to as the contested awareness of (*Southern*) *cultural Toyotism*; and (4) efforts to *manufacture dual-conjuncturalism of the global through prismatics of the Southern sporting local.*

First, over the past two seasons, NASCAR executives have deployed new layers of advertising and symbolic leverage onto their (intra)"national" market, particularly in attempts to hail the country's growing Latina/o consumer populace. In a U.S. marketplace where the "Latina/o segment" increasingly matters, brand managers navigate profit maximization schemes that synthesize dislocated labor exploitation with America's new, "untapped" consumer market—while carefully diffusing a still-pervasive NAFTA-inspired anti-immigrant backlash in the national imaginary. In turn, NASCAR has attempted to seize these heretofore disengaged consumer markets through the twin commercial exploits of America's most popular icons: (1) the addition of internationally known race car driver Juan Pablo Montoya to the Sprint Cup circuit and (2) the creation of an extensive advertising campaign featuring one of South America's most popular balladeers, Juanes. The former has become a significant figure within NASCAR's celebrity-scape, as both a hero figure for some and the representative embodiment of interloping "Otherness" for many more (we discuss this point later). The latter, on the other hand, represents perhaps the more intrusive (into an ethnically defined, monolithic Latina/o "market segment"), and simultaneously inclusive (redefining NASCAR Nation as a postanxiety, bilingual, inclusive cultural geographic sphere), of NASCAR's recent efforts to engage the Latina/o market. Through their 2007 season-long running advertisement featuring his ballad *Me Enamora*, NASCAR marketers attempted to position Juanes, his body, his music, and his "Latinized" cultural politics as comfortable—if not normalized—fixtures within the otherwise exclusively white contemporary NASCAR spectacle.

Second, and to further attend to the sport's new globalizing impulses, NASCAR's team owners have in recent years lured a number of the world's most popular celebrity-drivers away from established international circuits such as Formula One and Indy Car. Along with Juan Pablo Montoya (Columbia), teams have replaced "All-American" drivers like Rusty Wallace, Sterling Marlin, Dale Jarrett, and Terry Labonte with Dario Franchitti (Scotland; competed 2007–2008), Marcos Ambrose (Australia; competed 2007–present), Max Papis (Italy; competed 2006–present), Mattias Ekström (Sweden; 2010–present), Patrick Carpentier (Canada; competed 2007–present), and Jaques Villanueve (Canada; 2007–present). This new internationalized division of cultural labor is revelatory of neoliberal NASCAR's global-local complexity, in that each drives for teams lying on the periphery and semiperiphery of the sport's established oligarchy. More importantly for NASCAR, these drivers are seen to be worker-commodities who can act as a cultural conduit into new markets, while at the same time working as "insourced" wage laborers whose variable costs are limited by the league's monopolistic economic structure. In short, Montoya, Villanueve, and Franchitti—as well as former open-wheel drivers Scott Speed, A. J. Almendinger, and Sam Hornish—have been brought to NASCAR to build the brands of "fringe" teams who otherwise cannot compete with stock car oligarchs such as Hendrick Motorsports, Joe Gibbs Racing, and Roush-Fenway Racing.

As a third technique for capitalizing on dialectics of the global and the local, NASCAR introduced Japanese automaker Toyota into its NEXTEL (later Sprint) Cup Series in 2007. For Toyota, this move into NASCAR was an attempt to localize their global brand; to situate, in cultural terms, the Japanese automaker's brand within the postindustrial American consumer psyche (Kelman, 1990; Watanabe, 2000). To this end, Toyota brand managers created the "Toyota in America" showcase shortly after their introduction into the racing league—which still features outside of NASCAR racetracks on most racing weekends. A large U.S. map illustrating Toyota's various domestic manufacturing plants in places like Ann Arbor, Michigan, Lafayette, Indiana, Jackson, Tennessee, Buffalo, West Virginia, and Blue Springs, Mississippi highlights the exhibit.

Drawing upon the work of Manuel Castells (1996), we follow Silk and Andrews (2001) in arguing that Toyota's promotional presence has thus been an attempt to suture the corporation and its vehicular products to the imaginary national (in terms of NASCAR Nation) context in which they seek a tangible (and intangible) market presence

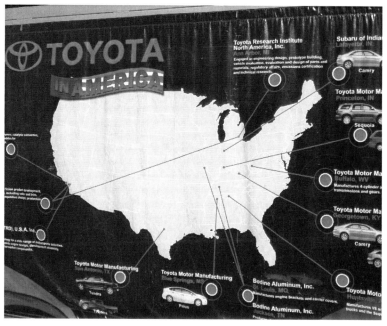

Americanizing Toyota through NASCAR (Phoenix, AZ, November 2010)

(p. 189). NASCAR Nation's "cultural Toyotism" (Silk & Andrews, 2001) is thus a *refractive* technique meant to divert consumer sensibilities away from their own apprehensions of "the global" within the cultural politics of the global brand and toward the newly NASCAR-ized branded local.

In financial terms, this marketing strategy resulted in Toyota subsidizing teams "with huge cash outlays that allow[ed] them to undercut sponsor bids by as much as 50 percent" in order to gain traction in NASCAR Nation (Ryan, 2006, p. 1). At a time when U.S. domestic automobile manufacturers sought billions of dollars in government subsidies, and NASCAR teams were simultaneously incurring a greater share of operating expenses, Toyota's offer to fund much of the partner teams' operating costs and potential sponsors could reduce the total amount for sponsorship packages—generating a higher propensity for sponsors to migrate away from current teams toward more cost prohibitive endeavors with Toyota teams. And despite well-documented struggles during their initial season in 2007 (Livingstone, 2007b; Pockrass, 2007), by 2010 Toyota (217 points) had finished second in the *NASCAR Manufacturer Standings* (besting stock car stalwarts Dodge [138 points] and Ford [176] and falling 44 points short of first-place Chevrolet [261]).

Finally, and most predictably, NASCAR's most recent expansion efforts have centered on holding racing events outside of the sport's traditionally Southern or even national boundaries. Over the past four years (2007–2010) league hierarchs have taken their products and spectacles to new markets outside of the United States, holding NASCAR-sanctioned events in Mexico City and Montreal (with plans to move into China in the coming years), opening new commercial spaces in Europe, Japan, and Central America, and partnering with local racing circuits in Australasia and Europe to cross-promote various racing ventures. Furthermore, Sprint Cup races are now broadcast in over 150 countries and in 30 different languages ("This Is Our NASCAR," 2009),[6] a seismic leap forward since the initial nationwide U.S. broadcast in 1979.

A CRISIS OF ACCUMULATION

But this growth has come at a high price. Many commentators have argued that by attending to this expansionist urge(ncy)—and in so doing re-articulating the spatial logics and cultural politics of the NASCAR brand—the racing league brought about an increased disenfranchisement amongst (Southern, white, male) stock car stalwarts. Columnist Marty Smith (2008a), ironically writing the following while on NASCAR's payroll, synopsizes a growing discontent among the sport's most faithful supporter-consumers this way:

> It is high time NASCAR took it back to the good ol' boys. And whoever it was in Daytona or Charlotte or Kalamazoo drawing that ire deserves a hearty pat on the back and a frothy, frosty Budweiser—the red-label kind that good ol' boys drink sittin' on a tailgate in the hayfield. A lot of fans feel like NASCAR over the past 10–15 years committed the ultimate sellout. It's the ol' "dance with the one that brought you" mantra—Wilkesboro and Rockingham brought you to the show, and when you arrived, you found a hotter partner in California...It is good to see the Daytona brass admit they need to steer back to the roots...Ultimately, perception from the rural roots says this: Ease off the suits and embrace the guy with his name on his shirt. Because that's the guy who spends his vacation time and savings account at Pocono Raceway. (p. 1)

In other words, in trying to expand its share of the global sport-consumer market, many observers believe NASCAR executives have abandoned the sport's traditional, "good ol' boy," Southern "roots." NASCAR's broadened quest for surplus capital has become a complicated enterprise for those millions of fans who have, for generations, identified with the sport's overtly pronounced geopolitical localness and cultural *locale*.

As early as 2005, MacGregor raised the question: "Despite its many recent successes, [NASCAR] seems hung somewhere between the city and the country, unsure how to shake its red-dirt past while grasping for its gold-lamé future. Is NASCAR Rockingham or is it Las Vegas? Can it be both?" (p. 176). Smith's (2008a) article three years later provided a partial answer; his rejoinder ignited a "firestorm of angst-filled feedback" (p. 1) from NASCAR fans longing for a medium to express their frustrations over the "oppressive" regime of the family-run, privately held sport-league conglomerate. One reader in particular questioned how NASCAR could return to their "roots" after they have associated themselves with foreign auto manufacturer Toyota (quoted in Smith, 2008c). Another commenter even proclaimed that he no longer watched NASCAR because of the influx of foreign drivers, asserting "if this continues at the pace it is now, it will diminish the sport extensively in the eyes of the good ol' boys and the fans that started it many years ago" (quoted in Smith, 2008c, p. 3)

Smith's readers also chastised league executives for suspending events at traditional Southern racetracks in Darlington and Rockingham, for increasing the ticket prices and related fees associated with attending race weekends, for allowing Toyota to compete in stock car racing's top circuit, and for developing and standardizing a more regulated, slower, Car of Tomorrow[7] (Smith, 2008a). Smith's column and the commentaries that ensued in no way claim to be rooted in globalization theory, nor are they exhaustive of the push-back that has surfaced against the "new global NASCAR," but they substantiate the accusations from many inside NASCAR Nation that the sport's executives must return to its local "roots" if it is to survive.[8]

While in the first instance these fans perhaps fail to realize that NASCAR has been "selling its fans out" for commercial ends from the league's inception, the entrance of Juan Pablo Montoya, the introduction of Japanese automaker Toyota, the internationalization of the sport's celebrity athletes (loosely defined as such), mass consolidation of teams and ownership, and the diffusion of competitions outside domestic borders invigorated a perceived *dislocation* of parochial sporting tradition (spectacles of paleo-conservative, Southern whiteness, etc.) from the commercial enterprise upon which that "tradition" was formulated. And just as George W. Bush's brand of U.S. conjuncturalism yielded to Obama's campaign of "change" (if less transformational in practice than was hoped for by many), so too did that conjuncturalism's most culturally entrenched sport backtrack against the changing tides of automobile sporting capital.

Indeed, NASCAR's recent financial reports tell us more about the sport's "National" crisis than any tirade in the blogosphere ever could. Television ratings in NASCAR-rich regional markets of the U.S. South were down starting from 2006, with fewer viewers tuning in to almost every race within that year's schedule (Thomaselli, 2007). In 2007, network ratings continued dropping, falling 11 percent from an average Neilson Rating of 5.4 in 2006 to 4.8 (Smith, 2008b). That downward spiral continued in 2008 and 2009, with mid-season race broadcast on TNT averaging a 3.4 rating in 2009 (~5.5. million viewers) and most races in the later part of that season yielding ratings below 3.7 for ABC and ESPN ("2010 NASCAR Sprint Cup TV Ratings," 2010). Things got worse for NASCAR and its broadcast partners in 2010. Fox network's early season NASCAR telecasts were down almost 10 percent from the previous season, while TNT mid-season races averaged nearly 12 percent fewer viewers. ESPN and ABC's coverage of the 2010 playoff races generated a remarkably low 2.6 average rating for the networks and their advertisers—more than 25 percent below the previous season's ratings (ibid.). All told, since 2005, television viewership of NASCAR Spring Cup races has fallen by more than 25 percent nationwide and at an even greater rate in the U.S. South. Most tellingly, the 2010 Daytona 500 race generated the lowest television ratings since 1991 (Gregory, 2010). Attendance numbers suggest things are getting worse for NASCAR at the track as well: For the first time in more than a decade, many of NASCAR's most high-profile 2010 races, both in the South and across the United States more generally, failed to fill to capacity (Gregory, 2010). Or put in more ironic terms, they failed to "sell out."[9]

In practical terms, one Ohio journalist put these corporate-cultural disjunctures into perspective:

> Some die-hard NASCAR fans complain about the sport's evolution, from a drive 'em if you got 'em, good-old-boys scene years ago to the multimillion-dollar corporate machine it's [*sic*] become. Old-timers complain about the cost of tickets, which have increased steadily from $30 for general passes to $200 and up for tickets that include bird's-eye seating, pit passes and private catering.... and they curse the cost of a $2.50 hot dog and $4 beer. (Battaglia, quoted in Hugenberg & Hugenberg, 2008, p. 638)

The contradictions emanating from the new face of old NASCAR is perhaps best summed up by *Time* magazine writer Sean Gregory (2010):

> NASCAR grew up lawless and positively redneck—the sport traces its heritage to moonshiners outrunning the law—but it's wrestling with an identity crisis. Can a sport appeal to both the chardonnay corporate crowd whose trackside condos at fancy new circuits fueled NASCAR's recent growth and the diehards whose unabashed passion for racin' and wreckin' built stock-car racing in the first place? (p. 2)

In effect, these fans' increased disenfranchisement and NASCAR's decreased popularity points to the complicated cultural and economic politics of the sporting local and the free market global, whereby expansion of NASCAR Nation is both a product of the convergence of the global upon the local (and vice versa). As Andrews and Ritzer (2007) suggest, this is typical within a neoliberal moment defined by "the imperialistic ambitions of nations, corporations, organizations, and the like and their desire, indeed need, to impose themselves on various geographic areas" (p. 135). In this way, by imposing itself on the global, NASCAR finds itself operating against the cultural insularity (either perceived or real) from which its local brand was formulated, celebrated, and eventually taken to market. In simpler terms, NASCAR's recent struggles point to a possible discordance between the very conjuncture—that of fusionist conservatism (as located within the aestheticized South) and market neoliberalism—upon which the brand and its expansionist platform were constructed. Citizen-spectators of NASCAR Nation, as political consumers, are turning away from the brand's corporate politics in protecting/preserving their own sportized cultural politics.

Or, Cultural Economies of Neoliberal Demise

A second, and perhaps related, argument regarding NASCAR's recent downturn is that the sport most entangled in the prevailing market logic and aesthetic has faltered in dialectic cadence with the broader global economic condition it helped bring to life. The story goes something like this: NASCAR's recent failures are imbricated in the extensive collapse of the neoliberal/fusionist conservative order that the sport had allied itself with many years ago. In turn, its portfolio shortcomings are a reflection of the economic hardships facing many of its most loyal consumer-citizens. Some observers (see Pierce, 2010) have suggested that NASCAR's legions of working-class fans are some of the nation's most vulnerable amidst these (as in past) uncertain economic times. Even those members of the investor class, who have in recent years shied away from NASCAR due to its poor financial results, have identified that NASCAR fans, as portrayed in an Morningstar Equity Research's (2009) investment profile, are "a less educated demographic, which has been hardest hit by unemployment." The report concludes: "We don't expect an immediate or rapid recovery in unemployment, or for demand in motor sports" (p. 5). The report then advises investors to wait until unemployment rates level off, as that might translate into renewed consumption of NASCAR-related goods. In short, they are suggesting that *NASCAR goes as the bottom of the neoliberal hierarchy goes*. We expand upon this thesis in the upcoming section.

First we point to the untenable structural formations of a global capitalist order that NASCAR played a role in creating; and in so doing explore how those breakdowns influence the state of stock car stagflation today. In this endeavor, we move beyond hackneyed public depositions that assume NASCAR's recent stammer is just a natural result of market-corrective recession, instead looking into how the neoliberal architecture(s) of capital, both in NASCAR in the its Nation, failed to establish a sustainable market-based producer-consumer relationship.

Systemic crises and collapses of various national and transnational market schemes—as well as environmental catastrophes and corruption scandals—have defined the global economy over the past decade. From economic instability in many developed nation-states (i.e., Ireland, Greece, Germany, the United Kingdom, the United States, etc.) to disasters of natural resource extraction (i.e., from mines in Greymouth, New Zealand to oil rigs in the Gulf of Mexico), from global pandemics (i.e., SARS, bird flu, etc.) to global "Wars on Terrorism," we have come to know these to be troubled times, indeed. In economic terms, the super profits from investment banking and real estate that defined Friedman's national success stories have collapsed about their shaky timber. In the same early millennial moment when these captains of the free market were relishing in the life's work of their visionary "savior," the rate of corporate expansion and growth brought about by his economic theories was producing considerably iniquitous capital distribution across the globe.

As Friedman's critics had predicted decades earlier (see Daly, 1977/1991; Galbraith, 1958/1998; 1996; 2001), the sharp rise of private growth was beginning to result in a crisis of "overcapitalization" (Mandel, 1975); whereby the system of controlling variable costs (wage labor in particular) and maximizing profits began to implode upon itself. No longer sheltered by labor unions or federal regulation of trade, wage-laboring masses in the United States earned less than their parents. In turn, individuals became increasingly unable to sustain the rate of consumption needed to continue the exponential growth necessitated by a deregulated marketplace (and its stock exchanges and members of the investment class). Moreover, as real surplus value failed to keep pace with the incessantly exponential modes of accumulation demanded by the investment-capitalist class, the domestic (and thus global) market turned to new forms of capitalization—those that could only be realized through radical, untenable forms of globetrotting speculation (Chancellor, 2000).[10]

The U.S. national debt had grown by nearly 900 percent during the neoliberal revolution (as the federal government became the free market's greatest consumer in order to sustain the growth bubble) (Giroux, 2008). This discordant distribution of capital culminated in a massive state- and consumer-based debt never before realized by any domestic economy in the world. To such an end, the U.S. debt pool now drowns out the combined consumer debts accumulated by the rest of the world's consumers in today's global marketplace (Li, 2008). Outstanding American consumer credit, including credit card and mortgage debt, recently surpassed $10 trillion. The average credit card and car loan debt per American household is currently more than $20,000. More telling, perhaps, is that from 1975 to 1999, the ratio of debt growth to Gross Domestic Product growth averaged 1.9 percent, while from 2000 to 2007 that ratio increased to 5.1 percent. Today, roughly 43 percent of American families spend more than they earn each year. Bankruptcies more than doubled each decade since Reagan's 1980 inauguration and credit card debt is now more than 200 percent higher than it was in 1990 (Amin, 2008). Foreclosures on home mortgages were up to a staggering 75 percent in 2007. In short, the rate of consumer debt accelerated at a much faster pace than the growth of the national economy. This dysfunction is perhaps best illustrated by the recent "crisis" in the housing market—particularly the subprime mortgage disaster and the subsequent government bailouts of the world's largest financial institutions—which is suggestive that that the neoliberal windfall has hollowed out (Beitel, 2008).

Whereas in the late 1960s and early 1970s, the United States was the dominant nation-state in terms of manufacturing, technology, and finance, under the throws of neoliberalism the domestic economy lost its place in each. Production of domestic-based products almost disappeared during the era of neoliberal deindustrialization

(Gereffi, Garcia-Johnson, & Sasser, 2001; Touraine, 1971). More relevant to our purposes here, economic data from the beginning of the Reagan administration to the end of George W. Bush's first term suggests that while corporations and their capitalist elites (the top 1 percent) grew their wealth more than 400 percent, during that same period American workers saw their real wages reduced by more than 14 percent ("United States Bureau of Labor Statistics Report, 1970–2005," 2005). Among the middle-class, the debt-to-income ratio reached its highest level in 24 years in 2010. By 2009, based on assessments made on changes in stock and housing prices, economists concluded that median wealth plunged by 36 percent and there was a fairly steep rise in wealth inequality, with the Gini coefficient advancing from 0.834 to 0.865 (Wolff, 2010).[11] Americans now work longer hours with less vacation time than they did three decades ago; and are now overburdened with the costs of subsidizing their health care, financing the public good, and buying into an increasingly privatized educational system more than ever before.

Moreover, working taxpayers have been required to "support economic growth" and in recent years "bail out" the private sector through tax amnesty, corporate welfare, and various "stimulus packages" at a rate that some estimate to be almost $10 trillion—or almost $50,000 per U.S. taxpayer (Pittman & Ivry, 2009). As part of a global market reaction to the forecasted profit potential for this massive debt, Middle Eastern investors now control a majority share in most U.S.-based banking conglomerates such as Citigroup and AIG. Ironically, the sheiks, princes, speculators, and tycoons from around the world who were once deeply indebted to the U.S. Federal Reserve have now flocked to the U.S. credit market to capitalize on the overextended consumerism that defined the national pathos in the era of neoliberal growth (Therborn, 2007). In short, "It looked good on paper, if all one read were the figures on the stock markets. But it was a super-credit bubble that was bound to burst, and is now bursting" (Wallerstein, 2008, p. 1).

However, if one were to survey recent mass-mediated pathologizing of neoliberalism's now-dominant galaxy of celebrity-economists (e.g., Alan Greenspan, Lawrence Summers, Ben Bernanke, and even, to a certain extent, Austan Goolsbee and Peter Orszag), we would get the impression that "everything's great with the free market," "it's just doing its thing," or "the market would be fine if not for the interference of big government." The investor class is finding out that the affectivity of such false discourse might be fleeting. As has been the case with every other failed *laissez-faire* system before it, our current neoliberal arrangement is faced with a growing disillusionment from wage laborers within "developed" nation-states longing for the yet-to-be-realized "glories of an unrestrained market":

> This (can) be seen in many developments: the return to power of more social-welfare-oriented governments in many countries; the turn back to calling for government protectionist policies, especially by labor movements and organizations of rural workers; the worldwide growth of an alterglobalization movement whose slogan (is) "another world is possible." (Wallerstein, 2008, p. 1)[12]

As David Harvey (2001a, 2006) has consistently argued, neoliberal states and corporate leviathans have expanded their quest(s) for "spatial-temporal fixes" to this neoliberal crisis—a term with double meaning that refers to both the historically stratified territorialization of capital and the globetrotting "solutions" to crises of accumulation. Through what former U.S. president Abraham Lincoln centuries ago predicted would emerge as a series of antidemocratic political and social techniques (cf. Bakan, 2004), these politico-corporatists have attempted to keep the global economy on "life support" by capitalizing on the cultural and political commons and interceding on the inner workings of the "free market" (Knauft, 2007).

One such "fix" has been *the privatization of the public good*. When the markets that had thrived under the *laissez-faire* economies of the late 1980s began to stagnate—realizing growth only in the form of speculative financial oligopolism and residual technological optimism—political and corporate intermediaries of Friedman's neoliberalism accelerated what Harvey (2006) refers to as new regimes of "accumulation by dispossession" (in much the same way colonizers of centuries past raided valuable resource-commodities from places like Brazil or Liberia). In the decade that followed—and having saturated a plurality of domestic marketplaces with their goods and services—elites of the megacorporate global order turned their attention inward again. By (political and/or military) force, coercion, and corruption, free market politicos such as Virginia Governor Ralph Stanley, Russian President Boris Yeltsin, and Chinese President Jiang Zemin "opened up" their states to the commodification of the centuries-old public sector (Klein, 2007). In simple terms, these political elites offered up their state's publically subsidized assets for wholesale to the corporate sector.

Locally, this transformation has resulted in the governments of many major U.S. cities "selling off" the public arms of their municipalities; such as those that once provided energy, transportation, waste management, education, social security, and health care to their constituents (Boyd, 2007; Chomsky, 2002; Giroux, 2007; "In an Era of Shrinking Government, Is Privatization the American Way?" 1995). Nationally, a fleeting neoliberal prosperity has resulted in a new, unbending advocacy for the privatization of social security; government pensions being almost completely replaced by market-parasitic 401(k) plans; the "homeland security" of shipping and airports being contracted to private companies; the health of the American people having been commodified into the most profitable sector of the economy; American "public" universities operating as quasi-private enterprises, with the professoriate researching to pay their own salaries and the student body incurring a disproportionate burden of previously state-administered costs;[13] and corporate welfare (~1.6 trillion per year) under the Obama administration burdening taxpayers at a rate nearly *100 times* higher than that of social welfare programs (~$16-$23 billion per year).

Under the reign of neoliberalism, the most fundamental element of the American republic—that of the democratic process itself—has become big business. At the intersection of a commodification of politics and the politicization of commodities, aspirant government officials of the 2008 and 2010 elections are now "made viable" via campaign funding, "leadership" and "dignity" are measured in terms of business acumen, and lobbyists direct the policies of Commanders in Chief.[14]

A second sustaining force of the failing neoliberal empire is politico-capitalists' ability to *create and advance* what Naomi Klein (2007) refers to as *"disaster capitalism."* The basic premise of Klein's (2007) argument is that as global free market entrepreneurialism has sputtered, investors and venture capitalists have successfully created a profitable system of accumulation that has commodified both unpredictable natural catastrophes (tsunamis, hurricanes, and pandemics) and strategically orchestrated disasters (such as imperialist war and genocide; see also Chapter Six). While at times slightly overstated, Klein's (2007) critique illuminates how the corporate sector has profited from the burgeoning disaster-based industries emanating from the U.S. government's War on Terror, the military-industrial-complex's *carte blanche* in the age of "Homeland Security," municipalities' fetish for vaccination to prevent "imminent" pandemics (such as SARS and the "bird flu"), the profit-based privatization of U.S. Gulf region, Indonesia, and Sri Lanka during the "rebuilding" of these region's communities, and the corporate contracts to harness oil and infrastructural collateral damage in the Middle East following the American government's post-9/11 military occupation (especially by Halliburton and its former subsidiary, KBR, Inc. [formerly Kellogg, Brown, and Root]). Klein (2007) argues that each of these events presented neoliberals with what Friedman often referred to as opportunistic "shocks"—periods when the traditions and structures of a society could be reshaped in order to maximize economic freedom and profitability. And in the years after the September 11 attacks, no sectors have turned greater profits than those of the "disaster-industrial-complex": oil, security technologies, military weapons, tourism and real estate development, biotechnology, and (each stimulated by the free market capitalization of catastrophe).

Under a corporate-capitalist state that at best has drastically reshaped the everyday lives of most Americans, and at worst often falls under the governance of a public polity oriented toward "profit over people" (Chomsky, 1999), a third, and ultimately tantamount mechanism for sustaining a neoliberal order, has emerged. These iniquitous economic policies and militaristic conquests are abetted, if not made possible, by an overwhelming consent of not only the ruling class, *but the middle and working-classes as well*. And in democracies such as the United States and Great Britain, intermediaries indefatigably endeavoring to "manufacture consent" for this neoliberal empire blur the boundaries of "political politics" and "cultural politics" (Morris, 1988b). As Jim McGuigan (2005) suggests, this consent toward neoliberal hegemony is made meaningful by "distorted communication motivated by unequal power relations" whereby "ideological sway is greatest at the popular level" (pp. 232–233). In the first instance, the global popular culture industry has been able to capitalize on individual needs, desires, and aspirations through the production of specific goods, services, and experiences. In the second, the technologies of identity and subjectivity active within the machinations of the "global popular" (Kellner, 1995) have been equally powerful by subordinating spectator/consumers to the laws of the neoliberal market.

In other words, public culture is being molded around the conventions of a dysfunctional neoliberal order, and consumers are often lining up to buy in. In the United States, debates around outsourcing and credit debt are glossed over in favor of arguments about illegal immigration and the failings of social welfarism. When an oil-rig off the Florida coast failed in 2010, creating one of the greatest environmental disasters in history, Americans' media attention was turned to chief executives in the United Kingdom or toward a new science of underwater oil plume rationality, rather than capitalism and Halliburton's profit maximization schemes (i.e., cost cutting measures, neglecting scheduled checks, etc.). Most tellingly, and as we detail further in the coming sections, the tensions of disjunctural neoliberalism reveal themselves through the dissonance of contemporary corporate and cultural nationalisms.

SPATIAL ANXIETIES AND THE CULTURAL POLITICS OF NEOLIBERALISM

This once again brings us back to NASCAR; an important space for appraising the cultural pedagogies of disjunctural neoliberalism. By 2010, mass apprehension toward heightened joblessness, mortgages crises, outsourcing and corporate downsizing, the (pre)eminence of Fox News-inflected terrorism alerts, and tensions surrounding the toiling U.S. economy manifest into Tea Party exhibitionism a national fervor. In contemporary NASCAR Nation we find a sport spectating populace languishing under the false promises of neoliberal mobility. We find a sport wrestling with its new multicultural identity and global aspirations amidst a cohesive rejection of this new corporate cosmopolitanism. In turn, NASCAR tracks have in recent years become veritable cultural battlegrounds; whereby the NASCAR "Old Guard" has mobilized against the superstructural logics of this failing market-based expansionism whilst, often against their own working-class interests, applauded the very economic base that undermines their own self-being.

NASCAR Nation's Ethnoracial Citizenship

Consider the places of both driver Juan Pablo Montoya and Juanes in the new NASCAR Nation. By integrating Juan Pablo Montoya and musician Juanes into their commercial scheme, NASCAR has sought to capitalize upon what Aihwa Ong (1998, 1999) might refer to as these celerity's new "flexible citizenship"—a media-produced, consumer-identified plurality that circumnavigates the imagined boundaries between "us" (NASCAR Nation) and "them" (the "immigrant Other"). Moreover, each of these icons' market flexibility is further complicated by the notion that sporting capitalists are juxtaposing the local (in this case the shared, if assumedly homogenous, cultural local of the Latina/o "outsider") against the relocalized global (NASCAR). Following Michael Giardina's work on global sporting icons David Beckham (2003) and Martina Hingis (2001) and the notion of "stylish hybridity" (2003, 2005), however, we might argue that this Latinization of NASCAR Nation is problematically bound to the market logics of "multiculturalism," "diversity," and inclusion; those that see cultural difference as that which must be folded into dominant *market* spheres:

> an influx of performative representations of hyphenated persons and culture(s) occupying leading spaces in mainstream media (television, film, and music). However, while purporting to be positive, progressive artifacts subverting the status quo, the majority of these popular iterations commonly wash over and efface harsh realities witnessed in the everyday interactions between and among diverse segments of a population. (Giardina, 2003, pp. 66–67)

This flexibility attempts to at once interpellate a viable market segment while simultaneously obscuring the anxieties of a post-9/11, anti-immigration dominant, backlash cultural politics.

During one detour through NASCAR Nation in early 2007, it became readily apparent to us that "Johnnie" Montoya is now one of the central "villain figures" in the pantheon of stock car-driver celebrities, despite no reasonable on-track explanation as to why such a reaction is warranted. Indeed, it is common practice during pre-race introductions for many NASCAR fans to hurl beer cans and racially charged epithets (such as "go home Chico" and "Go back to Mexico, Montoya"[15]) at NASCAR's only minority full-time Cup driver. Returning to the double entendre of NASCAR Nation, the overt demonization of Juan Pablo Montoya[16] parallels not-so-coincidentally with the dialectics of paleo-conservative backlash against nonwhite interloper/immigrants in both the spaces of NASCAR and the broader formations of American society.

These anxieties were captured during a recent ESPN college football telecast, when on-air analyst (and former Miami Dolphin great) Bob Griese called NASCAR star driver Juan Pablo Montoya what equated to a "Taco Eater." During the broadcast of an Ohio State versus Minnesota game in 2009, the ESPN commentator was promoting the NASCAR Martinsville race, which was scheduled to be broadcast on the network's ABC partner later that day. As Griese described an on-screen illustration of the top-five standing in that year's Sprint Cup race, one of his fellow announcers asked: "Where's Juan Pablo Montoya?" Griese, laughing, responded: "He's out having a taco."[17] This is but one example of a number of media gestures toward Montoya, or JPM as he is more commonly referred to in NASCAR circles.

In NASCAR Nation, Montoya elicits a coalition of white hypernationalistic anxieties. He is the counterpoint embodiment to xenophobic Senatorial legislation, a "Great Wall of Mexico," through which the jingoistic rantings of intolerant cable news pundits (e.g., Michelle Malkin, Ann Coulter, Glenn Beck, and Bill O'Reilly) and politicians alike (e.g., Palin, Gingrich, Barbour, etc.), and the distorted racial profiles of a media-constructed "homeland (in)security" are celebrated through the signified space and paranoiac physicalities of the sport's neo-tribalist contingent. "These anxieties," posits Lauren Berlant (1997), "are about whose citizenship—whose subjectivity, whose forms of intimacy and interest, whose bodies and identifications, whose heroic narratives—will direct America's future" (p. 6). Through the Confederate flag, white NASCAR Nation marks its territory. By way of these adversarial gestures toward the interloping "Other," the Nation more clearly classifies "aliens" it its midst.

Throughout our travels, we encountered a number of similarly anxious signifying acts representative of the politics of paranoia festering within post-9/11 white America. T-shirts, bumper stickers, baseball caps, and RV flags offered a range of backlash narratives:

- "I want YOU . . . to speak English" (borrowing from the World War II recruitment
- posters featuring Uncle Sam);
- "Tired of pressing '1' for English";
- "Illegal aliens are not immigrants, they are criminals";
- "Illegal aliens: uneducated, unlawful, unsanitary, & unwanted"; and
- "Stop the invasion: Build a fence, secure our borders, enforce laws."

To wit, this white supremacist backlash was on display during an anti-immigration Neo-Nazi rally held in Phoenix, Arizona, on the fall 2010 NASCAR racing weekend. The rally, while not held at or in conjunction with the NASCAR race (and certainly, we would stress, *not* sanctioned by the league), was strategically organized to evoke public response (in the form of support, monetary and civic) for various white nationalist groups in the area. Principal among these groups' causes has been the effort to raise monetary support for Arizona's SB-1070, both in its early stages as well as to its legal defense fund. The rally featured dozens of National Socialist Movement members parading about the downtown area, only to be met (and confronted) by hundreds of counterprotestors. In the report, news channels such as KSAZ Fox 10 reported that counterprotestors had attacked the Neo-Nazi activists. As a result, the television media coverage of the two most news worthy events of the weekend created an interesting, if unintentional, intertextual pedagogy of contemporary backlash whiteness: in one scene white supremacists were featured fighting for their "rights" to demonstrate support for an ill-conceived racial profiling law; in the second scene tens of thousands of white sports fans were shown congregating within a sporting spectacle that featured a much softer, more banal, and yet similarly problematic, racialism.

Drawing from the intellectual labors of Walter Benjamin and Michel Foucault, Berlant (1997) refers to this type of exercise in cultural politics as "hygienic governmentality," or a "ruling bloc's dramatic attempt to maintain its hegemony by asserting that an abject population threatens the common good and must be rigorously governed and monitored by all sectors of society." She continues, saying,

> Especially horrifying are the ways the ruling bloc solicits mass support for such "governing": by using abject populations as exemplary of all obstacles to national life; by wielding images and narratives of a threatened "good life" that a putative "we" have known; by promising relief from the struggles of the present through a felicitous image of a national future; and by claiming that, because the stability of the core image is the foundation of the narratives that characterize an intimate and secure national society, the nation must at all costs protect this image of a way of life, even against the happiness of some of its own citizens. (p. 175)

Where is this hate speech coming from? Better yet, in whose interests is it serving? And to what extent is it imbricated in the larger discursive system of signs operative within the paleo-conservative hegemony since 9/11? It can be surmised that in NASCAR Nation, such a discursive system is a two-part confederation: (1) a confederation of selectively apolitical, dominant, white, (Southern) neo-Confederate identities and (2) a confederation of the subject to broader forces of neoliberal subjectivity—subject to the culture of fear built on incessant terrorism, endless war, fears of losing influence, fear of the [immigrant, black, feminine, gay, and lesbian] Other. Frank Furedi (2004) has argued that this culture of fear "is underpinned by a profound sense of powerlessness, a diminished sense of agency that leads people to turn themselves into passive subjects who can only complain that 'we are frightened.'" It is the intellectual currency of a populace fearful of losing their jobs—exacerbated by local uncertainties of the global economic downturn—of the end of their nation's manifest destiny, and of a new world order where salsa is the new ketchup (or mustard) and state-endorsed multiculturalism strips back the imbedded powerful forms of whiteness.

Ever since the events of 9/11, Right-wing politicians and television pundits have tapped into this fear. Whether it is color-coded terror alert warnings, numerous airport security (non)"events" covered live on CNN, the "threat" posed by Saddam Hussein, the "threat" posed by al Qaeda, the "threat" posed by (dark-skinned) terrorists, to name but a few instances, or even President Bush or Vice President Cheney reminding us during most any speech or press conference about the "evildoers" who were out to get us, an ever-present specter of (manufactured) fear had emerged.

In broader terms, the ever-changing, enlightened modern world has been put on trial against the imagined simpler times of the "good old days" for which Jesus-worshipping, neo-Confederate commentators continuously argue. Cameron McCarthy and Greg Dimitriadis (2000) explain that such nostalgia for the so-called good old days of a perceived better bygone era is clearly "associated with a set of discourses that recode White middle-class identity as the identity of the oppressed...[in which]...The professional middle-class suburban dweller has appropriated the radical space of difference, the space of social injury, of social victim" (p. 328). In this way, defining one's identity through the negation of the other (what Nietzsche called "ressentiment") is a process governed by the strategic alienation of the other in forms of knowledge building, genres of representation, and the deployment of moral, emotional, and affective evaluation and investments (McCarthy, Giardina, Harewood, & Park, 2005). In so doing, it projects a mythologized worldview out into the social world as the barometer of public policy, displacing issues of inequality and poverty and replacing these with demands for balanced budgets, tax cuts, greater investment in surveillance and security, and calls for "moral values" to be promoted in schools. All of this is accompanied by a deep-bodied nostalgic investment in Anglo-American cultural form and its European connections (McCarthy et al., 2005, p. 157).

Much of this backlash is generated by a perceived attack on the (white, male) U.S. worker. NASCAR's turn toward the flexible (cultural and material) Toyotism was perceived by many within NASCAR Nation to be another way in which the league was "selling out" its fans, its traditions, and in this case, its national economy. NASCAR Nation is now awash with imagery of closed factories in Detroit, surrounded by the living embodiments of the "McJob revolution" (Ritzer, 1998), and cloaked by the realities of a nation's postindustrial demise (one where Toyota was now the top-selling automobile manufacturer in the North American marketplace). Consumer-fans, reflecting the Strictly Stock hegemony that had been cultivated through decades of domesticated Ford-Chevy on-the-track rivalries, responded with cacophonous tensions framed in the discursive formations of the neoliberal-neo-conservative impasse. On the website www.fansagainstracingtoyotas.com, fans "bandied about their racist, nationalist proclamations for a few days prior to the [2007] Daytona race" (Miller, 2007, p. 46). An army of insurrectionists came to occupy NASCAR tracks that season, donning T-shirts emblazoned with "No to Toyota" and "NASCAR: An American Sport."

This rejection of the localized global in some ways exposes the contradictions and incongruities of global accumulation and cultural logics of the commercial local; and in turn the ideological precepts upon which the "Nation" was economically imagined.

In some ways, these spatial anxieties surface in response to a perceived loss of freedom. As such, the very promises of neoliberalism—of individualization and freedom—are countenanced by the proximal paradoxes of the free market. As products, images, and bodies have been freed to move more seamlessly across national boundaries, the old pillars of national security, of ethnocentric territorialism, and of the embeddedness each within national framings of

The Boycott Toyota Movement, NASCAR 2006 (Dover, DE, September, 2006)

"economic growth" have been unsettled. In turn, the very outcomes of neoliberalism are seen as an imposition on free citizenship and the pursuit(s) of the individual. As David Theo Goldberg (2009) argues, in its failings neoliberalism produces an "ethnoracial rationalization" in which the cultural politics of the insecure market produce new contractions:

> invoked in the war on terror and exported as the neolibertarian impo-
> sition of "living free." Living free means buying (into) the American
> Dream: privatizing (i.e., corporatizing) national industries, dramati-
> cally diminishing trade union power, cutthroat competitiveness, a cul-
> ture of possessive individualism, reduced taxes and scaled-back welfare
> benefits, strongly encouraged foreign investment with few constraints
> on taking profits out, the freedom to choose (ultimately to starve).
> (pp. 93–94)

In this way, the individual worker in the automobile factory is seen to be under threat from the interloping (and possibly insurgent) migrant worker—whether *here* or *there*. Free market nomad-interlopers such as Juan Pablo Montoya or Toyota, each seen to present an imminent threat to the livelihood of American workers, are greeted with venomous mass hissing at NASCAR races. And yet at the same time, any attempt by the government to limit outsourcing is collectively chided within NASCAR Nation as unnecessary interference with market freedom. Furthermore, most folks argue that the maintenance of liberty neces-sitates big government investment in defense, in Homeland Security, in border control, and in activating conflicts in the Middle East.

Of Fools and Horsepower

What we might be seeing, then, is not only the demise of (at least this cycle of) neoliberalism, but also a passing of the cultural and economic mystifications of automobility. In the United States, we have in recent years witnessed a crisis of the car and all its parts. Factories are closing, American war machines have killed off many nations' vanguards of non-American natural resources, and in turn, oil fields are dying up (or bleeding into the ecosystem). The seduc-tive myth of endless modern prosperity is being retold as a tragedy of the commons—one in which short-term capital returns supersede the interests of the common good. As the United States auto indus-try loses its relevance as viable commercial enterprise in the global marketplace, so too does the culture that had been in place to pro-mote it. The NASCAR superspeedway, once the sporting beacon of auto-American exceptionalism, has become the public charnel house of a dying American industry.

The tenuous auto-imaginings of NASCAR Nation are interlaced within the spatial anxieties of neo-Confederate nationalism, theocratic paroxysm, and contradictions of the neoliberal immigrant state—a strange conservatism that cannot decide when capital and/or the state should act upon their everyday lives. Take the recent federal bailout of the "Big Three" domestic automobile manufacturing industry. In 2008, George W. Bush (and later Barack Obama) committed nearly $25 billion in government loans to aid struggling companies General Motors, Ford, and Daimler Chrysler in what was pejoratively referred to by commentators on the Left as "lemon socialism" (suggesting mass government support of failing private sector industries) and those on the Right as just another example of "big government."

Interestingly, Brian France wrote an open letter to key senators lobbying Congress in support of the corporate welfare. "I'm writing to you as a concerned American who wants what is best for our general country," France wrote. "Of course, the domestic automobile manufacturers play a very important part of the heritage of NASCAR, but, more importantly, it is vital for all of America." As a good corporate Samaritan, France implored: "For these manufacturers to survive, your assistance is urgently needed. By immediately supporting America's automobile industry, you can help our nation avoid a devastating economic blow" (quoted in Gomstyn, 2008). Drivers Jeff Gordon and Jimmie Johnson also "urg[ed] their fans to contact their members of Congress to push through the $25 billion Detroit bailout plan" (Winter, 2008, p. 1).

And so, on the one hand, we have many "anti-big-government" NASCAR fans opposing to the use of tax dollars to support a failing industry—the very industry that has come to define the sport and to provide jobs for many NASCAR Dads (and their dads). These NASCAR fans, many of whom abhor Toyota and Juan Pablo Montoya for intruding upon their All-American sport, cast aspersions upon the very companies (Ford in particular) that had paved their modern auto-mobile imaginaries. On the other hand, we have corporate executives and stock car celebrities who offered their support for government intervention—the very institution their brand antithesized for so many years—to secure the Nation's profitable auto-mobile future.

A 2009 "April Fool's" satire piece in a well-respected automotive publication, Car & Driver, brings these inconsistencies further into focus. Immediately upon it publication, the piece, headlined *Obama Orders Chevrolet and Dodge Out of NASCAR,* engendered intense outrage within NASCAR Nation. The article featured several fictitious quotes by President Obama and other members of the White House administration claiming U.S. automakers must demonstrate they are willing to spend judiciously to receive government assistance, and this included the termination of devoting financial resources toward stock car auto racing. Several of NASCAR's most influential website publications (Scene.com, Jayski.com) fell victim to the hoax, as well as local newspapers and news reporting organizations, as this news spread swiftly through the stridently conservative collective. As word reached NASCAR Nation, fans posted scathing critiques of President Obama in the comments section of the aforementioned mediums and the most popular NASCAR Internet message boards. Criticisms of big government, claims of socialism, accusations of class warfare, and racialized epitaphs directed toward the president flowed from the fingers of NASCAR Nation's most cyber-fervent members (motortrend.com, 2009; caranddriver.com, 2009; jayski. com, 2009; gminsidenews.com, 2009). A headline even read *The Socialist Experiment Continues* (autospies.com, 2009) and one comment on the *Orlando Sun-Sentinel* website read "Get this socialist out of NASCAR. It's bad enough he is going to trash this country" (Humphrey, 2009, p. 3). The circle, in effect, had become complete: NASCAR fans believing not only that (1) Obama was a socialist who would trash the country, but also believing (2) the absurd notion that the president of the United States would make such an "order" in the first place.

RELOCATING NASCAR NATION

To counter this crisis of (cultural political) location and in some assuage the anxieties brought about by an untenable sporting neoliberalism, NASCAR attempted beginning in 2008 to resituate itself within the imaginary spaces of the paleo-conservative U.S. South local through the various hybrid commercial forms. Motivated by changes in market and social conditions outlined above, NASCAR effectively reconsidered its profit motives, and in the words of Brian France, sought to "get back to the basics" (quoted in Caraviello, 2008, p. 2). In getting back to the basics, France brought back the Southern-themed advertising locus of NASCAR Nation. In early 2008, the league implemented a new "Our NASCAR" campaign of TV, print, online, and radio ads targeting "NASCAR's avid fans with an emphasis on great racing moments, fan passion and the sport's heritage" (Smith, 2008b). The campaign commenced with the 2008 Daytona 500 that featured prerace performances by popular country music performers Brooks & Dunn and Trisha Yearwood. During the race, organizers used the mediated and practiced spaces of the racetrack to emphasize the "history, tradition, and legacy" of the sport. Prior to the race, all 24 living past champions of the Daytona 500 were ceremoniously paraded around the track and their likenesses were used in various other promotional activities leading up to the event (Smith, 2008b).

To further augment NASCAR's "getting back to its roots" campaign, FOX Sports debuted new theme music for its 2008 NASCAR coverage that features country music artist Toby Lightman singing his stock car-tailored ballad "Let's go racing boys." The song's distinctly Southern language and twang came complete with steel guitars, stock car racing lyrics, dubs of broadcasting clips of historical NASCAR moments, and splices of Fox commentator Darrell Waltrip's signature "Boogity, Boogity, Boogity" catchphrase. In years past, NASCAR had featured in its race-day and advertising promotions global recording artists like Metallica, Lenny Kravitz, Pink, the Barenaked Ladies, and the Red Hot Chili Peppers, but in its attempts to appeal to the sport's self-described "redneck" traditionalists, NASCAR reinserted the aesthetic Southern local into their increasingly cosmopolitan cultural sphere.

Perhaps the most telltale reference point for the organization's back to its roots shift is the 60-second advertisement promoting the sixtieth anniversary of NASCAR. The commercial features U.S. recording artists Matchbox 20 perform their song "How Far We've Come" interlaced with a visual progression of NASCAR's evolution. The advertisement celebrates the heroic acts of drivers like Lee Petty, classic moments in NASCAR history, photo-finishes, spectacular crashes, good 'ol boys like Dale Earnhardt, Neil Bonnett, Bobby Allison, and Richard Petty, the rise of NASCAR Nation in the 1990s, and culminates with the champagne and confetti celebrating Jimmie Johnson's 2007 championship. This visual representation of the history of NASCAR as a site for American nationalism, while at the same time emphasizing a cultural maturation toward accepting NASCAR's open-ended politics of foreign drivers, international races, multinational sponsorship from financial oligarchies, and mass consolidation of team ownership.

NASCAR's cultural homecoming has been further abetted by a return to the sport's hyperregulatory business [infra]structure. The

Car of Tomorrow, while necessitating considerable expense for each of the independent racing teams within the circuit, has been mandated by NASCAR as a way of making for more competitive, compelling, and telegenic races for its expanding media markets. Further, NASCAR officials regularly intervene on race proceedings through unwarranted race stoppages, thus "resetting the field," and in turn forcibly clustering the cars for the effect of more competitive race action). In 2008, two-time NASCAR champion Tony Stewart accused NASCAR of "playing God with overzealous officiating" (quoted in Ryan, 2007b, p. 1) and likened NASCAR's constant rule changes, manipulations, and "staged performances" to those in Vince McMahon's WWE professional wrestling.

CODA

While for decades its ability to control both the product and the process permitted NASCAR to control the processes by which the boundaries of citizenship with the Nation were defined, in attending to the imperatives of neoliberalism, the league compromised the localness upon which consumer identification was moored. So contrived, it lacks seductiveness of the all-consuming global because it is so transparently local. In simple terms, NASCAR executives perhaps failed to consider that the reliance on the imperatives of neoliberal globalization came in direct conflict with the historical, cultural, and economic precepts of NASCAR Nation as paleo-conservative, Southern, local construct.

In short, there were cultural "limits to capitalism" (Harvey, 2007). Because NASCAR Nation was in fact a "nation"—or a collective space demarcated by local imagery and ideology (fireworks, American flags, Southern drawls, and Christian Ministries)—citizen-consumers consumed not only the signifiers and spectacles of the sport, but also *their* place within its cultural politics. Out of such cultural economic dissonance, NASCAR Nation has been awkwardly recapitulated as a globetrotting, cosmopolitan sporting enterprise *with a history*; a paleo-*mélange* of Southern, white, Christian, heteromasculine "American" norms and values mobilized against the invented transnational plural ensure continued profitability under the throws of the neoliberal market. The irony, and perhaps untenable paradox, is that NASCAR is returning to its "roots"—and the politics of the [white, conservative] South—while at the same time interpellating new markets that have been marginalized by the same paleo-conservative, exclusionary cultural practices from which that imaginary South sprung. Put another way, NASCAR hegemons have historically extracted the surplus value of Southern identities (the local), and are attempting to reproduce the commodified politics of the paleo-conservative, Southern, promilitary, hyperreligious, locally defined, conjunctural sporting brand in disjunctural times.

CONCLUDING THOUGHTS

[W]hat did this policy of society, this *Gesellschaftspolitik*, have to consist in for it to succeed in constituting a market space in which competitive mechanisms could really function despite their intrinsic fragility?

—Michel Foucault (2008, p. 240)

Sport. Politics. Neoliberalism. A veritable iron triangle of modern American life—awash with racism, sexism, class bias, greed, exploitation, oppression, imperialism, ideological warfare, monumental successes, and equally epic failures. As we have argued in this book, the racetrack is more than a sporting metaphor for the rotational counterbalance of welfare state economics and *laissez-faire* market economies—a back-and-forth history of economic stimulation and perpetual stagnation overlapped by state spending and private enterprise. In the 1970s, oil oligarchs, political and military elites, and global capitalists mobilized against the welfare state, positioning a free market catholicon of endless individual prosperity: thus setting the stage for the ascent of already-aligned corporate sport. And NASCAR, more so than any other U.S. sporting enterprise, was able to grow—and help facilitate growth—in tandem with this neoliberal political and cultural economy.

However, as Vladimir Lenin (1916/1969) nearly a century ago predicted would be the case, the global acceleration of capitalist enterprises (economic and cultural) such as NASCAR—those that prosper and serve the auspices of neoliberal empire (Pieterse, 2006)—have perhaps reached the "highest stage" of expansionist capital. As neoliberalism is rounding a proverbial "turn four" (and particularly in the context of a subprime mortgage crisis and mammoth credit card and consumer debt)—a new era of global conquest at the behest of *Syriana*-style oil investors and a growing military-industrial-media-congressional-complex,[1] and a backlash amongst American voters toward most elected officials[2]—a return to "imbedded" forms of economic regulation (such as the strange hypercorporatist state being constructed under the Obama administration) seems to be the order of the day. This might also mean the demise of cultural commodities that have been so closely aligned with the cultural and political politics of neoliberalism.

Against these tides, NASCAR, as both a product and a producer of neoliberal hegemony, will likely continue expanding its empire—searching both local and global "markets" for new forms of surplus value. But it will do so under the laws of a failing regime of unfettered accumulation. In short, worker/consumers of NASCAR Nation—like the United States in general—will not be able to keep up with the commercialized, mythologized spectacles forged in George W. Bush's and Bill France's NASCAR Nation. As a reflex to this incongruity, cultural, political, and religious intermediaries will further inundate NASCAR consumer-fans with the narratives and systems of a failing neoliberalism: ticket prices will rise, media saturation of NASCAR celebrities will continue, bailout banter will proliferate, and intermediaries will strive to maintain the delicate balance of (mass)-culturalized "Southern tradition" twinned to the market-driven aspirations for "goin' global." The mouthpieces of NASCAR will tell fans that times will be more desperate, a lack of faith more consequential, adherence to a specific set of "American" values more tantamount, more Wars on Terror™ needed, and so forth.

If we learned anything during our travels, however, it is that *NASCAR Nation is not made of dupes.* Profiteers of neoliberalism may rally around the sinking NASCAR ship, and those who have the most to gain through neoliberal imperatives (or importantly, those who think they stand to gain) may find ideological comfort in the phantasmagoria of the NASCAR spectacle. But for the consuming masses, there is no guarantee they will continue to worship at the altar of unfettered capital. And, while there is likewise no guarantee of a counterrevolution, the ancillary signs are there: for a corporate-sport entity that has hitched its soul to conservative politics (both social and economic), walking hand-in-hand down the aisle with it may prove to be a risky play: As we well know, 2008 saw the election of Barack Obama as U.S. president primarily through an energized and youth-oriented center-left coalition actively taking on issues of climate change, poverty, sustainability, racial issues, gender divides, and homophobia.

Though some may argue that Obama himself has not actualized the transformational promise of his campaign into the monumental change some heralded he would, it remains undeniable that the *fact* of his election pronounced a paradigmatic shift among *the people*—toward themselves, their country, and their global community. While the result of this shift has not always smiled brightly on the liberal-progressive side of the ledger (e.g., the extreme backlash politics of the so-called Tea Party, or the overtly racist invective on talk radio spewed almost daily at the president for being black), we would do well to recognize the de facto successes brought about by such a coalition, both in terms of policy (e.g., the repeal of "Don't Ask, Don't Tell," passage of the Lily Ledbetter Act, ratification of the START Treaty) and political perspectives (e.g., an ever-increasing introspective meditation on the "place" of the United States in the global village, the growing progressive bent among the under-30 crowd, or even the outwardly changing image of the United States away from that forged under Dubya).

Moreover, the seeds of resistance through *non*consumption, through the prospect of a transformational consumer shift (e.g., green consumerism), are fertile. As Arundhati Roy (2003) promises, "The corporate revolution will collapse if we refuse to buy what they are selling—their ideas, their version of history, their weapons, their notion of inevitability" (p. 112). And as NASCAR's plummeting attendance and television ratings numbers indicate, the NASCAR brand—with its entrenched white, neo-Confederate, patriarchal, proselytizing, militarized conservative alignments—has reached its own plateau in these transitional times. If we are indeed in the age of political consumerism, then perhaps NASCAR's cultural politics just aren't that appealing to many citizen-consumers in Obama's America.

Or maybe it is the unfulfilled promises of neoliberalism's spectacles of individualism that are failing NASCAR. Being in NASCAR Nation can, for many, serve as a painful reminder of the negative effects of free market reform. A sport built on the promise of free market prosperity has for some become a prolific reminder of America's neoliberal failings: lost factory jobs, outsourcing, government bailouts, certain environmental demise, infinite war, white rage, rapture, disastrous petrol capitalism, and performative consumer excess. Increasingly, these defining features of NASCAR Nation, especially when confronting those working-class Americans most disenfranchised by neoliberal reform, stimulate heightened senses of uncertainty, anxiety, and fear: fear for the individual's economic future; fear of the Jihadists in their midst; fear of end times; fear of a new national racialism; and so on. And why would a struggling family from Tennessee, Delaware,

South Carolina, or anywhere else pay $100 per ticket to enter into these spectacles of neoliberal dread?

This cultural extradition from NASCAR Nation, however, does not come easy, nor is it guaranteed. In *Ethics: Subjectivity and Truth*, Michel Foucault (1997) returns to that most basic of post-structuralist dictums: that subjectivity is *not* something that is given to or created independently by the individual, but rather is an effect of power, knowledge, and history. Following Foucault (1988, 1994), we have endeavored to illustrate throughout how the experiences of (NASCAR Nation's) sporting subjects are rationally polyvalent: First, the subject cannot create her or his identity outside these public pedagogies and, therefore, each spectator is the subject of market discourse (those of the market, its brands, and the corporation that produce those conditions). And, second, the spectator becomes subject to the discourses of neoliberalism if he/she puts him-/herself at the position from which discourse makes most "sense" (as a member of the atomized masses of the working-class "Nation"). Thus, the consumer—through the interplay of spectacularization and individualization—occupies a place within a "new habitat of subjectification." As such, the neoliberal self is constructed through *consumption* choices, choices that in total reaffirm the conditions by which those very consumer's livelihoods are destabilized.

This "neoliberal subjectivity" (Bondi, 2005) is largely regulated by *market* interests—and the technologies of the self-emergent thereof—often derivate from the idealized "economic man," or what Foucault and others often refer to as *Homo economicus*. In this way, the self is a projection of achievement in the hypercompetitive, individualized, ahistoricized market society:

> everyday experiences reflect a neoliberal ethos operative within almost every aspect of our individual and social lives with consequences that are dire for many and dangerous for most if not all of us. Indeed the central aim of neoliberal governmentality is the strategic production of social conditions conducive to the constitution of *Homo economicus*, a specific form of subjectivity with historical roots in traditional liberalism. However, whereas liberalism posits "economic man" as a "man of exchange," neoliberalism strives to en-sure that individuals are compelled to assume market-based values in all of their judgments and practices in order to amass sufficient quantities of "human capital" and thereby become "entrepreneurs of themselves." Neoliberal *Homo economicus* is a free and autonomous "atom" of self-interest who is fully responsible for navigating the social realm using rational choice

and cost-benefit calculation to the express exclusion of all other values and interests. (Hamann, 2009, p. 38)

In such a society, writes Trent Hamann (2009), "Exploitation, domination, and every other form of social inequality is rendered invisible *as social* phenomena to the extent that each individual's social condition is judged as nothing other than the effect of his or her own choices and investments" (p. 43, emphasis in original).

Under neoliberalism, *Homo economicus* is thus no longer a "partner in exchange" but instead is fashioned as "an entrepreneur and an entrepreneur of himself" (Hamann, 2009, p. 53). Through spectacles of consumption, such as the corporatized NASCAR spectacle we have described in earlier chapters, this normatively aestheticized *Homo economicus* self and all its discursive allusions (illusions) reaffirm for the citizen-consumer the *freedoms of the market*. However, this sense of "freedom can constitute a form of subjection" (Read, 2009, p. 25), as it produces techniques of self-awareness and self-regulation that, through norming and surveillance, proctor a form of governance over the performative space.[3] This is the challenge of our day: to transcend the frames and systems to which our identities, our politics, indeed our very sense of self, are subjugated and at the same time understood to be the pathways to freedom. And in some ways NASCAR has changed along these lines. It never really obfuscated the systems of neoliberalism, but rather selectively, if not mystifyingly, made them grand. As these systems fail and pathways dead end, the subjectivities created and reproduced in and through the NASCAR spectacle become articulated to broader formations of neoliberal demise. In other words, most NASCAR fans have long been aware of the (neoliberal) cultural politics of NASCAR Nation, but as the context changes, so too do the meanings, power relations, and interpellative qualities framed within those subjectivities. To buy NASCAR is in some ways, at least for some, to buy the lie.

NASCAR's fortunes may likely be tied to 1) the fate and reconciliation of a now-ruptured U.S. political Right (Tea Party, neo-conservatives, imperialists, libertarians, etc.); 2) the sport league's ability to depoliticize its brand, recasting it in the banalities of mainstream North American sport culture; and/or 3) delocalize itself in projecting a faux redneck cosmopolitanism into the global marketplace (an unlikely solution). NASCAR fans will undoubtedly be paying close attention, as will those political and cultural intermediaries who have invested various forms of capital into its success over the years. And perhaps this is the most important point in all of this: not the degree to which NASCAR fans are subjects or subjected to these broader political and power relations, *but the extent to which the interests of a few are projected onto the NASCAR experiences of so many.* While stock car subjectivities change with context, the pursuit of power (in and through NASCAR Nation, as elsewhere) is eternal.

NOTES

INTRODUCTION

1. Bush was making an effort to try and point out that he *had* shown up for flight training while in the Texas Air National Guard and thus quell media reports that had recently suggested that he had been AWOL from his Texas Air National Guard service.

2. Russell's observations mirror those reported by Mike Allen and Liz Clarke (2004) of the *Washington Post*, who noted the words of "Thomas," a 58-year-old self-employed contractor attending the race: "[Bush is] like me. His swagger, his confidence—I can relate to his thinking."

3. Of course, our use of the term "national culture" is not meant to signify either a singular, monolithic national culture shared by all self-identified "Americans," nor a cultural sphere limited only to the political, economic, or geographic boundaries of the United States of America. Rather, we are suggesting that for many self-identified "Americans," "America" is an inwardly and nonreflexively constituted free-floating, abstracted, and contested discursive formation through which the national narrative is framed. Further, our use of the terms "America" and "American" is specifically utilized through the text not to suggest that "America" is synonymous with the United States of America and its politics, culture, and economy—as to do so would problematically dismiss the multiplicities of the "Americas" and the privileged positioned the United States is often afforded in discussions thereof—but to evoke the homogenizing processes by which the national imaginary is often subjected and brought to life.

4. In the early part of the decade, NASCAR was lauded as North America's "fastest growing sport" in terms of the upsurge in gate receipts, television coverage, fan organizations, and sales of licensed merchandise when compared with other major professional sports leagues in recent decades (Rybacki & Rybacki, 2002). We detail this hypercommercialization of NASCAR later in the book.

5. Wright's aforementioned text, as well as Neal Thompson's (2006) concise cultural history of the early days of NASCAR, *Driving with the Devil: Southern Moonshine, Detroit Wheels, and the Birth of NASCAR*, being two exceptions.

6. And, of course, there is a plethora of mainstream press that focus in some fashion on NASCAR. These include such books as celebrity profiles of various drivers (e.g., Larry Cothren's series featuring Jeff Gordon, Dale Earnhardt, Sr., Tony Stewart, and others), fans' guides to auto racing (e.g., Mark Martin's [2000] *NASCAR for Dummies*),

or general automotive histories (e.g., Joe Menzer's [2001] *The Wildest Ride: A History of NASCAR [or How a Bunch of Good Ol' Boys Built a Billion-Dollar Industry out of Wrecking Cars]*).

7. A fantasy league is a virtual competition, usually hosted on a major sports-themed website such as ESPN.com, between contestants who select a set of drivers to make up their "team." Order is determined by the composite results of each contestant's team over the course of the NASCAR season.

8. Of course, our research did not exist in isolation from NASCAR's corporate practices, but rather in dialogue with them.

9. It is important to note that we *did* speak with administrators and other individuals within NASCAR's corporate hierarchy. In the best practices of critical ethnography, however, we did so in dialogue with the empirical conversations that we had with the folks consuming their events—never sharing any information about the people with whom we spoke, nor of their opinions or experiences at NASCAR events.

10. In practice, this meant spending entire weekends in NASCAR Nation—sleeping in local motels, eating sausages, and drinking beers hours before each event, wandering about (or what Guy Debord [1981c] refers to as "*derivé*") the spaces and spatial practices of NASCAR, speaking with various strategically identified and randomly selected cultural agents along the way—all the while performing the role of "researcher–fan" (and thereby not contesting or stepping outside the normative boundaries of fan conduct).

11. The student of society will undoubtedly recognize that there is no distinct chapter devoted to NASCAR's gender politics in this book. In its place, gender themes, issues, and problematics can be found "popping up" throughout the text, and specifically in discussions found in Chapters Four, Five, and Six. As issues of gender, patriarchy, and sexuality intersect across axes of consumerism, racism, fundamentalism, and militarism, we thought it best to weave this thread across, rather than in isolation of, these themes. That being said, we feel that in the future such a focused, protracted analysis of NASCAR's politics of gender and sexuality would certainly prove more than useful.

12. In the final chapters of this book, we extrapolate the untenable imperatives of both missile-guided and Wal-Mart commodified U.S. expansion, what Arundhati Roy refers to as the "checkbook and cruise missile" dynamic (Roy & Barsamian, 2004).

1 SPORTING AUTOMOBILITY: CONTEXTUALIZING NASCAR NATION

1. With regard to this autonomous auto patriarchy, David Gartman (2004) writes:

> [C]ar ownership and operation were considered culturally appropriate mainly for men. However, even when women in this early

period gained access to automobility, gender ideology segregated them in a different type of automobile, the electric car. Gasoline-powered cars were said to be too smelly, noisy, powerful, and difficult to operate and maintain for women. Cars driven by electric motors were considered more appropriate for women, for they were quieter, cleaner and less mechanical. (p. 174)

In short, the car—and the knowledge and fortitude to master its capabilities—reconstructed the norms of a burgeoning modern technological masculinity (Hall, 2002).

2. Which was roughly a quarter of the price of all other automobiles. The point is often made that Ford's assembly line efficiency and revolutionary processes of standardization and mass production transformed the exchange of commodities within the American marketplace. Equally important, yet oft overlooked, is that by paying his employees what was then an unprecedented wage of $5 per day, and offering various forms of buyer incentives, he simultaneously incited a revolution of middle-class *consumption*. When considering the residual effects of this regime of mass accumulation, it becomes all the more obvious why domestic automobile manufacturers of the neoliberal condition are unable to compete in the global marketplace (more on this in Chapter Seven).

3. For example, the largest public works project of the postwar period was the Federal Aid Highway Act of 1956, which dedicated an initial $25 billion (roughly $200 billion in 2010 dollars, adjusting for inflation) for the construction of 41,000 miles of interstate highway construction. As a result, by the late-twentieth century, 50 percent of the Los Angeles' (for instance) topography was covered with automobile-dedicated pavement

4. This critique of automobility is neither new nor unique to Urry. For example, in his novel *Second Generation*, Raymond Williams (1964) describes the *auto paralysis* consequential of this automobility. Writing from a British context, he offers a series of observations on traffic congestion within an industrial city located in the north of England. He maps the contradictions of movement, mobility, and flow offered by the automobile; whereby social order is determined (by backlog, limited navigation, roadway controls) and yet within the car—and its air-conditioned, musical ambience—the car-driver is seemingly afforded a limitless pursuit of self-determined private purposes. And hence myth and reality become one, whereby the car is both the conduit to freedom and the apparatus by which one's freedom (on the road, in traffic, at a stop light, etc.) is constricted. To drive a car was, and continues to be, an act of *engagement* (with capital, with modernity, with consumer culture, etc.) and of *disengagement* (from spatial and temporal constraint, from the social malaise of the transportive world, from the strictures of footpath or railway interdependency).

5. The examples are far-reaching and diverse in structure and design. In Nazi Germany, for example, the authoritarian regime was able to administrate the street space in spectacular ways and in so doing suppress the democratic and socialist resistance movements it had betrayed. More recently in the United States, corporate intermediaries, such as those at automobile manufacturer General Motors, have successfully become entrenched in the street planning and policy arms of the federal government, and in so doing configure public funding and programming to maximize the nation's auto centricity and hence GM's profitability. (As an example of U.S. automobile manufacturers' investments in free market political economics, GM famously distributed thousands of copies of Friedrich Hayek's *The Road to Serfdom* to workers, patrons, and policymakers in Detroit and Washington during the 1940s and early 1950s.)

6. In his novel *Crash*, which was later made into an Oscar-winning film, J. G. Ballard (1973) described the almost sensual fetish for the road and automobility as "a huge metallized dream" enlivened by "our sense of speed, drama and aggression, the worlds of advertising and consumer goods, engineering and mass manufacture, and the shared experience of moving together through an elaborately signalled landscape" (quoted in Wollen, 1993, p. 16).

7. The Bible Belt is an informal term referring to the Southern and Southwestern part of the United States where socially conservative evangelical Protestantism is a dominant feature.

8. Here, of course, we are referring to the scientific management theories of F. W. Taylor. Taylor is often lauded as the father of the modern science of production efficiency, with his 1911 book *The Principles of Scientific Management* often hailed by business scholars as a seminal text in management theory. His impetus for workplace efficiency is largely based on the scientific study of the task management and intensive work training: divide up the worker's discrete task, and divide work nearly equally between managers and workers, so that the managers apply scientific management principles to planning the work and the workers actually perform the tasks.

9. In building the largest, fastest track on the circuit, architects had neglected to address banking issues that created an impossible combination of speed and maneuverability.

10. The Mason-Dixon Line was demarcated by Charles Mason and Jeremiah Dixon in the 1760s to resolve a border dispute between British colonies in Colonial America. It forms a boundary line between four U.S. states, forming part of the borders of Pennsylvania, Maryland, Delaware, and West Virginia (then part of Virginia). During the U.S. Civil War, it became an important boundary that distinguished Confederate and Union territories.

11. For example, all but three of NASCAR's top 20 drivers for the 1964 season hailed from states east of the Mississippi River. During that

same period, just 9 percent of NASCAR's races were held outside of the Old Confederacy; namely North Carolina, South Carolina, Tennessee, Virginia, Georgia, Florida, Mississippi, and Alabama (Pillsbury, 1974).

12. Along with the aforementioned shifts toward unionization in the major North American sport leagues, teams in South America (such as the popular Brazilian club Corinthians) and Europe (most celebrated in the restructuring of Barcelona Football Club) were undergoing radically democratic transformations in the wake of the 1968 transnational workers' movement.

13. We saw similar inklings of NASCAR driver-celebrities openly supporting Republican politicians a few years earlier, in 1976, when Richard Petty served on Gerald Ford's Steering Committee for President in North Carolina. However, the public engagement with NASCAR personalities had not yet reached the explicit levels we document later in this book.

14. The derisive reaction to Clinton escalated in 1995, when as president he moved to ban cigarette advertising at sporting events as part of a larger policy move aimed at curbing teen smoking rates (at the time, NASCAR was sponsored by R. J. Reynolds Co., the maker of Winston cigarettes, from whence NASCAR's Winston Cup Series was named). Although some fans legitimately worried that such restrictions could have a deleterious impact on NASCAR, given its immense sponsorship agreements with RJR, Christopher Sullivan (1995) suggests that more was afoot, writing:

> Some [fans] were mad out of loyalty to the tobacco company sponsors "that brought us here".... But most were mad at something larger. Mad at Big Government. Mad about losing rights. Mad at the FDA. And President Clinton. And his wife, Hillary, for that matter. And just plain mad that a bunch of law-abiding, family-oriented, hard-working, six-pack-in-the-Igloo folks like themselves were getting jerked around again. (p. 1)

15. An "unofficial" poll commissioned by Maxwell House Racing in October 1992 showed that Bush had the support of 83 percent of NASCAR drivers, Clinton 10 percent, and third-party candidate H. Ross Perot 7 percent. ("Drivers Place Bush in 'Poll' Position," 1992).

16. On the other hand, some Southern "centrists" (read: neoliberals with a "moderate" social agenda) have found modest success among the NASCAR faithful, as former Florida senator Bob Graham, U.S. Representative Heath Shuler (D-NC), and former Virginia governor (now senator) Mark Warner were each able to ingratiate themselves with the sport and its followers in the run-ups to their respective elections.

17. Based on our archival research, NASCAR Nation was widely ignored during the 1996 Bill Clinton-Bob Dole election, save for a few appearances at NASCAR events by Dole, and the aforementioned tobacco sponsorship flare-up. Rather, the so-called Soccer Moms constituency

ruled the popular-political debate. In 2000, candidates made appearances at various races—John McCain, for example, drove a few laps around the track at Darlington prior to the South Carolina Republican primary—but it was not generally a large media spectacle.

18. Bush attended a March 1999 Winston Cup Primestar 500 race in Ft. Worth, Texas. Although Meserve refers to Bush as a "presidential hopeful," Bush did not actually declare himself a candidate until June 1999.

19. This nichefication of contemporary politics is obviously nothing new. Anna Greenberg (1998), in fact, reminds us that every presidential election since 1992 has had its own thematic frame organized or bracketed off by race or gender. She notes, for example, that, "[in] 1992, the 'Year of the Woman' was fueled by anger over the Anita Hill/Clarence Thomas hearings; in 1994, the 'Angry White Male' apparently elected a Republican Congress; and in 1996, the 'Soccer Moms' were responsible for the re-election of Bill Clinton" (p. 1).

20. David von Drehle's (1992) essay on the intersection of politics and NASCAR, which appeared in the *Washington Post*, provided one of the more raw examples of the racial dynamic in place at NASCAR events: "'You notice there's not many blacks here,' a race fan from Florence, S.C., observed, touching on another quality of stock car culture. Only he didn't say 'black'" (p. A10).

2 THE ROAD AND SERFDOM: THEORIZING THE CULTURAL POLITICS OF NEOLIBERALISM

1. For example, take the BP oil spill of 2010. Prior to the catastrophe, U.S. policymakers feuded for decades over whether oil-producing activities should be subjected to greater government regulation. Hayek's acolytes, from both political parties but certainly from the Right, argued that BP should be free to operate in the company's best interest. Conversely, opponents suggested that the company's sole interest was maximizing profits for its shareholders, and as such secondary and long-term interests such as environmental sustainability or safety would be important only if it affected the quarterly bottom line.

2. We should note here that Hayek's neoliberalism in not the exclusive enterprise of neo-conservatism or paleo-conservatism. In fact, many of the great free market reforms of recent decades were introduced by Left or "progressive" politicians such as Bill Clinton or Barack Obama. Here we are simply connecting U.S. free market ideologies to the political ideologues most pervasive in their construction.

3. Many observers from outside North American boundaries would shudder at the idea of "U.S. centrism," in that the "American" body politic has moved dramatically Rightward in recent decades. For what is today framed as "Center-Left" in U.S. political rhetoric would, in most developed nations, be considered Right to "Far-Right." Right-leaning

political beings within the United States are equally consternated at the sparse common ground, and disjointed viewpoints, of "conservative" stalwarts such as media personalities Rush Limbaugh, Ann Coulter, Sean Hannity, and Glenn Beck, and Tea Party–supporting politicians such as Sarah Palin, Rick Perry, and Michele Bachmann.

4. Consider a sampling of their publicly stated views, which would seem archaic to most readers in 2010: Paul holds a view of civil rights in which "while the federal government can enforce integration of government jobs and facilities, private business people should be able to decide whether they want to serve black people, or gays, or any other minority group" (Marsh, 2010); Miller stated in an interview with CNN's John King that, were he to be elected, he would be in favor of outright abolishing Social Security for those not already in the system or near to entrance in it in favor of a privatized, investment-oriented system (King, 2010 [September 1]); Buck has implied that the 1950s U.S. education system was the best in the world prior to government intervention (and by this it is clear he means 1954, as in, *Brown v. Board of Education*) (Milhiser, 2010); and Angle has supported everything from the abolition of federal funding for education, the revocation of unemployment benefits (which she has said "doesn't really benefit anyone"), and an extreme view of a women's right to choose her own reproductive healthcare, such as when Angle—who is against abortion even in the case of rape and incest—callously "insisted that a young girl raped by her father should know that 'two wrong don't make a right,'" calling instead for making "a lemon situation into lemonade" (Stein, 2010).

5. It is important to point out however, as Chomsky (2009) did in a speech to The Commonwealth Club of California, that the wider Tea Party constituency does have *real* anger and resentment. Discussing Beck, Limbaugh, and others cut from the same cloth who drive this narrative, Chomsky stated:

> I'm thinking about the part [of the right-wing media] that has substantive content—crazy content—but it *is* substantive. It does give answers, to the people who for the last thirty years have seen their wages, income, stagnate or decline, benefits decline, services, decline, there's nothing for their children, world's out of control. These are the people who on polls, maybe 80 percent of them, say the country's going in the wrong direction, the government's run by the few and the special interests, not the people, and so on—you know, *they're not wrong*. This *is* all happening to them. And the answers that they're getting, from say, you know, Rush Limbaugh, Michael Savage, and the rest of them are, well, we have an answer: the rich liberals own everything, they own the corporations, they run the government, they run the media, and they don't care about people like you, they don't care about the flyover people between the East Coast and the West Coast.

They only care about giving everything you worked for away, to illegal immigrants, or gays, or something. So we gotta protect ourselves from them. And furthermore they run the government, when they put up a health program, it's not to give you health care, it's to kill your granny. And that's an answer to something. It's a terrible answer. But it *is* an answer. And if you do suspend disbelief, if you forget about what's happening in the world, really, it's a coherent answer. Now they're not hearing anything else. ([emphases in original)

6. Andrew Sullivan (2009) makes this point in very concise terms, noting that

This axiom, while useful, has a problem. It is untrue. And this "country" that White Americans are allegedly losing is not, in fact, a country. It is merely a self-serving and solipsistic illusion of a country that some White Americans *feel* they are losing. From its very beginning, after all, America was a profoundly Black country as well. (emphasis in original)

7. In January 2009, *Carnegie Council for Ethics in International Affairs* senior fellow Jonathan Clarke (2009) summarily outlined the "main characteristics of neo-conservatism" as follows:

1. a tendency to see the world in binary good/evil terms;
2. low tolerance for diplomacy;
3. readiness to use military force;
4. emphasis on U.S. unilateral action;
5. disdain for multilateral organizations;
6. focus on the Middle East; and
7. an Us versus Them mentality. (p. 1)

8. In 2010, the Obama administration dramatically revised the *National Security Strategy of the United States of America*, shifting the language away from that of military might and preemptive strike in favor of "economic, moral, and innovative strength" in pursuing "a strategy of national renewal and global leadership—a strategy that rebuilds the foundation of American strength and influence" (quoted in DeYoung, 2010).

9. "Crises" that many scholars argue are brought about by a "restless" capitalist class seeking further expansion of their regimes of accumulation.

10. Many contemporary economists agree that the commitment to this balanced strategy (of growth, regulation, and social welfarism), even by the most conservative political regimes, resulted in the United States' ascent as a global power in the middle-to-latter half of the twentieth century (cf. Harvey, 2005a).

11. Milton Friedman was able to popularize an updated *laissez-faire* theory by skillfully guiding his adherents into high-ranking political spheres and capitalizing on Reagan's skilled campaign stylings.

12. In so doing, he rejected Adam Smith's famous declaration regarding working-class welfare, deskilling of labor, and state intervention. We quote at length:

> The man whose whole life is spent in performing a few simple operations, of which the effects are perhaps always the same, or very nearly the same, has no occasion to exert his understanding or to exercise his invention in finding out expedients for removing difficulties which never occur. He naturally loses, therefore, the habit of such exertion, and generally becomes as stupid and ignorant as it is possible for a human creature to become....It corrupts even the activity of his body, and renders him incapable of exerting his strength with vigour and perseverance in any other employment than that to which he has been bred....His dexterity at his own particular trade seems, in this manner, to be acquired at the expense of his intellectual, social, and martial virtues. But in every improved and civilized society this is the state into which the labouring poor, that is, the great body of the people, must necessarily fall, unless government takes some pains to prevent it. (Smith, 1776/1966, p. 782)

13. Friedman and a cadre of his colleagues and students (who came to be known as "the Chicago Boys") would go on to form an organization to promote neoliberal values in 1947 called the Mont Pelerin Society. This confluent group would outline a generation of economic theory that has come to influence American political activity over the past 40 years. Contorting the rudiments of Adam Smith's self-regulating, "invisible hand" doctrine with Darwinian prudence, Friedman and his adherents steadily rose to positions of prominence within government cabinets in Chile, Argentina, New Zealand, Brazil, the United Kingdom, and the United States of America (Munck, 2005). On the ground, and intent on eliminating the regulatory vestiges of the Keynesian "welfare state" (Hetzel, 2007) in these countries, Friedman and his Chicago Boys systematically redoubled a broad-sweeping demolition of Keynesian infrastructures and the collapse of macroeconomic plurality under the throws of a singular marketized global interconnectivity (Borzutzky, 2005; Carcamo-Huechante, 2006; Cowen, 2006; Klein, 2007; Nelson, 2007).

14. Historically speaking, the late-twentieth century fall of the Leftist governments in South America, Europe, and East Asia signaled the pinnacle of this new form of market empire (Ferguson, 2005; Hardt & Negri, 2000). According to numerous economists and political scientists, the end of the Cold War brought about a new macroeconomic hegemony—a new world order marshaled by leaders of Western capitalist nation-states (namely Chile under the dictatorship of Augusto Pinochet, the regimes of Margaret Thatcher in Great Britain, Roger Douglas in New Zealand, Joao Goulart in Brazil, General Suharto in

Indonesia, Deng Xiaoping in Communist China, and Reagan in the United States of America) who, in the years prior, had supplanted social welfare systems with the corporate capitalist imperatives of profit-first *laissez-faire* free marketization.

15. In the United States, the catalyst for this course of neoliberalization came in 1979, when then-chairman of the Federal Reserve, Paul Volcker, implemented a series of deregulatory measures—namely in the form of tax cuts for corporations, a reduction in trade regulations and corporate taxation, and severe cuts in the federal interest rates—each meant to curb inflation, and in turn reempower the corporate sector. By most accounts, these new policies brought about an epoch of unfettered, and unparalleled, capital accumulation in both the domestic American and the globally interconnected global economies (Roach, 2005; Treaster, 2004). In effect, by programmatically absolving the Federal Reserve of its commitment to full employment and refocusing its purpose on inflation control and corporate growth, Volcker was able to dismiss the Keynesian traditions that had moderated economic activity in both domestic and global markets during the preceding decades and usher in a new era of corporate-first "trickle-down economics." Seen at the time as a consequence of growth, the maneuvers also brought about the highest rates of unemployment the country had experienced since the Great Depression (Harvey, 2005a, 2005b). As further consequence, the relative influence of American workers, labor unions, and welfare advocates diminished and these neoliberals ushered in an age of market bullishness and worker disempowerment. Median salaries were slashed, middle-class jobs were downsized and ultimately outsourced to third world labor markets, major unions were busted or simply disappeared, and U.S. multinationals were allowed to "gallivant" across the globe in search of new consumer markets (Appadurai, 2001; Castells, 2000; Grzinic, 2007; Lechner & Boli, 2000; Wallerstein, 2000).

16. In the introduction to Virilio's (1977/2006) seminal work, *Speed and Politics*, Benjamin Bratton (2006) describes the concept of dromology as the "government of differential motility" (p. 8).

17. The phenomenon of speculative excess has less to do with free markets than with high profits. "When the profits of trade happen to be greater than ordinary," Adam Smith (1776/1976) once wrote, "overtrading becomes a general error" (p. 438). And rate of profit, Smith claimed, "is always highest in the countries that are going fastest to ruin" (p. 266).

3   Consuming NASCAR Nation: Space, Spectacle, and Consumer-Citizenship

1. We call into question the processes through which normative American nationalism(s)—in recent years gleaned from what Antonio Gramsci might refer to as the "common sense," "average American," imaginary

"new New South" (Cobb, 1992)—are articulated to the contemporary neoliberal condition.

2. According to the ISC 2009 annual report (p. 13), total revenues have decreased in each of the past two years for which data is available: to $787 million in 2008, and to a five-year low of $683 million in 2009. We return to this point in Chapter Seven.

3. In 2006, for example, global brands such as Anheuser-Busch, General Mills, and Home Depot spent a total of $650 million to sponsor the top 35 teams in NASCAR's premier circuit (Gage, 2006). By way of comparison, North America's most popular professional sports entity, the National Football League, at the same time commanded a total of only $485 million in sponsorship revenues per season (Gage, 2006). Nextel, the "title sponsor" of the championship cup, alone remunerated $700 million in 2003 for 10 years' worth of sponsorship rights (a significant increase from the $200 million over 5 years paid by the previous sponsor) (Elliott, 2004).

4. The "Big Three" faction rationalizes the large expenditures on stock car racing by selling consumers, employees, investors, and stockholders on the "win on Sunday, sell on Monday" mantra. "The idea, popularized in the 1960s, was that success on the racetrack translated quickly into success in the showroom for General Motors, Ford, and Chrysler, with the respective automakers seeing a surge in sales when one of their driver won a big race" (Jensen, 2009, p. 1). "Those closest to the racing action [in Detroit] demanded that their executives spend more and more money on racing, because, as the mind-set [goes], money equals wins, and wins equals more cars sold" (Margolis, 2008). Manufacturers utilize NASCAR racing programs as test environments to develop new safety gear, technical innovations, chassis designs, and to conduct engineering education and experimentation. "The same holds true for oil companies, tire companies, and pretty much any company that makes performance parts or cars that wind up on race tracks around the world" (Lemasters, Jr., 2005, p. 1).

5. Amidst the Great Recession of 2008–2009, revenue from gate receipts decreased slightly at first (from $253 million in 2007 to $236 million for 2008), then rapidly crashed (from $236 million for 2008 to $195 million in 2009). We explore this and other earnings trends for NASCAR in Chapter Seven.

6. McCarthy's prediction did not come to pass, however, as most business publications would by 2010 consistently rank Apple, Amazon, and Google among the most important U.S. brands.

7. We have chosen to forego the anthropological act of referencing every single conversation or observation as "fieldnotes." Unless otherwise stated, all quotes from race fans or observations pertaining to the physical environment of the NASCAR spectacle are to be presumed to have come from our notes.

8. In its marketing information, NASCAR has also made a point to illustrate that children under the age of 18 are more likely than other professional sports' young fans to consume sponsoring brands.

9. These sponsorships change frequently in the form of multiyear, year-to-year, or sometimes even week-to-week agreements, based on both driver performance and corporate sponsorship agenda (or lack of sponsorship monies). In turn, most fans are well versed in the etymology of most drivers' corporate symbols. In 2010, for example, Mark Martin fans could be distinguished by their race-day-adornment of GoDaddy.com merchandise. However, NASCAR aficionados will also likely recognize that a fan donning weathered U.S. Army, Kraft, or Viagra merchandise will likely have ties to Martin as well.

10. Here we take our understanding of space from the work of Michel de Certeau (1984), who posits that it is best understood as a kind of locus, specifically as "a plane, which is the order in accord with which elements are distributed in relationship of coexistence" (p. 117). Place, by contrast, is the cognitive, dynamic, representational, codified, and signified mechanism of meaning in practice. In *The Practice of Everyday Life*, de Certeau (1984) surmised that "place is constituted by a system of signs" (p. 117). In navigating the relation between place and space, de Certeau located the notion of space as a frequented system of the experienced, mobilized by and understood as an "intersection of moving bodies" (cf. Auge, 1995). In one sense, then, space is a physical and imagined geography constituted by dynamic elements that meet, intersect, unite, cross each other, or diverge. Or, as de Certeau (1984) posited, "space occurs as the effect produced by the operations that orient it, situate it, temporalize it, and make it function in a polyvalent unity of conflictual programs or contractual proximities" (p. 117). Taken together, the relationship between space and place can be described in this way: Place is a "fixed position," and space is a "realm of practices" (Crang, 2000, p. 138); or, more simply put, "*space is practiced place*" (de Certeau, 1984, p. 117; emphasis in original).

11. On the temporal nature of fashion and consumer culture, Barry Smart (2010) writes: "While a semblance of identity may now be purchased through individualized consumption, any sense of self-achievement in this manner is destined to be temporary, for the consumer process, and advertising, marketing, fashion, and popular culture lifestyling in particular, effectively contribute to the instability of identity through the perpetual generation and relentless promotion of new products, images, and values suggestive of further possible new identities and lifestyle choices" (p. 44).

12. To reproduce the power embedded in the spectacle, Debord (1994) asserts that the spectacular society must reinvent itself, always making and remaking itself as something new, something yet to be attained. For the spectator, the distance between what one has and what one wants, who one is and who one wants to be, and so on, is always availed through the spectacle; forever interpellating, impossible to achieve.

13. Although some might argue that they are really only being promised the "freedom to be formed and normed" (Ivison, 1997).

14. Beck and Beck-Gernsheim (2002) have similarly argued that this type of consumption does not offer "freedom of choice," but rather "insight into the fundamental incompleteness of the self" (p. xxi). In other words, this culture of consumption brings with it the mystification of the autocratic self—an economy of signs that transmits the myths of individual freedom.

15. These are contractions Marx problematized nicely in his *Sixth Thesis on Feuerbach*: "the human essence is no abstraction inherent in each single individual. In reality it is the ensemble of the social relations" (p. 23).

16. Beck and Beck-Gernsheim (2002) make this point clear: "the spiral of individualization destroys given foundations of social coexistence. So—to give a simple definition—'individualization' means disembedding without re-embedding" (p. xxii). Once inside the spectacle, the relationships of consequence are those between commodity and individual consumer, rather than individual consumer and the individual producer.

17. Bourdieu (1998a) explains the productive nature of insecurity in these times in this manner:

> One thus begins to suspect that insecurity is the product not of an *economic inevitability*, identified with the much heralded "globalization," but of a *political will*. A "flexible" company in a sense deliberately exploits a situation of insecurity which it helps to reinforce: it seeks to reduce its costs, but also to make this lowering possible by putting the workers in permanent danger of losing their jobs. The whole world of production, material and cultural, public and private, is thus carried along by a process of intensification of insecurity. (p. 84, emphasis in original)

18. Ironically, those who least ascribe to Darwin's theory of evolution are also those most likely supportive of a Darwinian economic system.

19. Again, the work of Bourdieu (1998b) is useful in understanding this point:

> Competition is extended to individuals themselves, through the individualization of the wage relationship: establishment of individual performance objectives, individual performance evaluations, permanent evaluation, individual salary increases or granting of bonuses as a function of competence and of individual merit; individualized career paths; strategies of "delegating responsibility" tending to ensure the self-exploitation of staff who, simple wage laborers in relations of strong hierarchical dependence, are at the same time held responsible for their sales, their products, their branch, their store, etc. as though they were in-dependent contractors. This pressure toward "self-control" extends workers'

"involvement" according to the techniques of "participative management" considerably beyond management level. All of these are
techniques of rational domination that impose over-involvement
in work (and not only among management) and work under emer-
gency or high-stress conditions. And they converge to weaken or
abolish collective standards or solidarities.

20. Foucault's definition of "subject position" highlights the productive
nature of these forms of disciplinary power—how it names and catego-
rizes people into hierarchies (of normalcy, health, morality, etc.).

4   NASCAR AND THE "SOUTHERNIZATION" OF SPORTING AMERICA

1. Although confessing his "non-Southern roots," Horwitz's (1999) rigor
and reflexivity take on a deeply invested perspective of a self-professed
"non-Southerner" who nonetheless identifies with the cultures of the
region. Furthermore, he maintains a reflexive voice throughout his travels and writings on "the South" and the people he meets.
2. NASCAR claims that more than 20 percent of its fans are "ethnic minor-
ities." When given this piece of information, race fans with whom we
spoke (confirming our own observations) suggested that this number
seems an incredible exaggeration, at least in terms of the proportions of
African American, Hispanic, and ethnicized "Others" attending races.
3. Taibbi continues, in rather pointed terms:

> The individuals in the Tea Party may come from very different
> walks of life, but most of them have a few things in common. After
> nearly a year of talking with Tea Party members from Nevada to
> New Jersey, I can count on one hand the key elements I expect
> to hear in nearly every interview. One: Every single one of them
> was that exceptional Republican who *did* protest the spending in
> the Bush years, and not one of them is the hypocrite who only
> took to the streets when a black Democratic president launched
> an emergency stimulus program. ("Not me—I was protesting!"
> is a common exclamation.) Two: Each and every one of them is
> the only person in America who has ever read the Constitution
> or watched *Schoolhouse Rock*. (Here they have guidance from
> [Richard] Armey, who explains that the problem with "people
> who do not cherish America the way we do" is that "they did not
> read the Federalist Papers.") Three: They are all furious at the
> implication that race is a factor in their political views—despite
> the fact that they blame the financial crisis on poor black home-
> owners, spend months on end engrossed by reports about how the
> New Black Panthers want to kill "cracker babies," support politi-
> cians who think the Civil Rights Act of 1964 was an overreach of

government power, tried to enact South African-style immigration laws in Arizona and obsess over Charlie Rangel, ACORN and Barack Obama's birth certificate. Four: In fact, some of their best friends are black! (Reporters in Kentucky invented a game called "White Male Liberty Patriot Bingo," checking off a box every time a Tea Partier mentions a black friend.) And five: Everyone who disagrees with them is a radical leftist who hates America.

4. The notion of a "visible" quality to whiteness, or more accurately the physical propagation of centralized identity politics around whiteness, is briefly introduced in Derald Wing Sue's (2004) article on "ethnocentric monoculturalism."

5. The distinction between racialism and racism is made quite clearly by David Theo Goldberg (2009) in his book titled *The Threat of Race: Reflections on Racial Neoliberalism*, and particularly in the opening chapter.

6. This dialogue between the omnipresent Southern signifiers, such as the Confederate flag and the proliferation of white bodies in NASCAR spaces, has created two interrelated arcs of interpretation and consumption for spectators allied with NASCAR. In relation to the meaningfulness of the Confederate symbol, both supporters and critics of the flag's public presence at NASCAR events agree that the meaning of the "Southern Cross" (as the flag is often referred to in the South) is neither fixed nor absolute but rather a malleable discursive formation through which ideologies have flowed since the first star was stitched onto the cotton banner. The flag has at once, and throughout its history, been a source of pride for Southern heritage groups, a marker of identity for white supremacist organizations, and a symbol of racial oppression for the marginalized peoples of the South (Newman, 2007c).

7. Although popular counternarratives of the flag as marginalizing, oppressive, iniquitous, symbolically violent symbol is gaining credence within the public sphere (e.g., the declarations offered by old-time sport icons such as University of South Carolina head football coach Steve Spurrier), such a discourse of resistance is noticeably absent from NASCAR spaces.

8. This colonization, or confederation, of space—by no means exclusive to races held in the South (races in Pennsylvania, Michigan, and Delaware are as equally saturated with these signifiers)—greets the consumer-spectator-subject the moment he or she enters the parking lot. On race days, these otherwise blank geometric canvasses are made meaningful through a sea of RVs, SUVs, trucks, and other automobiles casting images of the battle flag of the Confederacy, POW- and military-themed insignias, banners sporting the colors of popular NASCAR drivers, and a variety of American pennons.

9. It must also be pointed out that the uncontested, normalized nature of the Old South symbolic and the unequivocal white exclusivity in these

spaces are undoubtedly not lost on nonwhite subject-spectators who en masse stay away from these events.

10. A race held on the eve of the midterm U.S. elections that saw a sweeping voter swing back toward the paleo-conservative polity on offer by the likes of Kentucky's Rand Paul, Alabama's Jefferson Beauregard Sessions, South Carolina's Tim Scott, Texas' Rick Perry, or Louisiana's Jeff Landry.

11. Prior to a South-wide revitalization of Confederate History Month celebrations in 2009, Virginia's 1997 Confederate History Month celebration—initiated under that state's much-maligned, epithet-espousing former governor George Allen—was a rare exception to the otherwise eradicated practice in recent years.

12. Pierre Nora (1989) takes this line of thinking one step further, noting that history is often seen to hold a deathly quality; it comes to haunt our social lives through the processes of remembering. Over the course of some 40 texts on the subject, Nora (1989) develops the notion of "national memory"—broadly conceived (in order) as "founding memory" (or the period of defining and affirming the existence of the sovereign state); state-memory (circulations of representations of the state); "national-memory" (the recentering of national memories around collective machinations of the nation); and "citizen-memory" (the sense of "belonging to" the nation is diffused through the internalizing processes of the atomized masses). In his theorizing of French national memory, Nora contemplates the state as a generational mythology upon which modernity's longings for "place" are thrust unto the national imaginary.

13. In this instance, the neo-Confederate stylization presents itself as "the unique self-construction of the newest in the medium of what has been" (Benjamin, 1999, p. 64). And thus the re-articulated fusion of Confederate aesthetic and the "eternal return" of Old South public whiteness extended, and continues to extend, beyond fashion as *recherché*—what Walter Benjamin (1999) described as the "always vain, often ridiculous, sometimes dangerous quest for a superior ideal beauty" (p. 66)—into the realms of aesthetic governance and adornment as disciplinarity. The unreal bodies of the Confederate dead thus operated on, and continue to discipline, the active subjects of NASCAR Nation. To counter these racialized (and racist) historical renderings and imaginaries, Goldberg (2009) argues, requires a critical historical memory, one through which we recall "the conditions of racial degradation and relating contemporary to historical and local to global conditions" (p. 21).

14. Another popular example of this mass mediated absolution of stock car racing's racial and cultural homogeneity can be found in the 2006 film *Talladega Nights: The Ballad of Ricky Bobby* (see also Chapter Five). The movie follows the trials and tribulations of Ricky Bobby (played by *Saturday Night Live* alum Will Ferrell), a driver on NASCAR's top

circuit. Following a series of life-altering comedic highs and lows—each playing to overblown stereotypes of a bucolic, Southern, white, working-class vernacular (divorce and infidelity, lack of education, caricaturized faith, overprivileging the kitsch aesthetic, etc.)—Ricky Bobby faces the definitive moment of his racing career: a return to the fabled Talladega Super Speedway in his last act of racing redemption. In spite of the fact that the Talladega venue is notorious in NASCAR circles as one of the most Confederate-flag-saturated tracks on the circuit, the symbol is absent from Hollywood mediations of the space. Moreover, the track is transformed into a site of tolerance rather than of exclusivity in the film—as the protagonist reconciles his homophobic jingoism in the film's *dénouement* (a gay, French Formula One driver of Middle Eastern ethnic heritage named Jean Girard, played by famous English comedian Sacha Baron Cohen of *Borat* and *Bruno* fame).

15. Grant has said she followed the chain of command all the way to Nationwide Series director Joe Balash, but stopped short of telling human resources because she had been reprimanded by that department (for a separate incident) two weeks after lodging her complaint. She said she viewed the reprimand, which included a threat of termination, as retaliation for complaining to Balash (Hinton, 2008).

16. NASCAR's point of response to this critique would likely be to identify a recent upsurge in "minority ownership" in the sport. "Self-made" athletes from other sports (namely gridiron's Randy Moss, and basketball's Magic Johnson, Brad Daugherty) currently hold some investment in a racing team. This is roughly 5 percent of the total ownership of NASCAR teams. Nonetheless, in 2009 NASCAR felt it necessary to commission Bill Kimm to author a self-congratulatory article whereby the sport had proclaimed that these minority owners had helped "put the race issues in the rear view" (Kimm, 2009). In neoliberal parlance, Art Shelton, owner of an "all-minority" racing team in one of NASCAR's lower circuits, recently declared: "Trail Motorsport will race as a team that happens to be minority," Shelton said. "We're going to race as a team that's going to be competitive and happens to be minority. If you want to label that as diversity, yes. But we diversify only for the point of being successful. That's the only standard" (quoted in Kimm, 2009).

17. We would hasten to add that it is counterproductive and anti-intellectual to assume that those opposed to, say, affirmative action, are simply "racists" or "bigots," as a good number of those on the mainstream left seem to be offering up of late. Rather, the fear of losing one's job—or one's imagined "place" in society—to someone else (whether "Northern elite" or "unseen terrorist") was callously exploited by Bush for partisan political gain. As Larry Grossberg (2006) maintains, the answer to Thomas Frank's question ("What's the matter with Kansas?") is, simply, *nothing*. The problem, rather, lies in the morally corrupt political strategies seeking to further divide the nation along ideological grounds.

18. Grossberg (1996) proposes that scholars must escape the conventions of oppression, both the "colonial model" of "the oppressed and the oppressor" and the "transgression model" of "oppression and resistance" (p. 88). Rather than think in terms of binaries of oppression or forces of oppression versus forces of resistance, he proposes that we re-articulate the question of identity into a "question of constructing historical agency" (Grossberg, 1996, p. 88).

5   Racing for Jesus: Sport in Theocratic America

1. Newberry's (2004) analysis runs counter to the vast majority of journalistic musings and scholarly research on the sport that remain committed to exploring the increased relevance of stock car racing in the North American sporting popular—if not specifically fixed on its economic possibilities—in a decidedly banal tenor. In spite of the obvious labors of cultural and political intermediaries to construct a discursively and materially constituted cultural apparatus within speedway spaces, during television broadcasts, and in the print media coverage—one that carries with it a spectacular set of images, practices, institutions, rituals, commodities, and identities—there is but a scant critical discourse devoted to interrupting NASCAR as an important neo-conservative cultural technology within contemporary American society.

2. This religiosity is further compounded by a constant dialogue race car-drivers have with their own mortality. As racings fans new and old alike will concur, there is a palpable sense of *danger* shared by drivers and fans at a NASCAR event. This omnipresent anxiety is abetted by the fact that since 2001, some of racing's most-beloved icons—such as Dale Earnhardt, Sr., and Adam Petty (progeny of the Petty-family racing legacy), as well as lesser-known drivers Kenny Irwin and Tony Roper—have suffered life-ending injuries while competing in the NASCAR circuit. When asked why deaths in auto racing were six times more common than deaths in football, Bill France famously proclaimed: "because we go six times faster!" (quoted in Zweig, 2007, back cover). In the parlance of race car culture, a hard crash into "Turn Four" is all "that stands between these drivers and their maker" (see Newman & Giardina, 2009, p. 56).

3. Almost a decade after his death, Earnhardt's image—on T-shirts, flags, etc.—at any given speedway remains one of the most prevalent of all drivers (past or present).

4. Importantly, some fans point to Earnhardt's last act, whereby he effectively died protecting his son's place in the race (Junior went on to finish the race in second place) as the great sacrifice of a proud father.

5. As membership in groups such as the Promise Keepers has continued to rise over the past decade, the contentious ideologies propagated therein

have come under heavy scrutiny in both orthodox and nonorthodox circles:

> the discourse of masculinity found within conservative religious movements, such as the Promise Keepers...is inherently political. Any masculinity project aimed at restoring or reclaiming a "traditional" male role for privileged white, heterosexual males has a political impact within the tapestry of class, race, and gender power. (Schindler, 1998)

6. It is of no coincidence that Huckabee's views of same-sex marriage are equally regressive.
7. In recent years, many fans have turned on these inheritors of stock car racing lionization. Consider, for example, one fan's diatribe regarding Dale Earnhardt, Jr. in a January 2003 issues of *Scene Magazine*:

> Call me crazy, but I'm just not buying the hype about Dale Earnhardt, Jr....Granted, he has the name only, no real natural talent, just the name....I don't understand why everyone is cheering him. I cheer for drivers because they're good, clean racers and good clean guys. Junior doesn't personify either of those characteristics. I'm just not buying it. (January 23, 2003, quoted in Hugenberg & Hugenberg, 2008, p. 646)

8. Among other things, Palin has called prochoice feminists a "cackle of rads." For more see Jessica Valenti (2010), "The Fake Feminism of Sarah Palin" (*Washington Post*, May 30).
9. Similar hateful declarations were made by the very same individuals in the aftermath of Hurricane Katrina's devastation of New Orleans in 2005; in other words, that the devastation was caused by God as a rebuke against the people of New Orleans for their perceived cultural excesses.
10. According to its Wikipedia entry, South Barrington is one of the wealthiest towns in the United States, with a per capita income of $76,078, a median household income of $170,755, and a median home value of $689,200. Demographically speaking, the town is exceedingly White (~95 percent of residents). City-data.com and the 2000 U.S. census offer similar portraits of South Barrington.
11. A good friend of one of the authors was a member of the Willow Creek congregation; he attended several services with her in 2006.
12. Willow Creek has been consistently ranked as one of the largest and most (politically) influential churches in the United States for much of the 2000s. Its 7,000+ seat Worship Center was constructed in 2004 at a cost of more than $70 million, and contains massive 14'x24' high-definition LED screens and other state-of-the-art accoutrements that would seem to be more at home at STAPLES Center in Los Angeles (home to the NBA's Lakers and Clippers, and the NHL's Kings) or CONSOL Energy Center in Pittsburgh (home to the NHL's Penguins)

than a place of worship. Speakers to its annual Leadership Summit have included Bill Clinton, Colin Powell, Jimmy Carter, and U2's Bono.

13. For a detailed examination of the specific religious politics of various racing teams like that of Morgan Shepherd and Joe Gibbs, see Newman and Giardina (2009). For an example of this synergy in action, see Shepherd's website http://www.racewithfaith.com

14. In and of itself, there is nothing inherently problematic with a racing team being aligned with religion or deploying religion as part of its promotional agenda (Will Leitch makes this point very nicely in his [2008] book *God Save the Fan*). Rather, we seek to unravel how religion comes to be understood within the semiotic geometry of the track space at a particular point in history.

15. This brand of self-serving theocratic American exceptionalism is similarly found in the collective orgasm experienced by Republican politicians for all-things Ronald Reagan, and is mirrored in the title of Mitt Romney's (2010) *No Apologies: The Case for American Greatness* (a book that, as Chris Good's [2010] review in *The Atlantic* makes clear, reveals Romney to be "an inhabitant of fantasyland" when it comes to the realities of foreign policy in the present moment).

16. Just as George W. Bush and his cabinet had done two years prior, George Allen's politico-religious stumpings were an attempt to capitalize on NASCAR's pedagogies of belonging to a shared political ideology, to a collective religious movement, to the imagined spectatorship of NASCAR. That he was not reelected speaks more to his bigoted public pronouncements during the campaign than it does of a failing of the NASCAR constituency to support him. Also, his opponent, Jim Webb, was a centrist Democrat palatable to the Virginia electorate, and without the political baggage of Allen.

17. With the possible exception of the post-9/11 seventh-inning stretch renditions of "God Bless America" performed instead of "Take Me Out to the Ballgame" during Major League Baseball games in 2001 and 2002. Of note is the fact that the New York Yankees have continued this tradition through the 2010 season.

18. Where the living conditions are most desperate, particularly in the U.S. South, is where these evangelic modalities are most concentrated (Hedges, 2007). The stress to accumulate livable capital is more pronounced through the heightened demands of two-worker families in the context of a postindustrial rural labor climate. As the main employers of these regions tend to be Wal-Mart, Ruby Tuesday, and Exxon (or similar derivations thereof in the retail, food, and energy sectors), the wage labor is often suppressed and laborer oppressed. As a consequence, "Red States," and particularly those that are said to have the highest concentration of self-identified Christian fundamentalists, invariably have higher rates of murder, illegitimacy, teenage births, and divorce rates (Hedges, 2007).

19. The following two paragraphs are taken from Newman and Giardina (2009, p. 74).

6 Part I: NASCAR Nation as/in Petrol Empire; Part II: Militarizing NASCAR Nation

1. Oil has the best physical characteristics of any energy resource as it can exist in three different forms: solid, liquid, or gas. These forms can be given an "energy grade" and when measured against all other forms of energy, oil possesses more capability than any other similar resource.

2. Generally speaking, the lower and more stable the price of a barrel of oil, the greater the market will rally. This comes with two notable exceptions: in 1973, when the market experienced "stagflation," and in 1987, when a sharp rise in oil was offset by the Fed's pumping of sufficient money into the economy.

3. Consequently, those powerbrokers who retain strategic possession of the valuable commodity are beneficiaries of the *U.S. energy economy*—an economy that revolves around the continuous inexpensive flow of oil, petroleum, and natural gas products, but a highly lucrative industry within the broader economic infrastructure. From Rockefeller's Standard Oil monopoly at the height of U.S. industrialization, through the Seven Sisters' panics and oligopolization, and later the OPEC petrol hegemony during the postindustrial global transformation of the late twentieth century, one thing has been clear: those who have controlled the precious commodity have accumulated significant social, political, and economic capital. The oil industry had been quite profitable for petroleum producers historically, and by the 1990s, 7 of the top 20 wealthiest corporations in the world were in the business of petroleum (Yergin, 1991) with ExxonMobil, Royal Dutch Shell Group, ConocoPhillips, ChevronTexaco, and British Petroleum situated as the biggest of all big businesses in the world.

4. Interestingly, as Palast (2006) makes clear in *Armed Madhouse*, the language of a "peak-oil crisis" has been driven in large part by oil giants themselves. Of the logics of Chevron's PR efforts in particular, which have taken the form of billboards and multipage spreads in magazines such as *Harper's*, he writes: "The new oil Chevron is finding 'requires a greater investment to refine.' In other words, don't bitch about high prices—we need your cash to mix your next fix of crude" (p. 337).

5. There are, at present, differing interpretations and several schools of thought within Marxian political economy on interpreting crisis formation (Harvey, 2007). Indeed, Marx presents several modes of crisis formation in *Capital:* profit squeezes (labor organization and scarcity drives down rate of profit); underconsumption (deficiency of effective demand); overaccumulation (barriers to profitable surplus absorption); and the more controversial falling rate of profit crisis that sees labor saving innovations replace living labor in production.

6. There is debate among Marxists whether ecological Marxism constitutes a departure from all other previously mentioned formations of crisis, or

whether it is merely a subdivision of the profit squeeze crisis focusing on raw material capital inputs in commodity production rather than Marx's more emphasized labor power organization. For the purpose of this document, environmental destruction and raw material depletion is treated as an independent form of Crisis—a crisis external to the system.

7. Some might argue that the deliberate selection of fuel (in)efficient, eight-cylinder "gas hogs" becomes a means of (sub)cultural identification or badge of citizenship for partisans of NASCAR Nation. When asked if they would consider trading in their large truck for a fuel efficient hybrid vehicle, one NASCAR enthusiast responded: "Hell no! True NASCAR fans don't drive them. That's what [wimps] drive." Taking pride in these petrol-laden codes and rituals, attendants systematically rejected "alternative" fuel-saving technologies. Consider the following: Using NASCAR as a platform to showcase its own technological advancements, the Ford Motor Company, at a race in Martinsville, selected its newly designed Ford Fusion hybrid as the "official pace car vehicle" to escort competitors to the green flag. The propetroleum/antienvironment reactionary discourse was evident as a hundred thousand muscle car enthusiasts in attendance lustfully booed the fuel-saving hybrid as it paced the field.

8. Another automobile interactive experience, this time by Ford Motor Company, was erected at Daytona International Speedway in the days leading up to the 2009 Daytona 500 (Pockrass, 2009).

9. Indeed, NASCAR has a long history of these sponsorship-driver linkages as the sports' most successful and iconic driver-celebrity, seven-time champion Richard Petty, was sponsored by, and a prominent endorser of, STP motor oil.

10. Sunoco's interest in this is, of course, not coincidental. Prior to the 2004 race season, Sunoco Inc. replaced ConocoPhillips' Unocal "76" brand as the exclusive fuel supplier for NASCAR's highest touring series (Montgomery, 2003). Sunoco, the largest independent petroleum refiner/marketer in the United States, is currently entered into a 10-year agreement with NASCAR worth an estimated $100 million to supply fuel to over 30 regional touring series and furnish more than 400 national race tracks to an endless mean (Smith, 2008d).

11. With a field of 43 drivers for 10 races per weekend and stock cars averaging 4.5 miles per gallon on races that last on average 200 miles, we estimate that the weekly gasoline consumption approaches 400,000 gallons. This total surpasses 11 million gallons of gasoline annually for NASCAR's highest profile leagues. This, of course, does not include necessary supplementary petrol products such as motor oil and fuel additives that are vital to stock car engines. Still others—NASCAR columnist Marty Smith (2008d)—projects a much more conservative estimate calculating the number of gallons of gasoline is around 135,000 per year.

12. We found those residing in camping villages to be the most loyal and fervent stock car racing supporters—and there were quite a lot of them. The mobile camping and accommodation grounds stretched long into the distance at most venues, with all vehicles—almost without exception—saturated in their favorite driver's numbers, colors, and sponsors.

13. Examples of such externalities would be earth's natural features: the atmosphere, vegetation, and streams, lakes, and oceans. In addition, O'Connor identifies infrastructure and space as another source of destruction.

14. Only after a period of intense scrutiny from the environmental community and the threat of an investigation by U.S. Congress did NASCAR move in the direction of much safer unleaded gasoline.

15. Evidence supporting this claim could be referenced against the race team balance sheets that responded to recent petroleum increases. When, for instance, the average price of a gallon of diesel fuel increased from $1.29 to $4.14, it was easy to see how transporter fuel costs were up 15.4 percent and jet fuel consumption was up 15.9 percent for stock car teams (Smith, 2008d). Ty Norris, team director for Michael Waltrip Racing, claims that his race team's travel budget has increased over 35 percent as a result of rising fuel prices—a direct reflection of surging petroleum prices (Smith, 2008d).

16. Although the so-called Black Monday crash of 1987 yielded only a 508-point drop, it represented a 22.6 percent loss for the day. On May 6, 2010, the DJIA witnessed a 998.50-point drop (or 9.2 percent) in intraday trading, before regaining most of its loss later in the day.

17. Defense Secretary Donald Rumsfeld, Britain prime minister Tony Blair, and White House press secretary Air Fleischer (speaking on behalf of G. W. Bush) are all on record stating that the war in Iraq had nothing to do with oil (all quoted in Phillips, 2006, p. 69). However, an array of critical scholars and political journalists (Briody, 2004; Engdahl, 2004; Klare, 2004; Klein, 2007; Miller, 2006; Phillips, 2006) and academics (Chomsky, 2003a; Chomsky, 2003b, 2007; Denzin & Giardina, 2007b; Giroux, 2004b; Giroux, 2008; Harvey, 2003, 2005a; Kellner, 2003; Rutledge, 2005) have argued that oil was at least, below the surface, a major impetus for the military invasion of Iraq. Indeed, the Bush administration was well aware that any form of a peak-oil crisis "posed strategic dangers far beyond those publicly acknowledged" (Phillips, 2006, p. 69).

18. Vice President Cheney himself subscribed to the serious threat of proliferating energy scarcity when in 1990 he is quoted as saying: "by some estimates, there will be an average of two percent annual growth in oil supply demand over the years ahead, along with conservatively a three percent natural decline in production from existing reserves. That means by 2010 we will need on the order of an additional 50 million barrels a day" (see Phillips, 2006).

19. Indeed it was an inner circle comprising several petroleum power brokers who at one time either worked in the oil industry (e.g., Secretary of State Condeleeza Rice, Commerce Secretary Don Evans, and Bush himself) or in the case of Dick Cheyney, continued to receive annual deferred salary and stock options from his (current) former employer Halliburton (Engdahl, 2004).

20. Europe, Japan, and developing East and Southeast Asia are all dependent on Gulf oil, and controlling its delivery to world markets accords valuable political-economic power (Harvey, 2003).

21. The Carter Doctrine is pretext for current U.S. petroleum policy. In 1979, President Jimmy Carter responded to the Soviet Union's invasion of Afghanistan by informing the Congress that Washington would use any means necessary, including military force, to preserve free-flowing petroleum in the U.S. economy (Klare, 2004). The Carter Doctrine as it is often referred to has guided America's geopolitical policy in the Persian Gulf since its formation; the creation of Central Command (CENTCOM) in 1983, whose singular aim is to maintain the continued supply of oil in the Persian Gulf through the unlimited use of all military resources (Klare, 2004).

22. Following World War II, Secretary of State George C. Marshall unveiled a rebuilding plan for Europe to reconstruct cities, factories, and railroads that had been destroyed by a decade of conflict. In short, the United States provided the financial resources, while Europe was expected to provide the plan. Instead of American businesses dictating terms, they worked in cooperation with European nations to supply essential provisions and building materials.

23. Because Halliburton received no-bid contracts, they were able to exploit all Iraqi oil production to a large degree. "A Department of Defense audit in 2003 showed that Halliburton was charging $2.27 per gallon for more than 56 million gallons brought into Iraq, from Kuwait, since the ware began. That figure was $1.09 higher per gallon than the government was paying for the gas itself from another contractor. The result was a difference of $61 million" (Briody, 2004, p. 234).

24. One interrelated consequence of the removal of troops in Iraq will be the sudden shrinkage of America's more reliant, and profitable industry. Put simply, withdrawal from Iraq would mean the United States' most profitable economy bubble would burst (or at the least suffer a major set-back).

25. Options for policing the crisis so as not to threaten, contest, or overthrow the capitalist system are threefold. First, there lies the selection of devaluing commodities. But as most corporations and wealthy elite are unlikely to voluntarily lower the value of their assets or net worth. This is most often the last resort. The second solution is utilizing macroeconomic control measures through institutionalized or state policies and regulation. This is achieved through fiscal and monetary practices of Keynesian regulatory measures such as adjusting interest rates or an

adoption of Keynesian investment in public infrastructure and welfare state. However, this process is at one and the same time highly political and ineffective in massive market crises. These two choices are not without their own limits and ephemeral praxis. Thus, Harvey (2007) discusses spatiotemporal displacement as a temporary (and most likely) means for surplus absorption.

26. Giroux's (2004b) six characteristics that distinguish protofascism from its predecessor are these: a cult of traditionalists and reactionary modernists; ongoing corporatization of society; rampant nationalism; government regulation of the mass media; alterations to language, sound, and image; and the enmeshing of the church and state.

27. The Marines and Air Force were the first to arrive in 2000; the Navy in 2001; the Army in 2003 along with the Air National Guard; the Coast Guard in 2004 (Bernstein, 2005).

28. One thing must be pointed out, however, about these lucrative sponsorships inside the stridently conservative, pro-Republican space: the money funding the Department of Defense's advertising comes from taxpayers—many of whom are "outsiders" to NASCAR and (may) stand in opposition to U.S. militarism.

29. To ensure that the memory of the combative spectacle endures long after the race concludes, weapons and military arms are given as trophies to victorious drivers. At Texas Motor Speedway, the winners of the 500-mile pursuit were presented with twin Beretta cowboy pistols and celebrated their Texas conquest by donning a cowboy hat and spraying (blank) bullets into the nighttime sky—much to the enjoyment of anti-gun legislation activists in attendance—as 2007 race winner and two-time Spring Cup Champion Tony Stewart did (Ryan, 2007a).

30. The choice of which driver to sponsor is rather strategic; their end goal is driving enlistments, and, as we have argued elsewhere, it is important for corporations to select a driver and race team with the correct "matchup" to their "target market" (Braunstein et al., 2008). It is, of course, not coincidental that the U.S. Army has chosen to sponsor Aric Almirola, the only other nonwhite Hispanic driver on the NASCAR circuit (other than Juan Pablo Montoya). It is quite clear that this partnership is intentionally directed toward hailing young Latinos ages 18–24, who are disproportionately represented in the front lines of the war in Iraq (Roy, 2004). That the NASCAR-military partnership is remarkably successful in influencing impressionable young fans into enlistment is somewhat alarming; as one new recruit responded when asked what convinced him to sign up, "I saw David Stremme driving the Navy race car and I went down and saw the Navy recruiter" (quoted in Pate, 2008, p. 1).

31. Comedian Dave Chappelle once had an especially revealing riff about his decision to endorse both Coca-Cola and Pepsi at different times in the course of his career: whichever one was paying him at the time was the one he said tasted better.

32. These militarized spaces are highly effective means of recruitment, as each race produces nearly 2,000 new enlistment leads weekly, amounting to nearly 40,000 a year (Bernstein, 2005; Osunsami, 2005). This proliferation of prowar spaces at NASCAR events encourage men and women to "enlist" to play with the latest warfare technologies and to prove if they "can be all that they can be." Parents encourage their children to participate in these experiences at alarming rates, as the line to enter the Army Experience is usually one of the longest at any stop outside NASCAR track. Once inside, individuals are herded together in pep-rally-style celebrations for the military, and then cordoned off from one another in order to speak with recruitment officers. With events that routinely host over 100,000 fans over a three-day period with nothing much to do in the lead up to the event, army recruiters such as Col. Tom Nickerson envisage "a rich environment for soldiers and recruiters to talk to influencers and prospects. Influencers are parents and others who have influence over a military prospect's decision" (quoted in Bernstein, 2005, p. 1).

33. The categories listed on the laminated card read as follows—"HOT: Priority 1: High school junior, senior, grad, or college student who expresses an interest in the army AND has asked to be contacted by a recruit. Age = 17–29); Priority 2: High school junior, senior, grad, or college student who 1) expresses an interest in the Army or Army Reserves or 2), a career in the Armed Forces, or 3) in ROTC, AND has *not* opted to be contacted by a recruiter. Age = 17–29; Priority 3: High school grad, college student, college who expresses an interest in an Army career. Age = 29–41; AMEDD: College student or grads who express interest receiving more information on Army Medicine (AMEDD). *HOT AMEDD Prospect!*; ROTC: Interested in ROTC, high school junior through College Sophomore. *HOT ROTC Prospect!*" (Note: all grammar, spelling, and punctuation in original).

34. It is worth noting that the flight simulator's graphics engine was quite limited by the standards of high-end home video game consoles such as Playstation 3 or Xbox 360. Thus, the violence, of whatever form, was effectively limited in visual scope, not nearly approaching that of best-selling games like *Medal of Honor* and *Call of Duty*. However, the violent implications remain consistent despite the limited visual appeal.

35. This response—both by fan and researcher—also exists outside of the NASCAR environment. Attending an NFL game in Jacksonville, Florida in 2010, one of us witnessed four fighter jets do a pregame flyover at a similarly low altitude. Instead of "Git R Done," the common fan response was "Yeah, let's get some!"

36. For example, the NASCAR organization was a recipient of the Armed Forces Foundation's 2010 Bill and Beverly Young Humanitarian Award. Said Brian France on receiving the award: "patriotism and support for our troops goes into everything we do" ("Armed Forces Foundation's

Annual Tribute Event Draws Support from NASCAR and Fox Sports," 2010).

37. The press release from Lowe's Motor Speedway highlighting the prerace spectacle before the annual Memorial Day stock car race read as follows:

> Continuing a Memorial Day weekend tradition that started 30 years ago, Lowe's Motor Speedway's pre-race spectacular for the Coca-Cola 600 Nextel Cup Series race on Sunday, May 27, will celebrate the men and women of the U.S. Military and pay tribute to those who have served their country. The program begins with performances by the 82nd Airborne Division Chorus and the U.S. Army Drill Team, followed by the arrival of the U.S. Army Golden Knights parachute team. The U.S. Army will then "secure" the frontstretch during a demonstration that will include troops in full combat gear, military ground vehicles, helicopters and the firing of an M109 Howitzer gun. Once the frontstretch is "secured," 1,500 uniformed troops from Fort Bragg will march into the track and assemble at the start/finish line. Following driver introductions, the Fort Bragg Honor Guard will present the colors prior to the playing of Amazing Grace and the firing of a 21-gun salute. (Printed in Salem-News.com, 2007)

38. Klare (2007) sums up the features of energo-facism in this manner:

> ...increasing state involvement in the procurement, transportation, and allocation of energy supplies, accompanied by a greater inclination to employ force against those who resist the state's priorities in these areas. As in classical twentieth century fascism, the state will assume ever greater control over all aspects of public and private life in pursuit of what is said to be an essential national interest: the acquisition of sufficient energy to keep the economy functioning and public services (including the military) running. Either we will be compelled to participate in or finance foreign wars to secure vital supplies of energy, such as the current conflict in Iraq... This is not simply some future dystopian nightmare, but a potentially all-encompassing reality whose basic features, largely unnoticed, are developing today. (p. 1)

7   Selling Out NASCAR Nation

1. In 2004, for instance—and much to the derision of NASCAR's traditionalists—the new, "mainstream Jr." took members of his pit crew to see Michael Moore's polemic *Fahrenheit 9–11* (Moore, 2004).

2. In recent years, NASCAR has become further ensconced in the national popular by way of various popular films (e.g., Disney's animated feature film *Cars*).

3. And the "global vision of NASCAR" extends beyond the scope of NAFTA countries: "[We were] in Shanghai, talking to some people about international opportunities in the Far East," France noted in 2007. "Nothing to report other than every time I get on the road and talk to people they're very familiar with what we're doing, like our style, like our brand of racing, lots of interest.... we'll be looking at building our international platform" (quoted in Lemasters, 2007, pp. 1–2).

4. Studies unequivocally show that, in spite of popular belief to the contrary, the economic "development" (in terms of jobs, ancillary consumption, and tourism) brought about by the construction of new publicly subsidized sports stadia and arenas will never amount to the (fiscal and opportunity) costs paid by taxpayers.

5. The development of this new track has been met with tremendous resistance from many members within the community. To help their campaign, NASCAR launched a campaign lauding that a NASCAR track could restore the city's livelihood in the wake of 9/11.

6. The racing league had previously increased its profit margins, particularly in the mid-2000s, from surges in consumer activity in nontraditional markets in the western United States, Canada, Australasia, Mexico, and Europe (Miles, 2005; Spencer & Grant, 2005).

7. The "Car of Tomorrow," or CoT, was a standardized car design mandated by NASCAR starting in 2007. NASCAR claims the CoT is safer, costs less to maintain, and is intended to make for closer competition (due to numerous restriction in the weighting, instrumentation, and make-up of the car's engine). The CoT has received heavy criticism due to the initial outlay of capital required by racing teams, and namely those fringe teams, to conform its standards.

8. NASCAR president Mike Helton compounded this considerable ire of the sport's legions of "Southern-identified" fans when, just before the 2006 Daytona 500 race, he declared: "the old Southeastern redneck heritage that we had is no longer in existence" (quoted in Thompson, 2006, pp. 8–9). While his declaration was in response to mounting concerns within the public sphere about the primary role of the Confederate flag and lack of diversity within the NASCAR spectacle, it also echoed the organization's rhetorical shift away from the provincial "heritage" that they had long-mobilized in marking and marketing the sport's cultural boundaries.

9. The March 2010 Bristol race, for instance, failed to 'sell out' for the first time in more than 25 years ending a 55-race streak.

10. Two points should be noted here: (1) this inevitable feature of *laissez-faire* economics (that of overspeculation) is nothing new to the American economy. For a more detailed lesson on its effects, see the stock market crash of 1929 and the subsequent conditions of the Great Depression (Chancellor, 2000); and (2) this spectacular intensification

of the speculative financial sector was concomitant to the 1990s boon of the information technology sector (namely Internet-related commerce). Never was there a more perfect industry to build such a speculative empire; consumption was untraceable, the product intangible, expenses immeasurable, and market potential untenable.

11. The Gini Coefficient, named after Italian statistician Corrado Gini, is used to measure the inequality of a distribution. It is commonly used, as cited here, as an indicator of national income distribution and disparity. In this instance, the higher Gini Coefficient is indicative of an increased gap between the rich and the poor.

12. Writing in the *Monthly Review*, Minqi Li (2008) explained how the American working-class is learning to deal with this "age of transition"; redoubling their fiscal expectations for a nefarious state of economic well-being that threatens the neoliberal *pax Americana* by which neo-conservatives and "progressives" alike had come to understand the place of the nation-state within the global economy. As the next generation of outsourcing consumes the managerial sensibilities and investment machinations of market-savvy capitalists—a systematic relocation of semi- and highly skilled biotech, financial, and military-industrial-complex labor—many Americans find themselves contemplating their future within the global economy. This state of unrest is heightened by the omnipresent mediations of "threats" (Jihadism, universal health care, to the liberties that were seemingly afforded them by the "free market").

13. We see this as the practice of "voucher programs" has come into fashion across the nation, lower levels of education have been re-articulated as consumable services.

14. In only a few years, the U.S. government successfully flipped the New Deal on its head. Many critics have argued that, in effect, the neoliberal hegemony has left the American people dispossessed of the democratic fulcrum (e.g., Zinn, Chomsky, Arundhati Roy, Anthony Arnove, Peter McLaren, Henry Giroux). Likewise, this process is by no means exclusive to the United States. In fact, the most lucrative public sell-offs have evolved out of the collapse of former Communists and Socialist states such as the former Soviet Union. The streets of modern-day Moscow are now overflowing with bulletproof BMW and Mercedes-Benz luxury cars taxiing former mafia bosses-turned-post-Soviet magnates through the city's brutally impoverished neighborhoods (Appel, 2004). Immediately following the days of *perestroika*, these entrepreneurs were able to secure government subsidies to purchase grossly underpriced, state-held energy, transportation, and resource-mining companies. As these companies "went public," the free market revalued these companies at millions, and often billions, of dollars more than their purchase price (Goldman, 2003).

15. Montoya is actually from Colombia, not Mexico.

16. Never mind that Montoya's highly talented and well-known aggressive driving style (the primary reason Montoya failed to achieve long-term success in Formula One racing) was more representative of NASCAR cult hero Dale Earnhardt Sr. than most drivers currently claiming NASCAR as home, Montoya's polarizing character was displayed in his first victory, a NASCAR Busch Series international race in Mexico City in March of 2007 (Anderson, 2007). Montoya passed 18 cars in 26 laps including spinning out his own teammate, Scott Pruett, with 8 laps remaining to claim a controversial victory (Anderson, 2007).

17. At the end of the broadcast, Griese said: "Juan Pablo Montoya, he's one of the best drivers in NASCAR. Just want to apologize for the comment I made earlier in the ballgame."

CONCLUDING THOUGHTS

1. In which seemingly the only voice of reason on television is not NBC or CBS news anchors Brian Williams or Katie Couric, but rather Jon Stewart, comedian and host of the "fake news" program *The Daily Show* on *Comedy Central*, whom the *New York Times* referred to as having the cultural currency to be this era's Edward R. Murrow.

2. As of this writing (December, 2010), the U.S. Congress had an overall approval rating of only 13 percent (Gallup Poll, December 10–12, 2010) as it headed into its "lame-duck" session following shocking gains in the 2010 midterm elections that saw the Republican Party retake control of the House of Representatives.

3. This logic of self-governed freedom as consumer/embodied/aesthetic acts in this way to create power—power through which populations can be governed:

> The new governmental reason needs freedom; therefore, the new art of government consumes freedom. It must produce it, it must organize it. The new art of government therefore appears as the management of freedom, not in the sense of the imperative: "be free," with the immediate contradiction that this imperative may contain … [T]he liberalism we can describe as the art of government formed in the eighteenth century entails at its heart a productive/destructive relationship with freedom. Liberalism must produce freedom, but this very act entails the establishment of limitations, controls, forms of coercion, and obligations relying on threats, etcetera. (Foucault, 2008, p. 63)

In this way, neoliberalism constitutes a new mode of "governmentality," a "manner, or a mentality, in which people are governed and govern themselves. The operative terms of this governmentality are no longer rights and laws but interest, investment and competition" (Read, 2009, p. 29). This form of governmentality "is not a matter of a dominant force having direct control over the conduct of individuals; rather, it is a matter of trying to determine the conditions within or out of which individuals are able to freely conduct themselves" (Hamann, 2009, p. 55).

REFERENCES

2010 NASCAR Sprint Cup TV Ratings. (2010). *Jayski's Silly Season Site*. Retrieved December 22, 2010, from http://jayski.com/pages /tvratings2010.htm

Adamson, W. L. (1990). Economic democracy and the expediency of worker participation. *Political Studies, 38*(1), 56–71.

Adler, J. (2004). Frank Meyer: The Fusionist as federalist. *Publius: The Journal of Federalism, 34*(4), 51–68.

Adorno, T. (1991). *The culture industry*. London: Routledge.

Agger, B. (1989). *Fast capitalism: A critical theory of significance*: Urbana, IL: University of Illinois Press.

Agger, B. (2004). *Speeding up fast capitalism: Cultures, jobs, families, schools, bodies*. Boulder, CO: Paradigm.

Albert, M. (2003). *Parecon: Life after capitalism*. London: Verso.

Alderman, D. H., Preston, W., Mitchell, J., Webb, T., & Hanak, D. (2001). Carolina Thunder revisited: Toward a transcultural view of Winston Cup racing. *The Professional Geographer* (55), 239–249.

Allen, J. (1992). Fordism and modern industry. In J. Allen, P. Brahm, & P. Lewis (Eds.), *Political and economic forms of modernity* (pp. 229–260). Cambridge: Polity Press.

Allen, J. (1996). From Fordism and post-Fordism. In S. Hall, D. Held, D. Hubert, & K. Thompson (Eds.), *Modernity: An introduction to modern societies* (pp. 546–563). Oxford: Blackwell.

Allen, M., & Clarke, L. (2004). Gentlemen, start your campaigns: President takes the race for "NASCAR Dads" to the Daytona 500, *Washington Post*. Retrieved from http://www.washingtonpost.com/ac2/wp-dyn /A44551–2004Feb15?language=printer

Alleyne, S., & Witcher, T. R. (2004, April). The new face of NASCAR: Race, money, and politics, in motor sports' fast lane. *Black Enterprise*. Retrieved from http://www.blackenterprise.com/2004/04/01/the-new-face-of-nascar/

Althusser, L. (1971). *Lenin and philosophy* (B. Brewster, Trans.). London: New Left Books.

Alvarez, S. (2005). Despite rain, Pepsi 400 fans, drivers support troops. Retrieved from http://www.ourmilitary.mil/Content.aspx?ID=24098999

Amato, C. H., Peters, C. L. O., & Shao, A. T. (2005). An exploratory investigation into NASCAR fan culture. *Sport Marketing Quarterly* (14), 71–83.

Amin, S. (2008). "Market economy" or oligarchy-finance capitalism? *Monthly Review, 59*(11), 51–61.

Anderson, L. (2007). Busch league. *Sports Illustrated, 106,* 84.

Andrews, D. L. (1996). The fact(s) of Michael Jordan's blackness: Excavating a floating racial signifier. *Sociology of Sport Journal, 13*(2), 125–158.

Andrews, D. L., & Ritzer, G. (2007). The global and the sporting local. *Global networks: A journal of transnational affairs, 7*(2), 135–153.

Appadurai, A. (1996). *Modernity at large: Cultural dimensions of globalization.* Minneapolis, MN: University of Minnesota Press.

Appadurai, A. (2001). *Globalization.* Durham, NC: Duke University Press.

Appel, H. (2004). *A new capitalist order: Privatization and ideology in Russia and Eastern Europe.* Pittsburgh: University of Pittsburgh Press.

"Armed Forces Foundation's Annual Tribute Event Draws Support from NASCAR and Fox Sports" (2010, March 4). *PR Newswire.* Retrieved December 20, 2010, from http://www.prnewswire.com/news-releases /armed-forces-foundations-annual-tribute-event-draws-support-from-nascar-and-fox-sports-86459632.html

"Army reserve centennial commemoration at NASCAR's Chevy Rock & Roll 400" (2008). *ArmyReserve100th.com.* Retrieved from http://www .armyreserve100th.com/image_gallery.php?pi=19

Aron, J. (1999, March 29). Bush's potential campaign gets huge race-car audience. *Austin American-Statesman,* p. B2.

Aronson, R. (Writer). (2004). Frontline: The Jesus factor. In R. Aronson (Producer), *Frontline.* USA: PBS.

Ashbee, E. (1998). Immigration, national identity, and conservatism in the United States. *Politics, 18*(2), 73–80.

Ashbee, E. (2000). Politics of paleoconservatism. *Society, 37*(3), 75–84.

Assael, S. (1999). *Wide open: Days and nights on the NASCAR tour.* New York: Ballantine Books.

"At races, fans root for auto brands; NASCAR Chairman roots for help for automakers," *ABC News.* Retrieved from http://abcnews.go.com /Business/Economy/story?id=6293543&page=2

Auerswald, B. (2002). The economic impact of a racetrack is huge. *The Gloucester County Times.* Retrieved from http://www.nj.com/glouces-ter/index.ssf?/specialprojects/nascar/stories/sidebar2.html

Augé, M. (1995). *Non places: Introduction to an anthropology of supermodernity.* London: Verso.

Ayers, E. L. (1993). *The promise of the New South: Life after Reconstruction.* Oxford: Oxford University Press.

Babson, S. (1991). *Building the union: Skilled workers and Anglo-Gaelic immigrants in the rise of the UAW.* Piscataway, NJ: Rutgers University Press.

Bacevich, A. J. (2008). He told us to go shopping, now the bill is due. *The Washington Post.* Retrieved December 3, 2010, from http:// www.washingtonpost.com/wp-dyn/content/article/2008/10/03 /AR2008100301977.html

Bachmair, B. (1991). From motor-car to television: Cultural-historical arguments on the meaning of mobility for communication. *Media, Culture and Society, 13*(3), 521–533.

Bageant, J. (2007). *Deer hunting with Jesus: Dispatches from America's class war*: New York: Crown.

Bakan, J. (2004). *The corporation: The pathological pursuit of profit and power.* New York: Free Press.

Ballard, J. G. (1973). *Crash.* London: Jonathan Cape.

Balsley, G. (1950). The hot-rod culture. *American Quarterly, 2*(4), 353–358.

Barna, G. (1991). *The Barna Report: What Americans believe, an annual survey of values and religious views in the United States.* Ventura, CA: Regal Books.

Barnett, C. (2005). The consolations of "neoliberalism." *Geoforum, 36*(1), 7–12.

Barnett, C., Clarke, N., Cloke, P., & Malpass, A. (2008). The elusive subjects of neo-liberalism: Beyond the analytics of governmentality. *Cultural Studies, 22*(5), 624–653.

Barrett, R. (2005). The myth of Southern isolation. Retrieved March 20, 2005, from http://www.nationalist.org/docs/instruct/civics.html

Barthes, R. (1967). *Elements of semiology* (A. Lavers & C. Smith, Trans.). New York: Hill & Wang.

Baudrillard, J. (1983a). *Simulation and simulacra.* Anne Arbor, MI: University of Michigan Press.

Baudrillard, J. (1983b). *Simulations.* New York: Semiotext(e).

Baudrillard, J. (1989). *America* (C. Turner, Trans.). London: Verso.

Baudrillard, J. (1995). *The Gulf war did not take place.* Bloomington, IA: Indiana University Press.

Bauman, Z. (1998). *Globalization: The human consequences.* Cambridge: Polity Press.

Bauman, Z. (2002a). Forward: Individually, together. In U. Beck & E. Beck-Gernsheim (Eds.), *Individualization: Institutionalized individualism and its social and political consequences* (pp. xiv–xix). London: Sage.

Bauman, Z. (2002b). *Society under siege.* Malden, MA: Blackwell.

Bauman, Z. (2007). *Consuming life.* Cambridge: Polity Press.

Beaman, K. (Ed.) (2004). *Out of site: An inside look at HR outsourcing.* Austin, TX: Rector-Duncan.

Bechtel, M. (2010). *He crashed me so I crashed him back.* New York: Little Brown.

Beck, U. (1998). *Risk society: Towards a new modernity.* London: Sage.

Beck, U. (2000). What is globalization? In D. Held & A. McGrew (Eds.), *The global transformations reader: An introduction to the globalization debate* (pp. 99–104). Cambridge: Polity Press.

Beck, U., & Beck-Gernsheim, E. (2002). *Individualization: Institutionalized individualism and its social and political consequences.* London: Sage.

Beitel, K. (2008). The subprime debacle. *Monthly Review, 60*(1), 27–44.

Bell, D., & Kristol, I. (Eds.) (1981). *The crisis in economic theory.* New York: Basic Books.

Benedetto, R. (2004, February 16). Bush hopes NASCAR fans help steer him to victory. *USA Today*, p. 6A.

Benjamin, R. (2009). *Searching for Whitopia: An improbable journey to the heart of white America.* New York: Hyperion.

Benjamin, W. (1969). *Illuminations.* New York: Schocken Books.

Benjamin, W. (1999). *The arcades project* (H. Eiland & K. McLaughlin, Trans.). Cambridge, MA: Belknap Press (Harvard University).

Berlant, L. (1997). *The Queen of America goes to Washington City: Essays on sex and citizenship.* Raleigh, NC: Duke University Press.

Bernstein, V. (2005). Auto racing: In bid for recruits, military has allies in NASCAR and fans. *New York Times*, p. 1.

Bernstein, V. (2006, November 8). NASCAR's drive for diversity is producing mixed signals. *The New York Times.* Retrieved from http://www.nytimes.com/2006/11/08/sports/othersports/08nascar.html

Bernstein, V. (2010, August 31). NASCAR turns to BET Network to boost minority drivers, *The New York Times.* Retrieved from http://www.nytimes.com/2010/09/01/sports/autoracing/01nascar.html

Best, S., & Kellner, D. (1999). Debord, cybersituations, and the interactive spectacle. *Substance* (90), 129–154.

Bishop, R. (2001). Stealing the signs: A semiotic analysis of the changing nature of professional sports logos. *Social Semiotics, 11*(1), 23–41.

Blight, D. W. (2001). *Race and reunion: The Civil War in American memory.* Cambridge, MA: Belknap Press (Harvard University).

Bochon, D. (2008). Fueled by faith. *Living Light News.* Retrieved March 4, 2008, from http://www.livinglightnews.org/vpetty.html

Boettke, P. (Ed.) (2000). *The legacy of FA Hayek: Politics, philosophy, and economics,* 3 vols. Aldershot, UK: Edward Elgar

Böhm, S., Jones, C., Land, C., & Paterson, M. (2006). Introduction: Impossibilities of automobility. In S. Böhm, C. Jones, C. Land, & M. Paterson (Eds.), *Against automobility* (pp. 3–16). Malden, MA: Blackwell/Sociological Review.

Bondi, L. (2005). Working the spaces of neoliberal subjectivity: Psychotherapeutic technologies, professionalisation and counselling. *Antipode, 37*(3), 497–514.

Bonner, R. E. (2002). *Colors and blood: Flag passions of the Confederate South.* Princeton, NJ: Princeton University Press.

Bontemps, A. (2001). *The punished self: Surviving slavery in the colonial South.* Ithaca, NY: Cornell University Press.

Borzutzky, S. (2005). From Chicago to Santiago: Neoliberalism and social security privatization in Chile. *Governance, 18*(4), 655–674.

Bottum, J. (2004). Social conservatism and the new fusionism. *Varieties of Conservatism in America* (pp. 31–34). Stanford: Hoover Institution Press.

Bourdieu, P. (1998a). *Acts of resistance: Against the new myths of our time.* Cambridge: Polity Press.

Bourdieu, P. (1998b, December). The essence of neoliberalism. *Le Monde diplomatique*. Retrieved from http://mondediplo.com/1998/12/08bourdieu

Bourdieu, P. (2003). *Firing back: Against the tyranny of the market 2*. London: Verso.

Boyd, W. L. (2007). The politics of privatization in American education. *Educational Policy, 21*(1), 7–14.

Bradford, M., & Kirk, R. (1994). *A better guide than reason: Federalists and anti-federalists*: New Brunswick, NJ: Transaction.

Branham, H. A. (2010). *Bill France Jr.: The man who made NASCAR*. Chicago: Triumph Books.

Bratton, B. H. (2006). Logistics of habitable circulation: A brief introduction to the 2006 edition of *Speed and politics*. In P. Virilio (Ed.), *Speed and politics: An essay on dromology* (pp. 7–25). Los Angeles: Semiotext(e).

Braunstein, J. R., Newman, J. I., & Beissel, A. S. (2008). Inside BAM racing: Rethinking the sponsorship match-up process in "America's fastest-growing sport." *International Journal of Sports Marketing & Sponsorship, 9*(3), 219–233.

Briody, D. (2004). *The Halliburton agenda: The politics of oil and money*. Hoboken, NJ: Wiley.

Brown, W. (2004, July 25). NASCAR's diversity dearth may be sponsor-driven. *Washington Post*, p. G02.

Brown, W. (2005). *Edgework: Critical essays on knowledge and politics*: Princeton, NJ: Princeton University Press.

Brown, W. (2006). American nightmare: Neoliberalism, neoconservativism, and de-democratization. *Political Theory, 34*(6), 690–714.

Buchanan, P. J. (2009). Traditional Americans are losing their nation. *WorldNetDaily*. Retrieved from http://www.wnd.com/index.php?pageId=113463

Buruma, I. (2010). The great American Tea Party. *Project Syndicate*, pp. 1–2. Retrieved from http://www.project-syndicate.org/commentary/buruma41/English

Bush urges American to fly. (2001). *ABCNews.com*. Retrieved from http://abcnews.go.com/US/story?id=92410&page=2

Butler, J. (1990). *Gender trouble: Feminism and the subversion of identity*. London: Routledge.

Butler, J. (1993). *Bodies that matter: On the discursive limits of "sex."* London: Routledge.

Caldwell, D. (2001). Godspeed: Champion race-car driver Jeff Gordon faithfully examines the daily rewards—and risks—-of the sport. Retrieved March 2, 2008, from www.beiliefnet.com/story/85/story_8550.html

Campbell, D. (2005). The biopolitics of security: Oil, empire, and the sports utility vehicle. *American Quarterly, 57*(3), 943–972.

Canfield, J., Hansen, M. V., Adams, M. E., Autio, K., & Aubery, J. (Eds.). (2003). *Chicken Soup for the NASCAR Soul*. Deerfield Beach, FL: Health Communications.

Caraviello, D. (2008). In today's NASCAR, best change may be none at all. Retrieved from http://www.nascar.com/2008/news/opinion/01/21/dcaraviello.nascar.state.sport/index.html

Carcamo-Huechante, L. E. (2006). Milton Friedman: Knowledge, public culture, and market economy in the Chile of Pinochet. *Public Culture, 18*(2), 413–435.

Cash, W. J. (1941/1991). *The mind of the South.* New York: Vintage.

Castells, M. (1996). *The rise of the network society.* Oxford: Blackwell.

Castells, M. (2000). The global economy. In D. Held & A. McGrew (Eds.), *The global transformations reader: An introduction to the globalization debate* (pp. 259–273). Cambridge: Polity Press.

Chancellor, E. (2000). *The devil take hindmost.* New York: Penguin.

Chernick, H. (2005). *Resilient city: The economic impact of 9/11.* Russell: Sage.

Chomsky, N. (1999). *People over profit: Neoliberalism and the global order.* London: Seven Stories Press.

Chomsky, N. (2002, September 29). Assaulting solidarity—privatizing education. Retrieved June 1, 2005, from http://www.uct.ac.za/org/aa/chomsk.htm

Chomsky, N. (2003a). *Hegemony or survival: America's quest for global dominance.* London: Penguin Books.

Chomsky, N. (2003b). *Power and terror: Post 9–11 talks and interviews.* New York: Seven Stories.

Chomsky, N. (2007). *Interventions.* San Francisco: City Light Books.

Chomsky, N. (2009). *Philosophies of language and politics.* Paper presented at the Commonwealth Club of California, San Francisco.

Clarke, J. (2009). Viewpoint: The end of the neo-cons? Retrieved August 2, 2010, from http://news.bbc.co.uk/2/hi/americas/7825039.stm

Clarke, L. (2001, April 22). NASCAR races at God's speed: Ministry helps drivers keep faith amid danger. *Washington Post,* p. A01.

Clarke, L. (2008). *One helluva ride: How NASCAR swept the nation.* New York: Random House.

Cobb, J. C. (1992). *The most southern place on earth: The Mississippi Delta and the roots of regional identity.* New York: Oxford University Press.

Cokley, M. A. (2001). In the fast lane to big bucks: The growth of NASCAR. *Sports Lawyers Journal, 8*(1), 67–99.

Cole, C. L. (2007). Bounding American democracy: Sport, sex, and race. In N. Denzin & M. Giardina (Eds.), *Contesting empire, globalizing dissent: Cultural Studies after 9/11* (pp. 152–166). Boulder, CO: Paradigm.

Connolly, W. E. (2005). The Evangelical-capitalist resonance machine. *Political Theory, 33*(6), 869–886.

Coombe, R. J. (1998). *The cultural life of intellectual properties: Authorship, appropriation, and the law.* Durham, NC: Duke University Press.

Coski, J. M. (2005). *The Confederate battle flag: America's most embattled symbol.* Cambridge, MA: Belknap Press (Harvard University).

Cova, B. (1997). Community and consumption: Towards a definition of the "linking value" of product or services. *European Journal of Marketing, 31*(3/4), 297–316.

Cowden, J. A. (2001). Southernization of the nation and nationalization of the South: Racial conservatism, social welfare and white partisans in the United States, 1956–92. *British Journal of Political Science, 31*(2), 277–301.

Cowen, D. (2006). Fighting for "freedom": The end of conscription in the United States and the neoliberal project of citizenship. *Citizenship Studies, 10*(2), 167–183.

Cragg, J. (2008). NASCAR no. 88 to accelerate careers of 88 future sailors. *American Forces Press Service.* Retrieved from http://www.defense.gov/news/newsarticle.aspx?id=49788

Crang, M. (2000). Relics, places and unwritten geographies in the work of Michel de Certeau. In M. Crang & N. Thrift (Eds.), *Thinking space* (pp. 136–153). London: Routledge.

Daly, H. E. (1977/1991). *Steady-state economics.* Washington, DC: Island.

Dant, T. (2004). The driver-car. *Theory, Culture & Society, 21*(4/5), 61–79.

Dant, T., & Martin, P. (2001). By car: Carrying modern society. In A. Warde & J. Grunow (Eds.), *Ordinary consumption* (pp. 143–158). London: Harwood.

De Becker, G. (1998). *The gift of fear: And other survival signals that protect us from violence.* New York: Dell.

de Certeau, M. (1984). *The practice of everyday life.* Berkeley: University of California Press.

Debord, G. (1967/1994). *The society of the spectacle* (D. Nicholson-Smith, Trans.). New York: Zone.

Debord, G. (Writer/Director). (1981a). Critique of seperation [Transcript]. *Situationist international anthology.* Berkeley, CA: Bureau of Public Secrets.

Debord, G. (1981b). Definitions (K. Knabb, Trans.). In K. Knabb (Ed.), *Situationist international anthology* (p. 45). Berkeley, CA: Bureau of Public Secrets.

Debord, G. (1981c). Theory of derive (K. Knabb, Trans.). In K. Knabb (Ed.), *Situationist international anthology* (pp. 50–54). Berkeley, CA: Bureau of Public Secrets.

Debord, G. (1990). *Comments on the society of the spectacle* (M. Imrie, Trans.). London: Verso.

Debord, G. (2002). The society of the spectacle. Retrieved February 16, 2002, from http://www.bopsecrets.org/SI/debord/index.htm

Deffeyes, K. S. (2001). *Hubbert's peak: The impending world oil shortage.* Princeton, NJ: Princeton University Press.

Deffeyes, K. S. (2005). *Beyond oil: The view from Hubbert's Peak.* New York: Hill and Wang.

Deleuze, G., & Guattari, F. (1987). *A thousand plateaus: Capitalism and schizophrenia.* Minneapolis, MN: University of Minnesota Press.

Denzin, N. K. (2005). After the election: Surviving Bush's democracy. *Cultural Studies/Critical Methodologies, 5*(3), 273–275.

Denzin, N. K., & Giardina, M. D. (2006). Introduction: Qualitative inquiry and the conservative challenge *Qualitative inquiry and the conservative challenge* (pp. x–xxxi). Walnut Creek, CA: Left Coast Press.

Denzin, N. K., & Giardina, M. D. (2007). Introduction: Cultural studies after 9/11. In N. K. Denzin & M. D. Giardina (Eds.), *Contesting empire, globalizing dissent: Cultural studies after 9/11* (pp. 1–19). Boulder, CO: Paradigm.

Derbyshire, J. (2003, November 10). NASCAR nation. *National Review*, pp. 29–32.

Dery, M. (2006). "Always crashing in the same car": A head-on collision with the technosphere. In S. Böhm, C. Jones, C. Land, & M. Paterson (Eds.), *Against automobility* (pp. 223–239). Malden, MA: Blackwell /Sociological Review.

DeYoung, K. (2010). Obama redefines national security strategy, looks beyond military might. *The Washington Post*. Retrieved from http://www.washingtonpost.com/wp-dyn/content/article/2010/05/27/AR2010052701044.html

Diamond, S. (1995). *Roads to dominion: Right-wing movements and political power in the United States*. New York: Guilford Press.

Dianetics Racing Team to join NASCAR circuit. (2006). *Scientology*. Retrieved July 27, 2007, from http://www.scientology.org/news-media/briefing/2006/dianetics/060525.html

Domke, D. (2004). *God willing? Political fundamentalism in the White House, the "War on Terror," and the echoing press*. London: Pluto Press.

Domke, D., & Coe, K. (2008). *The God strategy: How religion became a political weapon in America*. London: Oxford University Press.

Doray, B. (1988). *From Taylorism to Fordism: A rational madness*. London: Free Association Books.

Dorrien, G. (1993). *The neoconservative mind: Politics, culture, and the war of ideology*. Philadelphia, PA: Temple University Press.

Drehs, W. (2004). Controversy doesn't resonate with NASCAR. Retrieved June 25, 2007, from http://sports.espn.go.com/rpm/news/story?id=1732991

Dutton, M. (2003). *Postcards from pit road: Inside NASCAR's 2002 season*. Dulles, VA: Potomac Books.

Dyer, L. (2007). Complaints about city run from driving to racism. *Charlotte Observer*. Retrieved June 15, 2007, from http://www.charlotte.com/mld/observer/living/home/17077242.htm?source=syn

Ecklund, Z. (2007, March 9). The checkered flag: Is NASCAR really a sport? *The Western Courier*, pp. Op 1–2.

Eco, U. (1976). *A theory of semiotics*. Bloomington, IN: Indiana University Press.

Egerton, J. (1974). *The Americanization of Dixie: The Southernization of America*. New York: Harper's Magazine Press.

Elder, L., & Greene, S. (2007). The myth of "security moms" and "NASCAR dads": Parenthood, political stereotypes, and the 2004 election. *Social Science Quarterly, 88*(1), 1–19.

Elias, N. (2001). *The society of individuals.* New York: Continuum.

Elliott, S. (2004, January 16). Nextel's in and Winston's out as NASCAR trades up. *New York Times,* pp. C1–C9.

Engdahl, W. (2004). *A century of war: Anglo-American oil politics and the new world order* (Revised ed.). London: Pluto Press.

Faram, M. D. (2008a). Earnhardt gets Navy recruitment quota. *Navy Times.* Retrieved from http://www.navytimes.com/news/2008/04/navy_earnhardt_042808w/

Faram, M. D. (2008b). Navy puts brakes on NASCAR sponsorship. *Navy Times.* Retrieved from http://www.navytimes.com/news/2008/07/navy_nascar_recruiting_071108w/

Faust, D. G. (1988). *The creation of Confederate nationalism: Ideology and identity in the Civil War South.* Baton Rouge, LA: Louisiana State University Press.

Featherstone, M. (1995). *Undoing culture: Globalization, postmodernism and identity.* London: Sage.

Featherstone, M. (2004). Automobilities: An introduction. *Theory, Culture & Society, 21*(4/5), 1–24.

Ferber, A. L. (1998). *White man falling: Race, gender, and white supremacy.* Lanham, MD: Roman & Littlefield.

Ferguson, N. (2005). *Colossus: The rise and fall of the American Empire.* New York: Penguin.

Fielden, G. (2004). *NASCAR chronicle.* Lincolnwood: Publications International.

Fish, M. (2001). The right stuff: NASCAR is a conservative crowd—and proud of it. Retrieved February 17, 2007, from http://sportsillustrated.cnn.com/motorsports/nascar_plus/news/2001/02/20/nascar_politics/

Forceprotection.net. (2007). Force protection to host ground zero museum at Darlington. Retrieved July 24, 2008, from http://forceprotection.net

Foster, G. M. (1987). *Ghosts of the Confederacy: Defeat, the lost cause and the emergence of the New South, 1865–1913.* New York: Oxford University Press.

Fotta, M. (2004). *God speed—NASCAR: A theological analysis.* [Thesis] Boston University, Boston, MA.

Foucault, M. (1977). *Discipline and punish: The birth of the prison.* New York: Pantheon Books.

Foucault, M. (1982). The subject and power. In H. Dreyfus & P. Rabinow (Eds.), *Michel Foucault: Beyond structuralism and hermeneutics* (pp. 208–226). Chicago: University of Chicago Press.

Foucault, M. (1983). Afterword: The subject and power. In H. L. Dreyfus & P. Rabinow (Eds.), *Michel Foucault: Beyond structuralism and hermeneutics* (pp. 208–226). Chicago: University of Chicago Press.

Foucault, M. (1984). Space, knowledge, and power. In P. Rabinow (Ed.), *The Foucault Reader* (pp. 239–256). New York: Pantheon.

Foucault, M. (1988a). Technologies of the self. In L. H. Martin, H. Gutman, & P. H. Hutton (Eds.), *Technologies of the self: A seminar with Michel Foucault* (pp. 16–49). Amherst, MA: University of Massachusetts Press.

Foucault, M. (1988b). Truth, power, self: An interview with Michel Foucault, October 25, 1982. In L. H. Martin, H. Gutman, & P. H. Hutton (Eds.), *Technologies of the self: A seminar with Michel Foucault* (pp. 9–15). Amherst, MA: University of Massachusetts Press.

Foucault, M. (1994). *The order of things: An archaeology of the human sciences.* New York: Vintage.

Foucault, M. (2008). *The birth of biopolitics: Lectures at the Collège de France, 1978–1979*: New York: Palgrave Macmillan.

Foucault, M., Rabinow, P., & Hurley, R. (1997). *Ethics: Subjectivity and truth*: New York: New Press.

Francis, S. (2005). Statement of principles. Retrieved December 6, 2009, from http://cofcc.org/introduction/statement-of-principles/

Frank, T. (2004). *What's the matter with Kansas? How conservatives won the heart of America.* New York: Metropolitan Books.

Freire, P. (2006). *Pedagogy of the oppressed.* New York: Continuum.

Freund, P., & Martin, G. (1993). *The ecology of the automobile.* Montreal: Black Rose Books.

Friaglia, L., & Yeransian, L. (2006). Scientology goes NASCAR with Dianetics race car. *ABC News.* Retrieved June 23, 2007, from http://abcnews.go.com/US/story?id=2044770

Friedman, M. (1962/2002). *Capitalism and freedom.* Chicago: University of Chicago Press.

Friedman, M. (1993). *Why government is the problem.* Palo Alto, CA: Stanford University/Hoover Institution.

Froymovich, R. (2007). Life in the fast lane: NASCAR driver charges full speed ahead. *Forward: The Jewish Daily.* Retrieved from http://www.forward.com/articles/10153/

Fryer, J. (2006, June 7). Dianetics to sponsor NASCAR race team. *The Washington Post.* Retrieved from http://www.washingtonpost.com/wp-dyn/content/article/2006/06/07/AR2006060702520.html

Fukuyama, F. (2004). The neoconservative moment. *The National Interest, 76*(2), 57–68.

Furedi, F. (2004). Dangerous state Fear: The history of a political idea by Corey Robin. *New Statesman (London),* pp. 53–53.

Gage, J. (2006, June 5). Racing for sponsors. *Forbes, 177,* 126–130.

Galbraith, J. K. (1958/1998). *The affluent society.* Boston: Houghton Mifflin.

Galbraith, J. K. (1969). *The new industrial state.* Harmondsworth: Penguin.

Galbraith, J. K. (1975). *Economics and the public purpose.* Harmondsworth: Penguin.

Galbraith, J. K. (1996). *The good society: The humane agenda*. Boston & New York: Houghton Mifflin Company.

Galbraith, J. K. (2001). *The essential Galbraith*. Boston: Houghton Mifflin.

Garcia, B. E. (2001, September 22). Stock Market ends worst week since Great Depression. *Miami Herald, The (FL)*. Retrieved from http://search.ebscohost.com/login.aspx?direct=true&db=n5h&AN=2W60609174030&site=ehost-live&scope=site

Garrett, G. (1993). The politics of structural change. *Comparative Political Studies, 25*(4), 521–547.

Gartman, D. (1994). *Auto opium: A social history of American automobile design*. London: Routledge.

Gartman, D. (2004). Three ages of the automobile: The cultural logics of the car. *Theory, Culture & Society, 21*(4/5), 169–195.

Gerard, J. (2005). Motor madness: Gas guzzling is business as usual at NASCAR. *Emagazine*. Retrieved from http://www.emagazine.com/view/?2947

Gereffi, G., Garcia-Johnson, R., & Sasser, E. (2001). The NGO-industrial complex. *Foreign Policy, 125*, 56–66.

Gerson, M. (1996). *The neoconservative vision: From the Cold War to the culture wars*. Lanham, MD: Madison Books.

Giardina, M. D. (2001). Global Hingis: Flexible citizenship and the transnational celebrity. In D. L. Andrews and S. J. Jackson (Eds.), *Sport stars: The cultural politics of sporting celebrity* (pp. 201–217). London: Routledge.

Giardina, M. D. (2003). "Bending it like Beckham" in the global popular: Stylish hybridity, performativity, and the politics of representation. *Journal of Sport & Social Issues, 27*(1), 65–82.

Giardina, M. D. (2005). *Sporting pedagogies: Performing culture and identity in the global arena*. New York: Peter Lang.

Giardina, M. (2010). One day, one goal? PUMA, corporate philanthropy and the cultural politics of brand "Africa." *Sport in Society, 13*(1), 130–142.

Gibbs, J., & Abraham, K. (2002). *Racing to win: Establish your game plan for success*. Colorado Springs, CO: Multnomah.

Giddens, A. (1990). *The consequences of modernity*. Cambridge: Polity Press.

Gilroy, P. (2010). *Darker than blue: On the moral economies of Black Atlantic culture*. Cambridge, MA: Belknap Press (Harvard University).

Giroux, H. (2003). Spectacles of race and pedagogies of denial: Anti-Black racist pedagogy under the reign of neoliberalism. *Communication Education, 52*(3), 191–211.

Giroux, H. (2004a). Public pedagogy and the politics of neo-liberalism: Making the political more pedagogical. *Policy Futures in Education, 2*(3), 494–503.

Giroux, H. A. (1997a). Rewriting the discourse of racial identity: Towards a pedagogy and politics of whiteness. *Harvard Educational Review, 67*(2), 285–320.

Giroux, H. A. (1997b). White squall: Resistance and the pedagogy of whiteness. *Cultural Studies, 11*(3), 376–389.

Giroux, H. A. (2004b). *The terror of neoliberalism: Authoritarianism and the eclipse of democracy.* Boulder, CO: Paradigm.

Giroux, H. A. (2006a). *Beyond the spectacle of terrorism: Global uncertainty and the challenge of new media.* Boulder, CO: Paradigm.

Giroux, H. A. (2006b). Reading Hurricane Katrina: Race, class, and the biopolitics of disposability. *College Literature, 33*(3), 171–196.

Giroux, H. A. (2007). *The university in chains: Confronting the military-industrial-academic complex.* Boulder, CO: Paradigm.

Giroux, H. A. (2008). *Against the terror of neoliberalism: Politics beyond the age of greed.* Boulder, CO: Paradigm.

Gitlin, T. (2003, January/February 2003). America's age of empire: The Bush doctrine. *Mother Jones.* Retrieved from http://motherjones.com /politics/2003/01/americas-age-empire-bush-doctrine

Goldberg, D. T. (2009). *The threat of race: reflections on racial neoliberalism.* Malden, MA: Wiley-Blackwell.

Goldberg, M. (2007). *Kingdom coming: The rise of Christian nationalism.* New York: W. W. Norton.

Goldberg, M. (2010). The governor-turned-reality-TV-star's new book dives into feminist history—distorting and misunderstanding it every step of the way. *The Daily Beast.* Retrieved from http://www.thedailybeast. com/blogs-and-stories/2010–11-26/sarah-palins-america-by-heart-distorts-feminist-history

Goldenbock, P. (1993). *American zoom: Stock car racing—from the dirt tracks to Daytona.* New York: Macmillan.

Goldfield, D. (2002). *Still fighting the Civil War: The American South and Southern history.* Baton Rouge, LA: Louisiana State University Press.

Goldman, M. I. (2003). *The piratization of Russia: Russian reform goes awry.* New York: Routledge.

Gomstyn. (2008, November 20). NASCAR banks on automakers' survival. *ABC News.* Retrieved from http://abcnews.go.com/Business/Economy /story?id=6293543&page=1.

Gordon, J. (2008). My faith and beliefs. Retrieved February 27, 2008, from http://www.jeffgordon.com/about_jeff/default.sps?itype=12225

Gottdiener, M. (1994). Semiotics and postmodernism. In D. R. Dickens & A. Fontana (Eds.), *Postmodernism and social inquiry* (pp. 155–181). New York: Guilford Press.

Gramsci, A. (1971). *Selections from the prison notebooks.* London: Lawrence and Wishart.

Gregory, S. (2010). NASCAR: A once hot sport tries to restart its engine. *Time Magazine.* Retrieved from http://www.time.com/time/magazine /article/0,9171,1982299,00.html

Groothuis, P. A., & Groothuis, J. D. (2008). Nepotism or family tradition? A study of NASCAR drivers. *Journal of Sports Economics, 9*(3), 250–265.

Grossberg, L. (1996). Identity and cultural studies: Is that all there is? In S. Hall & P. du Gay (Eds.), *Questions of cultural identity* (pp. 87–107). London: Sage.

Grossberg, L. (2006). Does cultural studies have futures? Should it? (or what's the matter with New York?): Cultural studies, contexts and conjunctures. *Cultural Studies, 20*(1), 1–32.

Grzinic, M. (2007). From transitional postsocialist spaces to neoliberal global capitalism. *Third Text, 21*(5), 563–575.

Guttmann, A. (1978). *From ritual to record: The nature of modern sports.* New York: Columbia University Press.

Guttmann, A. (1986). *Sports spectators.* New York: Columbia University Press.

Hadar, L. (2009). Birthers, deathers, and the fear of change. *Global Paradigms.* Retrieved from http://globalparadigms.blogspot.com/2009/08/birthers-deathers-and-fear-of-change.html

Hagstrom, R. (1998). *The NASCAR way: The business that drives the sport.* New York: Wiley.

Hale, G. E. (1999). We've got to get out of this place. *Southern Cultures, 5*(1), 54–66.

Hall, R. L. (2002). Before NASCAR: The corporate and civic promotion of automobile racing in the American South, 1903–1927. *The Journal of Southern History, 68*(3), 629–668.

Hall, S. (1979). The great moving Right show. *Marxism Today, 23*(1), 14–20.

Hall, S. (1980). Encoding/decoding. In S. Hall (Ed.), *Culture, media, language: Working papers in cultural studies (1972–1979)* (pp. 128–138). London: Hutchinson.

Hall, S. (1997). The spectacle of the "other." In S. Hall (Ed.), *Representation: Cultural representations and signifying practices* (pp. 223–290). London: Open University Press.

Hamann, T. (2009). Neoliberalism, governmentality, and ethics. *Foucault Studies* (6), 37–59.

Haraway, D. J. (1991). *Simians, cyborgs, and women: The reinvention of nature.* London: Free Association Books.

Hardball with Chris Matthews (February 13). (2004) [Live segment]: MSNBC.

Hardt, M., & Negri, A. (2000). *Empire.* Cambridge, MA: Harvard University Press.

Hardt, M., & Negri, A. (2004). *Multitude: War and democracy in the age of empire.* New York: Penguin Press.

Harris, D. (Writer). (2005). NASCAR takes religion to the raceway. *World News Tonight.* USA: ABC

Harvey, D. (1989). *The condition of postmodernity: An inquiry into the origins of cultural change.* Oxford, UK: Blackwell.

Harvey, D. (2001a). The postmodern condition. In S. Seidman & J. C. Alexander (Eds.), *The new social theory reader: Contemporary debates* (pp. 166–175). London: Routledge.

Harvey, D. (2001b). *Spaces of capital: Towards a critical geography.* New York: Routledge.

Harvey, D. (2003). *The new imperialism.* Oxford: Oxford University Press.

Harvey, D. (2005). *A brief history of neoliberalism.* Oxford: Oxford University Press.

Harvey, D. (2006). *Spaces of global capitalism: A theory of uneven geographic development.* London: Verso.

Harvey, D. (2007). *The limits to capital (new edition).* London: Verso.

Hawkins, R. (1986). A road not taken: sociology and the neglect of the automobile. *California sociologist, 9*(1–2), 61–79.

Hayek, F. (1944). *The road to serfdom.* Chicago: University of Chicago Press.

Hedges, C. (2007). *American fascists: The Christian Right and the war on America.* New York: Free Press.

Heinberg, R. (2003). *The party's over: Oil, war, and the fate of industrial societies.* Gabriola Island, BC: New Society.

Held, D. (Ed.). (2000). *A globalizing world? Culture, economics, politics.* London: Routledge.

Hemphill, P. (1998). *Wheels: A season on NASCAR's Winston Cup circuit.* New York: Berkley Books.

Henrie, M. (2004). Understanding Traditionalist Conservatism. *Berkowitz (2004),* Hoover Press.

Hetzel, R. L. (2007). The contributions of Milton Friedman to economics. *Economic Quarterly, 93*(1), 1–30.

Higgs, R. J. (1995). *God in the stadium: Sports and religion in America.* Lexington, KY: University of Kentucky Press.

Hill, M., & Fleming, T. (1995, October 29). The New Dixie Manifesto. *The Washington Post,* p. C3.

Hillhouse, R. J. (2007). Blackwater goes NASCAR. *The spy who billed me: Outsourcing the war on terror.* Retrieved from http://www.thespywho-billedme.com/the_spy_who_billed_me/2007/06/blackwater-goes.html

Hinton, E. (2007, March 23). NASCAR is not so color blind: Green still the color of money in stock-car racing. *South Florida Sun Sentinel.* Retrieved from http://www.sun-sentinel.com/sports/

Hinton, E. (2008). Lawsuit's settlement means we'll never know fact from fiction. *ESPN.com.* Retrieved from http://sports.espn.go.com/rpm/nascar/columns/story?columnist=hinton_ed&id=3782854

Hoelscher, S. (2003). Making place, making race: Performances of whiteness in the Jim Crow South. *Annals of the Association of American Geographers, 93*(3), 657–686.

Hofstetter, A. (2006). Selling it: NASCAR is a slave to sponsorships—and proud of it. Retrieved january 30, 2007, from sportsillustrated.cnn.com/2006/writers/adam_hofstetter/08/16/uncommon.sense/

Horwitz, T. (1999). *Confederates in the attic: Dispatches from the unfinished Civil War.* New York: Vintage.

Hossein-zadeh, I. (2006). *The political economy of U.S. militarism.* New York: Palgrave Macmillan.

Howell, M. D. (1997). *From moonshine to Madison Avenue: A cultural hisory of the NASCAR Winston cup series.* Bowling Green, OH: Bowling Green University Press.

Hsu, S. (2009). The end of white America. *The Atlantic* (January /February). Retrieved from http://www.theatlantic.com/magazine /archive/2009/01/the-end-of-white-america/7208/

Hua, V. (2005, June 27). Before starting engines, drivers pray: NASCAR racers face danger with ministries' support. *San Francisco Chronicle*, p. A1.

Huff, R. (1997). *The insider's guide to stock car racing: NASCAR racing, America's fastest growing sport.* Chicago: Bonus Books.

Hufford, M. (2002). Reclaiming the commons: Narratives of progress, preservation, and ginseng. In B. J. Howell (Ed.), *Culture, environment, and conservation in the Appalachian South* (pp. 100–120). Urbana, IL: University of Illinois Press.

Hugenberg, L. W., & Hugenberg, B. S. (2008). If it ain't rubbin', it ain't racin': NASCAR, American values, and fandom. *The Journal of Popular Culture, 41*(4), 635–657.

Humphrey, M. (2009). Did Obama tell Chevy, Dodge to ditch their NASCAR funding? *Orlando Sentinel.* Retrieved from http://blogs.orlandosentinel. com/sports_nascar/2009/04/did-obama-tell-chevy-dodge-to-ditch-its-nascar-funding.html

"In an era of shrinking government, is privatization the American way?" (1995). *Civil Engineering, 65*(10), 22–23.

In NASCAR, racing and religion intertwine. (2004). NASCAR.com. Retrieved January 23, 2008, from http://www.nascar.com/2004/news /headlines/cup/02/10/bc.racing.religion.ap/index.html

International Speedway reports record revenues for the 2007 fourth quarter and full year. (2008) (pp. 1–9). Daytona Beach, FL: International Speedway Corporation.

ISC Annual Report. (2008). Daytona Beach, FL. (pp. 1–81).

Itzkoff, S. W. (2008). *The world energy crisis and the task of retrenchment: reaching the peak of oil production.* Lewiston: Edwin Mellen Press.

Ivison, D. (1997). *The self at liberty: Political argument and the arts of government*: Ithaca, NY: Cornell University Press.

Jaher, F. (1968). The new nation: an introduction and appraisal. *Labor History, 9*(3), 376–379.

Jameson, F. (1991). *Postmodernism, or, the cultural logic of late capitalism.* Durham, NC: Duke University Press.

Jameson, F., & Miyoshi, M. (Eds.). (1998). *The cultures of globalization.* Durham: Duke University Press.

Jeffords, S. (1993). *Hard bodies: Hollywood masculinity in the Reagan era.* New Brunswick: Rutgers University Press.

Jenkins, C. (2001, March 2). Sunday morning service with twist: Motor Racing Outreach provides religious services for racing series. *USA Today*, p. 4C.

Jensen, T. (2009). CUP: Win on Sunday, sell on Monday. *Speedtv*, pp. 1–2. Retrieved from http://nascar.speedtv.com/article/cup-win-on-sunday-sell-on-monday/

Johnson, C. (2004). *The sorrows of empire*. London: Verso.

Kammen, M. (1993). *Mystic chords of memory: The transformation of tradition in American culture*. New York: Vintage.

Kaplan, E. (2005). *With God on their side: George W. Bush and the Christian Right*. New York: New Press.

Karr, G. (1992, September 1). Candidates speeding to speedways to woo "Bubba" vote.

Kay, J. H. (1997). *Asphalt nation: How the automobile took over America, and how we can take it back*. Berkeley, CA: University of California Press.

Keeping the faith: In NASCAR, lines blurred between racing and religion. (2004). *Sports Illustrated Online*. Retrieved from http://sportsillustrated.cnn.com/2004/racing/specials/daytona500/2004/02/10/bc.car.racing.religion.ap/index.html?cnn=yes

Kellner, D. (1995). *Media culture: Cultural studies, identity and politics between the modern and postmodern*. New York: Routledge.

Kellner, D. (1999). Virilio, war and technology: Some critical reflections. *Theory, Culture & Society, 16*(5–6), 103–125.

Kellner, D. (2003). *From 9/11 to terror war: The dangers of the Bush legacy*. Lanham: Rowman & Littlefield.

Kellner, D. (2007). The Katrina hurricane spectacle and crisis of the Bush Presidency. *Cultural Studies/Critical Methodologies, 7*(2), 222–234.

Kelman, S. (1990). The "Japanization" of America? *Public Interest* (98), 70–83.

Kimm, B. (2009). Noted owners in 2009 help put race issue in rear view, *NASCAR.com*. Retrieved from http://www.nascar.com/2009/news/opinion/02/04/bkimm.black.history.owners/index.html

Kincheloe, J. (2008, January 8, 2009). Interview with Joe Kincheloe for the 150th anniversary of the faculty of education at McGill University. Retrieved from http://freire.mcgill.ca/content/joe-kincheloe-interviewed

Kincheloe, J. L., & Steinberg, S. R. (1998). Addressing the crisis of whiteness: Reconfiguring white identity in a pedagogy of whiteness. In J. L. Kincheloe, S. R. Steinberg, N. M. Rodriguez, & R. E. Chennault (Eds.), *White reign: Deploying whiteness in America* (pp. 3–29). New York: St. Martin's Press.

Kincheloe, J. L., & Steinberg, S. R. (2006). An ideology of miseducation: Countering the pedagogy of empire. *Cultural Studies/Critical Methodologies, 6*(1), 33–51.

King, J. (2010, September 1). Anchor notes: John King on Joe Miller. *CNN Politics*. Retrieved from http://johnkingusa.blogs.cnn.com/2010/09/01/anchor-notes-john-king-on-joe-miller/

King, S. (2008). Offensive lines: Sport-state synergy in an era of perpetual war. *Cultural Studies ⟺ Critical Methodologies, 8*(4), 527–539.

Kitfield, J. (2007). Recruiting in wartime. *National Journal, 39*(14), 30–31.

Klare, M. (2004). *Blood and oil: The dangers and consequences of America's growing petroleum dependency*. New York: Metropolitan Books/Henry Holt.

Klare, M. T. (2007). The Pentagon's energy-protection racket. *Asia Times Online*, pp. 1–4. Retrieved from http://www.atimes.com/atimes /Middle_East/IA17Ak02.html

Klein, N. (1999). *No logo: Taking aim at brand bullies*. New York: Picador.

Klein, N. (2002). *No logo: No space, no choice, no jobs*. New York: Picador.

Klein, N. (2007). *The shock doctrine: The rise of the disaster economy*. New York: Metropolitan Books.

Kline, S. (2007). The morality and politics of consumer religion: How consumer religion fuels the culture wars in the United States. *Journal of Religion and Popular Culture, 17*(1), 1–15.

Knauft, B. M. (2007). Provincializing America: Imperialism, capitalism, and counterhegemony in the twenty-first century. *Current Anthropology, 48*(6), 781–805.

Knox, A. (2001). Kyle Petty: Racing for God and son. *The Chritian Broadcasting Network*. Retrieved from http://www.cbn.com/entertain-ment/sports/700club_kylepetty070407.aspx

Kristol, I. (1978). *Two cheers for capitalism*. New York: Basic Books.

Kristol, I. (1983). *Reflections of a neoconservative: Looking back, looking ahead*. New York: Basic Books.

Kristol, I. (2003). The neoconservative persuasion. *The Weekly Standard, 8*(47), 23–25.

Krugman, P. (2007, February 15). Who was Milton Friedman? *The New York Review of Books*, pp. 1–6.

Kruzel, J. J. (2007). NASCAR welcomes chairman, drives home commitment to military. *American Forces Press Service*. Retrieved from http://www.defense.gov/news/newsarticle.aspx?id=46958

Kubursi, A. (2006). Oil and the global economy. In R. Fawn & R. A. Hinnebusch (Eds.), *The Iraq War: Causes and consequences* (pp. 357–377). Boulder, CO: Lynne Reinner.

Kudlow, L. (2006, November 16). The hand of Friedman. Retrieved October 5, 2007, from http://www.nationalreview.com/corner/133137/hand-friedman/larry-kudlow

Kusz, K. (2007). From NASCAR to Pat Tillman: Notes on sport and the politics of white cultural nationalism in post-9/11 America. *Journal of Sport and Social Issues, 31*(1), 77–88.

Lakoff, G. (2004). *Don't think of an elephant: Know your values and frame the debate*. White River Junction, VT: Chelsea Green.

Lal, D. (2006). *Reviving the invisible hand: The case for classical liberalism in the twenty-first century*. Princeton, NJ: Princeton University Press.

Langdon, D., McMenamin, T., & Krolik, T. (2002). US Labor Market in 2001. *Monthly Labor Review, 125*(2), 3–34.

Lasn, K. (1999). *Culture jam: How to reverse America's suicidal consumer binge—and why we must*. New York: Quill.

Latimer, J., & Munro, R. (2006). Driving the social. In S. Böhm, C. Jones, C. Land, & M. Paterson (Eds.), *Against automobility* (pp. 32–53). Malden, MA: Blackwell/Sociological Review.

Lechner, F. J., & Boli, J. (Eds.). (2000). *The globalization reader.* Oxford, UK: Blackwell.

Leeb, S., & Leeb, D. (2004). *The oil factor: Protect yourself—and profit—from the coming energy crisis.* New York: Warner Business Books.

Leeson, R. (2000). *The eclipse of Keynesianism: The political economy of the Chicago counter-revolution.* New York: Palgrave.

Lefebvre, H. (1991). *The production of space* (D. Nicholson-Smith, Trans.). Malden, MA: Blackwell.

Leitch, W. (2008). *God save the fan.* New York: Harpercollins.

Lemasters, R. (2005). Win on Sunday, sell on Monday. *NASCAR.com.* Retrieved from http://www.nascar.com/2005/news/business/07/13/manufacturers/index.html

Lemasters, R. (2007). Business is good, France says in annual address. Retrieved October 5, 2007, from www.nascar.com

Lemasters, R. (2008). France hopeful fans can move past all the change: NASCAR chairman wants focus back on the race track. Retrieved January 24, 2008, from www.nascar.com

Lenin, V. I. (1916/1969). *Imperialism, the highest state of capital (a popular outline).* Moscow: Progress.

Levin, A. M., Beasley, F., & Gamble, T. (2004). Brand loyalty of NASCAR fans toward sponsors: The impact of fan identification. *International Journal of Sports Marketing & Sponsorship, 6*(1), 11–21.

Levin, A. M., Beasley, F., & Gilson, R. L. (2008). NASCAR fans' responses to current and former NASCAR sponsors: The effect of perceived group norms and fan identification. *International Journal of Sports Marketing & Sponsorship, 9*(3), 193–204.

Levin, A. M., Joiner, C., & Cameron, G. (2001). The impact of sports sponsorship on consumers' brand attitudes and recall: The case of NASCAR fans. *Journal of Current Issues and Research in Advertising, 23*(2), 23–31.

Li, M. (2008). An age of transition: The United States, China, peak oil, and the demise of neoliberalism. *Monthly Review, 59*(11), 20–34.

Lichtenstein, A. (1993). Good roads and chain gangs in the Progressive South: "The Negro convict is a slave." *The Journal of Southern History, 59*(1), 85–110.

Limbaugh, R. (1993). *See, I told you so.* New York: Simon & Schuster.

Lipovetsky, G. (1994). *The empire of fashion: Dressing modern democracy* (C. Porter, Trans.). Princeton, NJ: Princeton University Press.

Lipsitz, G. (2005). Whiteness and war. In C. McCarthy, W. Crichlow, G. Dimitriadis, and N. Dolby (Eds.), *Race, identity, and representation in education* (pp. 95–116). London: Routledge.

Lipsyte, R. (Writer). (2000). Gentlemen start your prayers. *Religion & Ethics.* USA: PBS.

Lipsyte, R. (2001, July 22). Auto racing: Wedded to Winston Cup, for better and for worse. *The New York Times,* p. D7.

Lipsyte, R. (2006). NASCAR values. *The Nation,* pp. 1–5. Retrieved from http://www.thenation.com/doc/20061204/lipsyte

Livingstone, S. (2007a). NASCAR seeks diversity but finds the going slow. *USA Today.* Retrieved from http://www.usatoday.com/sports/motor/nascar/2007-04-26-diversity-cover_N.htm

Livingstone, S. (2007b). Toyota teams struggle to make the field. *USA Today.* Retrieved from www.USAToday.com

Long, D. (2008, June 14). NASCAR's "racist culture" under fire, *The Roanoke Times.* Retrieved from http://www.roanoke.com/sports/racing/wb/165753

Lott, E. (1993). White like me: Racial cross-dressing and the construction of American whiteness. In A. Kaplan & D. E. Pease (Eds.), *Cultures of United States imperialism* (pp. 474–498). Durham, NC: Duke University Press.

Lott, E. (2001). The mirage of an unmarked whiteness. In B. B. Rasmussen, E. Klinenberg, I. J. Nexica, & M. Wray (Eds.), *The making and unmaking of whiteness* (pp. 214–233). Durham, NC: Duke University Press.

Luger, S. (2000). *Corporate power: American democracy and the automobile industry.* Cambridge: Cambridge University Press.

Luke, T., & Tuathail, G. (2000). Thinking geopolitical space: The spatiality of war, speed and vision in the work of Paul Virilio. In M. Crang & N. Thrift (Eds.), *Thinking space* (pp. 360–379). London: Routledge.

Macedo, S. (1999). Hayek's liberal legacy. *Cato Journal, 19*(2), 289–300.

MacGregor, J. (2005). *Sunday money: Speed! Lust! Madness! Death!—a hot lap around America with NASCAR.* New York: Harper.

MacGregor, S. (2005). The welfare state and neoliberalism. In A. Saad-Filho & D. Johnston (Eds.), *Neoliberalism: A critical reader* (pp. 142–148). London: Pluto Press.

Maffesoli, M. (1995). *The time of tribes.* London: Sage.

Makinen, G. (2002). *The economic effects of 9/11: A retrospective assessment.* Report for Congress (RL31617). Retrieved from http://www.dtic.mil/cgi-bin/GetTRDoc?AD=ADA469198&Location=U2&doc=GetTRDoc.pdf

Mandel, E. (1975). *Late capitalism.* London: NLB.

Mandelbaum, M. (2001). A note on history as narrative. In G. Roberts (Ed.), *The history and narrative reader* (pp. 52–58). London: Routledge.

Mansfield, S. (2004). *The faith of George W. Bush.* Lake Mary, FL: Charisma House.

Maresco, P. A. (2004). Mel Gibson's *The passion of the Christ*: Market segmentation, mass marketing and promotion, and the internet. *Journal of Religion and Popular Culture, 8*(Fall), NP.

Margolis, B. (2008). Detroit's big dilemma, *Yahoo! sports.* Retrieved from http://sports.yahoo.com/nascar/news?slug=bm-bigthree102208

Mathis, M. (2004). Sunoco and NASCAR forge winning team. *Philadelphia Business Journal*. Retrieved from http://www.bizjournals.com/philadelphia/stories/2004/05/10/focus3.html

McCade, D. (2004). Transcript. *CNN Sunday Morning*. Retrieved from http://edition.cnn.com/TRANSCRIPTS/0402/15/sm.03.html

McCarthy, C., & Dimitriadis, G. (2000). Mapping aesthetics within a global landscape: The work of art in the postcolonial imagination. In N. K. Denzin (Ed.), *Cultural studies: A research volume* (vol. 5, pp. 125–146). Stamford, CT: JAI Press.

McCarthy, C., Giardina, M. D., Harewood, S., & Park, J. K. (2005). Contesting culture. In C. McCarthy, W. Crichlow, G. Dimitriadis, & N. Dolby (Eds.), *Race, identity and representation in education* (pp. 153–178). New York: Routledge.

McCarthy, M. (2004, December 28). Gadgets, Google top consumers' 2005 "hot" picks, *USA Today*, p. 06B.

McGuigan, J. (2005). Neo-liberalism, culture and policy. *International Journal of Cultural Policy, 11*(3), 229–241.

McLaren, P. (1998). Whiteness is…the struggle for postcolonial hybridity. In J. L. Kincheloe, S. R. Steinberg, N. M. Rodriguez, & R. E. Chennault (Eds.), *White reign: Deploying whiteness in America* (pp. 63–75). New York: St. Martin's Press.

McLaren, P. (2005). *Capitalists & conquerors: A critical pedagogy against empire*. New York: Rowman & Littlefield.

McLaren, P., & Jaramillo, N. E. (2005). God's cowboy warrior: Christianity, globalization, and the false prophets of imperialism. In P. McLaren (Ed.), *Capitalists & conquerors: A critical pedagogy against empire* (pp. 261–334). Lanham, MD: Rowman & Littlefield.

McPherson, J. M. (2007). *This mighty scourge: Perspectives on the Civil War*. Oxford, UK: Oxford University Press.

McPherson, T. (2003). *Reconstructing Dixie: Race, gender, and nostalgia in the imagined South*. Durham, NC: Duke University Press.

McShane, C. (1994). *Down the asphalt path: The automobile and the American city*. New York: Columbia University Press.

Menzer, J. (2001). *The wildest ride: A history of NASCAR [or how a bunch of good ol' boys built a billion-dollar industry out of wrecking cars]*. New York: Simon & Schuster.

Merrifield, A. (2000). Henri Lefebvre: A socialist in space. In M. Crang & N. Thrift (Eds.), *Thinking space* (pp. 167–182). London: Routledge.

Meserve, J. (1999, March 30). Bush: Candidate in hiding? *The Hotline*, p. 1.

Micheletti, M. (2003). *Political virtue and shopping: Individuals, consumerism, and colelctive action*. New York: Palgrave Macmillan.

Miles, J. (2005, May 22). "Sunday money" and "Full throttle": NASCAR nation. *The New York Times*. Retrieved from http://www.nytimes.com/2005/05/22/books/review/22COVERCL.html?pagewanted=4

Milhiser, I. (2010). GOP candidate Ken Buck falsely blames federal government for imaginary decline in schools. Retrieved from http://thinkprogress.org/2010/09/03/buck-schools/

Milkman, R. (1997). *Farewell to the factory: Auto workers in the late Twentieth Century.* Berkeley: University of California Press.

Miller, G. W. (2002). *Men and speed: A wild ride through NASCAR's breakout season.* New York: PublicAffairs.

Miller, S. (2007). Race-ism: NASCAR fans pan Toyota. *Brandweek* (48), 46.

Miller, T. C. (2006). *Blood money: Wasted billions, lost lives, and corporate greed in Iraq.* New York: Little, Brown.

Miller, W. (2009). A green light for International Speedway. *Morningstar.* Retrieved from http://www.morningstar.com/artnet-art-1/361505.shtml

Mondaca, J. A. (2007). Does NASCAR need N.C. star to thrive? Retrieved from www.Foxsports.com

Montgomery, L. (2003). Sunoco to become official fuel of NASCAR. *NASCAR.com.* Retrieved from http://www.nascar.com/2003/news/headlines/wc/08/15/sunoco_deal/

Montville, L. (2001). *At the altar of speed: The fast life and tragic death of Dale Earnhardt.* New York: Doubleday.

Moore, M. (1991). Rhetorical criticism of political myth: From Goldwater legend to Reagan mystique. *Communication Studies, 42*(3), 295–308.

Moore, M. (2003). *Dude, where's my country?* London: Allen Lane.

Morgan's testimony. (2000, August 15). Retrieved November 22, 2007, from http://racewithfaith.com/morgantestimony.php

Mork, K. A., (1989). Oil and the macroeconomy when prices go up and down: An extension of Hamilton's results. *Journal of Political Economy*, 97, 740–744.

Morris, M. (1988a). At Henry Parkes Motel. *Cultural Studies, 2*(1), 1–47.

Morris, M. (1988b). *The pirate's fiancee: Feminism, reading, postmodernism.* London: Verso.

Morris, M. (1989). Tooth and claw: Tales of survival and "Crocodile Dundee." *Social Text* (21), 105–127.

Munck, R. (2005). Neoliberalism and politics, and the politics of neoliberalism. In A. Saad-Filho & D. Johnston (Eds.), *Neoliberalism: A critical reader* (pp. 60–69). London: Pluto Press.

NASCAR and religion. (2001). *Religion and ethics Newsweekly.* USA: PBS.

NASCAR's failed union. (2007). *FoxNews*, pp. 1–2. Retrieved from http://www.foxnews.com/wires/2007Feb07/0,4670,CARNASCARFailedUnion,00.html

Negri, A. (2003). *Time for revolution* (M. Mandarini, Trans.). New York: Continuum.

Nelson, E. (2007). Milton Friedman and U.S. monetary history: 1961–2006. *Review, 89*(3), 153–182.

Nethaway, R. (2006, June 8). Scientology off to the NASCAR races. *Waco Tribune-Herald*, p. 5.

Nevius, C. W. (2003, March 9). NASCAR rising: Why are sports' newest superstars paunchy white men? And how did they take over your TV? *San Francisco Chronicle*, p. CM12.

Newberry, P. (2004, February 9). NASCAR mixing religion, racing. *Deseret Morning News*, pp. 1–2. Retrieved from http://deseretnews.com/dn/view/0,1249,590042201,00.html

Newman, J. I. (2007a). Army of whiteness? Colonel Reb and the sporting South's cultural and corporate symbolic. *Journal of Sport and Social Issues, 31*(4), 315–339.

Newman, J. I. (2007b). A detour through "NASCAR Nation": Ethnographic articulations of a neoliberal sporting spectacle. *International Review for the Sociology of Sport, 42*(3), 289–308. doi: 10.1177/1012690207088113

Newman, J. I. (2007c). Old times there are not forgotten: Sport, identity, and the Confederate flag in the Dixie South. *Sociology of Sport Journal, 24*(3), 261–282.

Nora, P. (1989). Between memory and history: Les lieux de Memoire. *Representations* (26), 7–21.

NOW with Bill Moyers. (2003). Retrieved from http://www.pbs.org/now/transcript/transcript248_full.html

O'Connor, J. (1998). *Natural causes: Essays in ecological marxism.* New York: Guilford Press.

Offe, C. (1987). Democracy against the welfare state?: Structural foundations of neoconservative political opportunities. *Political Theory, 15*(4), 501–537.

Olson, J. S. (2002). *Encyclopedia of the industrial revolution in America.* Westport, CT: Greenwood Press.

O'Manique, C., & Labonté, R. (2008). Seeing (RED)-authors' reply. *Lancet, 371*(9627), 1836.

Ong, A. (1998). Flexible citizenship among Chinese cosmopolitans. In P. Cheah & B. Robbins (Eds.), *Cosmopolitics: Thinking and feeling beyond the nation* (pp. 134–162). Minneapolis: University of Minnesota Press.

Ong, A. (1999). *Flexible citizenship: The cultural politics of transnationality.* Durham, NC: Duke University Press.

Osunsami, S. (Writer). (2005). Army invades NASCAR nation to drive recruitment. USA: ABC News.

Ourand, J., & Mickle, T. (2010). ESPN on Chase for answers as race ratings fall. *Sports Business Journal.* Retrieved from http://www.sportsbusinessjournal.com/article/67188

Packer, J. (2008). *Mobility without mayhem: Safety, cars, and citizenship.* Durham, NC: Duke University Press.

Page, S., & Jagoda, N. (2010). What is the Tea Party? A growing state of mind. *USA Today.* Retrieved from http://www.usatoday.com/news/politics/2010–07-01-tea-party_N.htm

Palley, T. I. (2005). From Keynesianism to neoliberalism: Shifting paradigms. In A. Saad-Filho & D. Johnston (Eds.), *Neoliberalism: A critical reader* (pp. 20–29). London: Pluto Press.

Pate, J. (2008). Military sponsors pushing new lifestyle, not product. *NASCAR.com*. Retrieved from http://www.nascar.com/2008/news/headlines/cup/02/04/military.sponsorshipsbkeselowski.dearnhardtjr.mmartin.jwood/index.html

Patton, P. (2002). Nasculture: The graphic design aesthetic of stock car racing—cluttered, chaoitic, vernacular—goes mainstream. Retrieved from www.metropolismag.com/html/content_0302/nas/index.html

Pedley, J. (2008, October 25). NASCAR shares long history with the military, electronic. *Kansas City Star*. Retrieved from http://villagesracingclub.com/10–09.pdf

Perez, A. J. (2007, March 2). South of the border reunion. *USA Today*, p. 10C.

Perez, J. (2008). Joe Gibbs driven introduces new hot rod oil creation from NASCAR technology. *Street Import Online*. Retrieved from http://streetimportonline.com/sio/joe-gibs-driven-introduces-new-hot-rod-oil-created-from-nascar-technology.html

Phillips, K. (2006). *American theocracy: The peril and politics of radical religion, oil, and borrowed money in the 21st century*. London: Viking Penguin.

Phillips-Fein, K. (2009). *Invisible hands: The making of the conservative movement from the new deal to Reagan*. New York: W. W. Norton.

Pierce, D. (2001). The most Southern sport on earth: NASCAR and the unions. *Southern Cultures, 7*(1), 8–33.

Pierce, D. (2010). *Real NASCAR: White lightning, red clay, and Big Bill France*. Chapel Hill, NC: University of North Carolina Press.

Pierce, J. L. (2003). "Racing for innocence": Whiteness, corporate culture, and the backlash against affirmative action. *Qualitative Sociology, 26*(1), 53–70.

Pieterse, J. N. (1995). Globalization as hybridization. In M. Featherstone, S. Lash, & R. Robertson (Eds.), *Global moderntities* (pp. 45–68). London: Sage.

Pieterse, J. N. (2006). Neoliberal empire. In N. K. Denzin and M. D. Giardina (Eds.), *Contesting empire/globalization dissent: Cultural studies after 9/11* (pp. 78–94). Boulder, CO: Paradigm.

Pillsbury, R. (1974). Carolina thunder: A geography of Southern stock car racing. *The Journal of Geography, 73*(1), 39–47.

Pittman, M., & Ivry, B. (2009). U.S. taxpayers risk $9.7 trillion on bailout programs. *Bloomberg*. Retrieved from http://www.bloomberg.com/apps/news?pid=newsarchive&sid=aGq2B3XeGKok

Pockrass, B. (2007, Date). Toyota is stuck in first gear, at least for now. *Sporting News*, p. 53.

Pockrass, B. (2009). Ford still using NASCAR to launch new products. *Scenedaily.com*. Retrieved from http://www.scenedaily.com/news/articles/sprintcupseries/Ford_still_using_NASCAR_to_launch_new_products.html

Podobnik, B., & Riefer, T. (Eds.). (2005). *Transforming globalization: Challenges and opportunities in the post 9/11 era.* Leiden: Brill Academic.

Polanyi, K. (1944/2001). *The great transformation: the political and economic origins of our time* (2nd Beacon Paperback ed.). Boston, MA: Beacon Press.

Politician's "anti-gay" speech sparks outrage. (2008). *ABC News.* Retrieved from http://abcnews.go.com/TheLaw/story?id=4444956&page=1

Pollitt, K. (2004). Move over, NASCAR Dads. *The Nation*, p. 1. Retrieved from http://www.thenation.com/doc/20040412/pollitt

Promise keepers: Men of integrity. (2006). Retrieved November 27, 2007, from http://www.promisekeepers.org/

Putney, C. (2003). *Muscular Christianity: Manhood and sports in Protestant America, 1880–1920* Cambridge, MA: Harvard University Press.

Rajan, S. C. (2006). Automobility and the liberal disposition. In S. Böhm, C. Jones, C. Land, & M. Paterson (Eds.), *Against automobility* (pp. 113–129). Malden, MA: Blackwell /Sociological Review.

Read, J. (2009). A genealogy of *homo-economicus*: Neoliberalism and the production of subjectivity. *Foucault Studies* (6), 25–36.

Reed, J. S. (1986). *The enduring South: Subcultural persistence in mass society.* Chapel Hill, NC: University of North Carolina Press.

Reich, R. (1991). *The work of nations: Preparing ourselves for twenty-first-century capitalism.* New York: Knopf.

Rhee, A. (2005). God and NASCAR: On any given Sunday, drivers pray before they take the track. *Faith in America.* Retrieved February 17, 2007, from www.msnbc.msn.com/id/7286393/

Rich, F. (2010, April 17). Welcome to Confederate history month. *The New York Times.* Retrieved from http://www.nytimes.com/2010/04/18/opinion/18rich.html

Richardson, P. J., & Darden, R. (1997). *Wheels of thunder: Top NASCAR and Indy Car professionals share how they stay on track.* Nashville, TN: Thomas Nelson.

Riesman, D., Glazer, N., & Denney, R. (1950/2001). *The lonely crowd: A study of the changing American character.* New Haven, CT: Yale Note Bene.

Ritzer, G. (1998). McJobs: McDonaldization and its relationship to the labor process. In G. Ritzer (Ed.), *The McDonaldization thesis: Explorations and extensions* (pp. 59–70). London: Sage.

Ritzer, G. (2004). *The globalization of nothing.* Thousand Oaks, CA: Pine Forge.

Roach, S. S. (2005). Alan Greenspan. *Foreign Policy* (146), 18–24.

Roberts, P. (2004). *The end of oil: On the edge of a perilous new world.* Boston: Houghton Mifflin.

Robertson, R. (1992). *Globalization: Social theory and global culture.* London: Sage.

Robertson, R. (1995). Glocalization: Time-space and homogeneity-heterogeneity. In M. Featherstone, S. Lash, & R. Robertson (Eds.), *Global modernities: From modernism to hypermodernism and beyond* (pp. 25–44). London: Sage.

Robins, K. (1990). Global local times. In J. Anderson & M. Ricci (Eds.), *Society and social science: A reader* (pp. 196–205). Milton Keynes, UK: Open University.

Robinson, J. (2000). Feminism and the spaces of transformation. *Transactions of the Institute of British Geographers, 25*(3), 285–301.

Roche, M. (2000). *Mega-events and modernity: Olympics, expos and the growth of global culture.* London: Routledge.

Rodman, D. (2008). Wheeler's biggest asset in NASCAR: Promotional prowess. *NASCAR.com.* Retrieved from http://www.nascar.com/2008/news/headlines/cup/05/23/humpy.wheeler.promotional.expert/index.html

Ronfeldt, D. (2000). Social science at 190 MPH on NASCAR's biggest superspeedways. *First Monday, 5*(2), 1–29.

Rose, N. (1999). *Powers of freedom: Reframing political thought*: Cambridge: Cambridge University Press.

Ross, K. (1988). *The emergence of social space: Rinbaud and the Paris commune.* Minneapolis, MN: University of Minnesota Press.

Rothbard, M. (1998) Frank S. Meyer: The fusionist as libertarian Manqué. In G. W. Carey (Ed.), *Freedom and virtue: The conservative/libertarian debate* (p. 137). Wilmington, DE: ISI.

Roy, A. (2004). *An ordinary person's guide to empire.* Cambridge: South End Press.

Roy, A., & Barsamian, D. (2004). *The checkbook and the cruise missile: Conversations with Arundhati Roy.* Boston, MA: South End Press.

Royse, D. (2000, July 1). Bush greats NASCAR fans, racers, *Associated Press.*

Rubin, R. (2002). *Confederacy of silence: A true tale of the new Old South.* New York: Atria Books.

Rushin, S. (1999, February 22). A fun ride, I reckon. *Sports Illustrated,* p. 22.

Russell, A. (2004). NASCAR Dads: The high-octane patriots holding the keys to the White House. *The Telegraph.* Retrieved from http://www.telegraph.co.uk/news/worldnews/northamerica/usa/1454496/Nascar-Dads-the-high-octane-patriots-holding-the-keys-to-the-White-House.html

Russell, L. D. (2007). *Godspeed: Racing is my religion.* New York: Continuum.

Russello, G. (2004). Russell Kirk and territorial democracy. *Publius: The Journal of Federalism, 34*(4), 109–124.

Rutledge, I. (2005). *Addicted to oil: America's relentless drive for energy security.* London: I. B. Tauris.

Ryan, N. (2006). Toyota already making Cup teams nervous. Retrieved from http://www.usatoday.com/sports/motor/nascar/2006–05–11-darlington-preview_x.htm

Ryan, N. (2007a). Texas boasts unique experience in victory lane. *USA Today*. Retrieved from http://www.usatoday.com/sports/motor/nascar/2007-11-01-texas-victory-lane_N.htm

Ryan, N. (2007b). Tony Stewart accuses NASCAR of "playing God." *USA Today*. Retrieved from www.usatoday.com

Rybacki, K. C., & Rybacki, D. J. (2002). The king, the young prince, and the last confedrate soldier: NASCAR on the cusp. In P. B. Miller (Ed.), *The sporting world of the modern south* (pp. 294–325). Urbana, IL: University of Illinois Press.

Salem-News.com. (2007). NASCAR: Coca-Cola 600 pre-race show to celebrate U.S. military. Retrieved February 15, 2010, from http://www.salem-news.com/sports/may262007/nascar_news_052607.php

Sanger, D. E. (2004). The 2004 campaign: The president; at speedway, Bush courts race fans, dads included. *New York Times*. Retrieved from http://www.nytimes.com/2004/02/16/us/the-2004-campaign-the-president-at-speedway-bush-courts-race-fans-dads-included.html?scp=3&sq=Sanger%20NASCAR&st=cse

Sassen, S. (1998). *Globalization and its discontents: Essays on the new mobility of people and money*. New York: New Press.

Scherer, G. (2004, October 27). The godly must be crazy. *Main Dish*. Retrieved December 5, 2007, from http://www.grist.org/news/maindish/2004/10/27/scherer-christian/

Schindler, A. (1998). *Power, patriarchy, and the promise keepers: The pleasure of religious ecstasy*. Paper presented at the American Sociological Association, Toronto.

Schipani, D. S. (1988). *Religious education encounters liberation theology*. Birmingham, AL: Religious Education Press.

Schipani, D. S. (1997). Educating for social transformation. In J. Seymour (Ed.), *Mapping Christian education* (pp. 23–40). Nashville, TN: Abingdon Press.

Schnapp, J. T. (1999). Crash (speed as engine of individuation). *Modernism /Modernity, 6*(1), 1–49.

Schneider, B. (Writer). (2004). Bush promotes domestic high tech agenda; a look at NASCAR Nation. *CNN Live Today*. USA: CNN.

Scholte, J. A. (2000). *Globalization: A critical introduction*. New York: St. Martin's Press.

Schultz, J. (2006, June 8). Rubbing fenders with religion. *Atlanta Journal—Constitution*, p. 6.

Scotchie, J. (Ed.) (1999). *The paleoconservatives: New voices of the Old Right*. New Brunswick, NJ: Transaction.

Shaftel, D. (2008, February 15). Amid checkered flags, ministries keep faith. *The New York Times*, p. D4.

Shukin, N. (2006). The mimetics of mobile capital. In S. Böhm, C. Jones, C. Land, & M. Paterson (Eds.), *Against automobility* (pp. 17–31). Malden, MA: Blackwell/Sociological Review.

Silk, M. L., & Andrews, D. L. (2001). Beyond a boundary? Sport, trans-national advertising, and the reimagining of national culture. *Journal of Sport & Social Issues, 25*(2), 180–201.

Simmons, M. R. (2005). *Twilight in the desert: The coming Saudi oil shock and the world economy.* Hoboken, NJ: John Wiley & Sons.

Simons, H. C. (1934/1948). *Economic policy for a free society.* Chicago: University of Chicago Press.

Sirgy, M., Lee, D., Johar, J., & Tidwell, J. (2008). Effect of self-congruity with sponsorship on brand loyalty. *Journal of Business Research, 61*(10), 1091–1097.

Skocpol, T. (1985). What is happening to Western welfare states? *Contemporary Sociology, 14*(3), 307–311.

Smant, K. (2003). Paleoconservatives. *The Review of Politics, 65*(4), 473–475.

Smart, B. (2010). *Consumer society: Critical issues and environmental consequences.* London: Sage.

Smith, A. (1776/1966). *The wealth of nations.* New York: Hayes Barton Press.

Smith, G., & Wilson, P. (2004). Country cookin' and cross-dressin'. *Television & New Media, 5*(3), 175–195.

Smith, M. (2001). A renewed faith in the human race. Retrieved November 27, 2007, from http://www.nascar.com/2001/NEWS/09/27/smith_commentary/index.html

Smith, M. (2002). NASCAR observes National Moment of Remembrance. *NASCAR.com.* Retrieved from http://www.nascar.com/2002/news/headlines/wc/05/23/national_remembrance/index.html

Smith, M. (2008a). NASCAR's desire to return to its racing roots a very good thing. *ESPN.com.* Retrieved from http://sports.espn.go.com/rpm/columns/story?seriesId=2&columnist=smith_marty&page=DoorToDoor080123

Smith, M. (2008b). Returning to its roots. *Sports Business Journal, 10,* 1, 36.

Smith, M. (2008c). Welcome to diesel's dirt road: An open forum for fed-up fans. *ESPN.com.* Retrieved from http://sports.espn.go.com/rpm/columns/story?seriesId=2&columnist=smith_marty&page=DoorToDoor080130

Smith, M. (2008d). You think your fuel bill is high? NASCAR teams in a budget squeeze. *ESPN.com.* Retrieved from http://www.nascar.com/2003/news/headlines/wc/08/15/sunoco_deal/

Snyder, B. (2006). *Talladega Nights: The Ballad of Ricky Bobby*—Ridiculing the Bible Belt and white Southern Christian males. Retrieved from http://www.movieguide.org/reviews/movie/talladega-nights-the-ballad-of-ricky-bobby.html

The Socialist Experiment continues: Obama orders Chevrolet and Dodge out of NASCAR. (2009). autospies.com. Retrieved from http://www.autospies.com/news/The-Socialist-Experiment-Continues-Obama-Orders-Chevrolet-and-Dodge-Out-Of-NASCAR-42514/

Soja, E. (1989). *Postmodern geographies.* London: Routledge.

Spencer, L., & Grant, P. (2005). Going global. *Sporting News, 229*(8), 409.

Spitzer, G. (2001). Daytona 500 breaks 20-year ratings record. *Media Life*. Retrieved from http://www.medialifemagazine.com/news2001/feb01 /feb19/3_wed/news2wednesday.html

Stein, S. (2008, October 17). Michele Bachmann channels McCarthy: Obama "very Anti-American," Congressional witch hunt needed. *Huffington Post*. Retrieved from http://www.huffingtonpost.com/2008/10/17 /gop-rep-channels-mccarthy_n_135735.html

Stein, S. (2010, July 8). Sharon Angle's advice for rape victims considering abortion: Turn lemons into lemonade. *HuffingtonPost*. Retrieved from http://www.huffingtonpost.com/2010/07/08/sharron-angles-advice-for_n_639294.html

Stoler, A. (1997). On political and psychological essentialisms. *Ethos, 25*(1), 101–106.

Stubbs, D. (2006, May 13). Start your engines: NASCAR on way to Montreal. *Montreal Gazette*. Retrieved from www. canada.com/montrealgazette

Sue, D. W. (2004). Whiteness and ethnocentric monoculturalism: Making the "invisible" visible. *American Psychologist, 59*(8), 761–769.

Sullivan, A. (2009). Whose country? *The Atlantic*. Retrieved from http:// andrewsullivan.theatlantic.com/the_daily_dish/2009/10/whose-country.html

Sullivan, M. (1995). *US foreign policy in the periphery: A 50-year retrospective*. Los Angeles: International Studies Association.

Taibbi, M. (2010). Matt Taibbi on the Tea Party: How corporate interests and Republican insiders built the Tea Party monster. *Rolling Stone*. Retrieved from http://www.rollingstone.com/politics/news/17390/210904?RS_ show_page=0

Talley, H. L., & Casper, M. J. (2007). A response to the motion picture Talladega Nights: The Ballad of Ricky Bobby. *Journal of Sport and Social Issues, 31*(4), 434–439.

Therborn, G. (2007). After dialectics. *New Left Review* (43), 63–114.

This is our NASCAR. (2009). [PowerPoint Presentation]. Daytona, FL: NASCAR.

Thomaselli, R. (2007). How NASCAR plans to get back on the fast track. *Advertising Age, 78*(3), 26.

Thompson, N. (2006). *Driving with the Devil: Southern moonshine, Detroit Wheels, and the birth of NASCAR*. New York: Three Rivers Press.

Thrift, N. (1996). *Spatial formations*. London: Sage.

Thurmond, W. (2005, October 22). Virginia soldier killed in Iraq honored by NASCAR fans. Retrieved from http://www.forum.militaryltd.com /military-press/m12635-virginia-soldier-killed-iraq-honored-by-nascar-fans.html

Tomlinson, J. (1999). *Globalization and culture*. Cambridge: Polity.

Tonnies, F. (1887/2002). *Community and society*. Dover, DE: Dover.

Touraine, A. (1971). *The post-industrial society*. New York: Random House.

Transcript (2007). theautochannel.com. Retrieved March 15, 2010, from http://www.theautochannel.com Treaster, J. B. (2004). *Paul Volcker: The making of a financial legend.* New York: Wiley.

Trumper, R., & Tomic, P. (2009). The Chilean way to modernity: Private roads, fast cars, neoliberal bodies. In J. Conley & A. T. McLaren (Eds.), *Car troubles: Critical studies of auto-mobility and automobility* (pp. 165–180). Surrey, UK: Ashgate.

Tuggle, K. E. (2008). NASCAR profits on and off the track. Retrieved January 26, 2008, from www.foxbusiness.com

United States Bureau of Labor Statistics Report, 1970–2005. (2005). Washington, DC: United States Department of Labor.

Urry, J. (2004). The "system" of automobility. *Theory, Culture & Society, 21*(4/5), 25–39.

Urry, J. (2006). Inhabiting the car. In S. Böhm, C. Jones, C. Land, & M. Paterson (Eds.), *Against automobility* (pp. 17–31). Malden, MA: Blackwell/Sociological Review.

Vanberg, V. (1994). Hayek's legacy and the future of liberal thought: Rational liberalism versus evolutionary agnosticism. *Cato Journal, 14,* 179–179.

Vavrus, M. D. (2007). The politics of NASCAR Dads: Branded media paternity. *Critical Studies in Media Communications, 24*(3), 245–261.

Virilio, P. (1977/2006). *Speed and politics: An essay on dromology.* Minneapolis, MN: University of Minnesota Press.

Virilio, P. (1991). *The aesthetics of disappearance.* New York: Semiotext(e).

Virilio, P. (1995). *The art of the motor.* Minneapolis, MN: University of Minnesota Press.

Virilio, P. (2005). *The information bomb.* London: Verso.

Virilio, P., & Armitage, J. (2000). Ctheory Interview with Paul Virilio: The Kosovo War took place in orbital space. *CTHEORY*(a089), 1–4.

Virilio, P., & Lotringer, S. (1983). Pure war (M. Polizzotti, Trans.). *New York: Semiotext(e).*

Vogel, S. (2009, May 11). Military recruitment faces budget cut. *Washington Post.* Retrieved from http://www.washingtonpost.com/wp-dyn/content/article/2009/05/10/AR2009051002172.html

Wagner, M. B. (2002). Space and place, land and legacy. In B. J. Howell (Ed.), *Culture, environment, and conservation in the Appalachian South* (pp. 121–132). Urbana, IL: University of Illinois Press.

Wallerstein, I. (2000). The rise and future demise of the world capitalist system. In F. J. Lechner & J. Boli (Eds.), *The globalization reader* (pp. 57–63). Malden, MA: Blackwell.

Wallerstein, I. (2008). 2008: The demise of neoliberal globalization. *Commentaries: Fernand Braudel Center for the Study of Economies, Historical Systems, and Civilizations at Binghampton University* (226), 1–2. Retrieved from http://www.binghamton.edu/fbc/226en.htm

The war behind closed doors. (2003). In D. Fanning (Producer), *Frontline.* USA: PBS.

Warren, L. (2007). NASCAR's Reutimann: Faith-driven. *BPSports*, p. 1. Retrieved from http://www.bpsports.net/bpsports.asp?ID=5552

Watanabe, Y. (2000). "Japan" through the looking glass: American influences on the politics of cultural identity of post-war Japan. *Passages: A Journal of Transnational & Transcultural Studies, 2*(1), 21–36.

Weissberg, L. (1999). Introduction. In D. Ben-Amos & L. Weissberg (Eds.), *Cultural memory and the construction of identity* (pp. 1–18) Detroit: Wayne State University Press.

Wesbury, B. S. (2006). The post-9/11 economy. *Wall Street Journa—Eastern Edition*, p. A14.

Wetzel, D. (2006). Red flag. *Yahoo Sports*. Retrieved October 9, 2006, from sports.yahoo.com/nascar/news?slug=dwconfederateflag100906&prov=yhoo&type=lgns

Wilkey, L. (2006). NASCAR great Shepherd finds "victory in Jesus." *Associated Baptist Press*. Retrieved from http://www.abpnews.com/1384.article

Williams, R. (1964). *Second generation*. London: Chatto and Windus.

Williams, R. (1981). *The sociology of culture*. New York: Schoken Books.

Williamson, J. (1984). *The crucible of race: Black/white relations in the American South since emancipation*. New York: Oxford University Press.

Willis, S. (2002). Old Glory. *South Atlantic Quarterly, 101*(2), 375–383.

Wolf, N. (2007). *The end of America: Letter of warning to a young patriot*. White River Junction, VT: Chelsea Green.

Wolff, E. (2010). *Recent trends in household wealth in the United States: Rising debt and the middle-class squeeze—an update to 2007.* Levy Economics Instiute of Bard College. Retrieved from http://www.levyinstitute.org/publications/?docid=1235.

Wolfson, A. (2004). Conservatives and neoconservatives. *Public Interest*, pp. 32–48.

Wollen, P. (1993). *Raiding the icebox: Reflections on twentieth century culture*. Bloomington, IN: Indiana University Press.

Wood, W. M. (2003). *Empire of capital*. London: Verso.

Woodruff, J., Karl, J., & Black, C. (2000). Dole and Gore fight to change perceptions of their campaigns (Transcript # 99092005V15) [television show]: CNN.

Woolley, J. & Peters, G. T. (1984). Remarks of the president and Ned Jarrett of the Motor Racing Network during a radio broadcast of the Pepsi Firecracker 400 in Daytona Beach, Florida, from the American Presidency Project. Retrieved from http://www.presidency.ucsb.edu/ws/index.php?pid=40125&st=%20nascar&st1=

Woolley, J., & Peters, G. T. (1992). Remarks to the Pepsi 400 drivers and owners in Daytona Beach, Florida, from the American Presidency Project. Retrieved from http://www.presidency.ucsb.edu/ws/index.php?pid=21202&st=nascar&st1=

Wright, J. (2002). *Fixin' to git: One fan's love affair with NASCAR's Winston Cup*. Durham, NC: Duke University Press.

Yergin, D. (1991). *The prize: The epic quest for oil, money, and power.* New York: Simon & Schuster.

Zappia, C. (1999). The economics of information, market socialism and Hayek's legacy. *History of Economic Ideas, 7*(1/2), 105–138.

Zirin, D. (2008, July 11). Who is Mauricia Grant? NASCAR knows. *Huffington Post.* Retrieved from http://www.huffingtonpost.com/dave-zirin/who-is-mauricia-grant-nas_b_111913.html

Zweig, E. (2007). *Drive like hell: NASCAR's best quotes and quips.* Buffalo, NY: Firefly Books.

Zylinska, J. (2007). The secret of life. *Cultural Studies, 21*(1), 95–117.

Index